WITHDRAWAL

A DICTIONARY OF
NAMES NICKNAMES AND SURNAMES
OF
PERSONS PLACES AND THINGS

A DICTIONARY OF
NAMES   NICKNAMES
AND SURNAMES
OF PERSONS PLACES
AND THINGS

By

EDWARD LATHAM

Author of " Famous Sayings and their Authors " etc

LONDON
GEORGE ROUTLEDGE & SONS LTD
New York : E. P. DUTTON & CO.
1904

REPUBLISHED BY GALE RESEARCH COMPANY, BOOK TOWER, DETROIT, 1966

Library of Congress Card Number 66-22674

PREFACE

THE compilation of the present volume has been undertaken with the view of supplementing, and, to a certain extent, providing a key to the ordinary dictionaries of biography, geography, mythology, etc. A person or place is often alluded to by means of a surname or nickname without any clue being given to the reader, who does not happen to be aware of the actual name of the person or place, and in such cases it is hoped that the necessary information will be found in these pages. Sometimes, too, some particulars are required concerning celebrated ships, race-horses, etc., and a selection of the best known of these has been also included.

Owing to the numerous headings, considerations of space prevent more than the briefest particulars being given, but these are perhaps usually sufficient, or at all events give the necessary clue to enable fuller details to be obtained elsewhere.

Such additions to names as the Elder, the Younger, etc., which usually form, as it were, part of the actual surname, have not been noticed here.

Although the title may afford a better notion of the nature of its contents than seems to be the case in most of the existing works containing similar information, yet it may not be out of place to mention their general scope. In these pages will be found a selection of names, nicknames and surnames of noted persons, places and things (unless, as often happens, they are self-explanatory), comprising cities, districts, countries, popular resorts, old coffee-houses, taverns, gardens, theatres, monuments, prisons, bridges, tunnels, ships, rivers, walls, acts of parliament, laws, parliaments, diets, councils, alliances, treaties, battles, wars, peaces, armies, guns, anniversaries, eras, periods, ages, governments, political parties, ceremonies, moons, days, saints, exploits, offices (dignities), companies, schemes, trials, conspiracies, plots, rebellions, riots, insurrections, instruments of torture, railway engines, newspapers, periodicals, prizes, lectures, races, societies, clubs, sects, orders of knighthood, famous diamonds, nuggets, animals and trees.

The compiler has, of course, availed himself freely of the work of his predecessors, gleaning his materials from many sources, amongst which may be mentioned :—

The Cyclopædia of Names (Benjamin E. Smith). *Noted Names of Fiction* (William A. Wheeler). *Five Thousand Facts and Fancies* (W. H. P. Phyfe). *The Reader's Handbook* (Rev. E. C. Brewer). *Dictionnaire Universel d'Histoire, etc.* (M.-N. Bouillet). *Dictionary of National Biography*. *Encyclopædia Britannica*, etc.

EDWARD LATHAM.

DICTIONARY OF NAMES,
NICKNAMES AND SURNAMES.

Abbaye, L'.

A military prison in Paris, built 1522, and demolished 1854. In September, 1792, 164 persons imprisoned in L'Abbaye were murdered by the infuriated Republicans, led by Maillard.

Abderian Laughter.

A name given to derisive laughter, from Abdera, Democritus' birthplace (*v.* Laughing Philosopher, The).

Abderite, The, *v.* Laughing Philosopher, The.

Abecedarians.

A German Anabaptist sect (sixteenth century), led by Nicholas Stork, a weaver. Its adherents regarded all learning —even A B C—as inimical to religion.

Abencerrages (or Abencérages).

A Moorish tribe, said to have dominated Granada in the fifteenth century. The name has been rendered famous as the title of a work by Chateaubriand, "les Aventures du dernier Abencerrage."

Abraham-men.

The wards in Bethlehem Hospital (*v.* **Bedlam**) were named after saints or patriarchs, and that which bore Abraham's name contained a class of lunatics who were allowed to go out begging. They were known as Abraham-men, and wore a badge. The badge, however, came to be assumed by others who feigned lunacy. Hence the meaning of impostor attributed to the term, and the phrase "to sham Abraham."

Abraham Newland.

A nickname by which a Bank of England note was long known, from its being signed by Abraham Newland, the cashier of the Bank in the early part of the nineteenth century.

Academic Legion.

An insurrectionary corps of armed students who made themselves conspicuous at Vienna in 1848.

Acadia.

The name of a former French colony in America, bounded by the Atlantic, the Gulf and River of St. Lawrence and (westward) by a line running north from the mouth of the Penobscot. Colonized by France in 1604 on the Bay of Fundy and ceded (except Cape Breton) to Great Britain by the Treaty of Utrecht (*v.* **Peace of Utrecht**) in 1713.

Achilles of England, The.

A surname given to John, first Earl of Shrewsbury (c. 1373–1453). Also called the Terror of France.

Achilles of Germany, The.

Surname given to Albert (Albrecht), Elector of Brandenburg (1414–86). He was also surnamed Ulysses.

Achilles of Rome, The, v. Roman Achilles, The.

Acordad.

A court established at Queretaro, New Spain (Mexico), for the summary trial of brigands and others. It was suppressed in 1813.

Act of Indemnity (or of Oblivion).

Act of Oblivion.

An English statute of 1660, entitled " An Act of Free and Generall Pardon, Indempnity, and Oblivion," by which all political offences committed during the time of the Commonwealth were pardoned, certain offenders mentioned by name in the Act being excepted, especially those engaged in the trial and execution of Charles I. Also called Act of Indemnity.

Act of Settlement (or Succession Act).

An Act of Parliament passed in 1701, regulating the succession to the English throne (see Acland and Ransome, "Handbook of Political History," p. 124).

Act of Six Articles.

An Act passed in 1539. It asserted (1) transubstantiation ; (2) the sufficiency of communion in one kind ; (3) celibacy of the clergy ; (4) the maintenance of vows of chastity ; (5) the continuation of private masses ; and (6) auricular confession. The penalty for denying the first was death ; for the rest, forfeiture of property for the first offence, death for the second.

Act of Supremacy.

An English statute of 1534 (26 Henry VIII, c. 1) which proclaimed that Henry VIII was the supreme head of the English Church. Also an English statute of 1558–9 (1 Eliz., c. 1) vesting spiritual authority in the crown, to the exclusion of all foreign jurisdiction.

Act of Toleration.

The name given to the statute 1 William and Mary, cap. 18 (1689). By it the Protestant dissenters from the Church of England, except such as denied the Trinity, were relieved from the restrictions under which they had formerly lain with regard to the exercise of religious worship according to their own forms, on condition of their taking the oaths of supremacy and allegiance, and repudiating the doctrine of transubstantiation, and, in the case of dissenting ministers, subscribing also to the Thirty-nine Articles, with certain exceptions relating to ceremonies, ordination, infant baptism, etc.

Act of Union.

A statute of 1535–6, which enacted the political union of Wales to England.
A statute of 1706, which united the kingdoms of England

and Scotland on and after May 1, 1707. *v.* **Union, The.**

Adamantius (Latin, " The man of steel ").

A surname of Origen (Origenes), one of the Greek fathers of the church (c. 185– c. 253).

Adamites.

A sect pretending to have attained to the primitive innocence of Adam, rejecting marriage and (in their meetings, " paradises ") clothing. It was suppressed in 1421, owing to the crimes and immorality of its adherents. In 1781 it revived, and its latest appearance was in 1848–9.

Adams, *v.* **Wasp.**

Adam's Ale.

Water is sometimes jokingly so called.

Addison of the North.

A surname given to Henry Mackenzie, a Scottish novelist (1745–1831).

Addled Parliament.

A nickname of James I's second Parliament (1614), owing to its dissolution without having passed any Acts.

Admirable Crichton, The.

The surname " Admirable " was given to James Crichton, a Scottish scholar and adventurer (1561–83 ?), celebrated for his extraordinary attainments. He is said to have been the master of twelve languages and an accomplished swordsman. Cf. W. H. Ainsworth's novel, "Crichton."

Admirable, The.

A surname given to Abraham ben Meir ibn Ezra, a celebrated scholar of the Jewish-Arabic period in Spain, a philologist, poet, mathematician, astronomer and Bible commentator (1092–1167).

Admirable Doctor.

A surname given to Roger Bacon (c. 1214–94 ?). Called also the Wonderful Doctor (Doctor Mirabilis).

Admonitionists.

A name given to Thomas Cartwright's followers. In 1572 two of them published "An Admonition to Parliament," and this was followed by one by himself, advocating strongly the supremacy of the Church over the State, and Church government by presbyters instead of bishops.

Adria.

An abbreviated name for the Adriatic. Milton uses it in his "Paradise Lost."

Adullamites.

Name given to the group of Liberals seceding from the Whig party and voting with the Conservatives on the introduction of the measure in 1866 by Earl Russell and Mr. Gladstone for the extension of the elective franchise. The group was also known as " The Cave " and " The Cave of Adullam." The epithet originated in their being likened by John Bright to the discontented people taking refuge with David in the cave of Adullam (1 Samuel xxii, 1, 2).

Advance, The.

Vessel in which Elisha Kent Kane (1820–57) explored the Arctic regions in search of Sir John Franklin.

Adversity Hume.

Nickname given to Joseph Hume (1777–1855) about 1825, owing to his predictions of national disaster. (Cf. Prosperity Robinson).

Æsop of England, The.

A surname given to John Gay (1685–1732), an English poet and dramatist.

Æsop of France, The.

A surname given to Jean de La Fontaine, the most noted French fabulist (1621–95).

Æsop of Germany, The.

A surname given to Gotthold Ephraim Lessing, a celebrated German dramatist and critic (1729–81).

Affable, The.

A surname given to Charles VIII, king of France (1470–98).

African, The.

A surname given to Alfonso V (Affonso or Alphonso), king of Portugal (1432–81) from his conquests in Africa.

African Roscius, The.

A surname given to Ira Aldridge, a negro tragedian (c. 1810–66), in early life valet of Edmund Kean. Among his chief parts was "Othello."

Afrikander Bond.

An association in South Africa founded in 1879, aiming at the furtherance of Afrikander influence and the ultimate complete independence of South Africa. Afrikander is the Dutch word for " African," a name given to whites, particularly those of Dutch descent, born in South Africa.

Agnes' Eve, Saint, v. St. Agnes' Eve.

Agony Column, The.

A joking name given to the column in newspapers set aside for advertisements of missing persons, lost and found property, &c. The former are often couched in agonizing terms.

Ahasuerus, v. Wandering Jew.

Aitkenites.

Nickname given to a party in the Church of England led by Robert Aitkin (1800–73), who temporarily withdrew from the Church of England (1824–40). Their object was to graft certain Methodist practices and ideas upon the Anglican Church.

Alabama, The.

A wooden steamship of 1,040 tons, built at Birkenhead, England, for the Confederate States. She cruised from 1862–4, destroying American shipping and was sunk by the *Kearsage*, off Cherbourg, June 19, 1864 (See below).

Alabama Claims.

Claims made by the United States against Great Britain for losses caused by depredations of vessels fitted out or supplied in British ports under the Confederate government. The claims were referred to arbitration, and in the result a sum of $15,500,000 in gold was awarded to the United States in satisfaction of all claims.

Alabama Claims Commission.

The arbitration commission appointed to setttle the Alabama Claims mentioned above, composed of Earl de Grey and Ripon, Sir Stafford Northcote, Sir Edward Thornton, Sir John Macdonald, and Professor Montague Bernard, representing Great Britain ; and Hamilton Fish, Robert C. Schenck, Samuel Nelson, Ebenezer R. Hoar, and George H. Williams, representing the United States.

Alaric-Cotin.

A nickname given to Frederick (II) the Great, king of Prussia (1712–86) by Voltaire, in allusion to his military genius and his taste for literature. Alaric was a famous Visigoth king (c. 376–410) and the abbé Charles Cotin a mediocre poet (1604–82).

Albanian Alexander, The.

A surname given to Scanderbeg (or Skanderbeg) originally George Castriota, an Albanian commander (1403–68).

Albany Regency, The.

A name given to a clique of New York politicians who controlled the machinery of the Democratic party in New York State from about 1820 to about 1854. Among its members were Van Buren, Marcy, Wright and Dix.

Albemarle, The.

A Confederate ironclad ram, built during 1863. She did a great deal of damage to Union steamers in the spring of 1864, but was destroyed by Lieut. W. B. Cushing, during the night of October 27, 1864, who exploded a torpedo under the ram's overhang. She was afterwards raised, towed to Norfolk, and was stripped and sold in 1867.

Albigenses.

Name given to the members of several anti-sacerdotal sects in the south of France (twelfth and thirteenth centuries), from Albi, in Languedoc. Also called **Cathari.**

Albingians (properly North Albingians or Nordalbingisch).

A Saxon tribe living to the north of the Elbe, whence the name is derived. First made known to Europe by Charlemagne's campaigns (eighth century).

Albion.

The ancient name of Britain ; now only used poetically, and generally restricted to England, e.g., " the white cliffs of Albion."

Albion perfide (French, "Perfidious Albion ").

A name given (it is said) by Napoleon I to Great Britain.

Alcantara, Knights of, *v.* Knights of Alcantara.

Alcazar.

Palace of the Moorish kings, and, later, of Spanish royalty at Seville. Also a palace, originally Moorish, in Segovia, Spain, occupied by the sovereigns of Castile from the fourteenth century. Burned in 1862 and restored.

Alcibiades.

Surname given to Albert, Margrave of Brandenburg (1522-77) ; pseudonym used by Alfred Tennyson in *Punch.*

Alert, The, *v.* Discovery, The.

Alexander Column.

A column at St. Petersburg, erected in 1832 in honour of

Alexander I (1777–1825). Total height, 154¾ feet. The polished shaft of red granite, 84 feet high (diameter 14 ft.), is the greatest modern monolith.

Alexander of the North.

Surname of Charles XII of Sweden (1682–1718).

Alfred Club.

A club instituted in Albemarle Street, London, in 1808.

Alhambra.

A citadel and palace above the city of Granada, Spain, founded in the thirteenth century by the Moorish kings. The palace is the finest example of Moorish art.

Alliance of Teplitz.

A treaty of alliance between the monarchs of Russia, Austria, and Prussia against Napoleon, signed at Teplitz, Sept. 9, 1813.

Alliance of the Three Kings.

An alliance between the kings of Prussia, Saxony and Hanover, in 1849, for the furtherance of law and order in Germany.

Alliance of Torgau.

A league formed at Torgau, 1526, by Saxony and Hesse, and other Protestant powers, against the Roman Catholic states.

Allobroges.

A Celtic people of southeastern Gaul, living between the Rhône and the Isère, northward to Lake Geneva. Subjected to Rome 121 B.C.

All Red Cable, The.

The name given to a cable route from England to Australia, touching only soil belonging to Great Britain, completed in 1902.

All-the-Talents Administration.

Name given ironically to the English ministry of 1806–7. Grenville (Prime Minister), Fox (Foreign Secretary), Erskine and Lords Fitzwilliam, Sidmouth and Ellenborough were among the leading members.

Almack's.

A gaming club established earlier than 1763 by William Almack, in Pall Mall, London ; afterwards known as "Brooks's," the Whig Club. "Among the twenty-seven original members of Almack's Club were the Duke of Portland and Charles James Fox, and it was subsequently joined by Gibbon, William Pitt, and very many noblemen." ("Dict. Nat. Biog.") Also the name of the famous assembly-rooms in King Street, St. James's, built by Almack in 1764, and opened Feb. 20, 1765, afterwards called Willis's.

Almanach de Gotha.

An annual register published in French and German at Gotha from 1764. It comprises a genealogical detail of the principal royal and aristocratic families of Europe, and a diplomatic and statistical record for the time of the different states of the world.

Alnaschar of Modern Literature, The.

A surname given to Samuel Taylor Coleridge, an English poet, philosopher and literary critic (1772–1834), in allusion to his "Kubla Khan," which he said he dreamt one night and wrote out on awaking.

Alsatia.

At one time applied to White-friars (between the Thames and Fleet Street and adjoining the Temple), a district possessing certain privileges of sanctuary derived from the convent of Carmelites, or White Friars, founded there in 1241. The privileges were abolished in 1697, the locality having been the resort of rascals and libertines of every description. The word " Alsatia " is often used to typify a thieves' quarter or resort. Cf. Sir. W Scott's " The Fortunes of Nigel."

Alte Dessauer, Der (German, "The old Dessauer").

A nickname given to Leopold, Prince of Anhalt-Dessau, a Prussian field-marshal (1676–1747).

Amalfitan Code.

The oldest existing code of maritime law, compiled by the authorities of Amalfi about the period of the first Crusade. The town possessed considerable commerce and maritime power.

Amalfitan Tables, *v.* above.

Amalings (or Amals).

A royal Gothic family, said to have ruled over the Goths till the division of the nation into Ostrogoths and Visigoths, and then over the former until the extinction of the male line in Theodoric the Great, 526. *v.* Balthings.

Amals, *v.* Amalings.

Amaryllis, *v.* Tenth Muse, The.

Amateur Casual, The.

Pseudonym of James Greenwood, journalist and miscellaneous writer.

Amati.

Name applied to violins made by a celebrated family of violin-makers of that name, who flourished at Cremona in the sixteenth and seventeenth centuries. Its most noted members were Andrea, his sons Antonio and Geronimo, and Nicolo, son of Geronimo.

Amazon of the Revolution.

A surname of Anne Joseph Terwagne, called Théroigne de Méricourt, a heroine of the French Revolution (1762–1817). Also called " La Belle Lié-geoise," " the Fury of the Gironde," etc.

Amboise, Conspiracy of.

An unsuccessful conspiracy of the Huguenots under La Renaudie to seize Francis II, first at Blois and afterwards at Amboise (1560), and remove him from the influence of the Guises. Condé was the real chief.

Ambrosian Library.

A library at Milan (named after St. Ambrose), founded in 1609 by Cardinal Borromeo. Contains 164,000 printed volumes and 81,000 MSS.

America.

The name of a wooden-keel schooner yacht, designed and built by George Steers, of New York, for Commodore J. C. Stevens, of the New York Yacht Club, in 1851. Won a race (for a £500 cup) open to yachts of all nations, Aug. 22, 1851, the course being round the Isle of Wight. The cup was presented in 1857 to the New York Yacht Club, and although made a prize open to challenge by yachts of all nations, has remained in the club's possession. Known as the " America Cup."

America Cup, v. above.

American Bastille, The.

A surname given to Fort Lafayette, at the entrance of New York Bay, it having been used for political prisoners during the Civil War.

American Eclipse, v. Eclipse.

American Fabius, The.

A surname given to George Washington, first President of the United States (1732–99), his tactics being similar to those of Fabius the Cunctator.

American Federation of Labour, The.

The name of one of the largest labour unions in the world, organized in 1886 at Columbus, Ohio. Its objects and aims are officially stated to be to render employment and the means of subsistence less precarious by securing to the workers an equitable share of the fruits of their labour.

American Manchester v. Manchester of America, The.

American Montaigne, The.

A surname given to Ralph Waldo Emerson, a celebrated American essayist, lecturer, and poet (1803–82).

American Party, v. Anti-Masonic Party.

American Revolution.

The war, for redress of grievances, and later for independence, waged by the thirteen American colonies (States) against Great Britain. They were assisted by France, Spain and (in the latter part of the war) the Netherlands. The measures leading to the war were Writs of Assistance, 1761 ; Stamp Act, 1765 ; taxes on glass, paints, etc., 1767 ; Boston Port Bill, 1774. v. Boston Tea-party, The.

American Socrates, The.

A surname given to Benjamin Franklin, a celebrated American philosopher, statesman, diplomatist and author (1706–90), by Sir James Mackintosh.

American Tupper, The.

A surname given to Josiah Gilbert Holland, an American author, journalist and editor (1819–81), owing to his aphoristic style of writing.

Amidu Peuple, L', (French, "The Friend of the People ").

A surname given to Jean Paul Marat (1744–93), being the title of a democratic journal which he conducted.

Anabaptists.

A sect of Christians who hold that baptism in infancy is invalid, requiring adults to be rebaptized on joining their communion.

Anacharsis.

A name assumed by Jean Baptiste Clootz (or Cloots), a French revolutionary enthusiast (1755–94). He also styled himself the " orator of the human race."

Anacreon Moore.

A name sometimes given to Thomas Moore, an Irish poet (1779–1852) who published a translation of the "Odes of Anacreon" in 1801.

Anacreon of Painters, The.

A surname given to Francesco Albani (or Albano), a noted Italian painter (1578–1660). So called on account of the softness of his style.

Anacreon of Persia, The.

A surname given to Shams ed-din Muhammad Hafiz, a Persian poet, divine, grammarian and philosopher (b. beginning of fourteenth century—d.c. 1388–94).

Anacreon of the Guillotine, The.

A surname given to Bertrand Barère de Vieuzac, a French lawyer and politician (1755–1841). Also called the Witling of Terror.

Anacreon of the Temple, The.

A surname given to Guillaume Amfrye, abbé de Chaulieu, a French poet (1639–1720). He resided at the Temple, Paris, whence the surname.

Anak of Publishers, The, *v*. Emperor of the West, The.

Anatomie Vivante, L', *v*. Patriarch of Ferney, The.

Anatomist of Humanity.

A surname given sometimes to Jean Baptiste Poquelin Molière, the greatest French comedy writer (1622–73).

Andrassy Note, The.

A declaration relating to the disturbed state of Bosnia and Herzegovina, drawn up by the Governments of Austria, Russia, and Germany, with the approval of England and France, and presented to the Porte on Jan. 31, 1876. It was framed by Count Gyula [Julius] Andrassy, a noted Hungarian statesman (1823–90).

Andrea Ferrara.

A name often given to a sword, but originally only applied to the workmanship of a famous Italian sword-maker.

Âne de Buridan, *v*. Buridan's Ass.

Angelic Brothers.

A community of Dutch Pietists (founded by George Gichtel (sixteenth century), who believed that they had attained that state of angelic purity in which there is "neither marrying nor giving in marriage."

Angelic Doctor, *v*. Doctor Angelicus.

Angel of the Schools, The, *v*. Doctor Angelicus.

Anglo-Saxon Milton, The.

A name applied to Saint Cædmon (or Cedmon), an Anglo-Saxon (Northumbrian) poet (fl. c. 670), the reputed author of metrical paraphrases of the Old Testament. It has been doubted whether he was a real personage.

Anna Matilda.

Name adopted by Mrs. Hannah Cowley, dramatist and poet (1743–1809), in a poetical correspondence in the *World* with Robert Merry, who used the pseudonym of "Della

Crusca." The words have become a synonym for mawkish, namby-pamby sentimental verse and fiction.

Antarctic.

The name of a Norwegian whaler carrying an expedition to the Antarctic regions, 1894–5.

Anti-Burghers.

The members of one of the two sections into which the Scottish Secession Church was divided in 1747, by a controversy on the lawfulness of accepting a clause in the oath required to be taken by burgesses declaratory of "their profession and allowance of the true religion professed within the realm and authorized by the laws thereof." The Anti-Burghers denied that this oath was compatible with the principles of the church, while the Burghers were of the contrary opinion. The parties were re-united in 1820. *v.* **Burghers.**

Anti-Jacobin, or Weekly Examiner, The.

Title of a paper started Nov. 10, 1797, by George Canning, and principally contributed to by his friends, John Hookham Frere and George Ellis. It was edited by William Gifford, and the last number appeared July 9, 1798. Its avowed object was to ridicule the doctrines of the French Revolution and their advocates in England.

Anti-Jacobin Review, The.

Title of a monthly periodical started in 1798 by John Gifford ; it came to an end in 1821.

Anti-Masonic Party.

A political party in America, opposed to the alleged influence of Freemasonry in civil affairs It originated in western New York after the kidnapping of William Morgan in 1826. He had threatened, it is said, to disclose the secrets of the fraternity. In 1875 an "American Party" revived the principles of the Anti-Masonic Party, but its adherents have been very few.

Antonine Column, *v.* Column of Marcus Aurelius.

Apelles of his Age, The.

A surname given to Samuel Cooper (in his epitaph), a noted English miniaturist (1609–72). Walpole called him "Van Dyck in little."

Apollo Club.

A famous club held at the Devil Tavern, near Temple Bar, London, in the seventeenth century, frequented by Ben Jonson, Randolph, Herrick, and others.

Apostate, The.

A surname given to Julian (Flavius Claudius Julianus), a Roman emperor (c. 331–63), from his having renounced the Christian faith (in which he was brought up) for paganism.

Apostle of Andalusia, The.

Surname given to Juan de Avila, a Spanish pulpit orator, who preached forty years in Andalusia (1500–69.)

Apostle of Ardennes and of Brabant, The.

Surname of St. Hubert, a bishop of Liège, the patron saint of hunters (d. 727).

Apostle of Brazil, The.

Surname given to José de Anchieta (or Anchietta), a Jesuit missionary (1533–97).

Apostle of Caledonia, The, *v.* Apostle of the Highlanders, The.

Apostle of Culture, The.

A surname given to Matthew Arnold, an English poet and critic (1822–88).

Apostle of Free Trade, The.

Surname given to Richard Cobden, English statesman and political economist (1804–65). He was especially noted as an advocate of Free Trade and peace, and as the chief supporter of the Anti-Corn Law League (1839-46). Sometimes also applied to John Bright, a distinguished English Liberal statesman and orator (1811–89). Also called the " Tribune of the People."

Apostle of Germany, The.

Surname of St. Boniface (original name Winfrid or Winfrith), a celebrated English missionary (b. in Devonshire, d. in Friesland, 755).

Apostle of Greenland, The.

A surname of Hans Egede, a Norwegian missionary (1686–1758), who was stationed among the Eskimos of Greenland, 1721–36.

Apostle of Infidelity, The.

Surname given to François Marie Arouet, who assumed the name of Voltaire in 1718 (1694–1778). *v.* Patriarch of Ferney, The.

Apostle of Ireland, The.

Ireland's patron saint, St· Patrick (b. according to tradition, at Nemthur [now Dumbarton], Scotland, c. 396, and d. probably c. 469). He was a son of the deacon Calpurnius, son of Potitus, a priest.

Apostle of Liberty, The.

A surname given to Henry Clay (1777–1852) ; also to Thomas Jefferson (1743–1826), third President of the United States.

Apostle of Peru, The.

A surname given to Alonso de Barcena (or Barzena), a Spanish Jesuit (1528–98).

Apostle of Temperance, The.

A surname given to Theobald (Father) Matthew, an Irish priest and temperance advocate (1790–1856). Also called the " Sinner's Friend."

Apostle of the Anglo-Saxons, The.

Surname given to St. Augustine (or Austin), who d. at Canterbury, 604. A Benedictine monk sent in 597 by Pope Gregory I as a missionary to Kent. He became the first Archbishop of Canterbury c. 600. Also called the " Apostle of the English."

Apostle of the English, The, *v.* Apostle of the Anglo-Saxons.

Apostle of the French, The.

A surname given to St. Denis (or Denys), Apostle to the Gauls (*v.* **Apostle of the Gauls**), and patron saint of France. According to tradition he was beheaded at Paris in 272.

Apostle of the Friesians, The.

Surname of Willibrord (Wilibrord, Wilbrord or Wilbrod), an English missionary (b. in Northumbria, c. 657, d. c. 738). He settled among the Friesians c. 690.

Apostle of the Gauls, The.

Surname given to St. Irenæus, a celebrated Greek church father, who became bishop of Lyons in 177 (d. probably c. 202).

Apostle of the Gentiles, The.

Surname of St. Paul (originally Saul), who suffered martyrdom at Rome c. 67.

Apostle of the Highlanders, The.

Surname given to St. Columba (b. in Ireland 521, d. at Iona, Scotland, 597), a Celtic missionary in Scotland, who founded the monastery of Iona, c. 565. Alternatively called "the Apostle of Caledonia."

Apostle of the Hungarians, The.

A surname given to St. Anastasius (d. 628).

Apostle of the Indians, The.

Surname of John Eliot, a missionary to the Indians of Massachusetts (1604-90); v. also **Protector of the Indians.**

Apostle of the Indies, The.

Surname of St. Francis (Francisco) Xavier, a famous Spanish Jesuit missionary (1506-52). He went to the East Indies in 1541. Died near Canton.

Apostle of the Iroquois, The.

A surname given to the abbé F. Piquet.

Apostle of the Netherlands, The.

A surname given to St. Armand (589-679).

Apostle of the North, The.

Surname given to Ansgar (or Anscharius), a Frankish missionary to Denmark (827), Sweden (828-31), and Northern Germany (b. near Amiens, France, 801, d. at Bremen, 865). The first bishop of Hamburg. Also sometimes given to Bernard Gilpin, an English clergyman (1517-83), on account of his charities and gratuitous ministrations among the poor. Also called the "Father of the Poor."

Apostle of the Peak, The.

A surname given to William Bagshaw, a Nonconformist divine (1628-1702), from his missionary labours in Derbyshire.

Apostle of the Picts, The.

A surname given to St. Ninian, a British missionary among the Southern Picts (fl. c. 400).

Apostle of the Prussians, The.

A surname of St. Adalbert (originally Czech Vojtech), a Bohemian prelate, bishop of Prague (c. 955-997). *v.* **Apostle to the Prussians.**

Apostle of the Scots, The.

Surname given to John Knox, a celebrated Scottish reformer and writer (1505-72). Also the "Apostle of the Scottish Reformation."

Apostle of the Scottish Reformation, The, *v.* **Apostle of the Scots, The.**

Apostle of the Slavs, The.

Surname of St. Cyril (or Constantine), a scholar and prelate (c. 820–c. 869) ; also of Methodius (d. 885), brother of and co-labourer with Cyril ; also of Adalbert, a German missionary, archbishop of Magdeburg (d. 981).

Apostle of the Sword, The.

A surname given to Mohammed (570–632) owing to his enforcement of the religion of Islam at the sword's point.

Apostle's Creed, The.

A primitive creed of the Christian Church, a product of the Western Church during the first four centuries. Originally a baptismal confession. *v.* Athanasian Creed and Nicene Creed.

Apostle to the Gauls, *v.* St. Denis.

Apostle to the Prussians, The.

A surname given to Saint Bruno (c. 970, killed 1009). *v.* Apostle of the Prussians.

Apostolic Fathers, The.

Those Christian writers who were contemporary with any of the apostles. Their names are—Barnabas, Clement of Rome, Ignatius, Polycarp, Hermas and Papias.

Apostolic King.

A surname given by the Holy See to the kings of Hungary for the extensive propagation of Christianity by St. Stephen I (d. 1038), the founder of the royal line.

Apostolics, or Apostolicals.

A political party in Spain supporting the Catholic Church and absolute government. It dated from the restoration of the Bourbons, and lasted until about 1833, when it was absorbed by the Carlists.

Aquinian Sage, The.

A surname given to Juvenal (Decimus Junius Juvenalis), a noted Roman rhetorician and satirical poet (fl. c. 60–140), born at Aquinum, Latium.

Arabian, The.

A surname of Marcus Julius Philippus, a Roman emperor (r. 244–9).

Arabian Tailor, The, *v.* Learned Tailor, The.

Arctic, The.

A first-class passenger steamship belonging to the Collins Line (the first American line of steamships). Sunk in a collision in the Atlantic (1854) with the *Vesta*, off Newfoundland, during a dense fog.

Arians.

Name given to the followers of Arius, a deacon of Alexandria, who (fourth century), in opposition to both Sabellianism and Tritheism, that the son is of a nature similar to (but not the same as) the father, and is subordinate to him. *v.* Sabellians and Socinians.

Ariosto of the North.

One of the surnames given to Sir Walter Scott (1771–1832) (*v.* Great Unknown, The ; and Wizard of the North, Great Magician of the North). Cf. "And, like [the Ariosto of the North,"—Byron, "Childe Harold's Pilgrimage," can. iv, st. 40.

Ark, The, v. **Dove, The.**

Arlington House.

A mansion in the midst of the national cemetery, opposite Washington, district of Columbia, once the property of General Washington.

Armada, The Invincible (or Spanish).

Name given to the great fleet (or Armada) sent by Philip II of Spain against England in 1588. It was commanded by the Duke of Medina Sidonia, and consisted of about 129 vessels. The English fleet of about 80 vessels, under Lord Howard of Effingham, met and defeated it in Aug. 1588 in the English Channel and Straits of Dover.

Armagnacs.

The party of the house of Orleans, the house of Burgundy's opponents during Charles VI's reign (1380–1422), from Bernard of Armagnac, their leader. (v. **Burgundians,** also **Paix Fourrée, La.**) The name was also given to bands of lawless mercenaries, consisting chiefly of natives of the county of Armagnac, trained in the civil wars between the above-named parties. They were sent by Charles VII (in order to get rid of them) to help the Emperor Frederick III in enforcing his claims against the Swiss in 1444.

Armed Soldier of Democracy, The.

A surname given to Napoleon Bonaparte or Buonaparte (1769–1821), Also called the " Nightmare of Europe "; the " Modern Sesostris " (by Lord

Byron) ; the " Corsican Fiend " (by Sir John Stoddart) ; the " Corsican Ogre," the " Corsican General," " le Petit Caporal," the " Colossus of the Nineteenth Century," and " Redingote Grise."

Armenian, The.

A surname of Leo V, Byzantine emperor (d. 820).

Arminians.

The followers of Arminius (Jacobus Harmensen), a Protestant divine of Leyden (1560–1609). They presented their doctrines in a " remonstrance " (1610), which gave them the name of " Remonstrants " also.

Armistice of Znaim.

A truce between the French and Austrians, July 12, 1809, following the battle of Wagram and preparatory to the peace of Vienna.

Armorica.

The ancient (Latin) name of the north-western part of France now called Brittany (or Bretagne).

Armoury of Germany, The.

A name given to Suhl, Prussia, where manufactures of firearms are carried on.

Army of Northern Virginia.

The main Confederate army in the east during the Civil War. It surrendered to Grant at Appomattox, April 9, 1865.

Army of the Cumberland, v. **Army of the Ohio.**

Army of the James.

A Federal army in the American Civil War, which operated in 1864 in conjunction with the Army of the Potomac (q.v.). It was commanded by General B. F. Butler.

Army of the Loire.

A French army improvised after the battle of Sedan (Sept. 1, 1870), for the relief of Paris. Commanded by Aurelle de Paladines. After the beginning of December, 1870, the name was applied to the part of the first army commanded by General Antoine Eugène Alfred Chanzy, the remaining part being under General Charles Denis Sauter Bourbaki.

Army of the Ohio.

A Federal army in the American Civil War, organized by General Buell. In October, 1862, Buell was succeeded by Rosecrans, and the army was called the " Army of the Cumberland."

Army of the Potomac.

The principal Federal army in the American Civil War, organized by General McClellan in 1861. *v.* Army of the James.

Army of the Tennessee.

A Federal army in the Civil War. It was commanded after the battle of Shiloh by Halleck, and later by Grant, Sherman, McPherson, Howard and Logan.

Army of Virginia.

A Federal army in the Civil War, formed in August, 1862, out of the commands of Frémont, Banks and McDowell. It was commanded by General Pope, and took part in the second Bull Run campaign, after which it was discontinued.

Arthur's.

A London club established in 1765, so named from the keeper of White's Chocolate House, who died in 1761.

Articles of Confederation.

The compact or constitution adopted by the Continental Congress in 1777, and ratified by the separate colonies within the four years following. As it had no power to enforce its laws upon the States, it soon fell into contempt, and on March 4, 1789, it expired by limitation under the provisions of the present Constitution.

Arundel.

The steed of Sir Bevis of Southampton (or Bevis of Hampton). Cf. Michael Drayton's "Polyolbion," Bk. ii.

Arundel Society.

A society organized in 1849 for the cultivation of art, named after Thomas Howard, Earl of Arundel (1586-1646), who formed the first large collection of works of art in England.

Ascalon.

The sword of St. George, one of the "Seven Champions of Christendom " (q.v.).

Ascension Day, *v.* Holy Thursday.

Ascræan Sage, The.

A surname given by Virgil to Hesiod, a celebrated Greek poet (fl. c. 735 B.C.), who was born at Ascra, Bœotia.

Asparagus Gardens, The.

A low place of public entertainment, not far from Pimlico, from which a comedy by Richard

Brome (acted in 1635, published 1640) took its name ("The Sparagus Garden, or Tom Hoyden of Taunton Dean ").

Assassination Plot, The.

A conspiracy, detected in 1696, against the life of William III of England, by Sir George Barclay, Charnock, and Parkyns.

Assassins, The.

A military and religious order, founded in Persia by Hassan ben Sabbah, c. 1090. A colony migrated from Persia to Syria, settled in various places, with their chief seat on the mountains of Lebanon, and became remarkable for their secret murders in blind obedience to the will of their chief. Their religion was a compound of Magianism, Judaism, Christianity and Mohammedanism. One article of their creed was that the Holy Spirit resided in their chief, and that his orders proceeded from God himself. The chief of the sect is best known by the name of "old man of the mountain" (Arabic, "sheikh aljebal," chief of the mountains). These barbarous chieftains and their followers spread terror among nations far and near for almost two centuries. They were eventually subdued by the Sultan Bibars, c. 1272.

Assembly of Divines at Westminster, *v.* **Westminster Assembly.**

Assembly of Notables.

In French history, a council of prominent persons from the three classes of the state, convoked by the king on extraordinary occasions. The institution can be traced to the reign of Charles V (fourteenth century), but the two most famous assemblies were those of 1787 and 1788, summoned by Louis XVI in view of the impending crisis.

Asses' Bridge, *v.* **Pons Asinorum.**

Assize of Woodstock.

A code for the regulation of the forests, proclaimed by Henry II in 1184.

Associated Counties, The.

A name applied to the counties of Norfolk, Suffolk, Essex, Hertford, Cambridge, Huntingdon and Lincoln, they having combined (1642-6) to join the Parliamentary side in the Civil War.

Astor Place Riot, The.

A riot which took place May 9, 1849, when Macready was playing "Macbeth" at the Astor Place Opera House, New York. A mob of 20,000 persons attacked the theatre, but were at last dispersed by the military. The riot originated in a feud between Edwin Forrest, the American actor, and Macready. Sometimes referred to as the **Forrest-Macready Riot.**

Astronomer, The, *v.* **Wise, The** (Alfonso X).

Athanasian Creed.

One of the three great creeds of the Christian Church (cf. Articles of Religion, viii.), supposed at one time to have been composed by Athanasius, but now generally ascribed to Hilary, bishop of Arles, in 430. *v.* **Apostles' Creed and Nicene Creed.**

Athenian Bee, The.

A name applied to Plato, the famous Greek philosopher (c. 429–347 B.C.), the founder of the Academic school, alluding to the sweetness of his style. *v.* also **Attic Bee, The.**

Athens of America (or The Modern Athens).

A name given to Boston, Massachusetts. Also the **Athens of the New World.**

Athens of Ireland, The.

A name given to the city of Cork, also of Belfast.

Athens of Switzerland, The.

A name sometimes applied to Zürich.

Athens of the New World, The, *v.* Athens of America, The.

Athens of the North, The.

A name given to Edinburgh ; sometimes also to Copenhagen.

Athens of the West, The.

A name given to Cordova, Spain, which was an intellectual centre from the eighth to the thirteenth century.

Atherton Gag.

Name applied to a resolution introduced into Congress by Charles Gordon Atherton (1804–53). It provided that all bills or petitions on the subject of slavery should be " laid on the table without being debated, printed, or referred," and remained in force from 1838–45.

Attic Bee, The.

Surname of the Greek tragic poet Sophocles (c. 495–406 B.C.). Also called the **Attic Homer.**
D.N.

Also of Plato *v.* Athenian Bee, The.

Attic Homer, The, *v.* Attic Bee, The.

Attic Muse, The.

A surname applied to the Greek historian Xenophon (c. 430–after 357 B.C.). Also called the **Muse of Greece.**

Augsburg Confession, The.

The chief Lutheran creed, prepared by Melancthon and read before the Diet of Augsburg in 1530.

Augsburg Interim, The.

A provisional arrangement for the settlement of religious differences between Protestants and Roman Catholics in Germany. It was proclaimed by Charles V, May 15, 1548.

Augsburg, League of.

A treaty between Holland, the emperor, the kings of Sweden and Spain, and the electors of Bavaria, Saxony and the Palatinate, for maintaining the treaties of Münster and Nimeguen, as against France (July 9, 1686).

Augsburg, Religious Peace of.

A treaty (September 25, 1555), between the Lutheran and Catholic estates of Germany, concluded at a Diet held in Augsburg in conformity with the Convention of Passau. It provided that the individual states of the empire should be permitted to prescribe the form of worship within their limits.

Augusta, *v.* Trinovant.

Augustan Age of England.

A name by which the reign

c

(1558–1603) of Queen Elizabeth is sometimes referred to. Some use the term for the reign (1702–14) of Queen Anne.

Augustan Age of France.

A name given to the reign (1643–1715) of Louis XIV.

Augustan Age of Germany.

A name given, as regards Germany, to the period of the nineteenth century.

Augustan Age of Portugal.

A name given to the period, as regards Portugal, from the accession (1385) of John (I) the Great to the death (1557) of John III.

Auld Reekie.

Edinburgh was so named because of its smokiness or the uncleanliness of its streets.

Aulic Council.

Under the old German Empire, the personal council of the emperor, and one of the two supreme courts which decided without appeal. Instituted about 1501, and ceased to exist on the extinction of the German Empire in 1806. The title is now given to the council of state of the Emperor of Austria.

Auster.

Latin, the south wind.

Austerlitz, Sun of, *v.* Sun of Austerlitz.

Austin Friars.

The monastery of the Friars Eremite of the order of St. Augustine, on the north side of Broad Street, London, founded in 1253 by Humphrey Bohun,

Earl of Hereford and Essex. The site of the nave is now occupied by a Dutch church.

Austrian Hyena, The.

A nickname given to Julius Jakob von Haynau, from his cruelties in Italy and Hungary. The indignation caused by his flogging of women at the capture of Brescia, and his severity to the defeated Hungarians in 1849, was such that he barely escaped with his life when on a visit to Barclay and Perkins's Brewery, London.

Authentic Doctor, The.

Surname given to the schoolman, Gregory of Rimini (d. 1358).

Authorized Version (of 1611).

A term used to refer to the English translation of the Bible, authorized by James I of England. It is based upon the Bishops' Bible, which appeared in 1572, and is often called " King James's Bible," or the " King's Bible." *v.* Revised Version.

Avenger, The.

A surname given to Alfonso XI (or Alphonso), King of Leon and Castile (d. 1350), for his severity in repressing internal disorder.

Avon, *v.* Wasp.

Ayrshire Bard, The, *v.* Ayrshire Poet, The.

Ayrshire Poet, The.

A name given to Robert Burns, the Scottish poet (1759–96), who was born in Ayrshire. Also the **Bard of Ayrshire.**

Baanites.

Followers of Baanes, a Paulician of the eighth, and early part of the ninth, century.

Babes of the Wood, The.

A name given to insurrectionary bands of Irish, who infested the Wicklow mountains and the woods near Enniscorthy towards the end of the eighteenth century, and committed great atrocities.

Babists (or Babi).

A Persian sect of Mohammedans, so called from *bab*, "a gate," the name assumed by the founder, who claimed that no one could come to know God except through him. The founder, Seyd Mohammed Ali, a native of Shiraz, was executed in 1850.

Babism, *v.* **Babists.**

Baboon, Lewis, *v.* **Lewis Baboon.**

Baboon, Philip, *v.* **Philip Baboon.**

Bacon of Theology, The.

A surname given to Bishop Joseph Butler (1692–1752), author of "The Analogy of Religion."

Bacon-Shakspere Controversy, *v.* **Shakspere - Bacon Controversy.**

Bactrian Sage, The.

A surname given to Zoroaster (or Zarathustra), said to be a native of Bactria, but his actual existence has been denied.

Bad, The.

Surname given to Albert, landgrave of Thuringia (after 1265), and margrave of Meissen from 1268–93 (d. 1314), *v.* **Mauvais, Le**; also to William I, king of Sicily from 1154–66.

Baddeley Cake, The.

Name given to an annual festival held at Drury Lane Theatre, London, on Twelfth Night. Robert Baddeley, an English actor (1733–94) left in his will the interest of £100 to provide wine and cake for the actors of that theatre on Twelfth Night.

Badger State, The.

A popular name for the State of Wisconsin. A badger figures in its coat-of-arms.

Badinguet.

A nickname of Napoleon III (1808–73). Badinguet was the name of a Moor, in whose disguise Napoleon escaped from the fortress of Ham in 1846. *v.* **Prisoner of Ham, The.**

Badminton.

A cup made of special and sweetened claret, named after the Duke of Beaufort (of Badminton), who was a patron of pugilistics. Hence the slang term ' claret ' applied in the prize-ring to blood.

Badminton, The.

Name of a sporting and coaching club of 1,000 members, established in London in 1876.

Bad Old Man, The.

A nickname given to General Jubal Anderson Early (1816–94) by the Confederate soldiers during the Civil War.

Baedeker Guides.

A series of guide books, named

from the founder, Karl Baedeker a German publisher (1801–59). The word 'Baedeker' alone is often used as a synonym for a guide-book.

Bagimont's Roll.

A list of the ecclesiastical benefices of Scotland and their valuation in the latter part of the middle ages. "It took its name from an Italian churchman, Boiamond (or Bajimont), of Vicci, a canon of the Cathedral of Asti in Piedmont, who was sent by the Pope to Scotland in 1274, to collect the tithe or tenth part of all the church livings, for a Crusade" ("Chambers's Encycl." i. 657).

Bagnigge Wells.

A place of amusement in the time of George II, situated to the east of Gray's Inn Road, nearly opposite the present Mecklenburgh Square, and northeast of St. Andrew's burying-ground. It "included a great room for concerts and entertainments, a garden planted with trees, shrubs and flowers, and provided with walks, a fishpond, fountain, rustic bridge, rural cottages and seats. The admission was threepence."

Baker, The, and the Baker's Wife.

Nicknames given to Louis XVI (1754–93) and Marie Antoinette, his queen (1755–93), because they gave bread to the hungry mob at Versailles, October 6, 1789.

Baker's Wife, The, v. Baker, The, etc.

Balafré, Le.

Surname given to Henri I de Lorraine, third Duke of Guise (1550–88), also to François de Lorraine, second duke (1519–63) from the scars on their faces caused by sword-cuts. Sir Walter Scott gave this surname to Ludovic Lesly, a character in "Quentin Durward."

Bald, The, v. Chauve, Le.

Balsamo, Joseph, v. Cagliostro, etc.

Balthings.

A royal Gothic family, said to have ruled over the Visigoths. v. Amalings.

Bamberg Conference.

A conference of the middle German States at Bamberg (May 25, 1854), to determine their policy in regard to that of Prussia and Austria with reference to the Eastern Question (q.v.).

Bamboccio (The Deformed).

A surname given to Pieter van Laar (or Laer), a Dutch genre painter (c. 1613–74), noted for his pictures of *kermesses* or village fêtes.

Bampton Lectures.

A series of lectures on divinity at Oxford, founded by John Bampton, an English divine (c. 1689–1751). The first lecturer was chosen in 1779.

Banal Frontier.

A part of the former Military Frontier of the Austrian Empire.

Banbury Man.

A Puritan. The name "Banbury," however, was applied in a depreciatory sense before Puritan times. The town would appear to have been chiefly inhabited by Puritans, judging from the frequent allusions in writers of the sixteenth and seventeenth centuries.

Bande Noire.

One of the various infantry companies in the French service in the sixteenth century. Also applied, in France, to speculators who, especially during the Revolution, purchased confiscated church property and ancient buildings and estates, and often destroyed time-honoured relics, using the materials in the erection of new structures.

Bangorian Controversy.

A controversy arising out of a sermon preached before George I on March 31, 1717, by Dr. Hoadley, Bishop of Bangor, from the text, " My kingdom is not of this world " (John xviii. 36). His argument was that Christ had not delegated judicial and disciplinary powers to the Christian ministry.

Bank, The.

The name by which the Bank of England, London, is familiarly known.

Banker-Poet, The.

A surname of Samuel Rogers, an English poet and son of a London banker. Also called the **Bard of Memory**. Also applied to Edmund Clarence Stedman, an American poet and critic, who became a stockbroker in New York City (b. 1833).

Banks's Horse.

A celebrated trick-horse, named Morocco, belonging to one Banks, who lived about the beginning of the seventeenth century. Alluded to by Raleigh, Ben Jonson, Armin, Gayton, and others.

Bannatyne Club.

A Scottish literary club, taking its name from George Bannatyne, founded in 1823 under the presidency of Sir Walter Scott, and dissolved in 1859.

Banting.

Name applied to a particular course of diet for the reduction of corpulence, recommended by William Banting, a London undertaker (1797–1878), in a pamphlet (1863) entitled " A Letter on Corpulence." The diet was originally prescribed for Banting by William Harvey, and principally consists of the use of lean meats and abstinence from fats, starch and sugar.

Baphomet.

An imaginary idol or symbol which the Templars were accused of worshipping.

Barbarossa (or Redbeard).

A surname of Frederick I, the most noted emperor of the Holy Roman Empire. Crowned emperor at Rome by Hadrian IV in 1155. In 1189 he joined the third Crusade, during which he was drowned in the Kalykadnos in Asia Minor.

Barbary Roan, *v.* Roan Barbary.

Barber Poet, The, *v.* Last of the Troubadours, The.

Barberini Vase, *v.* Portland Vase.

Barcino.

Ancient name of Barcelona, Spain.

Barclay, Captain, *v.* **Captain Barclay.**

Bard of all Time, The, *v.* **Swan of Avon, Sweet.**

Bard of Avon, The, *v.* **Swan of Avon, Sweet.**

Bard of Ayrshire, *v.* **Ayrshire Poet, The.**

Bard of Hope, The.

A surname sometimes given to Thomas Campbell, a British poet and miscellaneous writer (1777–1844), author of " The Pleasures of Hope."

Bard of Memory, The.

A surname sometimes given to Samuel Rogers, an English poet (1762–1855), author of "The Pleasures of Memory." *v.* **Banker-Poet, The.**

Bard of Olney, The.

A surname sometimes given to William Cowper, a celebrated English poet (1731–1800), who resided for many years at Olney, Bucks. Also called the **Domestic Poet.**

Bard of Prose, The, *v.* **Prince of Story-Tellers, The.**

Bard of Rydal Mount.

A surname given to the poet William Wordsworth (1770–1850), from his residence at Rydal Mount, Lake Windermere. Also called the **Cumberland Poet** and the **Poet of the Excursion,** from the name of his principal poem.

Bard of Sheffield, The.

A surname given to James Montgomery, a Scottish poet (1776–1854). He entered the office of the *Sheffield Register* in 1792, and in 1795 became its proprietor.

Bard of the Imagination, The.

A surname given to Mark Akenside, an English poet and physician (1721–70), author of " The Pleasures of the Imagination."

Bard of Twickenham, The.

A surname given to Alexander Pope, a famous English poet (1688–1744), who resided at Twickenham for the last twenty-six years of his life.

Barebones' Parliament.

Name given to the " Little Parliament " (q.v.) of Cromwell (which lasted only from July 4 to December 12, 1653), from the name of one of its members " Praise God Barebones " (Barbon or Barebone), a Baptist preacher and leather dealer (c. 1596–1679).

Barefoot, *v.* **Barfod.**

Barfod (Barefoot).

A surname of Magnus III, King of Norway (d. 1103). Killed during an invasion of Ireland.

Barleycorn, John, *v.* **John Barleycorn.**

Barmecide's Feast.

Name used to signify a tantalizing illusion or disappointment, in allusion to the story of " The Barber's Sixth Brother," in " The Arabian Nights' Entertainments." A rich Barmecide gives a dinner, where all the dishes are empty, and makes Shacabac, a starving wretch, pretend to eat what is not before him.

Barnburners.

A nickname given to the extreme or radical wing of the Democratic Party in New York State in 1844–8. Also called the **Young Democracy** The origin of the name Barnburners is variously accounted for. The Conservative wing of the Democratic Party was called **Old Hunkers.** On the slavery question coming to the front, the Barnburners joined the **Free-Soil Party** (q.v.).

Barney Barnato, *v.* Kaffir King.

Barons, War of the, *v.* War of the Barons.

Barricades, Days of the, *v.* Journées des Barricades.

Barriers, Battle of the, *v.* Battle of the Barriers.

Barrier Treaty.

A treaty signed at Antwerp, November 15, 1715, by Austria, Great Britain and the Netherlands, determining the relations of the Dutch and Austrians in the strategic towns of the Low Countries.

Bas-Empire, Le.

A name given to the Byzantine Empire, from Constantine until its fall in 1453.

Basilidians.

The followers of Basilides, a teacher of Gnostic doctrines at Alexandria (Egypt) in the second century. "The Gnosticism of Basilides appear to have been a fusion of the ancient sacerdotal religion of Egypt with the angelic and demoniac theory of Zoroaster" (Milman. "Hist. of Christ." ii. 68).

Basket-Maker, The.

A surname given to Thomas Miller, an English poet, novelist, and writer on rural life (1807–74).

Basoche, La.

An association of clerks connected with the Parliament of Paris, founded 1303, and suppressed in 1791. Revived recently.

Bastard, The, *v.* Conqueror, The.

Bastard of Orleans, *v.* Bâtard d'Orléans.

Bâtard d'Orléans.

Surname given to the Comte Jean de Dunois (1402–68), an illegitimate son of Louis, brother of Charles VI. Figures in Sir Walter Scott's "Quentin Durward."

Battle Above the Clouds, The.

A name sometimes given to the Battle of Lookout Mountain, a part of the Battle of Chattanooga, a Federal victory by General Grant over the Confederates under General Bragg (November 24, 1863). The name alludes to the heavy mist on the mountain-side at the time.

Battle Bridge.

A locality in old London (King's Cross), marked by a bridge across the Upper Fleet, or Holborn, and supposed to have derived its name from a battle between Suetonius and Boadicea, or, more probably, between Alfred and the Danes.

Was the site of a hospital called Battle Bridge Hospital.

Battle of Dorking.

An imaginary narrative of an invasion and conquest of England by a foreign army, written by General Sir George T. Chesney in 1871. It called attention to the need for an improved system of national defence.

Battle of the Barriers.

A victory over the French under the walls of Paris, gained by the Allies in March, 1814.

Battle of the Brothers.

A name given to the Battle of Fontenay (or Fontenaille), fought June 25, 841, between the three sons of Louis le Débonnaire. Sometimes called the Judgment of God. *v.* also Treaty of Verdun.

Battle of the Dunes.

A victory gained by the French and English allies under Turenne over the Spaniards on the dunes, or sands, near Dunkirk, June 4 (o.s.) 1658.

Battle of the Giants.

The Battle of Marignano (or Melegnano), September 13–14, 1515, in which Francis I of France defeated the Duke of Milan and the Swiss, so called from the obstinacy with which it was fought, and the superior character of the troops on both sides.

Battle of the Herrings.

A name given to the engagement between the French under the Count of Clermont and the English under Sir John Fastolf, near Rouvray, February, 1429.

Sir John was carrying provisions to the English army besieging Orleans, and these provisions consisted chiefly of herrings intended for the Lenten fast. Hence the name.

Battle of the Nations.

A name given to the Battle of Leipsig, October 16, 18 and 19, 1813, in which the French, Prussians, Austrians, Russians, Swedes, Saxons, etc., were represented.

Battle of the Pyramids.

A victory gained near the Pyramids of Egypt, July 21, 1798, by the French, under Napoleon, over the Mamelukes, under Murad Bey.

Battle of the Spurs.

The victory of the Flemings over the French at Courtrai in 1302 was so called from the number of gilt spurs captured. The victory of the English over the French at Guinegate in 1513 was also so named, from the precipitate flight of the latter.

Battle of the Standard.

A victory of the English, led by Archbishop Thurston, over the Scots, under King David, near Northallerton, Yorks, in 1138, was so called from the English banner.

Battle of the Thirty.

A fight between thirty Bretons and thirty Englishmen in France, near Ploermel, in 1351, led by Jean de Beaumanoir and Bemborough respectively. The English were beaten.

Battle of the Three Emperors.

The Battle of Austerlitz (December 2, 1805) was so named

from the presence of the Emperors Alexander I, Francis and Napoleon.

Bavarian, The.

A surname of Louis IV, Emperor of the Holy Roman Empire (1286–1347), son of the Duke of Bavaria.

Bayard.

The name of the legendary horse given by Charlemagne to the four sons of Aymon. Also of Rinaldo's famous steed, formerly belonging to Amadis of Gaul.

Bayard of India, The.

A surname given to Sir James Outram, an English general (1803–61), by Sir Charles Napier.

Bayard of the Netherlands, The.

A surname given to Count Louis of Nassau-Dillenburg (1538–74), brother of William of Orange.

Bayeux Tapestry, The.

A strip of linen, 231 feet long and 20 inches wide, preserved in the Library at Bayeux, France, illustrating episodes in the Norman Conquest of England.

Baynard's Castle.

A strong fortification on the Thames just below Blackfriars, founded by Baynard, one of William the Conqueror's followers. It was burned in the Great Fire of London, 1666.

Bayonne Decree.

A decree issued by Napoleon I at Bayonne, April 17, 1808, directing the seizure of all American vessels then in the ports of France.

Bayou State, The.

A name sometimes given to Mississippi.

Bayreuth Festival.

A musical festival at Bayreuth for the performance of Wagner's works in the National Theatre (opened by Wagner in 1876).

Bay State.

A name often given to the State of Massachusetts. Called also, before the Federal Constitution, the Colony of Massachusetts.

Beagle.

The ship (commander Captain Fitzroy, R.N.) in which the scientific expedition to survey South American waters was sent, 1831–6. Darwin accompanied the expedition as naturalist.

Bear, The.

Surname given to Albert, margrave of Brandenburg (c. 1100–70), from his heraldic emblem.

Bearded, The (Latin, "Pogonatus").

A surname given to Constantine IV, Emperor of the East (d. 685); to George, Duke of Saxony (1471–1539).

Bear Flag Battalion.

In the early history of California, an American corps, which was active in expelling the Mexicans.

Béarnais, Le.

A surname given to Henry IV of France (1553–1610), who was a native of Béarn, a Béarnais.

Bear State, The.

A nickname of the State of

Arkansas, a great number of bears at one time having infested its forests.

Beau Brummel (or Brummell).

George Bryan Brummell, famous as a leader of fashionable society in London (1778–1840), was so named. He became imbecile, and died in an asylum.

Beauclerc (or Beauclerk).

A surname given to Henry I of England (1068–1135), on account of his scholarly attainments.

Beau Feilding.

Robert Feilding, an English rake of the Restoration Period (d. 1712) was so named. Also known as " handsome Feilding."

Beau Nash.

Richard Nash, an English leader of fashion and master of the ceremonies at Bath (1674–1761) was so named. Sometimes also called the " King of Bath." Oliver Goldsmith wrote his life in 1762.

Beau of Princes, The, v. First Gentleman of Europe, The.

Beau Sabreur, Le, v. Dandy King, The.

Beautiful Corisande, The, v. Belle Corisande, La.

Beautiful Parricide, The.

A surname given to Beatrice Cenci, a Roman lady of great beauty and high birth. Condemned to death, and beheaded September 10, 1599, for the murder of her father, who had violently outraged her. Cf. Shelley's tragedy, " The Cenci."

Beauty of Buttermere, The.

A surname given to a lovely English girl, Mary Robinson, who was deceived into a marriage with John Hatfield, an impostor, who was executed for forgery at Carlisle, September 3, 1803.

Bedford Coffee House.

A noted house, formerly standing in Covent Garden, London, the resort of Garrick, Foote, Fielding, and others.

Bedford Level.

A flat tract of land, situated on the eastern coast of England, about 60 miles in length and 40 miles in breadth, extending from Milton, in Cambridgeshire, to Toynton, in Lincolnshire, and from Peterborough, in Northamptonshire, to Brandon, in Suffolk. It comprises nearly all the marshy district called the Fens and the Isle of Ely. The name is derived from Francis, Earl of Bedford, who, in 1634, undertook to drain it. Extensive drainage works have since been established.

Bedlam.

The hospital of St. Mary of Bethlehem in London, originally a priory, founded about 1247, but afterwards a lunatic asylum. The name Bedlam is a corruption of Bethlehem, and has come to be a synonym for a scene of wild uproar (e.g. a regular Bedlam let loose).

Bedlam Beggar.

Same as Abraham-man (q.v.).

Bee, The.

Name of a periodical which appeared October 6, 1759, but

only eight numbers were published. Oliver Goldsmith wrote nearly all the essays.

Bee of Attica, The, v. Attic Bee, The.

Beefeaters.

A name given to the Yeomen of the Guard, whose function it has been, ever since 1485, when they first appeared in Henry VII's coronation procession, to attend the sovereign at banquets and other State occasions. The warders at the Tower of London are also called Beefeaters, fifteen having been sworn in as Yeomen Extraordinary of the Guard during Edward VI's reign.

Beefsteak Club.

A club founded in the reign of Queen Anne (it was called a " new society " in 1709), believed to be the earliest club with this name. It was composed of the " chief wits and great men of the nation," and its badge was a gridiron. " The Sublime Society of the Steaks " was not established until some years later (in 1735).

Befreiungsknieg (German, **War of Liberation**).

A name given by the Germans to the war of the Allies against the French in 1813–14. A leading result was the freeing of various German states from French occupation and influence.

Beggars, The, v. Gueux.

Beghards, v. Beguins.

Bègue, Le (French, " The Stammerer ").

A surname of Louis II, King of France (846–79).

Beguins (or Beguines).

A name given to members of various religious communities of women, who professed a life of poverty and self-denial, and went about in coarse grey clothing, reading the Scriptures and exhorting the people. They originated in the twelfth or thirteenth century, and communities of the name still exist in Belgium. Also [Beguins], given to a community of men, founded on the same principles as those of the women. The sect continued to exist until about the middle of the sixteenth century. Also called " Beghards."

Bel, Le (French, " The Fair ").

A surname of Charles IV, king of France (1294–1328); also of Philip IV, king of France (1268–1314).

Belgica.

The name of the ship carrying the Belgian expedition, under M. de Gerlache, to the Antarctic reigons, 1897–1900, reaching 71° 35′ S. lat. (May 31, 1898).

Bell, The.

A noted old inn in Warwick Lane, London. Also the name of a noted inn at Edmonton, near London. The latter figures in Cowper's ballad of " John Gilpin."

Belle Cordière, La (French, " The Beautiful Ropemaker ").

A surname of Louise Labé, the most important French female poet of the sixteenth century (1526–66), the wife of one Perrin, a ropemaker. She was a soldier in her youth, and was sometimes called "Captain Loys."

Belle Corisande, La (French, "The Beautiful Corisande").

A surname given to Diane d'Andouins, countess of Guiche and Grammont (d. 1620). Henri IV of France promised to marry her, but did not keep his promise.

Belle France, La.

A surname given to France. Cf. Merry England.

Belle Gabrielle, La.

A name given to Gabrielle d'Estrées (1571–99), a mistress of Henry IV of France, celebrated for her scandalous life and luxury, and for her beauty. An opera entitled "Gabrielle d'Estrées ou les Amours de Henri IV," was produced in 1806.

Belle Indienne, La.

A surname given to Madame de Maintenon (1635–1710), who spent part of her early years in the Island of Martinique.

Belle Jardinière, La (French, "The Beautiful Gardener").

A surname given to a mistress of Henry IV, king of France (1553–1610).

Belle Liégeoise, La, v. Amazon of the Revolution.

Belle Mignonne, La (French, "The Pretty Darling").

A name given in France (eighteenth century) to a skull, illuminated with tapers and highly decorated, used as furniture in devout ladies' boudoirs.

Bellerophon.

A British line-of-battleship of 74 guns and 1,613 tons. Served in the Channel Squadron 1793 & 4, was disabled at the Nile, August 1, 1798, and engaged at Trafalgar October 21, 1805. Napoleon was a prisoner on board this vessel July 15–26, 1815. (v. Northumberland). Also one of the first armoured warships launched in 1866, designed by Sir E. Reed. Length, 300 feet, breadth 56 feet.

Belle Sauvage.

A noted London tavern, formerly standing on Ludgate Hill. Its inn yard (La Belle Sauvage Yard) was one of those used in the sixteenth century as a theatre and for bear-baiting and other spectacles.

Bell-the-Cat.

A surname of Archibald Douglas, fifth Earl of Angus (d. c. 1514). Derived from his remark in answer to the question who would bell the cat at a meeting for the purpose of deciding how the removal of Cochran, James III's obnoxious favourite, was to be effected. Also sometimes called the Great Earl.

Beloved Merchant, The.

A surname given by Edward III of England to Michael de la Pole, an eminent London merchant, who became Lord Chancellor, and was afterwards created Earl of Suffolk

Belted Will.

A nickname of Lord William Howard, an English border nobleman, warden of the western marches (1563–1640).

Ben Block.

A nickname for a sailor.

Benedick.

Name of a character in Shakspere's " Much Ado About Nothing," often used, as Benedict, to mean a newly-married man.

Benedict, *v.* **Benedick.**

Benicia Boy.

A nickname of John C. Heenan, an American pugilist, from his residence at Benicia, in California. He fought for two hours, May 31, 1860, with Tom Sayers, the champion of England, at Farnborough.

Bennett Law, The.

A law passed in Wisconsin, 1889, for the regulation of schools. It was repealed in 1891.

Bentinck's Act, Lord George.

An English statute of 1845, restricting unlawful gaming and wagers.

Benton.

An iron-clad gunboat of 1,000 tons, altered in 1861 from a powerful United States snag-boat. Belonged to the Mississippi flotilla, and took part in the fighting at Island No. 10, Fort Pillow, Vicksburg, and the Yazoo and Red River Expeditions.

Berkshire Lady, The.

A surname given to Miss Frances Kendrick, daughter of Sir William Kendrick, second baronet, whose father was created a baronet by Charles II.

Berlin Conference.

A conference of the European Powers, held at Berlin in the summer of 1880, to settle the boundary dispute between Turkey and Greece. Also a conference at Berlin between representatives from all the European nations (except Switzerland) and the United States (November 15, 1884, to January 30, 1885), respecting the partition of Africa, etc.

Berlin Congress

A congress at Berlin, consisting of representatives from the German Empire, Austria, France, England, Italy, Russia and Turkey (June 13–July 13, 1878), for the purpose of settling the affairs of the Balkan Peninsula. The deliberations resulted in the **Berlin Treaty**.

Berlin Treaty, *v.* **Berlin Congress.**

Bermondsey Spa Gardens.

A place of entertainment in the time of George II, about two miles from London Bridge. *Besant.*

Bermudas, The.

A cant name for a group of courts and alleys between the bottom of St. Martin's Lane, Half Moon, and Chandos Street, London, the resort and refuge of thieves, fraudulent debtors and prostitutes in the sixteenth and seventeenth centuries. Called also **The Streights and the Caribbee** (corrupted into **Cribbee**) **Islands.**

Bernese Friedli, The, *v.* **Raphael of Cats, The.**

Bertha with the Large Foot.

Daughter of Caribert, Count of Laon, wife of Pépin le Bref (Pepin the Little), and mother of Charles the Great. She died at Choisy in 783 at an advanced age.

Berthe au Grand Pied, v. Bertha with the Large Foot.

Bess, Good Queen, v. Good Queen Bess.

Bess o' Bedlam, v. Tom o' Bedlam.

Bianchi, The (or Whites).

An Italian political faction, dating from about 1300. Their opponents were called the Neri (or Blacks).

Biddenden Maids, The.

A name given to two unmarried sisters, Mary and Elizabeth Chulkhurst, born at Biddenden, Kent, in 1100. Tradition says that they were joined together by the shoulders and hips (cf. Siamese Twins, The), and when one died, at the age of thirty-four, the other expired six hours after.

Bideford Postman, v. Postman Poet, The.

Bien-aimé, Le (French, " The Well-beloved ").

A surname given to Charles VI, king of France (1368–1422); also to Louis XV, king of France (1710–74).

Big Beggarman, v. Liberator, The.

Big Ben.

Name given to the bell in the clock-tower of the Houses of Parliament, London, cast in 1858. It is said to be the largest bell in England, and to have derived its name from Sir Benjamin Hall (afterwards Lord Llanover), the Chief Commissioner of Works at the time the bell was cast.

Bill of Rights, v. Declaration of Right.

Birkenhead.

An English troop steamer, wrecked off the Cape of Good Hope, February 26, 1852. The troops formed at the word of command, and went down at their posts, having put the women and children in the boats. More than 400 men were drowned.

Birmingham Festival.

A musical festival held triennially at Birmingham, established in 1768. The proceeds of the festivals are given to the funds of the General Hospital.

Birmingham of Belgium, The.

Liège, Belgium, is sometimes so called, from its manufactures of firearms, engines, zinc, etc. The centre of an important mining region of coal, iron, etc.

Birmingham of Russia, The.

A surname given to Tula, one of the chief manufacturing centres of Russia, especially noted for the manufacture of small arms.

Birmingham Poet, The.

A surname given to John Freeth, a wit, poet and publican (1730–1808). He wrote the words of his own songs, set them to music and sang them.

Bishop Bunyan, v. Immortal Dreamer, The.

Bishop of Hippo, The.

A name by which St. Augustine (354–430), who was made Bishop of Hippo in 395, is often alluded to. *v.* Hammer of Heretics.

Bismarck of Asia, The.

A name given to Li Hung Chang, a noted Chinese statesman (1823–1901). He joined General Gordon in quelling the Taiping Rebellion. He became Prime Minister of China in 1895.

Black, The.

A surname of Fulc, Fulk or Foulques III, Count of Anjou (972–1040). He carried on wars against the Duke of Bretagne and the Count of Blois; also of Henry III, emperor of the Holy Roman Empire (1017–56), son of Conrad II, whom he succeeded as king of Germany in 1039; also of Sir Evan Cameron of Lochiel (d. 1719).

Black Act, The.

An English statute of 1722, so called from its being originally designed to suppress associations of lawless persons calling themselves *blacks*. It made felonies certain crimes against the game laws, the sending of anonymous letters demanding money, etc. Scottish Acts of Parliament (from James I of Scotland's reign down to 1586 or 1587) were also called **Black Acts,** from their being printed in Saxon or black characters.

Black Agnes.

Agnes, Countess of Dunbar (c. 1312–69), a Scottish heroine, was so called from her dark skin. She is famous for her successful defence of Dunbar Castle in 1337–8.

Black Assize, The.

A name given to the Oxford Assize of 1577, in which year Oxford was ravaged by jailfever. Sometimes the epidemic alone is implied.

Black Band, *v.* Bande Noire.

Black Bess.

The famous mare of Dick Turpin, a notorious highwayman (executed in 1739).

Black Box.

A box supposed to contain the marriage-contract of Charles II and Lucy Walters (or Barlow), the Duke of Monmouth's mother, and said to have been stolen from her. (Cf. R. D. Blackmore's novel, " Lorna Doone.")

Black Brunswickers (or Death's Head Corps).

A corps of 2,000 horsemen, equipped by the Duke of Brunswick to operate against Napoleon in Germany. It attempted, vainly, to co-operate with the Austrians in 1809.

Black Captain, The, *v.* Capitaine Noir, The.

Black Charlie.

A surname given to Sir Charles Napier, a British admiral (1786–1860).

Black Code, The.

The system of law which prevailed in the southern United States before the emancipation of the slaves, regulating the treatment of the coloured race.

Black Country, The.

The name by which the mining and manufacturing region in the neighbourhood of Birmingham is familiarly known.

Black Death.

A name given to the fearful epidemic that ravaged Asia and Europe in the fourteenth century. Several visitations occurred in Edward III's reign in 1348-9, 1361 and 1369. It carried off 13 millions in China and 24 millions in other parts of Asia, 1333-47, and first appeared in Europe in 1342.

Black Diamond, The.

A nickname given to Tom Cribb, a noted English pugilist (1781-1848), from his occupation as a coal-porter.

Black Dick.

A nickname of Richard Howe, first Earl Howe (1726-99).

Black Douglas, The.

A surname given to Sir James Douglas (c. 1286-1330), a Scottish nobleman. Also called the **Good Sir James**. He was killed in battle (Spain) when on his way to the Holy Land with Bruce's heart. It was carried back to Scotland and buried in Melrose Abbey (cf. Mrs. Hemans' poem, "Heart of Bruce in Melrose Abbey"). Also to William Douglas, Lord of Nithsdale (d. 1390). (Cf. Sir Walter Scott's "Tales of a Grandfather," ch. xi.)

Black Flags.

Bands of irregular soldiers infesting the upper valley of the Red River in Tonquin. Originally survivors of the Taiping Rebellion in Cina. They fought against the French in their wars with Annam.

Black Friday.

Good Friday is so called, because on that day, in the Western Church, the vestments of the clergy and altar are black. The name is also given to any Friday marked by a great calamity, notably (1) December 6, 1745, the day on which news reached London that the Young Pretender, Charles Edward, had reached Derby; (2) the commercial panic caused by the failure of the house of Overend and Gurney, May 11, 1866; (3) the sudden financial panic and ruin caused by reckless speculation in gold on the exchange in New York, September 24, 1869; (4) another similar panic there, beginning September 18, 1873.

Black Hole of Calcutta.

The garrison strong-room or black hole at Calcutta, measuring about 18 feet square, into which 146 British prisoners were thrust at the point of the sword by the Nawab Siraj-ud-Daula, June 20, 1756. Next morning all but twenty-three were dead.

Black Horse, The.

A nickname given to the 7th Dragoon Guards, from their black velvet facings. At one time they rode black horses also.

Black Hussar of Literature, The.

A surname given to Sir Walter Scott (1771-1832) by his son-in-law and biographer, John Gibson Lockhart. *v.* also **Great Unknown**.

Black Jack.

A nickname given to General John Alexander Logan (1826–86) by his soldiers during the Civil War, on account of his long black hair and dark complexion. Also applied to John Philip Kemble, a celebrated English tragedian (1757—1823) for a similar reason.

Black Man, The.

One of the many familiar names given to the devil.

Black Maria.

A popular name of the covered van, usually painted black, in which criminals are conveyed to and from jail. The name is said to have originated in Philadelphia (1838).

Black Monday.

A name sometimes given to Easter Monday, from a terrible storm on Easter Monday, 1360, from which the English army before Paris suffered severely. (Cf. Shakspere's "Merchant of Venice," Act. 2, sc. 5.) Also applied to February 27, 1865, when a terrible sirocco swept over Victoria, Australia, and did immense damage.

Black Prince, The.

Edward, Prince of Wales (1330–76), son of Edward III of England, was so called, from the colour of his armour.

Black Republic.

A name given to the republic of Hayti, or St. Domingo, which is composed for the most part of negroes.

Black Republicans, *v.* Republican Party.

D.N.

Black Rod.

The title of a gentleman usher, with special duties, in the Houses of Lords and Commons. He carries a black rod of office surmounted with a gold lion.

Black Saturday.

In Scottish history, a name given to August 4, 1621, when the Edinburgh Parliament passed certain Acts favouring Episcopacy.

Black Thursday.

A name given in Victoria, Australia, to February 6, 1851, the date of the most terrible bush fire hitherto known in the colony.

Blacksmith of Antwerp, The.

A surname of Quentin Matsys, a Flemish painter (c. 1460–1530), in allusion to his original occupation. Also the **Flemish Blacksmith.**

Black Watch.

A body of Scottish Highlanders employed by the English Government to watch the Highlands in 1725, and enrolled as a regiment in the regular army in 1739; so named from their dark tartan uniform.

Bladud.

A mythical British king, who is said to have founded the city of Bath, England.

Blair Athol.

A celebrated English racehorse, bred in 1861, by Stockwell, out of Blink Bonny. Derby winner in 1864, and was sire of Prince Charlie, sire of Salvator in America.

D

Blanche Nef (French, " White Ship ").

The name of the ship in which Prince William, only son of Henry I of England, was drowned in the English Channel in 1120.

Bland Silver Bill.

A United States statute of 1878 (20 Stat., 25), so named from its author, Richard P. Bland, a member from Missouri. It re-established the silver dollar containing 412½ grs. troy of standard silver as a legal tender, but its main feature was a clause requiring the Treasury to purchase every month not less than two million, and not more than four million dollars' worth of silver bullion, and to coin it into dollars. *v.* **Sherman Bill.**

Blanketeers.

The name given to a body of half-starved Manchester operatives, who met at St. Peter's Field, March 10, 1817. Each man was provided with provisions and a blanket, and their purpose was to walk to London to petition for some legislative remedy against capitalistic oppression, and especially for the great panacea of Parliamentary reform. The leaders were seized and imprisoned, and those who persisted in their intention were intercepted, searched, and either sent back or imprisoned.

Blarney Stone.

A famous stone in the ruins of Blarney Castle, Ireland, which, according to tradition, confers great persuasive powers upon any one kissing it. This operation used to be a very difficult one, owing to the almost inaccessible position of the stone.

Blasphemous Balfour.

A surname given to Sir James Balfour, a Scottish judge and political intriguer (d. 1583).

Bleeding Kansas.

The territory of Kansas was so called, previous to the Civil War, on account of the bloody contests that had occurred there concerning the question of slavery. Kansas finally was admitted as a free state (1861). *v.* **Kansas-Nebraska Bill.**

Blenheim Spaniels.

A nickname given to Oxford electors on account of their obedience in returning any candidate supported by the Duke of Marlborough.

Blessed, The.

Surname given to Cadwalader, or Cadwallader, a British king (d. c. 664). He became in time to be regarded as a saint, hence the surname. The name has also been given to Gerard, the founder of the Order of St. John of Jerusalem, guardian of a hospital at Jerusalem, c. 1100 (c. 1040–c. 1120).

Blind, The.

A surname given to Didymus, an Alexandrian scholar and theologian (c. 308 or 314–c. 394 or 9). He lost his sight in childhood, but became nevertheless one of the most learned men of his time. Also to John (Johann), king of Bohemia (c. 1296–1346), who was killed at the battle of Crecy; of Vasili II

(III), grand prince of Moscow from 1425–62.

Blind Bard on the Chian Strand, The, *v.* **Father of Epic Poetry, The.**

Blind Emperor, The.

A surname given to Louis III, emperor of the Holy Roman Empire, from 901–5 (d. 929 or 917). Blinded by Berengarius I of Italy, by whom he was deposed.

Blind Harper, The.

A surname given to John Parry (d. 1739).

Blind Harry.

A Scottish minstrel who died c. 1492, author of a poem on Sir William Wallace.

Blind Mechanician, The.

A surname given to John Strong, a mechanical genius, who was blind from his birth. (1732–98).

Blind Naturalist, The.

A surname given to François Huber, a Swiss naturalist (1750–1831). He early became blind from excessive study, and thereafter conducted his scientific work with the aid of his wife.

Blind Old Man of Scio's Rocky Isle, The.

A surname given (by Lord Byron in " The Bride of Abydos " ii. 2) to Homer. *v.* **Father of Epic Poetry, The.**

Blind Poet, The (Italian, " Il Cieco ").

A surname given to Luigi Groto, an Italian poet (1541–85). Also applied to John Milton, a celebrated English poet

(1608–74), author of " Paradise Lost." By May, 1652, he had become totally blind. *v.* **British Homer, The**

Blind Preacher, The.

William Henry Milburn, a blind Methodist minister (b. 1823 in Philadelphia).

Blind Traveller, The.

A surname given to James Holman (1787–1857), a lieutenant in the British navy, and author of various books of travels. Lost his eyesight in 1812.

Blink Bonny.

A celebrated English thoroughbred mare, bred in 1854 by Melbourne, sire Gladiator, out of Queen Mary. She won both the Derby and Oaks in 1857. *v.* **Blair Athol.**

Blondin.

Professional name of Charles Emile Gravele (b. 1824, at Saint Omer, France—d. 1897, at Ealing), a famous tight-rope walker. He crossed Niagara in 1855, 1859, and 1860.

Blood-Bath, The.

A name given to a massacre of Swedish nobles and leaders three days after the Coronation as king of Sweden (1520) of Christian II, king of Denmark and Norway. This provoked a revolt under Gustavus Vasa, and led to the liberation of Sweden.

Bloody, The.

A surname given to Otto II, emperor of the Holy Roman Empire (955–83).

Bloody Assizes, The.

The popular name for the

trials for participation in Monmouth's rising of 1685, held in the western counties of England, and presided over by Lord Jeffreys. Over 300 persons were supposed to have been executed. King James II called them **Jeffrey's Campaign.**

Bloody Bill, *v*. Force Bill.

Bloody Butcher, The.

A name applied to the Duke of Cumberland, in allusion to his cruelty in suppressing the Jacobite rising after the battle of Culloden, 1746. Also called the **Butcher of Culloden.**

Bloody (Queen) Mary.

A name given to Queen Mary of England (1516–58), on account of the persecutions which she sanctioned.

Bloody Shirt.

" To wave the bloody shirt," means to keep up, by appealing to passion, the animosities engendered by the Civil War in the United States. This was a current political phrase during the decade following the Rebellion of 1861–5. By some it is derived from an old Corsican custom of hanging a murdered man's blood-stained shirt above his head before burial, his friends and relatives excitedly calling down curses upon his enemies. Another version, however, traces the origin to a massacre at Glenfruin, in Scotland, when some 220 widows, each bearing on a spear the bloody shirt of her husband, rode to Stirling Tower, the sight so rousing the people that a terrible revenge was inflicted upon their enemies.

Bloody Wedding, The, *v*. Massacre of St. Bartholomew, The.

Bloomers.

A name given to a reformed costume, consisting of Turkish trousers and a dress with short skirts, first introduced by Elizabeth Smith Miller, but taking its name from Mrs. Amelia Jenks Bloomer, an American lecturer and reformer (1818–94).

Bloomsbury Gang, The.

A name given to a political clique, influential about 1790. Its leader was the Duke of Bedford, and its headquarters, Bloomsbury House, London.

Bluebacks.

The name given to the paper-money of the Confederate American States, to distinguish it from that of the North, known as " greenbacks." On the paper-money of the South becoming worthless, it was known as " shucks."

Bluebellies.

During the American Civil War the Federal soldiers were so called by the Confederates, in allusion to the light blue overcoats and cloaks worn by them. *v*. **Graybacks.**

Blue-Coat School.

A name given to Christ's Hospital, a celebrated school in Newgate Street, London. The building is now demolished, and the school removed to Horsham. So called from the ancient dress of the scholars, still worn by them. It was founded by Edward VI on the site of the monastery of Gray Friars, given by Henry VIII to the city, for the relief of the poor, near the end of his reign.

Blue-Grass State.

A surname given to Kentucky, in allusion to its blue-grass region, famous for raising horses.

Blue Hen.

A popular nickname for the State of Delaware. Said to have originated from the fondness of Captain Caldwell, an officer of the First Delaware regiment in the Revolutionary War, for cock-fighting. His opinion was that no cock could be truly game unless its mother was a blue hen (*Delaware State Journal*, July, 1860).

Blue Laws.

A nickname given to the severe regulations of the early government of New Haven. *v.* **Code of 1650.**

Blue Nose.

A popular nickname for an inhabitant of Nova Scotia or New Brunswick. Origin variously accounted for, but probably the theory of the appearance caused by the prevailing easterly winds is the correct one. Cf. Haliburton's "Sam Slick."

Blue Peter.

The name given to a blue flag with a white square in the centre, indicating that a ship is about to sail.

Blue Ribbon of the Turf, *v.* Derby, The.

Blues.

In Canadian politics, the Conservatives of Quebec.

Blueskin.

A nickname given to Joseph Blake, an English burglar (executed November 11, 1723), from his dark complexion.

Blue-Skins.

A nickname applied to the Presbyterians.

Blue-Stocking Clubs.

A name applied to assemblies held in London, c. 1750, at the houses of Mrs. Montagu (Elizabeth Robinson) and other ladies. These were characterized by a studied plainness of dress on the part of some of the guests, and literary conversation was substituted for cards and gossip. Among the guests was Mr. Benjamin Stillingfleet, who always wore blue stockings, and in reference to whom the coterie was called in derision the " Blue-Stocking " Society, or Club, and its members, especially the ladies, " blue-stockings," or " blue-stocking ladies," and afterwards simply " blue-stockings," or " blues." Mrs. Montagu was born at York, 1720, and died at Montagu House (now 22, Portman Square), London, 1800.

Bluestring, Robin, *v.* Robin Bluestring.

Blue-tooth (Danish, " Harald Blaatand ").

A surname of Harold, King of Denmark (d. c. 985).

Bluff City.

A name sometimes bestowed on Hannibal, Missouri, from its position.

Bluff King Hal.

A nickname given to Henry

VIII of England (1491-1547), referring to his bluff, hearty manner. Also called **Burly King Harry** and **Stout Harry.**

Boar, The.

A surname given to Richard III, king of England (1452-85), from his cognizance. Also called **Crookback.**

Boar of Ardennes, Wild, *v.* **Wild Boar of Ardennes.**

Boar's Head, The.

A tavern in Eastcheap, London, celebrated by Shakspere as the scene of Falstaff's carousals. Destroyed in the Fire of London, rebuilt, and demolished to form one of the approaches to London Bridge. A statue of William IV marks the spot.

Bobbies, *v.* **Peelers.**

Bobbin Boy, The.

A nickname given to Nathaniel Prentiss Banks, an American politician and general (1816-94), because he worked as a boy in the cotton-factory of which his father was superintendent.

Bobs, or Bobs Bahadur (Hindustani, "Hero," "Champion," a title of respect).

Nickname given to Lord Roberts (b. 1832) by the British soldiers in India.

Bocca di Leone (Italian, "Lion's Mouth").

A famous hole or opening in the wall of the ante-chamber of the Great Council in the Doge's palace, Venice, through which anonymous communications were passed in. *Wheeler.*

Bodleian Library.

A library of Oxford University, England, originally established in 1445, formally opened in 1488, and re-established by Sir Thomas Bodley (1545-1613) 1597-1602. Formally opened November 8, 1603; and James I in 1604 granted letters patent, styling it by Bodley's name. It contains about 460,000 printed volumes, 27,000 vols. of MS., and 50,000 coins, many portraits, models of ancient buildings, and literary antiquities.

Boer War, The.

The war between the Transvaal Republic and Great Britain following the proclamation of the former, December, 1880, and ending with the treaty of March, 1881, by which the independence of the Republic was recognized, but the Boers acknowledged the suzerainty of Queen Victoria. (Dutch, "Boer," farmer.) Since, together with the Orange Free State, after the completion of the South African War, made a colony of the British Empire.

Bohemia.

In its figurative sense, used to indicate a *place* where people, especially artists and literary people, lead an irregular, unconventional life, or such people collectively. The adjective Bohemian is also applied to such *people* or their existence. Thackeray is credited with having introduced the word in this sense from the French, who associated Bohemia with gipsies. Cf. Henri Murger's "Scènes de la vie de Bohème."

Bohemian Brethren.

A religious sect in Bohemia (fifteenth to seventeenth century), a branch of the Hussites.

Bohemian Paradise, The.

A name given to the district round Leitmeritz, Bohemia, a rich agricultural region.

Bold, The.

Surname given to Albert, Duke of Saxony, younger son of Frederick the Gentle, and founder of the Albertine Saxon line (1443–1500). *v.* **Téméraire, Le; Hardi, Le.**

Bold Beauchamp.

A surname given to Thomas de Beauchamp, Earl of Warwick, who, in 1346, with one squire and six archers, defeated a hundred armed men at Hogges, in Normandy.

Bomba, King, *v.* **King Bomba.**

Bon, Le (French, " The Good ").

A surname of John (Jean) II, king of France (d. at London, 1364). Captured by the British under the Black Prince at Poitiers (1356), and restored to liberty by the Peace of Brétigny (1360) ; of John III, duke of Brittany (r. 1312–41); also of Philip, duke of Burgundy (1396 1467).

Boney.

An English nickname for Napoleon Bonaparte (1769–1821).

Bonhomme, Jacques, *v.* **Jacques Bonhomme.**

Bonhomme Richard.

One of a fleet of five vessels fitted out by the French Government, under the advice of Benjamin Franklin, and placed under the command of John Paul Jones. It was a merchantman changed to a man-of-war, and named the *Duc de Duras* and then *Bonhomme Richard* (" Poor Richard ") at Jones's suggestion in honour of Franklin. The fleet, reduced to three ships, fell in (September 23, 1779) with the North Sea merchant fleet under convoy of the *Serapis* (44 guns),' and *Countess of Scarborough* (20 guns) off Flamborough Head. The *Bonhomme Richard* engaged the *Serapis* (Captain Pearson) at 7.30 p.m. by moonlight, in the presence of thousands of spectators, and the latter struck at 10.30. The *Bonhomme Richard* went down on September 25.

Boniface.

A name applied to innkeepers in general. Derived from a landlord in G. Farquhar's comedy, " The Beaux' Stratagem " (1707).

Bonne Reine, La.

A surname given to Claude de France (1499–1524), daughter of Louis XII, and wife of Francis I. So named for her virtues, for she was lame and ugly.

Bonnets Rouges, *v.* **Red Republicans.**

Bono Johnny.

A name by which an Englishman is popularly designated in the East.

Bon roi Réne, Le.

A surname given to René I, Duke of Anjou, Count of Provence and (titular) King of Naples (1408–80).

Book of Mormon.

One of the authoritative writings of the Mormon Church.

According to the Mormons, it is the record of certain ancient peoples in America, abridged by the prophet Mormon, written on golden plates, and discovered by Joseph Smith at Cumorah (western New York), and translated by him. By anti-Mormons it is generally regarded as taken from a romance written about 1811 by Solomon Spaulding, whose manuscript was used by Smith and Rigdon.

Border Minstrel, The, *v.* Wizard of the North, The.

Border States.

Formerly the slave states, Delaware, Maryland, Virginia, Kentucky and Missouri, situated near the free states. In a wider sense, the term comprised also North Carolina, Tennessee and Arkansas.

Border-Thief School.

A collective name, sometimes given to Sir Walter Scott and his poetical imitators, who celebrated the adventures of various predatory chiefs of the Scottish border.

Born in the Purple, *v.* Porphyrogenitus.

Borough English.

The name of an ancient system of land tenure still existing in some districts, where real estate passes to the youngest (instead of eldest) son.

Boston Massacre.

A street affray in Boston, Massachusetts, on March 5, 1770, between the citizens and the British soldiery. The soldiers, irritated by snowballs thrown at them by the crowd, fired and killed several persons. The affair probably hastened the beginning of hostilities.

Boston Tea-Party, The.

A concourse of American citizens at Boston, December 16, 1773, as a demonstration against the attempted importation of tea into the colonies. The same evening about fifty men, disguised as Mohawks, boarded the three British tea-ships in the harbour, and threw 342 chests of tea (valued at £18,000) into the water.

Bottled Beer.

A nickname given to Alexander Nowell, an English ecclesiastic (c. 1507–1602).

Bottle Riot, The.

A disturbance at the theatre in Dublin, December 14, 1822, in consequence of the unpopularity of the Marquis of Wellesley (Richard Colley) (1760—1842), Lord-Lieutenant of Ireland. So called from a bottle having been thrown into his box.

Bottomless Pit, The.

A humorous nickname given to William Pitt, a celebrated English Whig statesman (1759–1806), in allusion to his remarkable thinness. Also called the **Heaven-sent Minister** and the **Pilot that Weathered the Storm.** The storm of course was the general European disturbance caused by Napoleon.

Boucher Royaliste, Le (French, the "Royalist Butcher").

A surname given to Blaise Lasseran-Massencome, Seigneur de Montluc, a noted French marshal (1501–77), alluding to his cruelty towards Protestants.

Boulangists.

Partizans of Georges Ernest Jean Marie Boulanger, a French general and politician (1837–91). He organized democratic reforms in the army, and became immensely popular as the leader of the party of revenge against Germany. Was exiled, and committed suicide at Brussels.

Bounty, The.

An English ship, whose crew, led by Fletcher Christian, after leaving Tahiti, mutinied in 1789. The captain, Bligh, and eighteen of the crew, were set adrift in a small boat, and eventually reached England. The mutineers, under the leadership of John Adams, settled on Pitcairn Island in the Pacific, and mingling with the natives formed a curiously isolated but civilized community.

Bourignonists.

A sect of Quietists founded in the seventeenth century by Antoinette Bourignon (1616–80). Her doctrines were essentially pietistic, and she claimed to be inspired by God.

Boustrapa.

A nickname given to Napoleon III, Emperor of the French (1808–73), in allusion to his unsuccessful attempt at a *coup d'état* at *Bou*logne (1840) and *Stra*sburg (1836), and his successful attempt at *Pa*ris (1851).

Bow Bells.

A chime of bells in the Church of St. Mary-le-Bow (Bow Church), Cheapside. The phrase "to be born within the sound of Bow Bells," is used to define a true London cockney.

Bow Street Runner.

The name given to special officers attached to Bow Street Police Court, and other police offices of the metropolis. Townsend was the most famous among them. Also called **Robin Redbreasts**, from their red waistcoats. Abolished in 1829.

Bowery Boys.

Name given to the ruffians formerly haunting the Bowery, a wide thoroughfare in New York, which took its name from the fact that it ran through Peter Stuyvesant's farm or bouwerie (a Dutch word).

Boy-Bishop, The.

A surname given to St. Nicholas, the patron saint of boys (fl. c. 300). An ancient custom, now extinct, was the election of a boy bishop on St. Nicholas's Day (December 6).

Boyle Lectures.

A course of eight lectures in defence of Christianity, delivered annually at St. Mary-le-Bow Church, London, instituted by Robert Boyle (1627–91), and commenced in 1692.

Bozzy.

A nickname given by Dr. Samuel Johnson to James Boswell, his friend and biographer (1740–95).

Braganza Diamond, The.

The largest diamond in existence, found in Brazil in 1741, and now one of the Portugal crown jewels. It is uncut, weighs 1,680 carats, and has been valued at £58,350,000. If, as is thought by many, it is a white topaz, the Rajah of Mattan's diamond would be the largest known, weighing, cut, 367$\frac{9}{16}$ carats.

Brandy Nan.

A nickname of Queen Anne of England (1665–1714) from her fondness for spirits. Also called **Mrs. Bull** in J. Arbuthnot's "History of John Bull. *v.* **Queen Sarah.**

Bras de Fer.

Surname of Baldwin, first Count of Flanders (d. c. 879), son-in-law of Charles the Bold of France. Also of the Huguenot leader, François de La Noue (1531–91). He lost his arm at Fontenay-le-Comte in 1570, and supplied its place with an iron one. Hence his surname. Cf. **Gotz with the Iron Hand.**

Brave, The.

A surname given to Alfonso IV (Affonso or Alphonso), King of Portugal (1290–1357). Also called the **Fierce.**

Brave des Braves, Le.

Surname given by Henri IV of France to Crillon (1541–1615); also applied by the French Army to Marshal Ney (1767–1815), after the Battle of Friedland, 1807.

Bravest of the Brave, *v.* Brave des Braves, Le.

Bread and Cheese Folk.

The insurgent party who held temporary possession of Haarlem, Netherlands, in 1492.

Breeches Review.

A nickname formerly given, among booksellers, to the "Westminster Review." Derived from the trade (leather-breeches maker and tailor) of a Mr. Francis Place, a great authority with the "Westminster" at one time.

Bref, Le (French, "The Short").

A surname given to Pepin, King of the Franks (d. 768), son of Charles Martel.

Brewer of Ghent, The.

Surname given to Jacob von Artevelde (c. 1285–1345) derived from the fact that, although an aristocrat by birth, he was enrolled in the Guild of Brewers. He was killed in a popular tumult, having, it was said, attempted to secure the succession in Flanders for Edward, the Black Prince.

Briareus of Languages, The, *v.* Pentecôte Vivante, La.

Bride of the Sea.

A poetical surname given to Venice, from the medieval ceremony by which the city was wedded to the Adriatic. The Doge, in the presence of his courtiers and amid much pomp and splendour, threw a ring into the sea, at the same time saying: "Desponsamus te, mare, in signum veri perpetuique dominii" (We wed thee, O sea, in sign of a true and perpetual dominion). *v.* also **Bucentaur.** The ceremony was instituted in 1174 by Pope Alexander III, who gave the Doge a ring from his own finger in token of the victory of the Venetian fleet over Frederick Barbarossa at Istria.

Bridewell.

A name often given to prisons or lock-ups generally, derived from a celebrated London prison, or house of detention, of the name, most of which was demolished in 1863. It was founded upon a favourite palace of Henry VIII, which stood at the mouth of the Fleet, between Blackfriars and Whitefriars.

Bridge of Sighs.

A name sometimes given to Waterloo Bridge, London, in allusion to the number of suicides committed from it by jumping into the river Thames.

Brilliant Madman, *v.* Madman of the North.

Bristol Boy, The.

Surname given to Thomas Chatterton, an English poet, born at Bristol, 1752, and who committed suicide at London, 1770.

Britannia Tubular Bridge.

A famous railway bridge across Menai Strait, Wales, built by Robert Stephenson between 1846 and 1850. It consists of two parallel rectangular tunnels of wrought iron, supported by three piers between the two shore piers. Total length, 1,840 feet, each of the central spans being 460 feet long. The central tower is 230 feet high.

British Aristides, The.

A surname given to Andrew Marvell, an English poet and satirist (1621–78), an influential member of the House of Commons, and a steadfast opponent of Charles II. He refused every offer of promotion and bribery, and died in poverty.

British Bayard, The, *v.* English Petrarch, The.

British Cicero, The, *v.* Great Commoner, The.

British Homer, The.

A surname given to John Milton, a celebrated English poet (1608–74). *v.* Blind Poet, The.

British Jeremiah, The.

A surname given by Gibbon to Gildas (or Gildus), a British historian (b. probably 516; d. probably 570). Also called the Wise.

British Legion.

A body of British troops commanded by Colonel Evans, who fought for Queen Isabella of Spain against the Carlists in 1836.

British Pausanias, The.

A surname given to William Camden, a noted English historian and antiquary (1551–1623). Sometimes called the British Strabo. Cf. Camden Society, The.

British Pindar, The.

A surname given to Thomas Gray, an English poet (1716–71).

British Samson, The, *v.* English Milo, The.

British Solomon, The.

A surname given to James I of England (1566–1625), owing to his literary tastes. Also called the Solomon of England, the English Solomon, the Second Solomon, the Scottish Solomon, and the Wisest Fool in Christendom, but the Duc de Sully really called him the "most learned fool in Christendom."

British Strabo, The, *v.* **British Pausanias, The.**

British St. Stephen, The.

A surname given to St. Alban, protomartyr of Britain (d. 303).

British Varro, The.

A surname given (by Watson) to Thomas Tusser, an English poet (c. 1527–80).

Broad Arrow, The.

The official mark of the British Government, which is stamped, cut or fixed upon Government property, such as guns, soldiers' clothing, ordnance, etc., to prevent embezzlement. Its use by private persons is forbidden by law.

Broad Bottom Administration.

A name given to the Pelham Administration (1744–54), because it was formed by a coalition of parties.

Brooks's.

A London (Conservative) Club established in 1764 by the Duke of Roxborough, the Duke of Portland, and others. It was formerly a gaming-house kept by Almack and afterwards by "Brooks, a wine merchant and money-lender," after whom it was named.

Brother Jonathan.

A popular nickname for the American people. Said to be derived from Jonathan Trumbull, an American magistrate and patriot (1710–85), a friend and adviser of Washington, who called him, familiarly "Brother Jonathan."

Brother Paul (Italian, "Fra Paolo").

A surname of Pietro (or Paolo) Sarpi, a Venetian historian (1552–1623). Also called **Servita.**

Brothers, The.

A political club of wits and statesmen, established in London in 1713. Swift was treasurer. In 1714 it was merged in the Scriblerus Club (q.v.).

Brown Bess.

A nickname popularly applied to the English regulation flintlock musket towards the end of the eighteenth century.

Brown, Jones and Robinson.

Names used to typify English snobbery, especially as shown abroad. Derived from the names given to three Englishmen travelling together, whose adventures by Richard Doyle (1824–83) were published in "Punch,"

Brumaire, The 18th (November 9, 1799).

The date of the beginning of the *coup d'état* by which the Directory was overthrown. It was completed on the following day.

Brussels Conference.

A conference of representatives from Great Britain, France, Germany, Italy, Austro-Hungary, Belgium and Russia, which met at Brussels in 1876 and 1877. It decided to establish an International African Association, to explore and civilize Central Africa, and provided for branch national committees.

Brute's City, *v.* **Trinovant.**

Bubble Act, The.

A popular name for an Act passed in 1719 (6 Geo. I, c. 18), designed to punish unprincipled adventurers who proposed schemes or Bubbles to extract money from ignorant or thoughtless persons. Repealed July 5, 1825. Cf. **South Sea Bubble.**

Bucentaur.

The name of the state-barge or galley in which the Doge of Venice with his nobles sailed annually on Ascension Day, in order to perform the ceremony of wedding the Adriatic. The third and last of the vessels used for this purpose was destroyed by the French in 1797. *v.* **Bride of the Sea.**

Bucephalus.

The favourite horse of Alexander the Great (356–323 B.C.). His master was the only person who could ride him.

Buchanites.

Followers of Elspeth Buchan, or Simpson, a Scottish religious enthusiast (1738–91). The sect became extinct in 1848.

Buckeye State, The.

A popular name for Ohio, from the number of buckeyes in that state.

Bucktails.

A name originally given to the members of the Tammany Society in New York City, but extended c. 1817–26 in its application to members of that faction of the Democratic Republican Party in the state which opposed De Witt Clinton.

Buffalo Bill.

A nickname given to William Frederick Cody, a Government scout (b. 1845), from his having contracted with the Kansas Pacific Railway to supply its labourers with buffalo meat; in eighteen months he killed 4,280 buffaloes. In 1883 he organized the " Wild West," an exhibition of life on the frontier.

Bulgarian Quadrilateral.

The four fortresses of Rustchuk, Schumla, Silistria and Varna.

Bull, John, *v.* John Bull.

Bull-dogs.

The name given to the menservants who attend a university proctor in his rounds, to assist him in apprehending students who are infringing the university rules.

Buller of Brazenose.

A name given (in Wilson's " Noctes Ambrosianae ") to John Hughes (of Oriel—not Brazenose—College, Oxford), author of " An Itinerary of the Rhone."

Bullion State, The.

A popular name for the State of Missouri, arising from the exertions of Senator Thomas H. Benton (1728–1858), in favour of gold and silver currency in opposition to papermoney.

Burghers.

A body of Presbyterians in Scotland, constituting one of the divisions of the early Secession Church. This church became divided in 1747 into the Associate Synod, or Burghers, and the General Associate Synod, or Anti-Burghers, in respect of the lawfulness of accepting the oath then required to be taken by the burgesses in Edinburgh, Glasgow and Perth. *v.* **Anti-Burghers.**

Burgundians.

The party of the House of Burgundy, opponents of the House of Orleans (*v.* **Armagnacs**) during Charles VI's reign (1380–1422). The dispute between the Duke of Burgundy and the Duke of Orleans (the king's brother) arose on Charles VI becoming deranged in 1392. The former, who gained the ascendancy, died in 1404, and his son Jean procured the murder of the Duke of Orleans (1407). This led to civil war, the so-called war of the Burgundians and Armagnacs.

Buridan's Ass.

Name applied to a sophism attributed to Jean Buridan, a noted French logician (d. c. 1358), in which an ass placed between two measures of oats must die of hunger, without free will, having no reason for eating the oats on his right any more than those on his left.

Burly King Harry, *v.* Bluff King Hal.

Burnett Prizes.

Prizes awarded every forty years, in accordance with the will of Mr. Burnett, a Scottish gentleman (1729–84), for the best essays on the Christian evidences. Lectureships now take the place of the essays.

Burns of France, The, *v.* Last of the Troubadours, The.

Butcher, The.

A surname given to Olivier de Clisson, Constable of France (succeeding Du Guesclin) (1336–1407).

Butcher, The Bloody, *v.* Bloody Butcher.

Butcher of Culloden, *v.* Bloody Butcher.

Butcher of England, The.

A surname given to John Tiptoft, Earl of Worcester (d. 1470), for his cruelty.

Bye, or Surprise, Plot.

A conspiracy in 1603 to seize the person of James I of England and extort certain religious concessions. Markham, Brooke, Lord Grey of Wilton and others were concerned in it. *v.* **Main Plot.**

Byerly Turk, The.

One of the three Oriental horses, from which all names in the stud-book trace descent. He was ridden by a Captain Byerly in the first Irish campaign of King William III, 1689; and from him springs the Herod family of thoroughbreds. *v.* **Darley's Arabian** and **Godolphin Barb.**

Bywell Castle, *v.* Princess Alice.

Cabal, The.

An unpopular ministry of Charles II, consisting of Clifford, Ashley, Buckingham, Arlington, and Lauderdale, the initials of whose names compose the word. It held office 1667–73.

Cagliostro, Count Alessandro di.

The assumed name of Guiseppe Balsamo, an Italian adventurer (1743–95), who was involved in the affair of the **Diamond Necklace** (q.v.). Died in confinement at San Leone Urbino, Italy.

Cagots.

A people of uncertain origin inhabiting Gascony and Béarn

(France) and the Basque provinces (Spain). They are considered a degraded race, and before 1793 were without political and social rights. Also called " Colliberts."

Cahensly Agitation, The.

An agitation in 1891 in the Roman Catholic Church to induce the Pope to appoint bishops and priests of their own nationality for the Roman Catholic immigrants in the United States. So called from the memorial addressed to the Vatican by Herr Cahensly and other Europeans.

Cainites.

A Gnostic sect of the second century, reverencing Cain, Esau, Korah and Judas Iscariot.

Ça ira (" It will go ").

Name of the first popular song of the French Revolution. Probably first sung by the insurgents as they marched to Versailles in 1789, and the words were suggested by Lafayette to Ladré, a street singer. The expression " ça ira " was used by Franklin when asked for news at various stages of the American Revolution. Here is one of the verses:

" Ah ! ça ira, ça ira, ça ira !
Les aristocrat', a la lanterne ;
Ah! ça ira, ça ira, ça ira!
Les aristocrat' on les pendra!"

The music was that of a contredanse, which was extremely popular under the name of the " Carillon national." *v.* also **Carmagnole, La.**

Calamity Jane.

A surname given to Mrs. Martha Burke (d. August 1, 1903), a noted female character in America. She donned male attire in 1870, and acted as a scout in Indian raids. Christened " Calamity Jane " by Captain Egan, whose life she saved in 1872. She figures as Cherokee Sal in Bret Harte's "The Luck of Roaring Camp."

Calculator, The.

A surname given to Jedediah Buxton, an English mathematical prodigy (1705–72), the son of a schoolmaster. He remained throughout life a farm labourer, owing to his incapacity to acquire an education, his mind being occupied by an absorbing passion for mental calculations.

Caledonia.

Name originally given by Roman writers to the northern portion of Great Britain. Now used as a poetical designation for Scotland. Also called **Scotia.**

Caliburn, *v.* Excalibur.

Calixtines.

A sect of Hussites in Bohemia. In 1421 they published their confession, of which the leading article was a demand to partake of the cup (calix), as well as the bread in the Lord's Supper. Also called Utraquists (Latin, *uterque,* both).

Calker, The.

A surname of Michael V (Calaphates), Byzantine Emperor from 1041–2.

Calligrapher, The.

A surname given to Theodosius II (401–50), Emperor of the East, for his skill in illuminating manuscripts.

Calves' Head Club.

A club said to have been instituted in ridicule of the memory of Charles I. First noticed in a tract called "The Secret History of the Calves' Head Club," etc., reprinted in the "Harleian Miscellany." An axe was reverenced, and a dish of calves' heads represented the king and his friends.

Cambria.

The Latin name for Wales, said to be derived from Camber, the son of Brute.

Cambridge Platform.

A declaration of principles respecting Church government and doctrine adopted by a synod composed of representatives of the Congregational churches of New England, held at Cambridge, Massachusetts, in 1648. *v.* Saybrook Platform.

Cambridgeshire Handicap, The.

An annual horse-race run in the autumn at Newmarket. Distance about one mile.

Camel-Driver of Mecca.

A surname given to Mohammed, the founder of Mohammedanism (571–632).

Camden Society.

An English historical society, formed in 1838 for the publication of documents relating to English history. Named after William Camden, a noted English historian and antiquary (1551–1623). Cf. British Pausanias, The.

Cameronians.

The followers of Richard Cameron in Scotland (d. 1680). They refused to accept the indulgence granted, under Charles II, to the Presbyterian clergy, for fear of being understood to recognize his ecclesiastical authority. At first known as "The Societies," but afterwards as the Reformed Presbyterian Church of Scotland, most of which was merged (1876) in the Free Church. The name was also given to the 26th regiment of British infantry, it having been originally composed of the Cameronians, who flocked to Edinburgh during the revolution of 1688. *Their* nucleus consisted of the men who fought under Richard Cameron (*v.* supra) at Aird's Moss, where he was killed.

Cameronites.

A group of French Protestants, professing a modified form of Calvinism, led by John Cameron (b. c. 1579 at Glasgow—d. at Montauban 1625), professor of theology at Saumur and elsewhere. They were condemned by the Synod of Dort.

Camisards.

A name given to the French Protestants of the Cévennes, who took up arms in defence of their civil and religious liberties early in the eighteenth century. From the white blouses worn by the peasants, who were the chief actors in the insurrection. Also called "Enfants de Dieu."

Camorristi.

The members of a secret society (Camorra), formerly existing in Naples. They terrorized the country for many years, but were tolerated for a long time for political reasons, and rendered efficient aid to Garibaldi in expelling the Bourbons. Some years after, however, they became so obnoxious to the new government that 200 of their number were banished in 1874.

Campbellites.

Otherwise known as the "Disciples of Christ," a denomination founded about 1827 by the Rev. Alexander Campbell (1788–1866). They were also called **New Lights.** The followers of the Rev. John McLeod Campbell, a minister of the Church of Scotland, were also called Campbellites. When deposed in 1831 for teaching the universality of the Atonement, he founded a separate congregation.

Camperdown, *v.* Victoria.

Cannucks.

A nickname given to Canada by people in the United States. Also **Cunnucks.**

Cantab.

A name given to a member of Cambridge University. A contraction of the Latin word *Cantabrigia.*

Capability Brown.

A nickname of Launcelot Brown, a famous English gardener (1715–83). Laid out Kew, Blenheim, etc. He was in the habit of using the word "capability."

Cape, The.

Name by which the Cape of

Good Hope is familiarly known. Also applied to Cape Colony.

Capel Court.

A court leading to one of the entrances to the London Stock Exchange, but often used figuratively and collectively to refer to financial magnates or members of the Exchange. Cf. **Wall Street.**

Cape of Storms (Portuguese, " Cabo Tormentoso ").

The name first given to the Cape of Good Hope by Bartholomew Dias in 1486. Its present name was substituted by King John II. Also called **Leão do Mar** (the "Lion of the Sea ").

Capet.

A surname of the kings of France, beginning with Hugh Capet, 987. Also **Capetians.**

Capetians, *v.* Capet.

Capitaine Noir, Le (French, " The Black Captain ").

A surname given by the French to Lieut.-Col. Denis Vassilievitch Davidov, an officer in the Russian army, and poet (1784–1839).

Capitol, The.

That part of the Capitoline Hill at Rome which was occupied by the Temple of Jupiter Optimus. The Piazza del Campidoglio, on the Capitoline Hill, with the palaces facing it on three sides. Name also given to the seat of the National Congress, at Washington, founded in 1793, and completed in 1830, but since enlarged to twice its original area.

D.N.

B

Capitoline Hill, The.

One of the seven hills of ancient Rome, on the left bank of the Tiber, north-west of the Palatine. Its south-western summit was the famed Tarpeian Rock (q.v.).

Caporal, Le Petit (French, " The Little Corporal ").

An affectionate nickname given to Napoleon Bonaparte (1769–1821) by his soldiers. Also called the Corsican General.

Caporal la Violette (French, " Corporal Violet ").

A nickname of Napoleon Bonaparte (1769–1821), given to him by his friends in France while he was in exile, expressing their hope that he would return with the violets in the spring. Also called " Papa la Violette " (Papa Violet) and L'autre.

Captain.

An English line-of-battleship of 72 guns. Served in Lord Hood's squadron in the Mediterranean in 1794–5; Nelson's flagship in 1796; in the battle off Cape St. Vincent, February 14, 1797; burned March 22, 1813. One of the earliest English armoured turret-ships, launched March 29, 1869 ; foundered off Cape Finisterre with 500 men, September 6, 1870.

Captain Barclay.

The name by which Robert Barclay Allardice, a British officer and pedestrian, was known. He performed the feat of walking one mile in each of 1,000 successive hours at Newmarket, June 1 to July 12, 1809.

Captain Jack.

A settler in America was known by this name, also the " Black Hunter " or the " Black Rifle." His cabin was said to have been burned by Indians, and his wife and children murdered during his absence. He vowed undying vengeance, raised a band of kindred spirits, and, dressed and painted like Indians, they became the scourge of the red man and the champions of the whites. Parkman, *Montcalm and Wolfe*, i. 204.

Captain Loys, *v.* Belle Cordière, La.

Captain of Kent, The.

A surname (self-bestowed) of John (Jack) Cade (d. 1450), the leader of " Cade's Rebellion," a rising chiefly of Kentishmen. Also called Jack Amend-all.

Captain Right.

A title given to an insurgent leader in Ireland (in the eighteenth century), whom the peasants were sworn to obey.

Captain Rock.

A name assumed by the leader of a band of Irish insurgents in 1822, and affixed to notices, summonses, etc.

Captain Thresher.

The assumed name of the leader of a number of Irish lawbreakers, c. 1806.

Caramurce.

Nickname of a political party in Brazil, which, after the Emperor Pedro I's abdication in 1831, sought to procure his restoration. After Pedro's death most of the members of the party joined the Conservatives.

Carbonari (Italian, " Charcoal-Burners ").

A secret society formed in the kingdom of Naples during the reign (1805–15) of Murat by republicans and others dissatisfied with the French rule. About 1820 they played an important part in French politics until the revolution of 1830.

Carders, The, *v.* **Terry Alts.**

Carlists.

The partisans of the Spanish pretender Don Carlos, brother of Ferdinand VII, and subsequent claimants under his title. Ferdinand d. 1833, and Carlos, who was heir presumptive to the throne under the Salic law, refused to recognize the pragmatic sanction and inaugurated a civil war, lasting from 1833 till 1840. His nephew, Don Carlos III, headed a formidable insurrection from 1873 to 1876. *v.* **Cristinos.**

Carlo Khan, *v.* **Young Cub.**

Carlovingians, *v.* **Carolingians.**

Carlton House.

A house formerly standing in what is now Carlton House Terrace, London. It was built for Henry Boyle, Lord Carlton, in 1709 ; occupied in 1732 by the Prince of Wales, and afterwards by the Prince Regent (George IV). Demolished in 1827 to make room for Waterloo Place.

Carmagnole, La.

A popular song and dance of the French Revolution, rivalling " Ça ira " (q.v.). The tune originated in Provence, probably a *contre-danse*, and was adapted to a patriotic song written in 1792. The last lines were—

" Dansons la Carmagnole,
Vive le son, vive le son !
Dansons la Carmagnole,
Vive le son du canon! "

Carnival of Venice (French, " Carnaval de Venise ").

A popular air, heard by Paganini in Venice, and to which he added a series of burlesque variations. Ambroise Thomas introduced the air into the overture of his opera of the same name (produced December 9, 1853).

Car of Juggernaut, *v.* **Juggernaut Car.**

Carolingians (or **Carlovingians**).

A royal house descended from Frankish lords in Austria in the seventh century. It furnished the second dynasty of French kings (751–987), a dynasty of German emperors and kings (752–911), and a dynasty of Italian sovereigns (774–961).

Carpet-Baggers.

An opprobrious term applied to a set of Northern political adventurers who invaded the Southern States soon after the Civil War, and, by the help of the negro vote, for ten years (1866–76), caused themselves to be elected to all the chief offices, and plundered the people. President Hayes refusing federal protection to them in 1877 caused the downfall of their system, and the whites regained Government control. The term implied persons whose interest in any region was restricted to their own carpet-bags.

Carpocratians.

A sect of Gnostics of the second century, followers of Carpocrates or Carpocras of Alexandria, who lived probably in the reign of Hadrian (117–38).

Caracci of France, The.

A surname given to Jean Jouvenet, a French historical painter (1644–1717). Becoming paralysed on his right side, he painted with his left hand.

Carse of Gowrie.

A low-lying tract of fertile land in Perthshire, Scotland, extending along the north bank of the Tay for about fifteen miles, between Perth and Dundee.

Carthage of the North, The.

A surname given to Lübeck a free city of Germany, at one time the leading city of the Hanseatic League (q.v.).

Carthaginian Lion, The.

A surname of Hannibal, a famous Carthaginian general (247–c. 183 B.C.).

Case of the Seven Bishops.

A famous English trial in 1688. Archbishop Sancroft, and Bishops Ken (of Bath and Wells), Lake (of Chichester), White (of Peterborough), Turner (of Ely), Lloyd (of St. Asaph), and Trelawney (of Bristol), were arraigned on a charge of libel in protesting, in a petition to James II, against his order that his "declara- tions for liberty of conscience" be read in the churches. They were acquitted on the day (June 30) that the invitation was sent to William of Orange to land in England.

Casa de Contratacion de las Indias, v. Council of Seville.

Castle, The.

Name by which Dublin Castle, especially regarded as the seat of Government, is familiarly known.

Castle of Maidens, The, v. Maiden Town, The.

Cathari, v. Albigenses.

Cathay.

Name given by Marco Polo to a region in eastern Asia, supposed to be northern China. Used poetically to designate China.

Catholic, The.

A surname given to Alfonso I (or Alphonso or Alonzo), King of Asturias (693–757), on account of his zeal in erecting and endowing churches and monas- teries; to Ferdinand V (II of Aragon and Sicily, and III of Naples), King of Castile (1452–1516), also called the Wily; and Isabella, Queen of Castile (1451–1504), wife of Ferdi- nand V.

Catholic Majesty.

A title used by the kings of Spain, at times after the Council of Toledo, and permanently since Ferdinand the Catholic (r. 1474–1516).

Cat Nation (French, " Nation du Chat ").

A surname given to the Erie

tribe of North-American Indians, formerly living in western New York, and along the southern shore of Lake Erie. Derived from their Huron name, signifying " Cat People."

Cato Street Conspiracy.

A conspiracy under the leadership of Arthur Thistlewood, having for its object the assassination of Castlereagh and other ministers. So called from the rendezvous in Cato Street, near Edgware Road, London, where it was discovered February 23, 1820. Thistlewood and others concerned in the plot were executed.

Cautionary Towns.

A name given to the four towns in the Netherlands— Briel, Flushing, Walcheren, Rammekens—held from 1586 to 1616 by England as security for payment due.

Cavalier Parliament, v. Pensioned (or Pension) or Cavalier Parliament.

Cavaliers.

The adherents of Charles I and Charles II during the civil war; also called Royalists.

Cave, The, v. Adullamites.

Caveau (French, " small (wine) cellar ").

A Parisian literary and convivial club, founded in 1729, dissolved in 1739, and refounded in 1806 and 1834, so called from a tavern of the name " Caveau."

Cave of Adullam, v. Adullamites.

Cecil's Fast.

A nickname given to an Act of Parliament introduced by William Cecil, Lord Burleigh (or Burghley) (1520–98), enjoining fish to be eaten on certain days. The object of the Act was to restore the fish trade, which had been almost ruined by the Reformation. No one would buy fish for fear of being thought a Papist.

Celestial City, The.

Bunyan, in his " Pilgrim's Progress," gives the name to Heaven. v. Celestial Empire, The.

Celestial Empire, The.

A popular name for the Chinese Empire. Pekin is called the Celestial City, and the Chinese are often called the " Celestials." Derived from the Chinese, " Tien Chao " (Heavenly Dynasty).

Celestials, The, v. Celestial Empire, The.

Celtic Homer, The.

A surname given to Ossian (or Oisin), a semi-historical Gaelic bard and warrior, son of Finn (fl. c. end of third century).

Censor, The.

Surname of Marcus Porcius Cato, a Roman statesman, general and writer (234–149 B.C.).

Censor of the Age, The, v. Sage of Chelsea, The.

Centennial State.

A surname given to the State of Colorado, from its having been admitted as one of the United States of America in 1876, one hundred years after the Declaration of Independence (q. v.).

Cent Jours, Les, v. **Hundred Days, The.**

Centralists (Spanish, " Centralistas ").

A political party in Mexico which began in 1823, was reorganized in 1837, and has ever since been prominent. The Centralists favour a single centralized republican government, and are opposed by the Federalists, who desire [autonomy of the states. The struggles for ascendency of these two parties have caused most of the civil wars which have desolated Mexico.

Century White.

A nickname given to John White (1590-1645) from his work, " First Century of Scandalous Malignant Priests," etc.

Ceremonious, The.

A surname given to Peter IV, King of Aragon (1319-87), from his attention to the etiquette of the court.

Cerinthians (or **Merinthians**).

A sect of early heretics, followers of Cerinthus, who probably lived in the latter part of the first century, A.D.

Cesarewitch Handicap.

An annual horse-race run in the autumn at Newmarket, Cambridgeshire. Distance, 2 miles, 2 furlongs, 35 yards.

Chaldeans, v. **Nestorians.**

Challenger Expedition.

A British scientific expedition, under the direction of Professor Wyville Thomson, for deep sea exploration, undertaken by H.M.S. " Challenger," 1872-6.

Chambers of Reunion.

Special courts established by Louis XIV at Metz, Besançon, Tournai and Breisach, 1680. They decided on the annexation to France of various territories along the eastern frontier (Saarbrücken, Luxemburg, etc.).

Chambre Introuvable ("Undiscoverable Chamber").

A nickname of the French Chamber of Deputies 1815-16, noted for its reactionary measures. Louis XVIII invented the expression, believing that, after the long years of the Revolution and the Empire, a Chamber purely monarchic, *serait introuvable* (was not to be found).

Chambres Ardentes (French, " Fiery Chambers ").

Extraordinary French tribunals sometimes convened under the old monarchy for the trial of cases of malversation, etc.

Champion, The.

A journal first appearing in 1739, edited by Henry Fielding and one Ralph. It ridiculed the Jacobite party.

Champion of England.

A feudal office held since 1377 by a Lincolnshire family named Dimoch, Dymoch, Dymoke or Dimocke.

Champion of the Virgin, v. **Doctor of the Incarnation, The.**

'Change.

A popular abbreviated name for the market held in the Royal Exchange, London.

Channel, The.

The English Channel is familiarly so called.

Chapter Coffee House.

A London coffee-house situated at the corner of Chapterhouse Court, on the south side of Paternoster Row, noted in the eighteenth century as the resort of men of letters, and for its punch, pamphlets and good supply of newspapers. Closed as a coffee-house in 1854, and then altered to a tavern.

Charge of the Light Brigade.

A celebrated charge made by the Light Brigade, of 670 men, under Lord Cardigan, on a Russian battery at Balaclava, October 25, 1854. Cf. Tennyson's poem with this title. Of the 670 men who had gone into action, only 195 were mounted when the brigade re-formed on the ground from which they had moved off.

Charlies.

Nickname of the London night-watchmen, c. 1640, from Charles I, who improved the police system.

Charlotte Dundas.

The name of the first practical British steamboat, built by William Symmington, and tried on the Forth and Clyde Canal in 1802. Cf. Clermont.

Charmante Gabrielle, La, v. Belle Gabrielle, La.

Charter, The Great, v. Magna Charta.

Charter Oak, The.

A tree formerly standing in Hartford, Connecticut, in which, according to tradition, the colonial charter was hidden in 1687. The tree was overthrown by a storm in 1856.

Chartist Clergyman, The.

A surname given to the Rev. Charles Kingsley, an English clergyman and author (1819–75), in allusion to his novel, "Alton Locke" (1850).

Chartreuse, La Grande.

The leading Carthusian monastery, 13 miles north-east of Grenoble (Isère), France, founded by St. Bruno, c. 1084. The Chartreuse liqueur is manufactured there.

Chassepot.

A rifle so named, from its inventor, Antoine Alphonse Chassepot (b. 1833), was adopted for the French army in 1868.

Chaste, The.

A surname given to Alfonso II (or Alphonso), King of Asturias (d. 842).

Chat, Nation du, v. Cat Nation.

Châtelet, Le Grand.

An ancient fortress in Paris on the site of the present Place du Châtelet, used for a prison and courts of justice until 1802, when it was destroyed.

Châtelet, Le Petit.

An ancient fortress in Paris, on the right bank of the Seine, near the Hôtel-Dieu, used for a prison. Destroyed in 1782.

Chaucer of France, The.

A surname given to Clément Marot, a noted French poet (1497–1544).

Chauffeurs or Garrotteurs.

A band of French brigands, under the leadership of Johann Bückler, surnamed Schinderhannes, who, during the Reign of Terror (q.v.) infested the forests of Argères, near Chartres, and were dispersed by the consulate in 1803. The name is derived from their practice of garrotting or burning (*chauffer*) the feet of their victims to make them reveal their treasures.

Chauve, Le (French, " The Bald ").

A surname given to Charles II, King of France and Emperor of the Romans [Charles I as King of France], (823–77).

Chelsea Philosopher, *v.* Sage of Chelsea, The.

Cheronean Sage, The.

A surname given to Plutarch, a Greek historian, born at Chæronea, c. 46. Chiefly known as the author of " Plutarch's Lives."

Cherub, *v.* Essex.

Chesapeake.

An American frigate of 38 guns, built at Norfolk, Virginia, in 1799. On June 1, 1813, an engagement between the " Shannon " (38 guns), under Captain Philip Vere Broke, and the " Chesapeake " (Captain James Lawrence), took place off Boston Harbour. Captain Lawrence was mortally wounded early in the fight, and was carried below exclaiming, " Don't give up the ship! " Fifteen minutes after the first shot was fired the " Chesapeake's " flag was struck.

Chevalier de St. George.

A title assumed by James Francis Edward Stuart (1688–1766), the Old Pretender, son of James II of England and Mary of Modena. Also called the **Warming-pan Hero**, he, it is said, having been conveyed to Mary d'Este, wife of James II, in a warming-pan. (Cf. Macaulay's *Hist. of England*, ii. 308).

Chevalier Sans Peur et Sans Reproche, Le (" The Knight Without Fear and Without Reproach ").

Surname given to Pierre du Terrail, seigneur de Bayard (1476–1524).

Chickamauga, Rock of, *v.* Rock of Chickamauga.

Chicken, The.

A nickname given to Michael Angelo Taylor, a barrister, he having alluded to himself in his maiden speech (1785) as but " a chicken in the profession of the law."

Child, The.

A surname of Louis, King of Germany (893–911), son of the Emperor Arnulf. He acceded to the throne at the age of six, the government being conducted chiefly by Hatto, Archbishop of Mainz. Louis was the last of the Carolingians in Germany.

Chiltern Hundreds.

The three hundreds of Stoke, Desborough and Bodenham, in Buckinghamshire. The office of Steward of the Chiltern Hundreds is a purely nominal one, and conferred upon a member of Parliament who wishes to resign his seat, such resignation being impossible unless he is disqualified by the acceptance of a place of honour and profit under the Crown. The place is in the gift of the Chancellor of the Exchequer.

China Wedding, v. Wedding Anniversaries.

Chinese Gordon.

A name given to General Charles George Gordon (1833–85), alluding to his services in China in 1863 against the Taiping rebels. He resigned his command in 1864, after putting down the rebellion, and received from the Chinese Emperor the yellow jacket and peacock's feather of a mandarin of the first class. He was Governor of the Equatorial Provinces of Central Africa in the service of the Khedive of Egypt in 1874–6, and was created " Pasha " in 1877 (hence Gordon Pasha). In 1884 he was sent by the British Government to the Soudan to assist the Khedive in withdrawing the garrisons of the country, which could no longer be held against the Mahdi. The Mahdi besieged Khartoum on March 12, 1884, and Gordon was killed in the storming of the city, January 26, 1885. His death was fully avenged by the troops under General Kitchener (b. 1850) in the Battle of Omdurman, September 2, 1898.

Chouans.

During the French Revolution, a name given to the royalist insurgents of Brittany (derived, perhaps, from Jean Cottereau, called Chouan, one

of their leaders ("Chouan" a corruption of "chat-huant," screech-owl). v. War of La Vendée, and cf. Balzac's novel, " Les Chouans."

Christian Atticus, The.

A surname given to Reginald Heber, an English prelate and hymn-writer (1783–1826), made Bishop of Calcutta in 1823. He wrote the hymn " From Greenland's icy mountains."

Christian Cicero.

A surname given to Firmianus Lactantius, Lucius Cælius (or Cæcilius), a Christian apologist and preceptor of Crispus in Gaul, c. 313.

Christian Seneca, The.

A surname given to Joseph Hall, an English bishop and author (1574–1656). Also called the English Seneca.

Christian Virgil, The.

A surname given to Marco Girolamo Vida, an Italian Latin poet (c. 1480—1566). Also to Jacopo Sannazaro, an Italian poet (1458–1530). Also called the Parthenope of Naples.

Christ's Hospital, v. Blue-coat School.

Cicero of France, The.

A surname given to Jean Baptiste Massillon, a noted French pulpit orator (1663–1742).

Cicero of Germany, The.

A surname given to Johann, elector of Brandenburg from 1486–99, on account of his eloquence.

Cicero of the (British) Senate, The.

A surname given to George Canning, a celebrated English statesman and orator (1770-1827), in allusion to his eloquence. Called (by Charles Lamb) the " Zany of Debate." Also **Clemency Canning**, in allusion to his leniency to the rebels after the Indian Mutiny (q.v.).

Cicero's Mouth.

A surname given to Philippe Pot, Louis XI of France's Prime Minister (1428-94).

Cid, The (Spanish," Master ").

A title given to the principal national hero of Spain, Ruy or Rodrigo Diaz de Bivar (c. 1040-99), famous for his exploits against the Moors. Also known as " el Campeador " (the champion or challenger), or " El Cid Campeador " (the lord champion). Cf. Southey's translation of the " Chronicle of the Cid " (1808); also Corneille's tragedy of " Le Cid " (1636).

Cider Cellars, The, v. **Coal Hole, The.**

Cincinnati, Society of the, v. **Society of the Cincinnati.**

Cincinnatus of the Americans, The, v. **Father of his Country, The.**

Cinque Ports (French, " Five Ports").

A collective name given to Hastings,Romney,Hythe,Dover, and Sandwich. Winchelsea and Rye were afterwards added. They are governed by a lord warden, under the title of Lord Warden of the Cinque Ports.

Cinthio (or Cintio).

A surname given to Giovanni Battista Giraldi, an eminent Italian novelist and tragic poet (1504-73).

Circe of the Revolution, The.

A surname given to Madame Roland, in allusion to her fascinating manners (1754-93).

Circumlocution Office.

A satirical term applied by Dickens in " Little Dorrit " to the system of red-tape in English Government offices.

Citizen King, The, v. **Roi Citoyen, Le.**

Citizen of Geneva.

A name by which Jean-Jacques Rousseau, an eminient Swiss-French philosopher (b. at Geneva 1712-78), is sometimes known.

City and Suburban Handicap.

An annual horse-race at Epsom, Surrey. Distance, 1¼ miles.

City of a (the) Hundred Towers.

A name bestowed upon Pavia, Italy.

City of Brotherly Love.

A nickname given to Philadelphia, Pennsylvania (from the Greek φιλαδελφία, brotherly love, instead of Φιλαδέλφεια, city of Philadelphus in Asia Minor, from which Philadelphia takes its name).

City of Churches.

Brooklyn, New York, is so called, on account of the large number of its churches.

City of Destruction.

The starting-point of Christian in his journey in Bunyan's "Pilgrim's Progress."

City of Elms.

New Haven, Connecticut, is so called from the numerous elms which shade its streets.

City of Homes.

A surname given to the city of Philadelphia, in allusion to the comparatively large number of private dwellings contained in it.

City of Intelligence.

A surname given to Berlin, Prussia.

City of Lilies, The.

A surname given to Florence, Italy.

City of Magnificent Distances.

A name sometimes given to Washington, District of Columbia, from its wide avenue and fine vistas.

City of Masts.

A surname sometimes given to London, referring to the number of ships, and consequent number of masts, in the Thames. Also called the **City of Smoke.**

City of Notions.

A surname sometimes given to Boston, Mass.

City of Oaks.

Raleigh, North Carolina.

City of Palaces, The.

A name given to Genoa, Italy; also to ancient Rome, Calcutta, Edinburgh, St. Petersburg, and modern Paris.

City of Peace.

A surname given to Jerusalem, *salem*, its old name, meaning "peace." Also applied to Bagdad.

City of Refuge, The, *v.* City of the Prophet, The.

City of Rocks.

A surname given to Nashville, Tennessee.

City of Smoke, *v.* City of Masts.

City of Spindles.

A popular name for the city of Lowell, Massachusetts, from the number of spindles employed in its cotton-mills.

City of the Golden Gate.

A popular surname for the city of San Francisco, California, on account of its proximity to the Golden Gate, a narrow strait connecting the Bay of San Francisco with the Pacific.

City of the Prophet, The.

Medina, Arabia, to which Mahomet fled from Mecca in 622. His tomb is at Medina. Also called the **City of Refuge.**

City of the Seven Hills, *v.* Seven-hilled City, The.

City of the Straits.

Detroit, Michigan, is so named from its geographical situation.

City of the Sun.

Baalbec (or Baalbek), an ancient city of Syria, the Greek Heliopolis, "City of the Sun."

City of the Three Kings.

A surname given to Cologne, Germany, as being the reputed burial-place of the **Three Kings of Cologne** (q.v.).

City of the Tribes, The.

A surname given to Galway,

Ireland, from its having been the residence of thirteen " tribes," or chief families, who settled there c. 1235.

City of the Violated Treaty.

Limerick, Ireland, is so called, on account of the frequent infringements of the " Pacification of Limerick," concluded at Limerick in 1691.

City of the Violet Crown, The, *v.* Violet-Crowned City, The.

City of the West.

A surname of the city of Glasgow, Scotland, in allusion to its situation.

City of Victory.

Cairo, Egypt.

Claimant, The, *v.* Tichborne Trial.

Clarendon Press.

A printing establishment at Oxford, belonging to the University. It was founded partly with profits from the sale of Clarendon's " History of the Rebellion."

Clarisses, Les.

A religious sisterhood of the order of Sainte-Claire, founded in 1212.

Claus, Santa, *v.* Santa Claus.

Cleanest City in the World, The.

A name given to Broek, Holland, famous for its neatness.

Clemency Canning, *v.* Cicero of the (British) Senate, The.

Clementine League, *v.* Holy League of Cognac.

Cleopatra's Needles.

Name given to a pair of Egyptian obelisks of pink granite, transported from Heliopolis to Alexandria in the eighteenth year of Augustus. One was taken to London, and was set up on the Thames Embankment in 1878, and the other was soon after taken to New York and erected in Central Park.

Clermont, The.

The name of the steamboat used by Robert Fulton on his first trip from New York to Albany (1807), in the beginning of steam navigation. Nicknamed in derision "Fulton's Folly." Cf. Charlotte Dundas.

Clicquot.

A nickname given by " Punch " to Frederick William IV (1795–1861), in allusion to his liking for that brand of champagne.

Clink, The.

A prison situated at one end of Bankside, London. It belonged to the " Liberty of the Clink," a part of the manor of Southwark not included in the grant to the City of London. It was burned down in the riots of 1780.

Clinton's Ditch.

A nickname given, in derision, to the Erie Canal, connecting the Hudson River with the Great Lakes, referring to the zeal shown by De Witt Clinton (then Governor of New York) in its construction in face of great opposition.

Closter-Seven, Convention of, *v.* Convention of Closter-Seven.

Club, The.

A body of malcontents in the

Scottish Parliament (1689–90). Its chief members were Montgomery, Ross and Annandale. Also the name of the **Literary Club** (q.v.), previous to Garrick's funeral in 1779.

Coal Hole, The.

A nickname given to a place of entertainment in Fountain Court, Strand (subsequently called the Cider Cellars), founded by John Rhodes, who died in 1847. The last manager before the house was demolished was Charles Wilmot.

Cobden Club.

An association (founded in London in 1866) for the promulgation of free trade doctrines, named after Richard Cobden, the chief supporter of the Anti-Corn Law League.

Cocaigne, The Land of.

A fabled land of perfect happiness and luxury, overflowing with milk and honey. The English poets of the sixteenth century called it "Lubberland." The name is usually, with or without reason, associated with Cockney.

Cock, The.

A famous tavern, formerly existing in Fleet Street, London. Celebrated by Tennyson in "Will Waterproof's Lyrical Monologue."

Cockade City, The.

A popular surname for the city of Petersburg, Virginia.

Cockaigne or Cocagne, v. Cocaigne, the Land of.

Cock Lane Ghost.

A noted imposture perpetrated in 1672 in Cock Lane, Smithfield, London, by a man named Parsons and his daughter of eleven. Knockings and other strange noises were heard, and a "luminous lady," supposed to be the ghost of a Mrs. Kent, was seen. Dr. Johnson, among others, visited the house, and was attacked for his credulity by Churchill in a long poem, "The Ghost." Parsons was pilloried.

Cockney.

A nickname given to any one born in London within the sound of Bow Bells. v. Cocaigne, The Land of.

Cockney School, The.

A name derisively applied by some English critics to a set of writers including Hazlitt, Shelley, Keats, Leigh Hunt and others. Leigh Hunt was the shining light of the coterie. (Cf. his "Carols of Cockayne.")

Cock of the North, The.

A surname given to the last Duke of Gordon *(George) (1770–1836). So called on a monument erected in his honour at Fochabers, Aberdeenshire.

Cockpit, The.

A London theatre which formerly stood in a narrow court, called Pitt Place, formerly Cockpit Alley, running out of Drury Lane. Erected c. 1615, but pulled down by a mob in 1617. A second theatre was built on the spot, called the "Phœnix"

* Charles Henry Gordon Lennox, Duke of Richmond and Gordon (b. 1818), sixth Duke of Richmond in 1860, was created Duke of Gordon in 1876.

(q.v.), and this was succeeded by " Drury Lane Theatre."

Cockpit of Europe.

A surname sometimes given to Belgium, it having been the scene of a larger number of important battles than any other European country.

Cocoa-tree Club.

A noted London club which was the Tory Cocoa-tree Chocolate-house of Queen Anne's reign, at 64, St. James's Street. It was converted into a gambling-house and club, probably before 1746, when the house was the headquarters of the Jacobite party, and the resort of the wits of the time. *Timbs.*

Code Frédéric.

A codification of the laws of Prussia by Frederick the Great in 1751.

Code Napoléon.

A compilation of the laws of France under the auspices of Napoleon Bonaparte, and promulgated 1804–10. It is founded on the civil law, and has been largely copied in other countries where the civil law prevails.

Code Noir (French, " Black Code ").

An edict of Louis XIV of France in 1685, regulating the West Indian colonies and the condition and treatment of negro slaves and freedmen.

Code of 1650.

A code of laws compiled for the colony of Connecticut by Roger Ludlow. Sometimes called " Ludlow's Code."

Codfish Aristocracy.

A name used to express the idea of vulgar, wealthy people or parvenus, and originally applied to certain Massachusetts families grown rich in the cod fisheries.

Cœur de Lion (French, " Lionhearted ").

A surname given to Richard I of England (1157–99) on account of his valour.

Coffee Club, The, *v.* Rota or Coffee Club.

Coldbath Fields.

A name by which the House of Correction or prison on that spot was popularly known. It was originally built in the reign of James I, closed in 1886, since pulled down, and the site now occupied by the Post Office buildings. Sometimes called the **English Bastille.**

Coldstream Guards.

Name given to a regiment of British foot-guards, first enrolled by General Monk at Coldstream 1659–60.

Colin-Tampon.

An ancient nickname for the Swiss.

Collegiants.

A sect founded near Leyden, Holland, in 1619, the societies of which are called colleges. In doctrine and practice the Collegiants resemble the Quakers, having no creed or organized ministry ; but they believe in the necessity of baptism, which they administer by immersion.

Colliberts, *v.* Cagots.

Collop Monday.

The day before Shrove Tuesday, so called from the custom of eating collops of salted meat and eggs on that day.

Colney Hatch.

Name by which the lunatic asylum at Colney Hatch (about six miles north of London) is known. Sometimes used as a synonym for a lunatic asylum.

Colonne de Juillet (French, " Column of July ").

A monument in Paris, erected on the site of the Bastille in 1840, in honour of the citizens killed in the attacks on the royal government in 1830. Total height, 154 feet ; diameter, 13 feet. It is a Corinthian column of bronze, rising from a square base surmounted by a gilded statue of the winged Genius of Liberty.

Colonne des Docteurs, La, *v.* Doctor Venerabilis.

Colonne du Congrès.

A monument erected in Brussels in commemoration of the Belgian Constitutional Congress in 1831. It is a Roman Doric column, 147 feet high, on the summit of which stands a statue of Leopold I. At the angles are four female figures in bronze, personifying types of liberty.

Colonne Vendôme.

A monument in the Place Vendôme, Paris. It is a Roman Doric column of masonry encased in bronze, imitating the Column of Trajan at Rome in design, and was erected by Napoleon I in honour of his victories over the Russians and Austrians in 1805. Height, 142 feet ; diameter, 13 ft. The shaft is encircled with reliefs referring to the campaigns in question, ascending in a spiral, and the column is surmounted by a figure of the emperor. Overthrown by the Commune in 1871, but restored in 1875.

Colossus of Independence, The.

A surname given to John Adams (1735–1826), the second President of the United States, in allusion to his earnest and persevering efforts towards colonial independence in the Continental Congress. Sometimes also called the **Colossus of the Revolution.**

Colossus of Rhodes.

One of the Seven Wonders of the World, an immense statue over 105 feet high, and made to commemorate the successful defence of Rhodes against Demetrius Poliorcetes (304 B.C.). It required twelve years for its completion, and Chares of Lindus, who lived c. 290–280 B.C., was its sculptor. It stood sixty-six years, and is said to have been made from the engines of war which Demetrius was obliged to abandon.

Colossus of the Nineteenth Century, The.

A surname given to Napoleon Bonaparte (1769–1821).

Colossus of the Revolution, The, *v.* Colossus of Independence, The.

Column of July, *v.* Colonne de Juillet.

Column of Marcus Aurelius (or Antonine Column).

A monument in the Piazza Colonna, Rome, erected 174 A.D., in honour of the campaigns against the Marcomanni. It consists of a Roman Doric column of marble on a square pedestal, the total height, excluding the statue of St. Paul of Sixtus V, being 123 feet. The shaft is sculptured in a spiral of twenty turns, with reliefs of the wars it commemorates. The column is of the Trajan type. *v.* Column of Trajan.

Column of the Congress, *v.* Colonne du Congrès.

Column of the Grand Army.

The name given to a column 166 feet high, erected on the high ground above Boulogne in honour of Napoleon I, on the occasion of the projected invasion of England. Begun in 1804, but not completed until 1841.

Column of Trajan.

A monument in Rome dedicated (114 A.D.) to the Emperor Trajan. Total height, excluding the present statue of St. Peter, 127½ feet. It is a Roman Doric column of marble, and the shaft is occupied by reliefs, ascending in a spiral, representing Trajan's campaigns.

Column of Vendôme, *v.* Colonne Vendôme.

Columns of Hercules, *v.* Pillars of Hercules.

Columns of St. Mark and St. Theodore.

Two columns in Venice, situated at the end of the Piazetta towards the Grand Canal. The massive plain cylindrical shafts are of granite, the western pink and the eastern grey, resting on spreading stepped bases. The figure of St. Theodore, with his crocodile, was erected on the western column in 1329. The eastern column bears the famous winged **Lion of St. Mark** (q.v.), in bronze, with eyes inlaid in precious stones. The existing lion is of the fifteenth century.

Comédie-Française, La.

The official name of the Théâtre-Français at Paris. The Comédie practically had its beginning in the Théâtre de l'Hôtel Bourgogne, established in 1552, which was followed by the Théâtre du Marais in 1600. A few years later the company of Molière was established in the great hall of the Hôtel Bourbon. Molière died in 1673. In 1680 there were three companies in Paris—that of the Hôtel Bourgogne, that of the Marais, and Molière's in the Théâtre Guénégaud. The two latter were amalgamated October 21, 1680, and the Comédie-Française organized by *lettre de cachet* of Louis XIV as " l'hôtel des Comédiens du Roi entretenus par Sa Majesté." The Comédie frequently migrated, and in 1782 played in what is now the Odéon (*v.* **Second Théâtre-Français**). After its suppression in 1793 it was reconstituted by Napoleon, then first consul, and established in the Théâtre-Français.

Commander of the Faithful.

A title of the caliphs, first assumed by Omar (r. 634-44). Often used in the Arabian

Nights' Entertainments. *v.* Emperor of Believers, The.

Commonwealth, The (also called the English Commonwealth or the Commonwealth of England).

The designation officially applied to the form of government existing in England from the abolition of the monarchy in February, 1649, after the execution of Charles I, until the establishment of the protectorate under Cromwell in December, 1653, but often loosely used of the whole interval from the death of Charles I to the restoration of Charles II in May, 1660. During the period of the real commonwealth the government was vested in a Council of State, composed of members of the House of Commons, and the House of Lords was abolished.

Compagnie Blanche, La (French, "The White Company").

A band of assassins organized in Toulouse in the thirteenth century by "the ferocious Folquet," Bishop of Toulouse. This company joined the army of Simon de Montfort when he besieged Toulouse. The name was also assumed by a band of freebooters (the "Grand Companies"), led by Bertrand du Guesclin in 1366, from the white cross which each wore on his shoulder. He was ransomed from English captivity for the purpose of ridding France of these adventurers, and, placing himself at their head, he led them out of the country into Spain. *v.* also White Company, The.

D.N.

Compromise of **1850**, *v.* Omnibus Bill.

Conciergerie, La.

The old prison of the Palais de Justice in Paris. When the palace, which was originally fortified, was inhabited by the kings of France, the part of the building containing the lodging of the concierge of the palace received this name. The Conciergerie became widely known during the Reign of Terror (q.v.). Three hundred and twenty-eight prisoners were butchered there in one week. The cell occupied by Marie Antoinette was destroyed in 1871 by the Communists, but the prison still exists.

Concordat of Francis I, The.

A convention concluded in 1516 between Francis I of France and Leo X. It replaced the pragmatic sanction of Bourges, adopted at the Assembly of Bourges in 1438, but which had never been recognized by the Pope. It re-established the *annato*, referred the *causæ majores* to Rome, and gave to the king the right of nominating bishops.

Concordat of Worms, The.

A convention concluded in 1122 between the Emperor Henry V and Calixtus II. The main point at issue between the emperors and the popes, the matter of the election of bishops and abbots, was settled in favour of the spiritual power, the concordat providing that the investiture should be conferred, not with the ring and staff, but with the sceptre. It was also provided that the

F

election should take place in the presence of the emperor or his representatives ; that investiture by the emperor should precede consecration; and that ecclesiastics holding secular benefices should perform feudal services. This instrument put an end to the contest regarding investiture, and became a fundamental ordinance of the Holy Roman Empire.

Concordat of 1801, The.

An agreement concluded July 15, 1801, between Napoleon Bonaparte, as first consul, and Pius VII. It re-established the Roman Catholic Church in France, and granted to the Government the right of appointing archbishops and bishops, who were to be confirmed by the Pope. It came into operation on April 8, 1802.

Concordat of 1855, The.

An agreement concluded at Vienna, August 18, 1855, between Francis Joseph of Austria and Pius IX. It gave the clergy control of public instruction, and placed cases of canon law, especially marriage affairs, under the jurisdiction of ecclesiastical courts. It was abrogated in July, 1870.

Confederate States of America.

A confederacy of eleven States which seceded from the United States in 1860 and 1861, and formed a government. They were re-admitted to the Union from 1866 to 1870.

Confederation, Articles of, v. Articles of Confederation.

Confederation of Bar.

A union of Polish patriots, led by members of the nobility, formed at Bar (1768) against the Russian influence and the dissidents. It was suppressed by the Russians and dissolved in 1772.

Confederation of the Rhine.

A confederation of most of the German states, formed in July, 1806, under the protectorate of Napoleon I, Emperor of the French, and dissolved in 1813.

Conference of Constantinople.

A conference of the six great Powers and Turkey for the purpose of preventing war between Turkey and Russia, the latter championing the cause of the Christian insurgents in the Balkan Peninsula. Formally opened December 23, 1876, but dissolved January 20, 1877, its demands being rejected by the Turks.

Confession of Bale.

A reformed confession, drafted by Œcolampadius, and revised by Myconius, published in 1534. Also the first Helvetic Confession.

Confession of Faith, v. National Covenant.

Confessor, The.

A surname of Edward, King of the West Saxons (c. 1004–66), from his reputed sanctity.

Congress of Berlin, v. Berlin Congress.

Congress of Rastatt.

A congress held in 1713–4, for putting an end to the war between Austria and France. Also a congress held in 1797–9, for the purpose of arranging the questions at issue between France and the Empire. It began December 8, 1797, and was dissolved April 8, 1799. The cession of the left bank of the Rhine to France and the secularization of various German dominions were agreed to. Two of the French envoys were murdered by Austrian hussars near Rastatt, April 28, 1799.

Congress of Troppau.

A congress of the monarchs of Russia, Austria and Prussia, held at Troppau, October to December, 1820, for the purpose of deliberating on the Neapolitan revolution and other popular movements, and preserving the Holy Alliance.

Congress of Verona.

A congress of representatives from the principal European governments, held at Verona, October to December, 1822, occasioned by the disturbances in Spain and south-eastern Europe. It was attended by the monarchs of Prussia, Austria, Russia and the Two Sicilies and Sardinia, the Duke of Wellington, the Duke of Montmorency and others. Metternich presided. The chief result was the armed intervention of France in Spain in 1823.

Congress of Vienna.

A congress of the principal European Powers, for settling the affairs of Europe, held at Vienna September 1814–June, 1815.

Connoisseur, The.

A periodical begun January 31, 1754, by George Colman the elder and Bonnell Thornton, and continued weekly for three years. In it appeared, in 1756, the first publications of William Cowper. His first paper was on " Keeping a Secret."

Connubio (Italian, " Marriage ")

The union of the left-centre faction (under Rattazzi), in the Sardinian Chamber, with the right-centre (under Cavour), c. 1852.

Conqueror, The, *v.* **Father of Good Works, The.**

A surname of Mohammed II, Sultan of Turkey (c. 1430–81); also called " The Great "; of Alfonso I (Affonso or Alphonso), King of Portugal (c. 1109–85); of James I, King of Aragon (1206–76); of William I, King of England (1027 or 8–87). Also called " the Norman " and " the Bastard." *v.* also **Conquistador.**

Conqueror of the World, The, *v.* **Great, The (Alexander III).**

Also a surname of Aurung-Zeb (Aurang-Zebe, or Aureng-Zebe), Emperor of Hindustan (1619–1707).

Conquistador (Spanish, " The Conqueror ").

A surname given to Francisco Pizarro, a Spanish soldier (c. 1475–1541), from his conquest of Peru.

Conscience Whigs.

A faction of the Whig Party in Massachusetts, who were opposed to the Cotton Whigs en the slavery question, c. 1850.

Consensus Genevensis.

A confession of faith, drawn up by Calvin, which was dedicated by the pastors of Geneva to the syndics and council of the city, January 1, 1552. It was occasioned by Calvin's dispute with Bolsec, who denied the doctrine of reprobation, and was designed to unite the Swiss churches on the subjet of pre-destination, but failed to acquire symbolical authority outside Geneva.

Consensus Tigurinus.

A confession of faith drawn up by Calvin in 1549 at Zurich (Latin, *Tigurium*), in concert with Bullinger and the pastors of Zurich, for the purpose of uniting the Swiss churches on the doctrine of the Lord's Supper. It was published in 1551, and was adopted by all the reformed cantons except Berne.

Conservative Club, The.

A London political club estab-lished in 1840. The number of members is 1,200.

Conservative Party, The.

Name of the party in British politics, formerly called Tories (q.v.), dating from (c. 1832) the time of the Reform Bill, which the Tories opposed.

Consolato del Mare (Italian, " Consulate of the Sea ").

A code of maritime law, sup-posed to be a compilation of the law and trading customs of various Italian cities, as Venice, Genoa, Pisa and Amalfi, to-gether with those of the cities with which they traded, as Barcelona, Marseilles, etc. Its precise date is unknown, but a Spanish edition of it was pub-lished at Barcelona at the end

of the thirteenth or beginning of the fourteenth century. It has formed the basis of most of the subsequent compilations of maritime law.

Constance, Council of.

An important council of the Roman Catholic Church, held 1414-8. Its objects were the healing of the Papal schism, the suppression of the Bohemian heresy, and the reformation of the Church. It condemned Huss (1415) and Jerome of Prague (1416) to death, and elected Martin V as Pope (1417).

Constance, Treaty of.

A treaty of peace concluded between Frederick Barbarossa and the Lombard League in 1183, at the expiration of the truce established after the defeat of the emperor at Legnano in 1176.

Constant, The.

A surname of John (Johann), Elector of Saxony (1468–1532). Co-regent with his brother, Frederick the Wise, until the death of the latter (May 5, 1525).

Constellation.

A vessel of the United States Navy, built in 1798. Captured (Commodore Truxton com-manding) the French insur-gents in 1799.

Constituent Assembly, *v.* National Assembly.

Constitution.

An American frigate (1,576 tons and 44 guns rating, but carrying 32 24-pounders and 20 32-pounders), built at Boston

1797. On July 17, 1812, she fell in with a squadron composed of the "Shannon," "Africa," "Æolus," "Belvidera," and "Guerrière" (under Commodore Philip Vere Brooke), but after a chase lasting three days, in an almost dead calm, escaped. Fought the "Guerrière," which surrendered and was burned, August 19, 1812. The "Java" (Captain Lambert) also surrendered to her, off the coast of Brazil, December 29, 1812. On February 20, 1815, she fought and captured the "Cyane" and the "Levant." The indignation at the proposal to dismantle and sell her (September, 1830) found expression in Oliver Wendell Holmes' poem, "Old Ironsides." She was afterwards used as a training-ship and a receiving-ship. Taken to Boston in 1897.

Constitution of the United States, *v.* **Federal Constitution.**

Consulate, The.

The government existing in France from November 9, 1799, to May 18, 1804. Napoleon was First Consul.

Continental Divide.

The elevated ridge or waterparting in the Rocky Mountain region of the United States, separating the Pacific Ocean from the Atlantic Ocean tributaries. Also applied, in a more restricted sense, to a portion of the main divide, in the Yellowstone National Park, about its narrowest portion.

Continents, *v.* **Encratites.**

Contractor General, The, *v.* **Général Entrepreneur, Le.**

Convention, The, *v.* **National Convention.**

Convention of Bayonne.

A convention concluded May 10, 1808, between France and the grand duchy of Warsaw.

Convention of Closter-Seven (or Kloster-Zeven).

A compact concluded at Zeven (a village in Hanover, Prussia, 24 miles north-east of Bremen), September 8, 1757, between the Duke of Cumberland and the Duc de Richelieu, the French commander. By its terms the Hanoverian army was dispersed.

Convention of London.

A convention concluded between England and France, October 22, 1832, for the purpose of coercing Holland into withdrawing its troops from Belgium.

Convention of Pillnitz, *v.* **Pillnitz, Convention of.**

Convention of Rastatt.

A secret agreement between France and Austria, December 1, 1797, providing for the delivery of the left bank of the Rhine to the French.

Conversation Sharp.

A nickname given to Richard Sharp (1760–1835).

Conway Cabal.

An intrigue (1777–8), having for its object the superseding of Washington by Gates. So named from Thomas Conway, a general in the American service in the Revolutionary War, one of its members (1733–c. 1800).

Copenhagen.

The name of the Duke of Wellington's horse. Died at the age of twenty-seven.

Copperheads.

A popular nickname in the time of the Civil War in the United States ; applied to a northern faction generally considered to be in secret sympathy with the Rebellion. Allusion to a poisonous snake so named.

Corda Fratres.

The name given to an organization founded in 1902 by Italian students, with the object of defending all students wrongfully attacked.

Cordière, La Belle, v. Belle Cordière.

Corn-Cracker, The.

A popular nickname for the State of Kentucky, whose inhabitants are often called **Corn-Crackers.**

Corn-Crackers, v. Corn-Cracker, The.

Corneille of the Boulevard(s), The.

A surname given to Ch. Guilbert de Pixérécourt, a French dramatic author (1773–1844), who excelled in melodrama. Also the **Shakspere of the Boulevard(s).**

Cornelian Laws (Latin, " Leges Corneliæ ").

The body of laws introduced by the dictator L. Cornelius Sulla in Rome, c. 80 B.C., with a view to restore the aristocratic form of government, whose integrity had been destroyed by the democratic legislation of the Gracchi and of Marius.

Cornelia's Jewels.

The two sons of Cornelia, a distinguished Roman matron. Tiberius and Caius Gracchus (Roman tribunes) were so named by her. A wealthy lady, after showing Cornelia her jewels and ornaments, asked to see those of the matron, when Cornelia called her sons to her side, and pointed to them, saying, " These are my jewels ! " After her death a monument was erected to her memory, and inscribed, " Cornelia, Mother of the Gracchi."

Corniche, La (Italian, " Cornice ").

The celebrated coast-road, along the Riviera of France and Italy, from Nice to Geneva.

Corn-Law Rhymer.

A surname applied to Ebenezer Elliott, an English poet (1781—1849), author of " Corn-Law Rhymes."

Corporal, The Little, v. Caporal, Le Petit.

Corporal John.

A nickname given to John Churchill, Duke of Marlborough (1650–1722).

Corporal Violet, v. Caporal la Violette.

Corporation of Trinity House.

An English corporation, first chartered in 1514, charged with various naval matters, especially the erection of lighthouses, etc.

Corpus Christi Day.

A festival of the Romish

Church (in honour of the Conse-crated Host), founded in 1264 by Pope Urban IV. Held on the Thursday after Trinity Sunday, and still in the English calendar.

Corrector, The.

A surname (self-bestowed) of Alexander Cruden (1701-70), a London bookseller, and author of Cruden's " Concordance of the Holy Scriptures."

Correggio of Sculpture, The, *v.* French Phidias, The.

Corsican Fiend, The, *v.* Armed Soldier of Democracy, The.

Corsican General, The, *v.* Caporal, Le Petit.

Corsican Ogre, The.

One of the various nicknames of Napoleon Bonaparte (1769-1821), who was born in Corsica. Also called the **Corsican Sesos-tris.**

Corsican Sesostris, *v.* Corsican Ogre, The.

Corso.

One of the principal streets of Rome, extending for nearly a mile from the Piazza del Popolo. It is the chief scene of the annual carnival.

Coryphæus of German Litera-ture, The, *v.* Meister, Der.

Coryphæus of Grammarians, The.

A surname given to Aristar-chus, a celebrated Alexandrian grammarian and critic (fl. c. middle of the second century B.C.).

Cosmos Club.

A club in Washington, D.C.,

organized in 1878, whose mem-bers are chiefly scientific men. Located at the south-east corner of Lafayette Place and H Street, in the house formerly occupied by Dolly Madison.

Cotswold Lion.

Term applied to a sheep, the only " lions " to be found on the Cotswold Hills.

Cottonian Library.

A library, now in the British Museum, originally founded by Sir Robert Bruce Cotton, a noted English antiquary (1571-1631). It contains a large num-ber of original documents and manuscripts.

Cotton Wedding, *v.* Wedding Anniversaries.

Council of Ancients.

The upper chamber of the Corps Législatif under the French constitution of 1795, consisting of 250 members, each at least 40 years of age. *v.* **Council of Five Hundred.**

Council of Bâle.

A council held at Bâle (Switzerland), July 23, 1431-May 7, 1449, the last of the three great reforming councils of the fifteenth century.

Council of Blood, The.

A court established in the Netherlands by the Duke of Alva to suppress the popular agitation against the religious and political tyranny of Philip II. Its first session was held September 20, 1567, and 1,800 persons were put to death in less than three months, among the victims being the counts of

Egmont and of Hoorn (1568). Cf. Motley's " Dutch Republic."

Council of Constance.

An important council of the Roman Catholic Church, held 1414–8. Its objects were the healing of the Papal schism, suppression of the Bohemian heresy, and the reformation of the Church. It condemned Huss to death in 1415, and Jerome of Prague in 1416, and elected Martin V as Pope in 1417.

Council of (the) Five Hundred.

An assembly of 500 members (during the French Directory, 1795–9), forming the second branch of the Corps Législatif, the first being the Council of the Ancients (q.v.).

Council of Pisa.

An ecclesiastical council held in 1409 at Pisa, for the purpose of healing the Papal schism. It deposed the rival Popes Gregory XII and Benedict XIII. Alexander V was elected by the cardinals.

Council of Seville (or Consejo de Sevilla) (Spanish, Casa de Contratacion de las Indias, " House of Commerce with the Indies ").

An office established at Seville in 1503, for the regulation of commerce with the Indies. It maintained the strict Spanish monopoly of American commerce.

Council of Ten.

A secret tribunal of the ancient Republic of Venice, instituted 1310, and continued until the overthrow of the republic in 1797. It was com-posed at first of ten, and later of seventeen, members, and exercised unlimited power in the supervision of internal and external affairs, often with great rigour and oppressiveness.

Council of the Indies.

A body created in 1511 by King Ferdinand, for the regulation of Spanish colonial affairs, but its powers were enlarged by Charles V and his successors until they covered every branch of administration.

Council of Trent.

A famous council (usually reckoned as the Eighteenth Ecumenical), held (with several prorogations and suspensions) at Trent, in the Tyrol, December 13, 1545–December 4, 1563. It condemned the leading doctrines of the Reformation concerning the Bible, original sin and justification. Its decrees were confirmed by Pius IV, January 26, 1564. He also published in that year the Tridentine Profession of Faith.

Councils of Nice, *v.* Nicene Councils.

Country Party.

A political party in the reign (1660–85) of Charles II, which opposed the court and sympathised with the nonconformists. It developed into the Petitioners, and later into the Whig party. *v.* Whigs and Court Party.

Country's Muse, The, *v.* Muse de la Patrie, La.

County Council, The.

A name by which the London County Council is popularly referred to.

Court of Lions.

A celebrated court in the palace of the Alhambra, so named from the lions that once poured streams of water into the alabaster reservoir.

Court Party.

A political party in the reign (1660–85) of Charles II, supporting the policy of the court. To it succeeded the Abhorrers, and, later, the Tories (q.v.). *v.* Country Party.

Cousin Michael (or Michel).

A nickname of the German people.

Covenant, The, *v.* National Covenant.

Covenanters, The, *v.* Supplicants, The.

Covent Garden Journal.

A bi-weekly periodical, started in January, 1752, by Henry Fielding, under the name of "Sir Alexander Drawcansir, Knight,Censor of Great Britain." It was discontinued before the end of the same year.

Coventry Plays.

A series of forty-two religious plays performed at Coventry from an early date until c. 1591. First mentioned in 1416.

Cowboys.

A name given originally, during the American Revolution, to bands of marauders who plundered the people on the east bank of the Hudson River, for a distance of about forty miles north of New York City. This territory was considered neutral ground, and was the scene of many depredations, both by Americans and British. *v.* Skinners.

Cradle of (American) Liberty.

A name given to a market-house in Boston, Mass., built by Peter Faneuil, 1740–2. It contained a hall for public assemblies, which was a meeting-place of American patriots during the Revolutionary period. Hence its name. Burned in 1761, rebuilt 1763, and enlarged in 1805.

Craftsman, The.

A political periodical, originated in 1726 by Nicholas Amhurst under the signature of "Caleb D'Anvers of Gray's Inn." It gained a high reputation, and proved a powerful organ of the opposition against Sir Robert Walpole.

Crapaud, Johnny (or Jean), *v.* Johnny (or Jean) Crapaud.

Crazy Jane.

A nickname given to Joanna la Loca (1479–1555), daughter of Ferdinand (King of Castile) and Isabella, on account of her mental imbecility.

Crazy Poet, The, *v.* Mad Poet, The.

Creator of the New Comedy, The.

A surname given to Menander, an Athenian comic poet (342–290 B.C.), who created a new style of comedy, dealing with vices, etc., instead of personalities.

Crédit Mobilier (French, "Personal Credit").

A banking corporation formed

in 1852 in France under the style of the " Société Générale du Crédit Mobilier," with a capital of 60 million francs. It came to an end in 1867. Also a similar corporation in the United States (Pennsylvania, 1863), with a capital of 2,500,000 dollars.

Creed of Saint Athanasius, v. **Athanasian Creed.**

Cremorne Gardens.

A place of amusement near Battersea Bridge, north of the Thames. Closed in 1877.

Creole State.

A name sometimes given to the State of Louisiana.

Crescent City.

A name given to New Orleans, from its position on a bend of the Mississippi River.

Crichton, The.

A London, artistic, scientific and literary club, established in 1872.

Crichton, The Admirable, v. **Admirable Crichton, The.**

Crispin, Saint, v. **St. Crispin.**

Crispin-Cataline.

A surname given by Mirabeau to Jean Jacques Duval d'Éprémesnil (1746–94).

Criss Kringle (Corrupt form of the German, " Christ-kindel,-kindlein,-kindchen, the little Christ-child "), the Christ-child.

Cristinos.

The partisans of Donna Maria Christina, who was regent (1833–

40) for her daughter, Isabella Maria II (1830–68). v. **Carlists.**

Cristóbal Colón.

A Spanish armoured cruiser, bought from the Italian Government, of 6,840 tons displacement and a trial speed of 20 knots. In the battle of Santiago, July 3, 1898, under Captain Emilio Diaz Moren, it was the last Spanish ship to surrender, being forced ashore by the " Brooklyn " and the " Oregon " at Rio Tarquino.

Crittenden Compromise.

A measure promoted (1860–1), by John J. Crittenden, in the United States Senate, providing for the re-establishment of the slave-line of 36° 30' N., and for the enforcing of the fugitive-slave laws.

Crockford's.

A famous gaming club-house at No. 50 (west side) St. James's Street, London, opposite White's, It was built by William Crockford, originally a fishmonger, in 1827, who is said to have made a large fortune by gambling. He died in 1844, and the house was re-opened in 1849 for the Military, Naval and Country Service Club. It was again closed in 1851, was for several years a dining-house, and is now the Devonshire Club (q.v.).

Crookback, v. **Boar, The.**

Crotona's Sage, v. **Sage of Crotona, The.**

Crouchback.

A surname of Edmund, Earl of Lancaster (1245–96), second son of Henry III and Eleanor of Provence.

Crown of Iona, The.

A surname given to Smyrna, Asia Minor.

Crown of the East, The.

A surname given to Antioch, Syria. 'Also called " Antioch the Beautiful."

Cruel, The.

A surname of Pedro, King of Castile and Leon (1334–69). Cf. A. Dumas' novel, " Le Bâtard de Mauléon." *v.* **Nero of the North.**

Crystal Wedding, *v.* **Wedding Anniversaries.**

Cumberland Poet, The, *v.* **Bard of Rydal Mount, The.**

Cunctator (Latin, " The Delayer ").

A surname of Quintus Fabius Maximus Verrucosus, a Roman general (d. 203 B.C.). Also called the **Shield of Rome.** Cf. **Sword of Rome, The.**

Cunnucks, *v.* **Cannucks.**

Cupar Justice.

An expression used to mean " hang first and try afterwards." Jedbury (Jedburgh, Jeddart or Jedwood) Justice, and Lydford Law, mean the same thing.

Curé de Meudon, Le (French, " The Parish Priest of Meudon ").

A surname given to François Rabelais, the French humorist (1495–1553), who was during the latter part of his life the *curé* or parish priest of Meudon.

Curse of Cromwell.

Cromwell's campaign in Ireland (1649–50) is so called on account of the massacres of Drogheda, Clonmel, Wexford, etc.

Curse of Scotland, The.

Name given to the nine of diamonds in playing-cards. One version of its origin is that it alludes to the groups of nine lozenges in the coat of arms of the Dalrymple family, one of the members of which, the Master (afterwards Earl) of Stair, played an important part in the Massacre of Glencoe (q.v.).

Curtain, The.

A London playhouse, established in Shoreditch in 1576. It is said that the name arose from the green curtain being first used there. In 1678 John Aubrey calls it " The Green Curtain," and the name is still preserved in Curtain Road, Shoreditch. The church of St. James stands near the site, and a stained-glass window was placed in it in 1886 to commemorate the association of the theatre with Shakspere. It is believed that he acted there in his own plays.

Curthose.

A surname given to Robert II, Duke of Normandy (c. 1056–1134), eldest son of William the Conqueror.

Curtmantle.

A surname given to Henry II, King of England (1133–89).

Cutpurse, Moll, *v.* **Moll Cutpurse.**

Cyclic Poets, The.

A name given to the authors of Greek epic poems, composed between 800 and 550 B.C., relating to the Trojan war and the war against Thebes.

Cynics.

A sect of Greek philosophers founded by Antisthenes of Athens (b. c. 444 B.C.), a pupil of Socrates, whose teachings he sought to develop. Their chief doctrines were that virtue is the only good, and that pleasure, if sought for its own sake, is an evil. Accordingly they were characterized by ostentatious contempt for riches, art, science and amusements. The most famous cynic was Diogenes of Sinope.

Cyprian, Saint, v. St. Cyprian.

Cyrenaics (From Κυρήνη, Cyrene).

A school of Greek hedonistic philosophers, founded by Aristippus of Cyrene, a disciple of Socrates.

Czar Bell, v. Czar Kolokol.

Czar Kolokol.

The great bell in the Kremlin at Moscow. It was cast in its present form in 1733, but four years later, owing either to a flaw or a fall, a large piece was broken from the side. It now stands on a circular base of stone. Total height, 26¼ feet; base circumference, 67 feet 11 inches; greatest thickness 2 feet; and weight about 200 tons.

Dago.

A name applied, in the United States, to Spaniards, Portuguese and Italians in general, but originally referring to any one born of Spanish parents, especially in Louisiana. Said to be a corruption by American and English sailors of the frequently occurring Spanish name Diego.

Daily Courant, The.

The first British daily newspaper, begun March 11, 1702.

Damascus of the North, The.

A surname given to Bosnia-Serai (Serajevo or Sarajevo), the capital of Bosnia.

Dame de Beauté, La.

A surname of Agnes Sorel (1409–50), a favourite of Charles VII, derived from the Château de Beauté, presented to her by the king.

Damsel of Brittany.

A surname of Eleanor of Brittany, niece of John (Lackland), King of England, and sister of Arthur, Count of Brittany. She was imprisoned by John in Bristol Castle, and died 1241.

Dance of Death.

Originally, a kind of morality or allegorical representation, intended to remind the living of the power of death. Of German origin (fourteenth century), and consisting of dialogues between Death and a number of typical followers, acted in or near churches by the religious orders. It became very popular, and was treated in every possible way in pictures, bas-reliefs, tapestry, etc. In the reign of Henry VI a processional Dance of Death was painted round the cloisters of old St. Paul's, London; and Lydgate wrote a metrical translation of the Spanish poem (1400) "La Danza General de los Muertos," from the French, for the chapter of St. Paul's, to be placed under the pictures.

Dancing Chancellor, The.

A nickname given to Sir Christopher Hatton, Chancellor of England (1540–91), who is said to have first won favour in Queen Elizabeth's eyes by his graceful dancing at a court masque.

Dandie Dinmont.

A name given to a breed of terrier dogs, derived from the name of a Border farmer, in Sir Walter Scott's " Guy Mannering."

Dandy King, The.

A nickname given to Joachim Murat, a French marshal, King of Naples (1771–1815), and brother-in-law of Napoleon Bonaparte, in allusion to his fondness for display and dress. Napoleon called him " un roi de théâtre " (a theatrical king). Also called **le Beau Sabreur** (the handsome swordsman), and **King Franconi** (from a celebrated mountebank of that name).

Danish Luther, The.

A surname given to Hans Tausen, a Danish preacher (fl. 1528).

Danites, The.

Originally, the members of the Hebrew tribe of Dan, but later the members of a secret organization in the Mormon Church, sworn to support the heads of that church in everything they say or do, right or wrong.

Danse Macabre, *v.* Dance of Death.

Dan Tucker.

A negro song with the refrain, " Out o' de way, ole Dan Tucker." The name is said to refer to Captain Daniel Tucker, of Virginia, second Governor of Bermuda.

Darby and Joan.

A name often applied to happy old married couples, from a married pair who are said to have lived in the West Riding of Yorkshire in the eighteenth century, noted for their long and happy married life. There is an old ballad on the subject, " The Happy Old Couple," supposed to have been written by Henry Woodfall, although also attributed to Matthew Prior (1664–1721).

Darbyites, *v.* Plymouth Brethren (or Plymouthites).

Dark and Bloody Ground, The.

A name given to Kentucky, in allusion to its early associations with Indian warfare, and said to be a translation of the Indian word Kentucky.

Dark Continent, The.

A surname given to Africa. Cf. H. M. Stanley's " Through the Dark Continent."

Dark Day, The.

A name given to May 19, 1780, on account of a remarkable darkness on that date extending all over New England, lasting from about ten o'clock in the morning until the middle of the next night.

Darley Arabian, The.

One of the three Eastern stallions from which all horses in the stud-book trace descent. He was imported c. 1700 by a Mr. Darley, of Yorkshire, through his brother, an English agent in the Levant. Sire of Flying Childers (q.v.) and Bartlett's Childers, the sire of Squirt, the sire of Marske, the sire of Eclipse (q.v.), the founder of the chief male line of thoroughbreds. *v.* **Byerly Turk** and **Godolphin Barb.**

Daughters of the American Revolution.

A patriotic society organized at Washington, D.C., October 11, 1890. Any woman descended from a man or woman of recognized patriotism, rendering material aid to the cause of independence, is eligible for membership.

Daughters of the Revolution.

A patriotic society organized in New York City, August 20, 1891. Membership restricted to women lineal descendants of an ancestor in actual military or naval service under any of the thirteen colonies or states, or the Continental Congress, or of any one signing the Declaration of Independence, or actually assisting in the establishment of American independence and becoming liable to conviction for treason against the British Government.

Dauphins, *v.* Delphin Classics.

Davy Jones.

The name given by sailors (said to be a corruption of Jonah) to the evil spirit supposed to rule over the sea-demons. Hence, to go to Davy Jones' Locker, to drown or to die.

Davy Jones' Locker, *v.* Davy Jones.

Day of Dupes, *v.* Journée des Dupes.

Day of Flours, The, *v.* Journée des Farines, La.

Day of the Camel.

A name sometimes given to the battle of Bassorah (fought c. 656-9), from Ayesha (Mohammed's widow) having gone into battle on a camel.

Days of Barricades, The, *v.* Journeés des Barricades.

Dean of St. Patrick's (Dublin).

Name by which Dean (Jonathan) Swift (1667-1745) is sometimes alluded to.

Death Ride, The.

A name given to the Charge of the Light Brigade at Balaclava, September 20, 1854. Cf. Tennyson's poem, " The Charge of the Light Brigade."

Death Valley (or Amargosa Desert).

A desert region (160 feet below the sea-level) in Inyo County, eastern California, near the Nevada frontier.

Debatable Land.

A region on the borders of England and Scotland, between the Esk and the Sark, formerly claimed by both kingdoms.

Débonnaire, Le (French, " The Debonair "), *v.* Pieux, Le.

Decembrists.

Name given in Russia to the conspirators in the revolt of December, 1825, of which Kodrat Fedorovitch Rileiev (1792–1826) was the leading spirit.

Declaration of St.-Ouen.

A proclamation to the French nation, made by Louis XVIII, at St.-Ouen, May 2, 1814, promising a constitution.

Declaration of Independence.

The public act (July 4, 1776) by which the Continental Congress declared the American colonies to be free and independent of Great Britain. The anniversary is sometimes called the Glorious 4th of July.

Declaration of Right.

An affirmation of the ancient constitutional rights of the English nation, prepared by the Convention of the Commons, assented to by the Lords, and by William and Mary (who thereupon were declared king and queen, February 13) in 1689. Confirmed by Parliament as the Bill of Rights, December, 1689.

Decoration Day.

A day annually set apart in many American States (May 30 in the North, and April 26 in the South, where it is called Memorial Day) for decorating the graves of soldiers who fell in the Civil War.

Decree of the Trianon.

An edict issued by Napoleon I at the Grand Trianon (*v.* Trianon, Grand,) in 1810, imposing an import duty of 50 per cent. on colonial products.

Defender.

A sloop-yacht, built at Bristol, R.I., and owned by C. Oliver Iselin and others. Length, 88·45 feet. Defeated "Valkyrie III" (q.v.) in the race for the America Cup, September 1895.

Defender of the Faith.

A title, since retained by English sovereigns, conferred upon Henry VIII of England by Pope Leo X in 1521, in recognition of the former's treatise, "Assertio septem sacramentorum" (1521).

Defender of the Faith of God.

A title assumed in 929 by Abd-er-Rahman III, Caliph of Cordova (891–961).

Deformed, The, *v.* Bamboccio.

Deira.

An Anglian kingdom in the sixth century, extending from the Humber to the Tees. United c. 600 with Bernicia to form the kingdom of Northumbria.

Delectable Mountains.

In Bunyan's "Pilgrim's Progress," a range of mountains from which a view of the Celestial City is to be obtained.

Delight of Mankind.

A surname applied to Titus (Titus Flavius Salinus Vespasianus), a Roman emperor (c. 40–81). Also to Maximilian II, Emperor of the Holy Roman Empire (1527–76).

Della Cruscan School.

A small clique of English poets of both sexes who originally met in Florence c. 1785. They took their name from the Florentine Academia della Crusca, an academy founded at Florence in 1582 by the poet Grazzini, with the object of purifying the Italian language and literature.

Delphin Classics.

An edition of the Latin classics prepared by order of Louis XIV. for the use of the Dauphin ("In usum Delphini "). The first works were published in 1674. They are sometimes called " Dauphins."

Democratic Party.

A political party which arose c. 1792. It was called first the Republican, later the Democratic-Republican, and afterwards simply the Democratic Party. It has opposed a strong central government, and has generally favoured a strict construction of the Constitution. It may be regarded as the successor of the Anti-Federalist Party.

Democritus of the Sixteenth Century, The.

A surname given to John Calvin, the Protestant Reformer (1509–64).

Demosthenes of the Pulpit, The.

A surname given (by William Pitt) to Dr. T. Rennell, Dean of Westminster (1753–1840).

Denis, Saint, *v.* St. Denis.

Derby, The.

Name given to an annual race for three-year-olds at Epsom, established in 1780 by the Earl of Derby. " Derby Day " is the last Wednesday in May (sometimes the first in June), and the Oaks (q.v.) is run on the following Friday. The Derby has been twice won

by fillies : in 1801 by Eleanor, and in 1857 by Blink Bonny (q.v.), each of whom also won the Oaks of her year. The course is now 1½ miles wide at the start and with steep ascent, then level for three furlongs, descending again to " Tattenham Corner," where it turns and goes straight home. The " triple crown " (i.e. the 2,000 Guineas, the Derby and the St. Leger) has been won by five horses : West Australian, Gladiateur, Lord Lyon, Ormonde and Common.—*Rice*. The Derby is sometimes called " The Blue-Ribbon of the Turf."

Derby Dilly.

A nickname given in 1835 to a section of the Tory party following Lord Stanley, afterwards Earl of Derby.

Derrydown Triangle, The.

A nickname given by William Hone (in a parody on the Athanasian Creed) to Lord Castlereagh, afterwards Marquis of Londonderry (1769–1822). Cf. " Third Trial of William Hone before Lord Ellenborough " (1818, 3rd ed. p. 9).

Devil, The.

A surname given to Robert I, Duke of Normandy from 1028 to 1035, younger son of Richard the Good. Also called the **Magnificent.** Also to Robert François Damiens (1715–57), who attempted to assassinate Louis XV in 1757.

Devil Dick.

A nickname given to Richard Porson, an English classical scholar (1759–1808), famous for his knowledge of Greek.

Devil's Parliament, The (Latin, " Parliamentum diabolicum ").

A nickname given to the English Parliament which met at Coventry, 1459. It attainted the leading Yorkists. Also called the Diabolical Parliament.

Devil's Wall, The.

A popular name for the southern portion of the long line of Roman fortifications called the Pfahlgraben, built by the Romans, c. 70 A.D. They extended from Ratisbonne northwestward to Giessen, Ems and Hönnigen.

Devonshire Club.

A Liberal club established in 1875, at 50, St. James's Street, London.

Diable, Le, v. Devil, The.

Diabolical Parliament, The, v. Devil's Parliament, The.

Dial, The.

An American literary quarterly journal and organ of the Transcendentalists (published at Boston), edited by Margaret Fuller, assisted by Ripley, Emerson and others (1840-2), and by Emerson (1842-4).

Diamond Necklace, The.

A celebrated episode in French history. A necklace (valued at about £75,000), originally ordered for Madame du Barry, was (1783-4) negotiated for by the Cardinal de Rohan through an adventuress, the Countess de Lamotte. The cardinal, who hoped to gain the affection of Marie Antoinette, was duped by pretended signatures of the queen. Dumas' novel, " Le Collier de la Reine " (the Queen's Necklace), contains an account of the celebrated " affaire."

Diamonds, Famous.

v. The Braganza, Dudley, Florentine, Great Mogul, Hope, Koh-i-noor, Nassac, Orloff, Pitt or Regent, Sancy, Shah, and Star of the South Diamonds.

Diamond State, The.

Delaware.

Diamond Wedding, v. Wedding Anniversaries.

Diana of the Stage, The.

A surname given to Mrs. Anne Bracegirdle, a famous English actress (c. 1663-1748).

Dick's Coffee House.

An old coffee-house, No. 8, Fleet Street, London (on the south side, near Temple Bar), originally " Richard's," from Richard Torner, or Turner, to whom the house was let in 1689. Frequented by Cowper when he lived in the Temple. *Timbs.*

Dick Turpin of France, The.

A surname given to Louis-Dominique Bourguignon (Cartouche), a notorious French robber (1693-1721).

Dictator of Letters, The, v. Patriarch of Ferney.

Dictum of Kenilworth.

An award made between King Henry III and the Commons in 1266 during the siege of Kenilworth. It re-established Henry's authority, proclaimed amnesty, annulled the

D.N.

provisions of Oxford, and provided that the king should keep the charter according to his oath.

Diet of Augsburg, *v.* Augsburg, Religious Peace of.

Diet of Spires.

An assembly of German princes called by Charles V of Germany, and held at Spires, Bavaria, in 1529. It condemned the Reformation, and the " Protestation" then made by the Reformers is the origin of the name Protestants.

Diet of Worms.

A Diet, famous in the history of the Reformation, opened by the Emperor Charles V at Worms, January 28, 1521. Luther was cited (March 6) to appear before it, and he arrived in Worms on April 16. On April 17 and 18 he appeared before the Diet, and on the latter day refused to recant, and defended his position.

Dieu-Donné (French, " God-given ").

A name applied to Louis XIV (1638–1715) in infancy, alluding to his mother, Anne of Austria, having borne no children for twenty-three years previously. Also given to the Comte de Chambord (Henri Charles Ferdinand Marie Dieudonné d'Artois) (1820–83), son of the Duchesse de Berri. He was a posthumous child of the Duc de Berri, who was assassinated February 13, 1820, and was called by the people l'Enfant du Miracle.

Dilettanti Society, The.

A London society devoted to the encouragement of a taste for the fine arts, founded 1734.

Dinner-Bell, The.

A nickname given to Edmund Burke, a celebrated British statesman, orator and writer (1729–97), from his habit of speaking so long in Parliament that it interfered with members' dinners.

Dircæan Swan, The.

A surname given to Pindar, the greatest of the Greek lyric poets (c. 522–443 B.C.), from his residence near the river Dirce.

Directoire, Le, *v.* Directory, The.

Directory, The.

A body of five men holding the executive power in France from November 1, 1795, until the *coup d'état* of 1799 (November 9, 18th Brumaire). *v.* Brumaire. It succeeded the Convention.

Disciples of Christ, *v.* Campbellites.

Discovery, The.

One of the two vessels of the British Polar Expedition of 1875–6, commanded by Captain Sir George Nares. The other was named the " Alert." A small ship sent out in 1602 by the East India Company (Captain George Waymouth), to " find the passage best to lye towards the parts or kingdom of Cataya or China, or the backe side of America," was also called the " Discovery." In April, 1610, Henry Hudson sailed in the vessel, entering the strait which bears his name in June. Hudson's Bay was entered early in August. Three months were spent in exploring it, and in November the vessel was frozen in. In the following June she was released, and a mutiny occurred shortly after. Hudson and others were set adrift and never seen again. In 1615 and 1616 the ship made voyages with William Baffin and Robert Bylot, resulting in many important discoveries. Also the ship in which a British expedition, under Commander R. F. Scott, R.N., sailed for the Antarctic regions in 1901.

Dismal Swamp, Great, *v.* **Great Dismal Swamp.**

Distaff's Day, Saint, *v.* **St. Distaff's Day.**

Distressed Statesman, The.

A nickname given in 1761 to William Pitt, Earl of Chatham (1708–78), when compelled to resign his office as Secretary of State.

Divide, Continental, *v.* **Continental Divide.**

Divine Doctor, The (Latin, " Doctor Divinus ").

A surname of Jean de Ruysbroeck (1294–1381), a celebrated mystic. Also called the Ecstatic Doctor.

Divine Madman, The.

A surname given to Michael Angelo (Michelangelo Buonarotti), a famous Italian sculptor, painter, architect and poet (1475–1564), in allusion to his habit of secluding himself when meditating upon any great project.

Dixie's Land.

Said to have been originally a negro name for New York or Manhattan Island, and later applied to the South. The phrase originated in New York early in the nineteenth century, and developed into a number of songs whose refrains contained the word " Dixie " or " Dixie's Land." In the South, Dixie is regarded as meaning the Southern States, the word being supposed to be derived from " Mason and Dixon's Line," which formerly divided the free and slave states. It is said to have first come into use there when Texas joined the Union, and the negroes sang of it as " Dixie."

Dizzy.

A nickname of Benjamin Disraeli, created Earl of Beaconsfield in 1876 (1804–81).

Doctor, The.

A nickname given to the first Lord Viscount Sidmouth (1757–1844), he having been the son of Doctor Anthony Addington, of Reading.

Doctor Angelicus.

A surname of St. Thomas Aquinas (or Thomas of Aquino), Italian theologian and philosopher (1225 or 7–74). Also called " Doctor Universalis," the " Father of Moral Philosophy," the " Dumb Ox " (by his school companions), the " Eagle of Divines," the " Fifth Doctor of the Church," " the Angel of the Schools," " the Second Augustine."

Doctor Christianissimus (Latin, " The Most Christian Doctor ").

A surname given to Jean

Charlier de Gerson, a noted French theologian (1363–1429).

Doctor Dulcifluus (Latin, " The Dulcifluous Doctor ").

A surname given to Antony Andreas, a Spanish Minorite and theologian (d. 1320).

Doctor Evangelicus (Latin, " The Evangelical Doctor ").

A surname given to John Wickliffe, a celebrated English religious reformer (c. 1324–84). Also called the **Morning Star of the Reformation** and the **Gospel Doctor.**

Doctor Fundatissimus (Latin, " The Well-founded Doctor ").

A surname of Ægidius Romanus of Colonna, a scholastic philosopher, general of the Augustine order (c. 1247–1316).

Doctor Fundatus (Latin, " The Thorough Doctor ").

A surname given to William Varro, an English Minorite and scholastic philosopher of the latter half of the thirteenth century.

Doctor Illuminatus (Latin, " The Enlightened Doctor ").

A surname given to Raymond Lully, a distinguished Spanish scholastic and alchemist (c. 1235–1315). Also to Johann Tauler, a noted German mystic and preacher (c. 1300–61).

Doctor Irrefragabilis, *v.* **Irrefragable Doctor.**

Doctor Mirabilis, *v.* **Admirable Doctor.**

Doctor " My-book."

A nickname given to John Abernethy, the eminent English surgeon (1764–1831). The celebrated " My-book," to which he so often referred his patients, was his " Surgical Observations."

Doctor of the Incarnation.

A name given to St. Cyril of Alexandria, an ecclesiastic and theologian (d. 444), famous as an exponent of Nestorianism. His fête day is January 28. Also called the **Champion of the Virgin.**

Doctor Planus et Perspicuus (or **Conspicuus** (Latin, " The Plain and Perspicuous Doctor ").

A surname given to Walter Burleigh (or Burley), an English schoolman (1274 or 5–c. 1345), a pupil of Duns Scotus.

Doctor Profundus, *v.* **Profound Doctor, The.**

Doctor Resolutissimus (Latin, " The Most Resolute Doctor ").

A surname given to Guillaume Durand de St.-Pourçain, a famous French bishop (d. c. 1333).

Doctor Seraphicus (Latin, " Seraphic Doctor ").

A surname given to the scholastic theologian Saint Bonaventura (Giovanni di Fidenza), (1221–74).

Doctor Slop.

A nickname given to Doctor (afterwards Sir John) Stoddart (1773–1856), on account of his violent prejudices and the denunciations of the first Napoleon in the "Times" newspaper, of which Stoddart was editor, 1812–6 ; also on account of his action at the time of the Queen Caroline affair, 1820–1.

Doctor Solemnis (Latin, "The Solemn Doctor").

A surname given by the Sorbonne to Henry Goethals, an eminent schoolman (1227–93).

Doctor Subtilis (Latin, "Subtle Doctor").

A surname of Joannes Duns Scotus, a famous scholastic (b. at Duns, Scotland, c. 1265–c. 1308) and founder of the system called Scotism, which long contended with the system called Thomism, founded by Thomas Aquinas. *v.* **Thomists.** The surname of Doctor Subtilis was given to him on account of the ingenuity and resource he displayed in a dispute at Paris (1304) as to the Immaculate Conception of the Virgin Mary. It is said that his name, Duns, Dunse, Dunce, used at first as a synonym for a very learned man, being applied ironically to very ignorant and stupid persons, is the origin of dunce in its present sense.

Doctor Universalis (Latin, "Universal Doctor").

Surname given to Alain de Lille (or Alanus ab Insulis), a celebrated scholar and monk (1114—1203 ?). Also applied to **Albertus Magnus** (*v.* **Magnus**), and St. Thomas Aquinas (*v.* **Doctor Angelicus**).

Doctor Venerabilis (Latin, "Venerable Doctor").

A surname given to Guillaume de Champeaux (or Campellensis), a noted French scholastic philosopher (b. c. 1070, d. 1121), an opponent of Abelard, who was his pupil. Also called **La Colonne des Docteurs** (the pillar of the doctors).

Doe, John, *v.* **John Doe.**

Doggett's Coat and Badge.

An orange-coloured livery and a badge, given in honour of George I, as a prize in the Thames rowing-match, which takes place yearly on August 1. Established in 1716 by Thomas Doggett, an English actor (d. 1721). The custom is still kept up under the auspices of the Fishmongers' Company.

Dog of Montargis.

A dog belonging to Aubry de Montdidier, a gentleman of the court of Charles V, who was murdered in the forest of Montargis in 1371 by Richard de Macaire. It is said that the murderer would have escaped but for the fidelity of Aubry's dog, which followed Macaire continually, until, the attention of the king having been called to it, orders were given that Macaire should fight his accuser, the dog. Macaire, although armed with a club, was pulled down by the dog, and confessed his crime. The subject forms the theme of ballads in French, German and English, and there is a play called "Le Chien de Montargis," by Guilbert de Pixérécourt (1814).

Dolly's.

A well-known tavern in Paternoster Row, London, dating from the time of Queen Anne, and still in existence. *Wheeler.*

Domestic Poet, The, *v.* **Bard of Olney, The.**

Donatists.

An early Christian sect in Africa, originating in a dispute over the election of Cæcilian to the see of Carthage, A.D. 311, occasioned by his opposition to the extreme reverence paid to relics of martyrs and to the sufferers for the Christian faith called confessors, and by the rivalry of Secundus, primate of Numidia. The name was probably derived from Donatus the Great, under whom the schism became fixed.

Donatus the Great, *v.* **Great, The.**

Dongan Charter.

A charter for the City of New York, granted by Thomas Dongan, Lieutenant-Governor and Vice-Admiral of New York and its dependencies under James II of England, dated April 27, 1686. It remained in force until 1730. *v.* **Montgomery Charter, The.** An early charter of the city of Albany, by the same authority, is known by the same name.

Don Saltero's Coffee House.

A noted house formerly standing in Cheyne Walk, Chelsea, London, founded by John Salter, c. 1690, and torn down in 1866. It contained not only an eating-house, but a museum of natural curiosities. *Walford.*

Doomsday Book.

A book containing a digest, in Norman-French, of the results of a census or survey of England, undertaken by order of William the Conqueror, and completed in 1086. It consists of two volumes in vellum, a large folio of 382 pages and a quarto of 450. Now kept in the Public Record Office. In 1783 a facsimile edition, printed from types made for the purpose, was issued by the British Government. The counties of Northumberland, Cumberland, Westmoreland and Durham were not included in the survey.

Dorcas Societies.

A name given to societies for supplying the poor with garments, from Dorcas (Acts ix. 36), a woman who was full of good deeds, and made coats and garments for the poor.

Dorking, Battle of, *v.* **Battle of Dorking.**

Dorr's Rebellion.

A revolutionary movement, under the leadership of T. W. Dorr, to introduce a new State Constitution in Rhode Island (1840–2). A party, the so-called Suffrage Party, was organized by Dorr in 1840. An unsuccessful attempt was made by the party (May 18, 1842) to seize the arsenal at Providence, but they were dispersed June 25, 1842.

Dort, Synod of, *v.* **Synod of Dort.**

Doubting Castle.

In Bunyan's " Pilgrim's Progress " the abode of Giant Despair, in which he locked up Christian and Hopeful.

Douglas Larder, The.

A name given to the conglomeration of food and dead bodies made by Sir James Douglas (the Good Sir James) in 1307, when he took Douglas Castle from the English garrison. (Cf. Sir Walter Scott's " Tales of a Grandfather," ix.) *v.* also **Wallace's Larder.**

D'Outre-Mer (French, " From Beyond the Seas ").

A surname of Louis IV, King of France (921–54), derived from the fact that, on the death of his father (Charles the Simple), he was taken to England by his mother, Eadgifu, sister of Athelstan, King of England, to avoid falling into the hands of his rival, Rudolph of Burgundy, who had been elected King of France by the nobles. He returned to France in 936 on the death of Rudolph.

Dove, The.

A pinnace of about 50 tons, one of the vessels (the other was named the " Ark "), in which Lord Baltimore sent out a colony of " gentlemen adventurers," including his brothers George and Leonard Calvert, to Maryland in 1633. They landed at St. Clement's Island in the " Potomac " in 1634.

Dover, Treaty of.

A secret treaty concluded May 22, 1670, between Charles II and Louis XIV. The former was to aid France's designs against Holland, and the latter was to furnish subsidies and troops. The province of Zeeland and the adjacent islands were to be reserved for England, and Charles was to receive £200,000 a year if he declared himself a Roman Catholic.

Dowgate.

The original water-gate of the

city of London, situated at the mouth of the Walbrook, where it enters the Thames, and just under the great Roman citadel. —Loftie, " History of London," 1884.

Downing Street.

A street, leading from Whitehall, containing the Treasury and Foreign Office buildings. The name has come to be used in a figurative sense to mean the administration.

Dragonades (French, " Dragonnade, from "dragon," a dragoon.

A form of persecution inflicted by Louis XIV's Government upon the French Protestants in the period preceding the revocation of the Edict of Nantes (q.v.). It consisted in billeting troops upon the inhabitants as a means of converting them, licence being given the soldiery to commit all manner of misdeeds.

Drisheen City.

A popular name for the city of Cork. A drisheen is an article of food made of the serum of sheep's blood, mixed with milk and seasoned with pepper, salt and tansy. *Wheeler.*

Druids.

The members of a society named the United Ancient Order of Druids, founded in London in 1781, for the mutual benefit of the members, and now comprising numerous lodges, called *groves*, in America, Australia, Germany and elsewhere.

Drunkard, The, *v.* Sardanapalus of Germany, The.

Drunken Parliament, The.

A nickname of the Scottish Parliament which met in 1661.

Dryden of Germany, The.

A surname given to Martin Opitz, a German poet and writer (1597–1639). Also called the **Father of German Poetry.** He brought about a reform of German versification.

Dual Alliance.

An alliance between France and Russia, dating from a military convention in 1891, stipulating that either nation, in the event of Germany attacking it, should help the other with a certain force. The convention in 1897 became a definite alliance for defensive purposes, but without special reference to Germany.

Dublin Castle, *v.* **Castle, The.**

Duchesne, Le Père, *v.* **Père Duchesne.**

Dudley Diamond, The.

A diamond found in Africa in 1868, and bought from Nie Kirk, the master of the man who found it, by Hunt and Roskell, for £12,000. The Earl of Dudley purchased it from them for £30,000. It is heart-shaped, extremely brilliant, and weighs 44½ carats ; originally, before cutting, it weighed 88½ carats. *Brewer.* It was originally named the Star of South Africa Diamond.

Duke Humphrey's Walk.

A name given to the middle aisle of St. Paul's Cathedral, London, on account of the tomb of Duke Humphrey, the son of Henry IV, which was said to be there. Some derive the expression " to dine with Duke Humphrey," from the alleged custom of persons without money for a dinner frequenting this spot; others find in it an allusion to Duke Humphrey having been starved to death.

Duke of Exeter's Daughter, The.

The rack, which the Duke of Exeter introduced as an engine of torture in the Tower of London in 1447.

Duke's Theatre, The.

A London theatre built in 1660. Destroyed in 1666 in the Great Fire, and rebuilt in 1671 by Sir Christopher Wren. It stood until 1720, and was on the site of the Salisbury Court Theatre (q.v.).

Dumb Captain, The.

A name given by his fellow conspirators to the Prince de Condé (1530–69). *v.* **Amboise, Conspiracy of.**

Dumb Ox, The, *v.* **Doctor Angelicus, Eagle of Divines, Father of Moral Philosophy.**

Dum-dum Bullets.

A kind of explosive bullet, used by the Boers in the Transvaal War, against the rules of civilized warfare.

Dumping-ground of Europe, The.

A term applied to Great Britain, in allusion to its enormous imports from other European countries.

Dunces' Parliament, The, *v.* **Parliament of Dunces, The.**

Dunedin.

A poetical name for Edinburgh; also called Edin.

Dunes, Battle of the, *v.* **Battle of the Dunes.**

Dunmow Flitch, The.

A flitch of bacon awarded to any married pair who could take oath at the end of the first year of their married life that there had not only been no jar or quarrel, but that neither had ever wished the knot untied. The custom was originated at Great Dunmow, England, by Robert Fitzwalter in 1244, and the flitch has been claimed as late as 1876. (Cf. W. H. Ainsworth's novel, "The Flitch of Bacon, or the Custom of Dunmow," 1854.)

Dupes, Day of, *v.* **Journée des Dupes.**

Durandal.

The celebrated sword of Roland (Orlando), which he broke in twain at Roncevaux (Roncesvalles), so that it should not fall into the hands of a craven or an infidel. (Cf. "La Chanson de Roland," a *chanson de geste* ascribed to Théroulde or Turoldos, a Norman trouvère, dating from the end of the eleventh or the beginning of the twelfth century.) The sword is also called Durenda, Durandana, Durindana, etc.

Dutch Paradise, The.

A name given to Gelderland (or Guelderland), a province of the Netherlands.

Eagle of Brittany.

A surname of Bertrand Du Guesclin (or Duguesclin), a noted French commander (c. 1320–80).

Eagle of Divines.

A surname of Saint Thomas Aquinas (or Thomas of Aquino), a famous Italian theologian and scholastic philosopher. Also called "Doctor Angelicus" (q.v.), the "Father of Moral Philosophy" (q.v.) and (in his early days) the "Dumb Ox" (q.v.).

Eagle of Meaux.

A surname of Jacques Bénigne Bossuet, a celebrated French prelate, pulpit orator and theological writer (1627–1704).

Eagle of the Doctors of France, The, *v.* **Hammer of Heretics, The.**

East End.

A name by which that part of London lying east of the Bank of England is familiarly known, generally with reference to the poverty of the district. *v.* **West End.**

Eastern Empire (Called also Byzantine Empire, or Greek Empire or Lower Empire).

The eastern division of the Roman Empire, and, after 476, the Roman Empire itself, with its capital at Constantinople, and with greatly varying boundaries. It included, in its greatest extent, south-eastern Europe, western Asia, northern Africa, part of Italy, and various islands. After 800 its rival in the West was the Empire of the West, and the Roman Empire of the German nation. Overthrown in 1453 by the Turks under Mahomet II capturing Constantinople. *v.* **Western Empire.**

Eastern Question, The.

The collective name applied to the several problems or complications in the international politics of Europe connected with Turkey.

Eastern States.

A popular designation of the six New England States, Maine, New Hampshire, Vermont, Massachusetts, Rhode Island, and Connecticut.

East India United Service Club.

A London club established in 1848 at 16, St. James's Square.

Ebony.

A joking nickname given by James Hogg, the Ettrick Shepherd (q.v.) to William Blackwood (1777–1834), the original publisher of "Blackwood's Magazine." Sometimes used as a synonym for the magazine itself.

Eclipse.

A famous race-horse (so named from his having been foaled during the eclipse of 1764), descending, in the male line, from the Darley Arabian (q.v.). He was a chestnut with a blaze and one white leg. American Eclipse was an American horse foaled in 1814.

Economites, v. Harmonists.

Écorcheurs, Les.

Bands of armed adventurers who, favoured by the Hundred Years' War (q.v.), ravaged France and Belgium in the fifteenth century, beginning c. 1435. They were called Écorcheurs (or flayers), probably because they " not only waylaid and plundered their victims, but stripped them of every vestige of clothing, leaving but their shirts."

Ecstatic Doctor, v. Divine Doctor, The.

Eden of Germany (German, " Das Eden Deutschlands ").

A name sometimes given to Baden.

Edict of Milan.

An edict, promulgated (313) by Constantine and Licinius, proclaiming toleration of the Christians.

Edict of Nantes.

An edict of Henry IV of France, issued April 13, 1598, and ending the religious wars of the country. By it the Huguenots were put on an equality with the Catholics as regards political rights. It was annulled October 22, 1685, by a proclamation of Louis XIV of France, which forbade the free exercise of the Protestant religion. This was followed by the emigration of about 300,000 persons to Holland, Brandenburg, England, Switzerland, America, etc.

Edict of Nemours.

A treaty concluded in 1585 at Nemours between Henry III and the chiefs of the League. v. La Ligue.

Edict of Restitution.

An edict by the Emperor Ferdinand II, dated March 6, 1629, requiring Protestants to restore to the Roman Catholics sees and ecclesiastical property appropriated since the Treaty of Passau in 1552.

Edin, v. Dunedin.

Edinburgh Review.

A literary and political review, founded at Edinburgh in 1802 by Jeffrey, Sydney Smith, Brougham, Horner and others.

Edmunds Bill, The.

A law against polygamy in the United States, passed in 1882 by Congress. Specially directed against the practices of the Mormons in Utah. This and other measures were finally amended and supplemented by the Edmunds-Tucker Act of March, 1887, which became law without the President's signature.

Égalité, Philippe, v. Philippe Égalité.

Egyptian Expedition, The.

An expedition undertaken by the French against Egypt in 1798–1801 with the ultimate object of attacking the British empire in India.

Eiffel Tower.

A tower 984 feet in height, built of iron framework, in the Champ de Mars, Paris, for the exhibition of 1889. Its general form is that of a concave pyramid. There are three platforms at different heights ; the top one, over 900 feet from the ground, is surrounded by a balcony, and covered with a glass pavilion 54 feet square. A lantern fitted for scientific observations rises above this.

Eighth Wonder of the World, The.

The palace, etc., of the Escurial in Spain is sometimes so named.

El Campeador, v. Cid, The.

El Cid Campeador, v. Cid, The.

El Dorado (Spanish, " The Gilded ").

The reputed king or chief of a fabulous city of great wealth (Manoa), which, during the fifteenth century, was supposed to exist somewhere in the northern part of South America. In common and poetical language the name El Dorado has been transferred to the city or country referred to, and has come to be a synonym for any place rich in gold.

Eleatics.

A school of Greek philosophy founded by Xenophanes of Colophon, who resided in Elea (or Velia), in Magna Græcia. The most distinguished philosophers of this school were Parmenides and Zeno. The main Eleatic doctrines are developments of the conception that the One or Absolute alone is real.

Electioneer.

A bay horse by Hambletonian (10) out of Green Mountain Maid, foaled May 2, 1868, d. December 2, 1890. Second only to Hambletonian (10) as a trotting sire. Owned by Senator Stanford of California.

Electoral Rhine Circle, v. Lower Rhine Circle.

Elgin Marbles.

A collection of Greek sculptures comprising the bulk of the surviving plastic decorations of the Parthenon, and a caryatid and column from the Erechtheum, and recognized as containing the finest existing productions of sculpture. The marbles were brought from Athens between 1801 and 1803 by the Earl of Elgin, hence their name. The collection is in the British Museum, London, having been purchased by the Government from Lord Elgin for £35,000.

Elm City.

New Haven, Connecticut, has been so named from the number and beauty of its elms.

Elocution Walker.

A popular surname given to John Walker, English orthoëpist and lexicographer (1732–1807), who was also a teacher of elocution.

Eloquent Doctor, The (Latin, "Doctor facundus").

A surname given to Peter Aureolus, an archbishop of Aix in the fourteenth century.

Elzevir (Elsevier or Elzevier).

A name by which editions of works printed by the Dutch family of that name are known. Louis, the founder of the family, was born at Louvain, near Brussels, c. 1540, and died at Leyden in 1617. The last printers of the name were Peter, who printed a few volumes at Utrecht, 1667–72, and Abraham, who was university printer at Leyden, 1681–1712.

Emancipation Proclamation.

The proclamation by which on January 1, 1863, President Lincoln, as commander-in-chief of the armies of the United States, declared as a military measure, in accordance with notice proclaimed September 22, 1862, that within certain specified territory in armed rebellion all persons held as slaves "are and henceforward shall be free."

Emerald Isle, The.

Ireland is sometimes so called (or Green Isle), owing to its verdure; also called "Erin," "Hibernia," and "Innisfail" (Isle of Destiny).

Emigrés, Les.

The royalists who left France in 1789 and succeeding years, taking refuge in Germany, Switzerland, Great Britain and other countries.

Eminence Grise, L'.

A surname of Père Joseph (François Leclerc, Marquis du Tremblay), Cardinal Richelieu's *âme damnée*, or familiar spirit (1577–1638). *v.* **Eminence Rouge, L'.**

Eminence Rouge, L'.

A surname of Armand Du Plessis, cardinal, duc de Richelieu (1585–1642), alluding to his red cardinal's robe. *v.* **Eminence Grise, L'.**

Emmanuel's Land, *v.* Delectable Mountains.

Emperor of Believers, The.

A surname of Omar I, second caliph of the Mussulmans and father-in-law of Mohammed. Assassinated in 644. *v.* **Commander of the Faithful.**

Emperor of the Mountains, The.

A surname given to a notorious Calabrian robber chief named Peter (1812).

Emperor of the West, The.

A surname given to John

Murray, an eminent London publisher (1778–1843), owing to his having removed his business from Fleet Street to Albemarle Street, in the West End of London. Lord Byron styled him the **Anak of Publishers.**

Empire City.

A name sometimes given to New York as the metropolis of the Empire State.

Empire State.

A name popularly given to New York, on account of its leading position in respect of population, wealth and industrial enterprises.

Empire State of the South, The.

A surname given to the State of Georgia.

Empress of India.

A title conferred upon Queen Victoria by Parliament, May 1, 1876, and proclaimed at Delhi, January 1, 1877, in the presence of the Viceroy.

Encratites.

In the early history of the church, especially among the Gnostics, those ascetics who refrained from marriage and from the use of flesh-meat and wine. Also called **Continents.**

Encyclopædia Britannica.

An English dictionary of arts, sciences and general literature; first published, in parts, at Edinburgh, 1768–71. The tenth edition (35 vols.) was completed in 1903.

Encyclopédie.

A French encyclopædia (exact title, " Dictionnaire raisonné des sciences, des arts et des métiers "). Published at Paris (28 vols.) between 1751 and 1772, it was followed by a supplement (5 vols.), 1876–7, and an analytical index (2 vols.), 1780.

Encyclopædists.

The collaborators of Diderot and D'Alembert in the Encyclopédie (q.v.).

Endeavour, The.

A British ship commanded by Captain Cook (then lieutenant), sent out in 1768 to the Pacific by the Royal Society to observe the transit of Venus. Captain Cook returned in 1771, having made important explorations and discoveries.

Endymion, *v.* **President.**

Enfant Chéri de la Victorie, L'.
(French, " Victory's Darling Child ").

A surname given by Napoleon to André Masséna, a famous French marshal (1758–1817).

Enfant du Miracle, L', *v.* **Dieu-Donné.**

Enfants de Dieu (French, " Children of God ").

The Camisards (q.v.).

Engagement, The.

An agreement between Charles I of England and the Scottish commissioners, made at Newport, Isle of Wight, December 26, 1647. The Scottish army was to restore Charles, who consented to an establishment of Presbyterianism in England.

England's Pride and Westminster's Glory.

A surname given to Sir Francis Burdett, the most popular English politician of his time. (1770–1844). He represented Westminster in Parliament 1807–37. Sometimes called **Old Glory.**

English Achilles, The.

A surname given to John Talbot, first Earl of Shrewsbury (c. 1373–1453). Sometimes applied to the Duke of Wellington. *v.* **Great Duke, The.**

English Alexander, The.

A surname given to Henry V (1387–1422).

English Aristophanes, The.

Surname given to Samuel Foote, English dramatist and actor (1720–77), from his scathing wit. Also the **Modern Aristophanes.**

English Atticus, The.

A surname given to Joseph Addison, a famous English essayist, poet and statesman (1672–1719). Cf. Pope's " Prologue to the Satires."

English Bach, The.

A surname of Johann Christian Bach (b. Leipsig, 1735; d. London, 1782), from his residence in London (1759–82). Also surnamed " the Milanese," from his residence in Milan (organist of the cathedral there 1754–9).

English Bastille, The, *v.* Coldbath Fields.

English Ennius, The.

A surname given to Layamon (or Laweman), an English priest (fl. c. 1200), and author of a semi-Saxon paraphrase of Wace's " Roman de Brut."

English Hercules, The.

A surname given to Guy, Earl of Warwick, a legendary hero of English romance. (Cf. Michael Drayton, " Polyolbion," xiii.)

English Hobbema, The.

A surname given to John Crome, a noted English landscape painter (1768–1821); born and died at Norwich.

English Horace, The, *v.* Rare Ben Jonson.

Also applied to Alexander Pope, an English poet (1688–1744), famous for his " Imitations of Horace."

English Joan of Arc, The.

A surname sometimes given to Mary Ambree, who is said to have fought at the siege of Ghent in 1584 to avenge her lover's death. Frequently mentioned in old ballads.

English Justinian, The.

A surname given to Edward I, King of England (1239–1307), whose reign (1272–1307) is remarkable for the progress made in it towards the settlement of the laws and constitution of England. Also called **Longshanks** and the **Hammer of the Scots.**

English Juvenal.

A surname given to John Oldham, an English satirical poet (1653–83).

English Marivaux, The, *v.* Founder of the English Domestic Novel, The.

English Mersenne, The.

A surname given to John Collins, an English mathematician and physicist (1624–83); from Marin Mersenne, a contemporary French philosopher.

English Milo, The.

A surname given to Thomas Topham, a famous strong man (1710–52). Also the British Samson.

English Opium-Eater, The.

A surname often applied to Thomas De Quincey, an English essayist and miscellaneous writer (1785–1859), from his " Confessions of an English Opium-Eater." His habit of opium-eating eventually disabled him from protracted application to literary work.

English Pale, The.

That part of Ireland in which English law was acknowledged, and within which the English dominion was confined for some centuries after the conquests of Henry II.

English Palladio, The.

A surname given to Inigo Jones, a noted English architect (1573–1652).

English Petrarch, The.

A name sometimes given to Sir Philip Sidney (or Sydney), an English author and general (1554–86). Also called the British Bayard and the Flower of Chivalry.

English Plato, The.

A surname given to the Rev. John Norris, an English Platonist (1657–1711).

English Poussin, The.

A surname given tô Richard Cooper the younger, an English painter and engraver (1740–c. 1814).

English Rabelais, The.

A surname given to Jonathan (Dean) Swift (1667–1745); Thomas Amory (? 1691–1788), and Laurence Sterne (1713–68).

English Revolution.

The movements by which James II was forced to leave England and a purer constitutional government secured through the aid of William of Orange, who landed in England in November, 1688. In 1689 William and Mary were proclaimed constitutional sovereigns, and Parliament passed the Bill of Rights. *v.* Declaration of Right.

English Roscius, The.

A surname given to David Garrick, a celebrated English actor (1717–79). Also to Thomas Betterton, an English actor and dramatist (c. 1635–1710).

English Salvator Rosa, The.

A surname given to John Hamilton Mortimer, an English historical painter (1741–79).

English Sappho, The, *v.* Fair Perdita.

English Seneca, The, *v.* Christian Seneca, The.

English Socrates, The, v. **Great Moralist, The.**

English Solomon, The, v. **British Solomon, The.**

Also applied to Henry VII of England (1457–1509), who by his marriage with Elizabeth, eldest daughter of Edward IV, united the rival houses of Lancaster and York.

English Switzerland, The.

A name sometimes given to the neighbourhood of Ilfracombe, Lynton and Lynmouth, North Devon.

English Teniers, The.

A surname given to George Morland, an English painter (1763–1804).

English Terence, The, v. **Man without a Skin, The.**

English Tintoretto, The.

A surname given by Charles I to William Dobson, a distinguished English portrait and historical painter (1610–46). Also called the **English Van Dyck.**

English Van Dyck, The, v. **English Tintoretto, The.**

Enlightened Doctor, The, v. **Doctor Illuminatus.**

Enniskilleners.

The Sixth Dragoons regiment in the British service, so named from its origin among the defenders of Enniskillen in 1689.

Ephesian Poet, The, v. **Father of Parody, The.**

Epistle of Barnabas, The.

An anonymous epistle, dating from an early period of the church. It contains no mention of the readers for whom it was intended. Its authorship was ascribed to Barnabas, the apostle, in the early church, but by some modern critics it has been assigned to a post-apostolic writer, perhaps a converted Jew of Alexandria.

Era of Good Feeling.

An allusion to the period from 1817 to c. 1824, which in the United States was marked by internal harmony and the absence of strong party feeling.

Era of Spain.

An era, long used in Spain, which began with the first day of the year 38 B.C.

Erastians.

Those who maintain the doctrines held by or attributed to Thomas Erastus, a German polemic (1524–83), author of a work on excommunication, in which he proposed to restrict the jurisdiction of the church.

Ercles.

A corruption of Hercules. (Cf. Shakespeare, " Midsummer Night's Dream," act I, sc. 2.)

Erebus, v. **Terror.**

Eretrian Bull, The.

A surname given to Menedemus of Eretria, a Greek philosopher (b. c. end of fourth century, B.C.).

Erin.

Ireland ; also called " Hibernia," and the " Emerald Isle."

Erymanthian Boar, The.

A surname given to Hercules.

Essex.

A frigate of 860 tons, built at Salem, Massachusetts, in 1799. On August 13, 1812 (Captain David Porter) she fought and captured the "Alert." On February 6, 1814, she was blockaded in Valparaiso Harbour by the "Phœbe" (Captain Hillyar) and the "Cherub" (Captain T. T. Tucker), and fought these ships in a storm, March 28, 1814, when, after about three hours' fighting, she surrendered.

Essex, *v.* **Wasp.**

Essex Junto.

A name (first used about 1781) chiefly applied to a group of extreme Federalist leaders, mostly connected with Essex County, Massachusetts, about the end of the eighteenth and beginning of the nineteenth century. Later the name was applied to the Federalists in general.

Est-il possible? (French, "Is it possible?")

A nickname given by James II of England to Prince George of Denmark (1653–1708), the husband of James's daughter (afterwards Queen) Anne. The words had been a common phrase with the prince at the time of the Revolution of 1688, as reports of successive desertions of the king arrived.

Etats-Généraux (French, "States General").

The name given to the legislative assemblies of France before the Revolution of 1789, and to those of the Netherlands.

Eternal City, The.

Rome, Italy. Title of a novel
D.N.

by Hall Caine. Also called the **Imperial City,** the **Queen of Cities,** the **Seven-hilled City,** the **Niobe of Nations** (Cf. Byron's "Childe Harold," iv. 79).

Ethiopia.

In ancient geography a country south of Egypt, corresponding to the kingdom of Meroë, from the neighbourhood of Khartoum northward to Egypt. It comprised, in a more extended sense, Nubia, northern Abyssinia, Sennaar and Kordofan.

Étiquette, Madame, *v.* **Madame Étiquette.**

Ettrick Shepherd, The.

A surname given to James Hogg, a Scottish poet (1770–1835), from his occupation. He was born at Ettrick, Selkirkshire.

Eunuch, The.

A surname of Eutropius, a Byzantine statesman (fl. c. 395–9).

Europe's Liberator.

A surname given to the Duke of Wellington (1769–1852), in allusion to the victory at Waterloo freeing Europe from Napoleon Bonaparte's despotic rule. *v.* also **Iron Duke, The; Saviour of the Nations, The; Hero of a Hundred Fights, The.**

Eurydice.

A training ship that foundered off Dunnose headland, near Ventnor, Isle of Wight, through a squall, March 24, 1878. She was returning from the Bermudas. Captain A. J. Hare and about 300 men perished.

H

Evangelical Alliance.

The name of an association of Christians belonging to the Evangelical denominations, organized in 1846 in London with the object of promoting Christian intercourse between the different orthodox Protestant denominations, and more effective co-operation in Christian work.

Evangelist, The.

A surname of Philip, a deacon and preacher in the early Christian church, who lived in the first century.

Everglade State, *v.* Peninsular State, The.

Ever-Loyal City, The.

A surname given to Oxford, in allusion to its steadfast loyalty to Charles I during the Parliamentary wars.

Ever-Memorable, The.

A surname of John Hales, an English scholar and Arminian divine (1584–1656) ; also called (by Wotton) a **Walking Library.** Cf. **Living Dictionary.**

Ever-Victorious Army.

A name given to the Chinese troops (commanded by Gordon in 1863–4) organized by Frederick Townsend Ward, an American adventurer (1831–62). He was made a high-grade mandarin and admiral-general.

Evil May-day, The.

A name given to May 1, 1517, owing to the excesses then committed against foreigners, particularly the French, by the apprentices and populace.

Excalibur (Excalibar or Escalibor).

The sword of the mythical King Arthur. Arthur received it from the hands of the Lady of the Lake. It had a scabbard, the wearer of which could lose no blood. It is called Mirandoise in some versions of the romance. There seems, however, to have been another sword called Excalibur in the early part of the story. This was plunged deep into a stone, and could only be withdrawn by the man who was to be king. After two hundred knights had failed, Arthur drew it out without difficulty. Also named Mordure and Caliburn.

Excelsior State.

A popular surname for the State of New York, alluding to the motto, " Excelsior," on its coat-of-arms.

Exchange, The.

The name by which the Royal Exchange, London, is familiarly known.

Expounder of the Constitution.

A surname popularly bestowed on Daniel Webster, a famous American statesman, orator and lawyer (1782–1852).

Expunging Resolution.

A resolution introduced into the United States Senate by T. H. Benton, of Missouri, to erase from the journal the censure passed by the Senate on President Jackson, March 28, 1834, relating to the bank controversy. It was first introduced in 1834, and was carried January 16, 1837.

Exterminator, The (Spanish, "El Exterminador").

A surname of Montbars, a French buccaneer (b. c. 1645), from his ferocity. His uncle having been killed by the Spaniards, he joined the buccaneers, rose to high command, and for several years ravaged the Spanish colonies about the Caribbean Sea.

Eye of Greece, The.

A surname given to Athens, and sometimes also to Sparta.

Eye of the Baltic.

A name sometimes given to the island of Gothland (Gotland, Gottland or Gutaland), 60 miles east of Sweden, to which it belongs.

Factory King, The.

A surname given to Richard Oastler, of Bradford (1789–1861), alluding to his success in promoting the "Ten Hours' Bill."

Fainéant, Le (French, "The Sluggard").

A surname of Louis V, King of France (966–987). The last of the Carolingians in France.

Fair, The, *v.* **Bel, Le.**

A surname of Edwy (or Eadwig), King of Wessex (c. 938–58).

Fair City, The.

A popular surname in Scotland for the town of Perth, remarkable for the beauty of its appearance and situation.

Fair Geraldine, The.

A surname of the supposed mistress (c. 1528–89) of Henry Howard, Earl of Surrey (c. 1517–47), celebrated in a sonnet by him and in other poems. The lady referred to in the sonnet was an Irish lady named Lady Elizabeth Fitzgerald, daughter of Gerald Fitzgerald, ninth Earl of Kildare, first married to Sir Anthony Browne, and after his death to the Earl of Lincoln (Edward Fiennes de Clinton).

Fair-haired (Norwegian, "Harfagr or Haarfager").

A surname of Harold I, King of Norway (d. 933), who reigned from 860–930.

Fair Maid of Anjou, The.

A surname given to Lady Edith Plantagenet, a kinswoman of Richard Cœur de Lion, and an attendant of Queen Berengaria. She married David, Earl of Huntingdon, Prince Royal of Scotland.

Fair Maid of Galloway, The.

A surname given to Margaret, only daughter of Archibald (*v.* **Bell-the-Cat**), fifth Earl of Douglas (d.c. 1514), wife of her cousin William, to whom the earldom passed in 1443, and, after his death, reluctantly obeying the royal command, she married his brother and successor, James, last Earl of Douglas.

Fair Maid of Kent, The.

Joan, daughter of Edmond Plantagenet, Earl of Kent, and wife of Edward, "the Black Prince" (q.v.).

Fair Maid of Norway, The.

Margaret, daughter of Eric II of Norway, and grand-daughter of Alexander III of Scotland (1283–90, at sea).

Fair Maid of Perth, The.

A surname of Catherine Glover, a beautiful young woman of Perth, Scotland. The heroine of Sir Walter Scott's novel of the name (1828).

Fair of Lincoln.

A battle fought at Lincoln, England, 1217, in which the Earl of Pembroke defeated the French under Louis, son of Philip II.

Fair Perdita.

A surname of Mrs. Mary Darby Robinson, an English actress, novelist and poet (1758–1800). In the part of Perdita ("Winter's Tale") she attracted the notice of George IV, then Prince of Wales, and became his mistress. Also called the **English Sappho.** The prince was nicknamed **Florizel.**

Fair Quakeress, The.

A surname given to Hannah Lightfoot, whom George III is said to have married when he was Prince of Wales (1759).

Fair Rosamond.

Rosamond Clifford, a daughter of Walter de Clifford (d. c. 1176), and mistress of Henry II of England. A subterranean labyrinth in Blenheim Park is said to have been built by Henry II as a retreat for her.

Falcon.

A ship commanded by Sir Walter Raleigh in Sir Humphrey Gilbert's Expedition to America in 1578. The other ships were soon obliged to return, but Raleigh reached the Cape Verde Islands. Owing to scarcity of provisions he was obliged to turn back, and reached England in May, 1579.

Falcon, The.

A famous London tavern (pulled down in 1808) at Bankside, said to have been patronized by Shakspere and his company.

Falk Laws, *v.* **May Laws.**

Falls City.

A name given to Louisville, Kentucky, from the rapids or falls of the Ohio River, near the city.

False Prophet, The.

A surname of Mohammed Ahmed (c. 1841–85), who claimed to be the Mahdi. According to the Mohammedan belief, the Mahdi is a spiritual and temporal ruler, destined to appear on earth during the last days. There have been a number of pretended Mahdis.

Family Compact, *v.* **Pacte de Famille.**

Family Party, The.

An aristocratic political party in Quebec, Canada, c. 1835.

Faneuil Hall, *v.* **Cradle of Liberty.**

Farmer George.

A nickname of George III of England (1738–1820) on account of his simple appearance and manners. He is said to have actually derived profit from a farm near Windsor. Also the **Farmer King.**

Farmer King, The, *v.* **Farmer George.**

Farmers' Alliance.

An organization in United States politics (founded c. 1873)

devoted to the interests of farmers. It absorbed the Farmers' Union and the Agricultural Wheel, and developed rapidly, especially in the west and south, c. 1885–90. In May, 1891, it united at Cincinnati with several industrial organizations, and formed the People's Party (q. v.).

Fat, The.

A surname given to Alfonso II (or Affonso or Alphonso), King of Portugal (1185–1223). *v.* **Gros, Le.**

Fat Adonis of Forty (or Fifty), The, *v.* **Fum the Fourth.**

Father Abraham.

A nickname of Abraham Lincoln, sixteenth President of the United States (1809–65).

Father Cats.

A popular surname given to Jakob Cats, a Dutch poet (1577–1660).

Father Fritz.

A popular name given to Frederick (II) the Great, King of Prussia (1712–86).

Father of America, The.

A surname of Samuel Adams, an American patriot and statesman (1722–1803), one of the leaders of the Revolution.

Father of Angling, The.

Izaak Walton, an English author (1593–1683), so named from his famous work, " The Compleat Angler."

Father of British Inland Navigation.

A surname given to Francis Egerton, third and last Duke of Bridgewater (1736–1803), noted as the projector of a canal from Worsley to Manchester (the first in England entirely independent of a natural stream throughout its course), and of one from Manchester to Liverpool.

Father of Burlesque Poetry, The, *v.* **Father of Parody, The.**

Father of Chemistry, The.

A surname given to Arnaud de Villeneuve, a distinguished French chemist, astrologer and theologian (1238–1314).

Father of Church History, The, *v.* **Father of Ecclesiastical History.**

Father of Comedy, The.

Aristophanes (b. c. 450– c. 380 B.C.), the greatest of the Greek comic poets. Hence the surname. Also called the **Prince of Ancient Comedy.** Cf. **Creator of the New Comedy, The.**

Father of Dutch Poetry (or Poets), The.

A surname given to Jakob de Coster van Maerlant, an early Belgian poet (d. after 1291). Also called the **Father of Flemish Poets.**

Father of Ecclesiastical History The.

Eusebius of Cæsarea (c. 264– c. 349), surnamed " Pamphili," a celebrated theologian and historian, sometimes called the **Father of Church History,** *v.* also **Venerable Bede, The.**

Father of English Cathedral Music, The.

Thomas Tallis (Tallys, or Talys), an English composer

(c. 1515–85), organist of Waltham Abbey, and, later, gentleman of the Chapel Royal and music-printer.

Father of English Geology, The.

A surname given to William Smith, an English geologist (1769–1839).

Father of English Natural History.

A surname given to John Ray (or Wray), a noted English naturalist (1628–1705).

Father of English Poetry, The.

Geoffrey Chaucer (c. 1340–1400), a celebrated English poet, author of the " Canterbury Tales," also called the **Flower of Poets**; **Tityrus** (by Spenser); the **Morning Star of Song** (by Campbell and Tennyson).

Father of English Printing, The.

A surname of William Caxton, the first English printer (c. 1422–91).

Father of English Prose, The.

Roger Ascham, a noted English classical scholar and author (1515–68).

Father of English Unitarianism.

Surname given to John Biddle, an English Unitarian divine (1615–62). Died in prison.

Father of Epic Poetry, The.

Homer, the celebrated Greek poet and author of the "Iliad" and the "Odyssey" (lived c. 850 or later, or, according to some, as early as 1200 B.C.). Also called the **Father of Poetry**, the **Father of Song**; the **Maeonian Swan**; the **Man of Chios**; **Scio's Blind Old Bard**; the **Blind Old Man of Scio's Rocky Isle**; **Swan of the Meander** (from the river); the **Blind Bard on the Chian Strand**.

Father of Equity, The.

A surname given to Heneage Finch, Earl of Nottingham (1621–82), an English lawyer and statesman.

Father of Flemish Poets, The, v. **Father of Dutch Poetry (or Poets), The.**

Father of French History, The.

André Duchesne, a noted French historian (1584–1640).

Father of French Satire, The.

A surname given to Mathurin Regnier, a French satirical poet (1573–1613).

Father of French Surgery, The.

A surname given to Ambroise Paré, a French surgeon (1517–90).

Father of French Tragedy, The.

A surname given to Pierre Corneille (1606–84); also the **Homer of the French Drama, The.** Robert Garnier, a French dramatic author (1534–90) has also been called the former.

Father of German Literature, The.

Gotthold Ephraim Lessing, a celebrated German dramatist and critic (1729–81).

Father of German Poetry, The, v. **Dryden of Germany, The.**

Father of German Rationalism, The.

A surname given to Johann Salomo Semler, a German Protestant theologian, critic, and church historian (1725–91).

Father of Good Works, The.

A surname of Mohammed II, Sultan of Turkey (c. 1430–81). Also called the " Conqueror " and the " Great."

Father of Greek Music, The.

Terpander, a famous Lesbian musician and lyric poet, who settled in Sparta (fl. first half of the seventh century B.C.) ; probably so called from his development of the lyre.

Father of Greek Prose, The. *v.* Father of History, The.

Father of Greek Tragedy, The.

A surname given to Æschylus, the greatest of the Greek tragic poets (525–456 B.C.). Also applied to Thespis, an Attic poet (fl. middle of sixth century B.C.).

Father of Harlequins.

A name given to John Rich, a noted English harlequin (1692–1761). He was manager at Lincoln's Inn Fields 1713–32, and then built the first Covent Garden Theatre, opened December 7, 1732. During the season of 1718–9 Rich frequently produced French plays and operas at Lincoln's Inn Fields. Also called **Lun.**

Father of the Country, The. (Latin, " Pater Patriae.")

A surname of Cicero, a celebrated Roman orator, philosopher and statesman (106–43 B.C.), conferred upon him by the Roman senate. The title was also borne by several of the Cæsars. Also applied to George Washington, first President of the United States (1732–99). Sometimes called the **Cincinnatus of the Americans.** Cf. **Father of America, The.**

Father of History, The.

Herodotus, a celebrated Greek historian (c. 484–c. 424 B.C.). Also called the **Father of Lies** and the **Father of Greek Prose.**

Father of Iambic Verse, The.

A surname given to Archilochus, a Greek lyric poet of Paros (fl. c. 700 B.C.), famous for his satiric iambic poetry.

Father of Inductive Philosophy, The.

A surname given to Francis Bacon, Viscount St. Albans, a celebrated English philosopher (1561–1626).

Father of Italian Prose, The, *v.* Prince of Story-Tellers, The.

Father of Jests, The.

Joseph (Joe) Miller, an English comedian (1684–1738). The collection of jests known as " Joe Miller's Jests " originally appeared in 1739 as " Joe Miller's Jest Book, or the Wits' Vade Mecum," etc. It was made by John Mottley, and received its name unwarrantably from Joseph Miller, who is popularly said never to have made a joke in his life, and could neither read nor write. The word " Joe Miller " is now synonymous with any stale jest, the idea being that it emanated from this source, or is old enough to have been included in that collection.

Father of Landscape-Gardening, The.

A surname given to André Lenôtre, a noted French architect and landscape-gardener (1613-1700). In England he laid out Kensington Gardens, St. James's and Greenwich Parks.

Father of Letters, The, *v.* **Père des Lettres, Le,** and **Magnifico, Il.**

Father of Lies, The.

Satan. *v.* also **Father of History, The.**

Father of Medicine, The.

Hippocrates, a famous Greek physician (c. 460–c. 377 B.C.).

Father of Modern French Songs, The.

A surname given to Charles-François Panard, a French vaudevillist and song-writer (1694–1765).

Father of Modern Prose Fiction, The.

A surname given to Daniel Defoe (or De Foe), a celebrated English novelist (c. 1661–1731). Author of " Robinson Crusoe."

Father of Monks, The.

A surname given to Ethelwold of Winchester (d. 984).

Father of Modern Painting, The.

A surname given to Giovanni Cimabue, a noted Italian painter (1240–c. 1302).

Father of Moral Philosophy, The. *v.* **Doctor Angelicus; Dumb Ox;** and **Eagle of Divines.**

Father of Music, The.

Giovanni Pierluigi da Palestrina, a celebrated Italian musician (c. 1524–94), also called " Princeps Musicæ " (Prince of Music) and the **Michelangelo of the Lyre.**

Father of Ornithologists, The.

A surname sometimes given to George Edwards, an eminent English ornithologist (1693–1773).

Father of Orthodoxy.

Surname given to Saint Athanasius (c. 296–373), one of the fathers of the Christian Church and defender of the orthodox faith against Arianism

Father of Parody, The.

A surname given to Hipponax, a Greek iambic poet (fl. during second half of sixth century B.C.). Also called the **Ephesian Poet** (b. at Ephesus) and the **Father of Burlesque Poetry.**

Father of Peace, The.

A title given by the Senate of Genoa to Andrea Doria, a celebrated Genoese admiral and statesman (1468–1560). Also styled the " Liberator of Genoa," which he freed from the French in 1528.

Father of Philosophy, The.

A surname given to Roger Bacon, a celebrated English philosopher (c. 1214–94). Also to Albrecht von Haller, a distinguished Swiss physiologist, anatomist, botanist and poet (1708–77). Also called the **Father of Physiology.**

Father of Physiology, The, *v.* **Father of Philosophy, The.**

Father of Poetry, The.

A surname sometimes given to Orpheus, a Greek poet, who is said to have flourished before Homer, but whose existence has been questioned, besides others, by Aristotle. Also sometimes applied to Homer, *v.* **Father of Epic Poetry, The.**

Father of Reform, The.

Surname given to John Cartwright, an English Radical politician and publicist (1740–1824), an advocate of parliamentary reform and the abolition of slavery.

Father of Ridicule, The.

François Rabelais, a celebrated French humorist (c. 1495–1553).

Father of Roman Philosophy, The.

A surname given to Cicero, a celebrated Roman orator, philosopher and statesman (106–43 B.C.).

Father of Roman Satire, The.

A surname given to Caius Lucilius, a Latin satirical poet (c. 180—103 B.C.).

Father of Russian History, The.

A surname given to Nestor, a Russian historian and monk of the convent of Kiev-Petchersk (c. 1054–d. probably after 1113).

Father of Satire, The.

A surname given to Archilochus, a Greek lyric poet of Paros (fl. c. 700 B.C.), famous for his satiric iambic poetry.

Father of Song, The. v. Father of Epic Poetry.

Father of Swiss History, The.

A surname given to Ægidius (or Gilg) Tschudi, a Swiss historian and Roman Catholic theologian (1505–72).

Father of Symphony, The.

A surname given to Joseph Haydn, a celebrated Austrian composer (1732–1809).

Father of the Country, The.

A surname given to Cosmo de Medici, the elder, ruler of Florence (1389–1464), from his having fed the people during a famine.

Father of the English Novel, The.

A surname given (by Sir Walter Scott) to Henry Fielding, a celebrated English playwright and novelist (1707–54).

Father of the Faithful, The.

Abraham, the first of the patriarchs, and founder of the Hebrew race.

Father of the French Drama, The.

A surname given to Étienne Jodelle, a French poet (1532–73), the first to compose tragedies with choruses and imitating the Greek.

Father of the Game of Whist, The.

A surname given to Edmund Hoyle, an English writer on games (1672–1769).

Father of the Halls, The (i.e. Music Halls).

A surname given to Charles Morton, the well-known music-hall and variety entertainment manager (b. 1819).

Father of the Locomotive, The.

A surname given to Richard Trevethick, a Cornish mining engineer (1771–1833), the first to use a steam-carriage on a railway in 1804.

Father of the People, The, v. Père du Peuple, Le.

A surname given to Christian III, King of Denmark (1502–59), and a title assumed by the kings of Denmark during the period of absolutism.

Father of the Poor, The, *v.* **Apostle of the North, The.**

Father of the Potteries, The.

A surname given to Josiah Wedgwood, a celebrated English potter (1730–95), noted for his copies of classical vases, etc.

Father of the Spanish Drama, The.

A surname given to Lope Felix de Vega Carpio, a celebrated Spanish dramatist and poet (1562–1635).

Father of the Vaudeville, *v.* **Père Joyeux du Vaudeville, Le.**

Father of Thought, The, *v.* **Père de la Pensée, Le.**

Father of Tragedy, The, *v.* **Father of Greek Tragedy, The.**

Father of War Correspondents, The.

The writer (signing himself " William Richardson ") of a letter that appeared in the " Daily Post " in 1740, accompanying an illustration of Admiral Vernon's attack on Portobello, purporting to come from a witness of the conflict.

Father of Waters, The.

The Mississippi River. Also called the **King of Waters.** The name is sometimes given to the Irrawaddy (Irawadi), the chief river of Burmah.

Father Rondo, *v.* **Père aux Rondeaux, Le.**

Faultless Painter, The.

A surname given (by R.

Browning) to Andrea del Sarto, a noted Florentine painter (1488-1530).

Fearless, The.

A surname of John, Duke of Burgundy (c. 1370–assassinated 1419). He assassinated the Duke of Orleans in 1407 ; also of Richard, duke of Normandy (d. 996), son of William Longsword, whom he succeeded in 942 or 943.

Feather-Heads, *v.* **Half-Breeds.**

Federal Constitution, The.

The fundamental or organic law of the United States. It was formed by the Constitutional Convention, which met in Philadelphia on May 25, 1787, and adjourned September 17, 1787. It became operative on March 4, 1789, having been ratified by eleven of the thirteen states, the remaining two (North Carolina and Rhode Island) ratifying it November 21, 1789, and May 29, 1790, respectively.

Federalists, The.

A political party formed in 1787 to support the Federal Constitution (q.v.) of the United States. Among its leaders were Hamilton and John Adams, and it controlled the executive of the national government under the administration of Washington and Adams. From 1789 it favoured a broad construction of the Constitution and a strongly centralized government. It opposed the war of 1812, and after that time ceased to be of importance in national politics ; but it figured for some years longer in local New England politics. Also the name of a political party in Mexico, *v.* Centralists.

Félibres, Les.

A brotherhood of modern Provençal poets, originated by Joseph Roumanille, who revived Provençal as a literary language, c. 1835. He was followed by Frédéric Mistral and five other poets, all living in or near Avignon. In the course of years this brotherhood came to be a great literary society, with affiliated organizations in other parts of France and in Spain. Among the members are— Aubanel, Brunet, Camille Reybaud, Mathieu and Félix Gras. The brotherhood of the Félibrige was formally founded May 21, 1854, at Fontségugne. The etymology of Félibre, an old Provençal word, is unknown.

Female Howard, The.

A surname given to Mrs. Elizabeth Fry, an Englishwoman, celebrated for her exertions in improving the conditions of prisoners and lunatics (1780–1845).

Fen Country, or The Fens.

That part of eastern England which formerly abounded in fens, now in great part drained. *v.* Bedford Level.

Fénelon of Germany, The.

A surname given to Johann Caspar Lavater, a Swiss poet and theologian, the founder of the so-called science of physiognomy (1741–1801).

Fénelon of the Reformation, The.

A surname given to John Arndt, a German theologian (1555–1621).

Fenians.

A modern English form of Irish *Fiann, Fianna,* a name applied in Irish tradition to the members of certain tribes, who formed a militia of the ardrigh or king of Eire or Erin (the *Fianna Eirionn,* or " Champions of Erin "). The name is applied to an association of Irishmen known as the Fenian Brotherhood, founded in New York in 1857 with a view to secure the independence of Ireland.

Fennel.

The name of Richard Cœur de Lion's horse.

Fens, The, *v.* Fen Country.

Ferney, The, Patriarch of, *v.* Patriarch of Ferney, The.

Feuillants, Les.

A political club established in Paris during the Revolution. It was at first called the Club of 1789, receiving its later name from the convent of the Feuillants, where its meetings were held.

Field Codes.

A series of codes intended to embody all the general laws of the State of New York, several of which were in substance adopted by that State, and all of which have been adopted in a number of other states. They were prepared by a commission appointed in New York, Mr. David Dudley Field being the chief member.

Fielding of the Drama, The.

A surname given to George Farquhar, an Irish dramatist (1678–1707). Also the **Smollett of the Stage.**

Field of Lies, The.

A name sometimes given to the battle near Colmar, Alsace (833). His three sons had revolted and Louis (I) le Débonnaire was compelled to surrender owing to the defection of his troops.

Field of Mourning, The.

A name given to the site of a battle, near the city of Aragon, between the Christians and the Moors, July 17, 1134.

Field of the Cloth of Gold.

The scene of a meeting between Francis I of France and Henry VIII of England in 1520. A plain near Ardres, Pas-de-Calais, France, was so called from the magnificence of the display.

Field of the Forty Footsteps.

Tradition has it that the fields behind Montagu House, London, at about the period of the Duke of Monmouth's rebellion, were the scene of a conflict to the death between two brothers, since which their footsteps were said to remain, " nor could any grass or vegetable ever be produced where these ' forty footsteps ' were thus displayed. This extraordinary area was said to be at the extreme termination of the north-east end of Upper Montagu Street. They were built over c. 1800."— *Rimbault.*

Fierce, The, *v*. Brave, The (Alfonso IV).

Also a surname of Alexander I, King of Scotland (c. 1078–1124).

Fifth Doctor of the Church, The, *v*. Doctor Angelicus.

Fifth-Monarchy Men.

A sect of millenarians of the time of Cromwell, differing from other Second-Adventists in believing not only in a literal second coming of Christ, but also that it was their duty to inaugurate this kingdom by force. It was to be the fifth and last in the series of which those of Assyria, Persia, Greece, and Rome were the preceding four ; hence their self-assumed title. They unsuccessfully attempted risings against the government in 1657 and 1661.

Fighter, The.

A surname given to Alfonso (or Alphonso) I, King of Aragon and Navarre from 1104–34 and, as Alfonso VII, King of Leon and Castile. He fought in twenty-nine battles.

Fighting Joe, *v*. Fighting Joe Hooker.

Fighting Joe Hooker.

A popular nickname for General Joseph Hooker, an American soldier (1814–79). Also called **Fighting Joe.**

Fighting Nat.

A nickname of Nathaniel Fitz-Randolph, an intrepid soldier in the American Revolutionary War.

Fighting Parson, The.

A nickname of William Gannaway Brownlow (" Parson Brownlow "), an American journalist and politician (1805–77), originally an itinerant preacher in the Methodist Church. He became a United States senator in 1869.

Fighting Phil.

A nickname of Philip Kearny, an American general (1815–62).

Fighting Prelate, The.

A surname given to Henry Spenser, a warlike bishop of Norwich in the reign (1377–99) of Richard II. (Cf. **Peaceful Prelate, The.**)

Fighting Téméraire, The.

A line-of-battle ship of 98 guns, captured from the French at the battle of the Nile, August 1, 1798. She fought next to the "Victory" in the line at the battle of Trafalgar, October 21, 1805; under Captain Harvey. Broken up in 1838. Turner's picture of "the Fighting Téméraire" was exhibited at the Royal Academy in 1839. *v.* also **Téméraire.**

Filia Dolorosa (Latin, "Daughter of sorrow").

A surname given to Marie Thérèse Charlotte, Duchesse d'Angoulême (1778 – 1851), daughter of Louis XVI. Also called the **Orphan of the Temple** in allusion to her imprisonment for three years in the Temple (*v.* **Temple, Le**). Louis XVIII called her the Modern Antigone.

Finality John, *v.* **John Finality.**

Firebrand of France, The.

A surname given to John of Lancaster, Duke of Bedford (1389–1435), Regent of England and France.

Firebrand of the Universe, The.

A surname given to Tamerlane (Timur, or Timour, or Timur-Leng, or Timur the Lame), a Tartar conqueror (1333–1405). Also the **Prince of Destruction.**

First English Magazine, The.

"The Gentleman's Magazine," founded by Edward Cave in 1731, was the first monthly magazine of the modern type.

First Gentleman of Europe.

A popular surname of George IV of England (1762–1830). Also called the **Beau of Princes,** while Prince of Wales and Prince Regent. *v.* **Fum the Fourth.**

First Grenadier of France, The, *v.* **Premier Grenadier de la République, Le.**

First Grenadier of the Republic, The, *v.* **Premier Grenadier de la République, Le.**

First Scotch Reformer, The.

A surname given to Patrick Hamilton (1504–28), who was burned at the stake for disseminating Lutheran doctrines.

Five Boroughs, The.

A name applied in early English history to Derby, Leicester, Lincoln, Stamford and Nottingham. They were under Danish rule until their conquest (completed 922) by Edward and Ethelfleda.

Five Members, The.

The five members of Parliament—Hampden, Pym, Holles, Haselrig and Strode—who were leaders in the opposition to Charles I in the Long Parliament (q.v.), and whom he attempted to arrest January 4, 1642.

Five Nations, The, *v.* **Six Nations, The.**

Five P's.

A nickname given to William

Oxberry, who was a printer, publisher, poet, publican and player (1784-1824).

Flagellants.

A body of religious persons who believed that by whipping and scourging themselves for religious discipline they could appease the divine wrath against their sins and the sins of the age. An association of flagellants, founded c. 1260, spread throughout Europe, its members marching in processions, publicly scourging their own bare bodies till the blood ran. Having by these practices given rise to great disorders, they were suppressed ; but the same scenes were repeated on a larger scale in 1348, and several subsequent years, in consequence of the desolating plague called the " Black Death."

Flagellum Dei, *v*. Scourge of God.

Flamberge, *v*. Floberge.

Flammock's Rebellion.

A rebellion in Cornwall, under the leadership of Thomas Flammock in 1497, occasioned by the imposition of a tax to defray the cost of a Scottish war. The insurgents marched on London, but were defeated at Blackheath, June 17, 1497.

Fleet, The, *v*. Fleet Prison, The, and Fleet Ditch, The.

Fleet Ditch, The.

A tidal stream which flowed by the western wall of old London City. The stream took its rise in the clay beds east of the Hampstead Hills. At Battle Bridge, near King's Cross, it entered a deep valley between high clay banks, from which it did not emerge until it reached the river. In olden times the only road from the city westward crossed the Fleet by a bridge from Snow Hill, Newgate, to Holborn Hill (High Holborn). Later another was made opposite Ludgate, and this crossing was called Fleet Bridge, the road leading to it being named Fleet Street. The tidal portion of the Fleet was navigable in the reign of Edward I. The brook is now a main sewer of London. The allusion to the Fleet Ditch in the literature of the sixteenth and seventeenth centuries is accounted for by the fact that the water from the bed of the brook or river having been diverted from its course, the offal, etc., thrown into it was not carried off, and became a nuisance.

Fleet Prison, The.

An old London prison, formerly standing on the east side of the Fleet brook or ditch, where it now runs under Farringdon Street. Destroyed in 1846, having been in existence nearly 800 years. It was a debtor's prison as early as 1290. Burned by Wat Tyler's men in 1381, in 1666 during the Great Fire, and again in 1780 by rioters. In the seventeenth and early part of the eighteenth century persons wishing to be married secretly came within the rules of the Fleet, where degraded clergymen were easily found, among the debtors, to perform the ceremony. This practice was stopped in 1754 by Act of Parliament.

Flemish Blacksmith, The, *v.* **Blacksmith of Antwerp, The.**

Flemish Raphael, The.

A surname given to Frans Floris (De Vriendt), a Flemish historical painter (1520-70).

Fleshly School, The.

A name applied to a school of English nineteenth century poets, in allusion to the alleged sensuous style of their writings. It included William Morris, Charles Swinburne and Gabriel Rossetti.

Fliegende Hollander, Der, *v.* **Flying Dutchman, The.**

Flint Jack.

A surname given to Edward Simpson, of Whitby, who used to sell spurious flint arrow-heads, etc. Imprisoned for theft in 1867.

Floberge (or **Flamberge**).

The sword of Renaud de Montauban, one of the four sons of Aymon, and one of Charlemagne's knights.

Flora Temple.

A celebrated bay trotting mare, foaled in 1845; sire, a Kentucky hunter; dam, Madame Temple. She held the world's trotting record for many years.

Florence of the North, The, *v.* **German Florence, The.**

Florentine Diamond, The.

The fourth largest cut diamond in the world, of a pale yellow tint, and weighing 139½ carats. It is one of the Emperor of Austria's crown jewels, and is valued at over £100,000.

Florian's.

A celebrated café in Venice, on the Piazza of St. Marco, so named from its founder, Floriano. About 200 years old. Now the rendezvous chiefly of strangers in Venice, but was formerly the headquarters of the most illustrious men of the city and of Italy.

Florida.

The first of the three commerce-destroyers built in England for the Confederate Government. She left Liverpool March 22, 1862, and received her armament at the Bahamas, August 7. On October 7, 1864, she was captured by the " Wachusett " (sister ship to the " Kearsage "), under Captain Napoleon Collins. She was taken to Hampton Roads, where she was afterwards sunk by a collision.

Florizel, *v.* **Fair Perdita.**

Flour City, The.

A popular surname for the city of Rochester, New York, alluding to its flour-mills.

Flower City, The.

A surname sometimes given to the city of Springfield, Illinois, in allusion to the beauty of its suburbs.

Flower of Chivalry, The.

A surname given to Sir William Douglas, Lord of Liddesdale. *v.* **Knight of Liddesdale, The,** also **English Petrarch, The.**

Flower of Kings.

A surname of King Arthur, a British chieftain, who lived in the sixth century.

Flower of Poets, The, *v.* **Father of English Poetry, The.**

Flower of Strathearn.

A surname given to Carolina Oliphant, Baroness Nairne, a Scottish poetess (1766–1845).

Flower of the Levant, The.

A surname given to Zante, Greece.

Flowery Kingdom, The.

China. The Chinese designations are: Chung Kwoh (Middle Kingdom), Chung Hwa Kwoh (Middle Flowery Kingdom), etc. *v.* **Cathay.**

Flying Childers.

A chestnut racehorse, foaled in England c. 1715, a descendant of the Darley Arabian. He was never beaten.

Flying Dutchman, The.

A spectral ship, according to sailors' superstition supposed to haunt the seas near the Cape of Good Hope in stormy weather. There are various legends as to why it can never enter port. *v.* **Vanderdecken.** Name also given to the principal Great Western Railway express train to the West of England, from one of the Company's best engines so named.

Flying Highwayman, The.

A surname given to William Harrow, a notorious highwayman, executed at Hertford, March 28, 1763. So called from his habit of leaping his horse over turnpikes when pursued.

Flying Scotchman.

A popular name for an express train between London and Scotland and the North (Great Northern Railway).

Fools' Paradise, *v.* **Limbo.**

Force Bill.

A Bill passed by Congress to enforce the tariff. It was occasioned by the ordinance passed by South Carolina, November 24, 1832, nullifying the Tariff Acts of 1828 and 1832, and became law March 2, 1832. Also called the "Bloody Bill." Also a bill for the protection of political and civil rights in the South, passed in 1870. A bill, with the same purpose as the preceding, passed in 1871. A popular name for the Lodge Election Bill, which passed the Republican House of Representatives in 1890, but failed to pass the Senate in 1891. It became a leading party measure, and was designed "to amend and supplement the election laws of the United States, and to provide for the more efficient enforcement of such laws, and for other purposes."

Ford's Theatre.

A former theatre in Washington. President Lincoln was assassinated there April 14, 1865. It was afterwards used by the Government for the record division of the War Department. It collapsed June 9, 1893, and a number of lives were lost.

Forefathers' Day.

The anniversary of the landing of the Pilgrim Fathers (q.v.) at Plymouth Rock, Mass., December 22, 1620.

Forest Cantons.

A collective name for the cantons of Lucerne, Schwyz, Uri and Unterwalden, in Switzerland.

Forest City, The.

A name given to Cleveland, Ohio, on account of the number of its shade-trees. Portland, Maine, and Savannah, Georgia, are also sometimes called by this name.

Foresters.

Members of the Ancient Order of Foresters Friendly Society are often so called.

Forrest-Macready Riot, The, *v.* **Astor Place Riot, The.**

Forth Bridge, The.

A bridge erected (1882–9) by the North British Railway across the Firth of Forth at Queensferry, Scotland ; the largest bridge yet built. The two main spans are each 1,710 feet long, and are formed of two cantilevers, each 680 feet long, united by a girder of 350 feet clear span. Each of these spans is 100 feet longer than that of the Brooklyn Bridge. The steel towers which support the cantilevers are 361 feet high, with a clear headway above high-water (spring-tides), of 150 feet. Total length, 8,296 feet, and cost £1,600,000.

Fortunate, The.

A surname of John IV, King of Portugal (d. 1656). The first of the House of Braganza. .

Fortunate Islands, The.

An ancient name of the Canary Islands. The Fortunate Islands, Islands of the Blest, D.N.

or the Happy Islands, were originally imaginary isles in the Western Ocean, where the souls of the good are made happy. With the discovery of the Canary and Madeira Islands, the name became attached to them.

Fortune.

A ship which arrived at Plymouth, Mass., November 11, 1621, from London, bringing out thirty-five colonists; and a patent, granted June 1, 1611, by the President and Council of New England to John Pierce and his associates, allowing 100 acres to be taken up for every emigrant, and empowering the grantees to make laws and set up a government. *Winsor.*

Fortune, The.

A London theatre, built in 1599 for Henslowe (the pawnbroker and moneylender) and Alleyne (the comedian). It stood in the parish of St. Giles, Cripplegate, and in the street now called Playhouse Yard, connecting Whitecross Street with Golden Lane. It was a wooden structure, which was burned down in 1621, and replaced by a circular brick edifice. In 1649 a party of soldiers broke into the building and pulled it down.

Forty, The, *v.* **Immortals, The.**

Forty-two Articles, *v.* **Thirty-nine Articles.**

Fosse-way (or The Fosse).

An ancient Roman road, running from Bath through Cirencester and Leicester to Lincoln.

Foul Raid, The.

The raid of the Duke of

I

Albany on Roxburgh Castle and the town of Berwick in 1417, during the absence in France of Henry V of England. He was compelled to retire by the Dukes of Exeter and Bedford.

Foul-Weather Jack.

A nickname given to Admiral John Byron, a British naval officer (1723–86), from his bad fortune at sea.

Founder of Christian Eloquence, The, v. Roi des Predicateurs, Le.

Founder of Peace.

A surname given to St. Benedict (c. 480–543), an Italian monk, who founded the order of the Benedictines at Monte Cassino, c. 529. His fête in the Roman and Anglican calendars is March 1, and in the Greek calendar March 14.

Founder of the English Domestic Novel, The.

A surname given to Samuel Richardson, an English novelist (1689–1761). Also sometimes called the English **Marivaux.**

Fountain of Life, The, v. Irrefragable Doctor, The.

Four Cantons, Lake of the, v. Lake of the Four Cantons.

Four Cities, v. Six Cities, The.

Four-eyed George.

A nickname of George Gordon Meade, an American general (1815–72), alluding to the spectacles which he wore.

Four Lakes, The.

A chain of lakes (Mendota and others) in Dane County, Southern Wisconsin.

Fourth Estate, The.

A surname applied by Edmund Burke (when speaking in the House of Commons) to the newspaper press (Cf. Carlyle's "Hero Worship," Lecture V.).

Fourth Party, The.

A name given c. 1880 to a knot of English Conservatives, of whom Lord Randolph Churchill was the leading spirit. It frequently opposed the Conservative Party.

Fowler, The.

A name given to Henry I, King of Germany (876–936). When they came to announce his election to the throne he was found "fowling" with a hawk on his wrist.

Fox.

A yacht sent out in 1857 by Lady Franklin (Captain Leopold McClintock), in search of traces of the missing Arctic expedition commanded by her husband, Sir John Franklin, consisting of the "Erebus" and the "Terror" (Captain Crozier), sent out in 1845, but which never returned. McClintock ascertained from papers found that Franklin died June 11, 1847 (b. 1786). v. **Terror.**

Fra Diavolo (Italian, "Brother Devil").

A name by which Michele Pezza, an Italian robber (c. 1760–1806), a Bourbon partizan leader, 1799–1806, was known. He was hanged at Naples.

Fram.

A specially constructed steam

schooner, in which Fridtjof Nansen attempted to reach the North Pole. Length, 113 feet on the water-line, and built at Raekvik, near Laurvig, Norway. She sailed from Christiania June 24, 1893, and Nansen left her to continue his journey on sledges March 14, 1895. Under command of Captain O. N. Sverdrup she reached, drifting with the ice, 85° 55·5′. N. lat., 66° 31′ E. long. on November 15, 1895, and, returning, passed Spitzbergen in August, 1896, having circumnavigated Nova Zembla and the Franz Joseph and Spitzbergen archipelagoes.

Franklin of Theology, The.

A surname given to Andrew Fuller, an English Baptist preacher and theologian (1754–1815).

Frederick the Noble, *v.* Our Fritz.

Free-and-Easy.

Periodical meetings at certain taverns, at which songs are sung under the direction of a chairman, are so called. Also **Sing-Songs.**

Free-born John.

A surname given to John Lilburne, a famous English republican (c. 1613–57), alluding to his defence of his rights as a free-born Englishman before the **Star Chamber** (q.v.).

Freeman, Mrs., *v.* Queen Sarah.

Free-Soil Party.

A political party in the United States, which opposed the extension of slavery into the Territories. Formed in 1848 by a union of the Liberal Party with the Barnburners (q.v.).

It nominated Van Buren for the presidency in 1848 and, under the name of the Free Democratic Party, nominated John P. Hale in 1852. Was one of the principal elements in the formation of the Republican Party in 1854.

Freestone State.

A surname given to the State of Connecticut, from the quarries of freestone which it contains.

Free Trade.

A name given to the principles first advocated by Adam Smith (1723–90), in his "Wealth of Nations," published in 1776. The origin of the expression, however, is attributed to Henry Grattan, who used it in 1779 in the Irish Parliament. Cobden's prediction that within twenty years every other nation would follow England's example has not been fulfilled, and at the present time (1903) a policy of protection is favoured in the United States.

French Anacreon, The.

A surname given to Pontus de Thiard, a French poet; one of the poets of Ronsard's Pleiad (c. 1521–1605).

French and Indian War (or Old French War).

The last of the series of wars between France and Great Britain in America. It was the American phase of the Seven Years' War (q.v.). The French were assisted by several Indian tribes, and the seat of the war was mostly the frontiers of Pennsylvania and New York, and Canada. It ended with the

Battle of Quebec, September 13, 1759, surrender of Montreal, 1760, Peace of Paris (q.v.), and the surrender of Canada to Great Britain, February 10, 1763.

French Aristophanes, The.

Surname given to Molière (Jean Baptiste Poquelin), the great French dramatist (1622–73).

French Burns, The, *v.* **French Horace, The.**

French Byron, The.

A surname given to Louis Charles Alfred de Musset, a celebrated French poet (1810–57).

French Calliope, The, *v.* **Tenth Muse, The.**

French Chaucer, The, *v.* **Chaucer of France.**

French Defoe, The.

A surname given to Rétif de la Bretonne (Nicolas Edme Restif), a French romancer and *littérateur* (1734–1806).

French Derby, The, *v.* **Grand Prix, Le.**

French Devil, The.

A surname given by the English, Dutch and Spanish to Jean Bart, a famous French naval commander (1650–1702).

French Dickens, The.

A surname given to Alphonse Daudet, a French humorist and novelist (1840–97).

French Ennius, The.

A surname given to Jehan de Meung, a French poet (c. 1260–c. 1318), who wrote a continua-

tion of Guillaume de Lorris's "Roman de la Rose."

French Fabius, The.

A surname given to Anne, Duc de Montmorency, Grand Constable of France (1492–1567), on account of his dilatory policy in Provence in 1536. *v.* Cunctator.

French Fury, The.

A treacherous attack on Antwerp by 4,000 French soldiers under the Duc d'Anjou, January 17, 1583. The attack was repelled by the citizens ; about one-half of the French were killed, and the rest made prisoners. *v.* **Furia Francese.**

French Horace, The.

A surname given to Pierre-Jean de Béranger, a celebrated French song-writer (1780–1857). Also the **Horace of France** and the **French Burns.**

French Isocrates, The.

A surname given to Esprit Fléchier, a French bishop and pulpit orator (1632–1710).

French Michelangelo, The, *v.* **Michel-Ange français, Le.**

French Ovid, The.

Joachim du Bellay, a French poet and prose-writer, was so styled (c. 1524–60). Also called "Prince of the Sonnet."

French Phidias, The.

A surname given to Jean Goujon, a celebrated French sculptor and architect (1515–68). Also called the **Correggio of Sculpture.** Also to Jean Baptiste Pigalle, an eminent French sculptor (1714–85).

French Pindar, The.

A surname given to Jean Dinemandy or Dorat (Latin, "Auratus"), a French poet (c. 1510–88). Charles IX created expressly for him the office of **Poète Royal.** Ponce-Denis Écouchard Lebrun, a French lyric poet (1729–1807), styled himself "Lebrun-Pindare."

French Poet, The.

A surname given to Pierre de Ronsard, a celebrated French poet (1524–85). He was proclaimed "le Poète français par excellence" by the Toulouse magistrates. Considered the father of lyric poetry in France.

French Plutarch, The, *v.* Plutarch of France, The.

French Quintilian, The.

A surname given to Jean François de La Harpe, a celebrated French critic and poet (1739–1803).

French Raphael, The.

A surname given to Eustache Le Sueur, a distinguished French painter (1616–55).

French Revolution, The.

The name specifically given to the revolution in France at the close of the eighteenth century. The meeting of the States-General, May 5, 1789, marks the beginning, and the end is taken either as 1795 (end of the Convention), or 1804 (end of the Directorate).

French Roscius, The.

A surname given to François Joseph Talma, a famous French tragic actor (1763–1826). He was the first to introduce, on the French stage, the custom of wearing the costume of the period represented in a play. Also to Michel Baron (or Boyron), a celebrated French actor (1653–1729).

French Sappho, The.

A surname given to Madeleine de Scudéri, a French poetess (1607–71). Also called the Tenth Muse.

French Shore, The.

Portions of the western and northern coasts of Newfoundland, where the French have the privilege (secured by the Treaty of Utrecht, 1713) of catching and drying fish.

French Solomon, The, *v.* Solomon of France, The.

French Switzerland (French, "La Suisse Romande ").

That part of Switzerland in which the vernacular language is French (or a French patois). It comprises the cantons Geneva, Vaud, Neuchâtel and Valais, the greater part of Fribourg, and a small part of Berne.

French Tibullus, The.

A surname given (by Voltaire) to Evariste Désiré Deforge, Chevalier de Parny, a French elegiac and erotic poet (1753–1814).

French Titian, The.

A surname given to Jacques Blanchard, a French painter (1600–38).

French Van Dyck, The.

A surname given to Hyacinthe Rigaud, a French portrait painter (1659–1743).

Friday Club, The.

A club instituted at Edinburgh by Sir Walter Scott in June, 1803.

Friend of Man, The (French, "L'ami des hommes").

A surname ironically given to Victor Riquetti, Marquis de Mirabeau (father of the orator), from the title of his work, "L'ami des hommes."

Friend of the People, The, v. Ami du Peuple, L'.

'Frisco.

A familiar abbreviation of the name of the city of San Francisco, California.

Frog's March.

A familiar name for a method of conveying refractory prisoners to the police station. Four policemen each take hold of an arm or leg of the prisoner, who is thus carried along face downwards.

Frolic, The.

A British sloop-of-war, taken in 1812 by Captain Jacob Jones in the American sloop-of-war "Wasp" (q.v.).

From Beyond the Seas, v. D'Outre-Mer.

Fronde, The (French, lit. "A Sling").

The name of a party which, during Louis XIV's minority, waged civil war against the court party, on account of the humiliations inflicted on the high nobility and the heavy fiscal impositions laid upon the people. The movement began with the resistance of the Paris Parliament to the measures of the minister, Mazarin, and was sarcastically called by one of his supporters there " the War of the Fronde," in allusion to the use of the sling then common among the street-boys of Paris. The contest continued from 1648 to 1652, during which period Mazarin was driven from power, but soon restored. The name "frondeur" afterwards became a term of political reproach.

Fructidor, The 18th (Sept. 4, 1797).

The date when the majority of the Directory executed a *coup d'état* against the royalist reaction. Two of the Directors were ejected, and more than fifty members expelled from the Council of Five Hundred (q.v.), where the royalists had succeeded in obtaining a majority.

Fruit-bringing Society, v. Order of the Palm.

Fugitive-Slave Law.

An Act included in the Omnibus Bill (q.v.), securing to slave-holders additional facilities in the recovery of runaway slaves.

Fulton's Folly, v. Clermont, The.

Fum the Fourth.

A nickname given (by Lord Byron) to George IV, King of Great Britain and Ireland (1762–1830). Cf. "Don Juan," xi. 78). Also called the **Fat Adonis of Forty** (or **Fifty**).

Furia Francese (Italian, "French Fury").

A name given by the Italians to the impetuosity shown by the French at the Battle of

Fornovo, Parma (July 6, 1495), where from 35,000 to 40,000 Italians were routed by 16,000 Frenchmen. Cf. **Spanish Fury, The.**

Furies of the Guillotine, *v.* **Tricoteuses, Les.**

Furioso, Il.

A nickname of Jacopo Robusti (Tintoretto or Tintoret, from the trade of his father, a dyer), a celebrated Venetian painter (1518–94), from the furious rate at which he worked. Also called the **Thunderbolt of Painting.**

Fürstenbund, Der (German, " The League of the German Princes ").

A league formed at the instance of Frederick the Great in July, 1785, between Prussia, Hanover and the electorate of Saxony, aganist the Emperor Joseph II. Afterwards joined by Brunswick, Mainz, Hesse-Cassel, Baden, Mecklenburgh, Anhalt, and the Thuringian lands.

Fury.

One of Captain (afterwards Sir) W. E. Parry's ships, the other being the " Hecla," in which an expedition to the Arctic regions was undertaken 1821–3. Fury and Hecla Strait, in the Arctic regions, about 70° N. lat. and 80°–86° W. long., is named after them.

Fury of the Gironde, The, *v.* **Amazon of the Revolution.**

Fusberta.

The name of the sword of Rinaldo, a warrior in many romantic tales of Italy and France. Cf. Tasso's " Gerusalemme Liberata " and Ariosto's " Orlando Furioso."

Gabriel.

One of the ships of Frobisher's first expedition in search of the North-West Passage in 1576.

Gadsden Purchase.

A treaty negotiated December 30, 1853, by James Gadsden, United States Minister to Mexico, by which the United States acquired from Mexico a tract of 45,000 square miles, now included in the southern part of Arizona and New Mexico, for $10,000,000.

Galenists.

A Mennonite sect founded in 1664 by Galen Abraham de Haan, a physician and preacher of Amsterdam, constituting the Arminian division of the Waterlanders.

Galilean, The (or " The Gaulonite ").

A surname of Judas, a Jewish popular leader in the revolt against the census under the prefect Quirinus.

Gallia.

The ancient Latin and modern poetic name for France.

Galloping Dick.

A popular surname given to Richard Ferguson, a celebrated highwayman (executed at Aylesbury, April 4, 1800).

Garden City.

A name by which Chicago is sometimes alluded to.

Garden of England.

A name given to Worcestershire, on account of its fertility ; also to Hereford for a similar reason, and sometimes to Kent.

Garden of Erin, The.

A surname given to Carlow, Leinster.

Garden of Europe, The.

A surname often given to Italy, on account of its fertility. Also applied to Belgium.

Garden of France.

A name given to Touraine, a former province of France.

Garden of Helvetia.

A name given to Thurgau.

Garden of India, The.

A surname given to Oude.

Garden of Italy, The.

A surname given to the island of Sicily, on account of its fertility. For similar reasons, the name is also applied to the Campania and Lombardy.

Garden of Spain, The.

A surname given to Andalusia (Spanish, Andalucia). Also the **Granary of Spain** and **Goldpurse of Spain**.

Garden of the Argentine, The.

A surname given to Tucuman, an interior province of the Argentine Republic.

Garden of the Gods.

A remarkable region near Colorado Springs, Colorado, comprising about 500 acres, covered with extraordinary rock-formations (resembling cathedral spires, etc.).

Garden of the West, v. Garden State.

Garden of the World, The.

A surname often given to the vast tract of land (of more than 1,200,000 square miles) drained by the Mississippi and its tributaries, a region of great fertility.

Garden Sect, The.

A name often given to the followers of Epicurus, the founder of the Epicurean school of philosophy (342–270 B.C.). In 306 he opened a school in a garden at Athens, where he spent the remainder of his life.

Gardens of the Sun, The.

A surname given to the East Indian (Malayan) Archipelago.

Garden State, or Garden of the West.

A name given to Kansas ; also to Illinois and others of the Western States, in allusion to their fertility.

Garraway's Coffee House.

A noted London coffee-house, standing for two centuries in Exchange Alley, Cornhill. Tea was first sold here ; the promoters of the South Sea Bubble met here ; and sales of drugs, mahogany, and timber, were held here periodically. The original proprietor, Thomas Garway, was a tobacconist and coffee-dealer.

Garrick Club.

A London club, instituted in 1831 for the patronage of the drama, and as a rendezvous for men of letters. Since 1864 it has occupied a house in Garrick Street.

Garrotteurs, *v.* **Chauffeurs or Garrotteurs.**

Gate City.

A name given to Atlanta, Georgia, and also to Keokuk, Iowa.

Gate House Prison.

A London prison at Westminster, memorable as that from which Sir Walter Raleigh was taken to execution.

Gate of Italy.

A gorge in the valley of the Adige, near Roveredo, Tyrol.

Gate of the Mountains.

The gorge in which the Missouri breaks through the Rocky Mountains, about 40 miles above Great Falls, Montana.

Gaulonite, The, *v.* **Galilean, The.**

Gelert or Gellert.

The faithful hound of Llewellyn, according to Welsh tradition. He was killed by his master under the impression that he had killed the child he was set to guard. A huge wolf was found dead, killed by the dog, and the child unharmed. Llewellyn, overcome by remorse, erected a monument to his memory at Bethgelert, North Wales. (Cf. "Beth-Gelert," by W. R. Spencer.)

Gem of Normandy, The.

A surname given to Emma Ælfgifa (d. 1052) daughter of Richard (II) the Fearless (q.v.) of Normandy, who married Ethelred the Unready (q.v.), and afterwards Canute the Great (q.v.).

Général Entrepreneur, Le (French, "The Contractor General ").

A nickname given by the people of Paris to Napoleon Bonaparte (1769–1821) in allusion to the public works he undertook, but did not always complete.

General Lud.

A name given to the leader, real or supposed, of the Luddites (q.v.).

Generous, The, *v.* **Great, The** (Khusrau).

Genesta.

A cutter designed by J. Beavor-Webb and launched at Glasgow, April, 1884. Won 19 prizes in England in that year. She was built expressly for the race for the America cup, but was beaten by the Puritan (q.v.) in two races, Sept. 14 and Sept. 16, 1885.

Geneva Bull, The.

A surname given to Stephen Marshall, a Nonconformist divine (d. 1655).

Geneva Convention.

An international convention of various European States held at Geneva, Switzerland, Aug., 1864, designed to lessen the needless suffering of soldiers in war. It provided for the neutrality of the members and buildings of the medical departments on battle-fields.

Geneva Tribunal.

A tribunal of arbitration provided for by the treaty of Washington for the settlement of the Alabama claims (q.v.).

Gentil Belleau, Le (French, "the agreeable Belleau ") v. Painter of Nature, The.

Gentle Lochiel, The.

A surname given to Donald Cameron (d. 1748) grandson of Sir Evan Cameron, the **Black** (q.v.). Cf. Thomas Campbell's "Lochiel's Warning."

Gentleman Smith.

A surname given to William Smith, an English actor (1730-90) noted for his gentlemanly deportment.

Gentle Shepherd, The.

A nickname given to George Grenville (1712-70) by William Pitt, in allusion to an old ditty, "Gentle shepherd, tell me where ! *Dict. Nat. Biog.*

George's Conspiracy.

A conspiracy to assassinate Napoleon Bonaparte (when first Consul) and restore the Bourbons to the throne. Discovered in 1804, and Georges Cadoudal, Pichegru and others were arrested. Also called **Pichegru's Conspiracy.**

German, The.

A surname of Louis, king of Germany (c. 804-76) son of Louis I (v. **Pieux, Le**). He is commonly regarded as the founder of the German kingdom.

German Achilles, The, v. Achilles of Germany, The

German Athens, The.

A surname given to Saxe-Weimar.

German Cicero, The, v. Cicero of Germany, The.

German Florence, The.

A surname given to Dresden, Saxony. Sometimes called the Florence of the North.

German Hector, The, v. Hector of Germany, The.

German Milton, The.

A name sometimes given to Friedrich Gottlieb Klopstock, a noted German poet (1724-1803).

German Plato, The.

A name sometimes given to Friedrich Heinrich Jacobi, a noted German philosopher (1743-1819).

German Trismegistus, The, v. Prince of Alchemy, The.

German Voltaire, The, v. Voltaire of Germany, The.

Germinal Insurrection.

The insurrection (bread riots) at Paris against the Convention, 12th Germinal, year iii (April 1, 1795).

Ghibellines.

The imperial and aristocratic party of Italy in the middle ages : opposed to the Guelfs (or Guelphs), the papal and popular party.

Giant Despair.

In Bunyan's "Pilgrim's Progress," a giant who takes Christian and Hopeful while they are asleep and imprisons them in his dungeons in Doubting Castle.

Giant Grim.

A giant, in Bunyan's "Pilgrim's Progress," who is killed by Mr. Greatheart.

Giant of Literature, The, *v.* **Great Moralist, The.**

Giant's Causeway.

A group of basaltic columns situated on the coast of Antrim, northern Ireland, west of Bengore Head, about eleven miles north-east of Coleraine.

Giants of Guildhall, *v.* **Gog and Magog.**

Giants' Staircase.

A famous staircase in the Doge's Palace, Venice. So-called from the colossal statues of Mars and Neptune.

Gibelines, *v.* **Ghibellines.**

Gibraltar of America.

A name sometimes given to Quebec.

Gibraltar of North America, The.

A name given to St. John's, Newfoundland.

Gibraltar of the New World, The.

A surname given to Cape Diamond, Quebec.

Gilded Youth, *v.* **Jeunesse Doreé, La.**

Girondins, *v.* **Girondists.**

Girondists.

An important political party during the first French revolution, from Gironde, a party so called. They were sometimes called Brissotins, from Brissot. Gironde is the name of a department of France, from which the original leaders came.

Girouettes, Les.

A name given in the "Dictionnaire des Girouettes," pub-lished in Paris in 1815, to those who had deserted the tricolour for the white flag of the Bourbons after the fall of Napoleon, or vice versâ. After each name was engraved one or more weather-cocks, shewing the number of times the subject of the article had changed sides. *Larousse.*

Glamorgan Treaty.

A treaty made with the Roman Catholics of Ireland by the Earl of Glamorgan (afterwards Marquis of Worcester), acting (but apparently without authority) as agent of Charles I, Aug. 25, 1645. It made important concessions to the Roman Catholics in return for military aid,

Glassites.

A religious sect in Scotland, founded by John Glass (1695-1773). *v.* **Sandemanians.**

Glastonbury Thorn.

A tree at Glastonbury which bursts into leaf on Christmas Eve. The legend has it that Joseph of Arimathea, who visited it, planted his staff here, in sign of possession. It took root and became the famous Glastonbury thorn.

Globe, The.

A celebrated London theatre, built by Richard and Cuthbert Burbage in 1599. When their theatre in Shoreditch was taken down, the materials were carried to Bankside and used in the erection of the Globe. Burned down in 1613, but immediately rebuilt at a cost of £1,400. Pulled down in 1644 during the Puritan *régime*, and the site is now occupied by Barclay and Perkins' brewery. The Globe theatre in Wych Street, Strand, now also demolished, was built in 1868.

Glorious, The.

A surname given to Athelstan, king of the West Saxons and Mercia (895–940), a son of Edward the Elder.

Glorious John, v. Poet Squab.

Glorious Preacher, The.

A surname given to St. John Chrysostom, a celebrated father of the Greek Church. (c. 347–407). Also the Homer of Orators.

Glorious 1st of June, The.

A name given to the battle of Ushant, in which the French were defeated by Lord Howe, June 1, 1794.

Glorious 4th of July, The, v. Declaration of Independence.

Glory Hole.

A name given to a cupboard, box, chest, or other receptacle where anything may be stowed so as to be out of sight. Also applied to a cupboard for brooms, etc., at the head of a staircase.

Goddam.

A nickname applied by the French to the English, on account, it is said, of their frequent use of the phrase " God damn it ! "

Godless Florins.

A name given to English florins (issued in 1849) from which the letters F.D. (" Fidei Defensor, defender of the faith ")

were omitted. The master of the mint at the time, named Shiel, was a Roman Catholic. Also Graceless Florins.

God of All Philosophers, The.

A surname given to Marcus Tullius Cicero, a celebrated Roman orator, philosopher and statesman (106–43 B.C.), by Plato.

God of Dancing, The.

A surname given to Gaetano Apollino Balthazar Vestris, an Italian dancer (1729–1808).

Godolphin Barb, The.

One of the three Oriental sires from which the thoroughbred horse is derived. He was probably a barb foaled in 1729 and brought from Paris in the reign of George II. Died in 1753. The traditions surrounding this horse were woven into a novelette by Eugene Sue in 1825. From the Godolphin springs the Matchem branch of the thoroughbred horse.

God Save the King (or Queen).

The English national anthem: words and music probably composed by Henry Carey. First performed in 1740. Sometimes attributed to John Bull (1607), and has also been assigned a Scottish or French origin. The tune was adopted in France in 1776, and was afterwards used as the Danish, Prussian and German national air. Beethoven introduced it in his "Battle Symphony " ; Weber has used it in three of four compositions. The American national hymn, " My Country, 'tis of Thee," was written by Dr. Samuel Francis Smith, and published in 1843 : the music is that of "God Save the King."

Gog and Magog.

The names given to two effigies in the Guildhall, London. They are now thought to be intended for Gogmagog (q.v.) and Corineus. The original statues stood there in the days of Henry V (r. 1413–22). They were burned in the Great Fire of 1666, and new ones were put up in 1708. The older ones were made of wickerwork, pasteboard, etc., and were carried in procession at the Lord Mayor's Show.   Cf. Hood's poem, "Gog and Magog : A Guildhall Ditty" (ed. 1871, Moxon, vol. vi. 178).

Gogmagog (or Goëmot or Goëmagot).

A legendary king of the giants, killed by Corineus, a follower of Brut. Cf. Tom Hood's poem, "The Wee Man : a Romance" (last stanza) :

"Loud laughed the Gogmagog, a laugh
As loud as giant's roar——"

Gold-Bugs.

A popular nickname in the United States for the advocates of a single gold standard.

Golden Bull.

A bull (so named from its golden seal) published at the Diet of Nuremberg by the Emperor Charles IV in 1356, the latter part being issued at Metz. It was the electoral code of the empire, determining the prerogatives and powers of the electors, and the manner of the election of the king of the Romans. Andrew II, king of Hungary (r. 1205–35 or 36) also issued a Golden Bull (1222).

Golden City.

A name sometimes given to San Francisco.

Golden Fleece.

The fleece of the winged ram Chrysomallus (Greek mythology), the recovery of which was the object of the expedition of the Argonauts. A play by Corneille is entitled "La Toison d'Or" (The Golden Fleece).

Golden Gate, The.

A gate in the wall of Theodosius, Constantinople, now walled up on account of a Turkish tradition that the conqueror of Constantinople is destined to enter through it. It consists of three arches between two huge towers of white marble. The great central arch was reserved for the passage of the Emperor. Drake gave the name of the Golden Gate (c. 1578) to a strait about two miles wide connecting San Francisco Bay with the Pacific Ocean.

Golden Horn, The.

A surname given to the inlet of the Bosphorus on which Constantinople is situated. So called from its beauty and shape.

Golden Nose.

A nickname given to Tycho Brahe, a celebrated Danish astronomer (1546–1601). He lost his nose in a duel, and replaced it with an artificial one made of gold.

Golden Rose, The.

A jewel consisting of a cluster of roses and buds on one stem, all of gold, given each year by the Pope to the queen who has performed during the year the most pious deeds for the church.

Golden Staircase, The.

A celebrated staircase in the Doge's Palace, Venice.

Golden State, The.

A name sometimes applied to California.

Golden Stream, The (Greek, " Chrysorhoas ").

A surname given to John of Damascus (Joannes Damascenus), a theologian and father of the Eastern Church (b.c. end of 7th century-d.c. 760).

Golden Valley, The.

A surname given to the eastern part of Limerick, Ireland, from its fertility.

Golden Wedding, *v.* **Wedding Anniversaries.**

Gold Mine of Europe, The.

A surname formerly given to Transylvania, in allusion to the gold obtained from that region.

Gold-purse of Spain, The, *v.* **Garden of Spain, The.**

Goldsmith's Maid.

A bay trotting mare by Abdallah (15). Her racing career extended from 1866 to 1878. In 1871 she captured the great trotting record from Dexter (2.17¼) by a mile in 2.17. This she afterwards lowered to 2.14, and lost to Rarus (2.13¼) in 1874.

Goldy.

A nickname given by Dr. Samuel Johnson to Oliver Gold-smith, an English poet, novelist, dramatist, and miscellaneous writer (1728-74). *v.* **Inspired Idiot, The.**

Good, The.

A surname given to Alfonso IV (or Alphonso) king of Aragon (1299-1336) ; Alfonso IX (or Alphonso), also called the **Noble ;** to H.R.H. Francis Albert Augustus Charles Emmanuel, Prince Consort, Duke of Saxony, Prince of Coburg and Gotha (1819-61)—married to Queen Victoria, Feb. 10, 1840 ; to Hakon or Haco I, king of Norway (c. 920-c. 961) ; to Magnus I, king (1035-47) of Norway and of Denmark (1042-7), *v.* **Bon, Le ;** to James Graham, second Marquis of Montrose, a Scottish nobleman (c. 1631-69) ; to René I, duke of Anjou, count of Provence and (titular) king of Naples (1409-80) ; to Richard, duke of Normandy (996-1026), son of Richard the Fearless ; to William II, king of Sicily from 1166-89.

Good Duke Humphrey.

A name given to Humphrey, duke of Gloucester (1391-1447), noted as a patron of learning and a collector of books. He was the founder, by his gifts of books, of the library of Balliol College, Oxford. *v.* **Duke Humphrey's Walk.**

Good Earl, The.

A surname given to Archibald, 8th earl of Angus (d. 1588) for his many virtues.

Good Gray Poet, The.

A surname of Walt Whitman, an American poet (1819-92).

Good King René, The, *v*. Bon roi René, Le.

Goodman (or "Gudeman") of Ballengeigh (or "Ballinbreich"), The.

A name assumed by James V of Scotland (1512–42) who was accustomed to make midnight expeditions in Edinburgh in disguise. Also called the King of the Commons.

Goodman Palsgrave, *v*. Winter King, The.

Goodman's Fields Theatre.

A London theatre built in 1729. David Garrick made the success of the house in 1741. Pulled down c. 1746, and a second theatre built in 1802.

Good Parliament, The.

The name given to the English Parliament of 1376, noted for its efforts to reform political abuses. It impeached Lords Latimer and Neville, and others—the first instance of an impeachment.

Good Queen Bess.

A popular name for Queen Elizabeth of England (1533–1603).

Good Regent, The.

James Stuart, earl of Murray (or Moray) (1533–70), regent of Scotland 1567-70. Cf. Sir Walter Scott's "The Monastery" and "The Abbot."

Good Sir James, The, *v*. Black Douglas, The.

Goody Palsgrave, *v*. Winter Queen, The.

Goosey Goderich.

A nickname given [by Cobbett)

to Frederick John Robinson, an English statesman (1782-1859), created Viscount Goderich in 1827 and Earl of Ripon in 1833.

Gordon Pasha, *v*. Chinese Gordon.

Gordon Riots.

A rising of the London populace, June, 1780, the culmination of an anti-Roman Catholic agitation, instigated and abetted by Lord George Gordon (1751–93). He was tried in 1781 for complicity in the riots, but was acquitted for want of evidence. Cf. Charles Dickens's "Barnaby Rudge."

Gore House.

A house formerly occupying the site of the Albert Memorial, London. It was a famous resort for men of letters during the successive ownerships of William Wilberforce and the Countess of Blessington, in the early part of the nineteenth century.

Goshenland (or "Goosen"),

A republic set up by some Boer adventurers after the war of 1881, to the west of the Transvaal. The expedition of Sir Charles Warren in 1884 delimited the British and Transvaal boundaries, and Goshenland was absorbed in the Transvaal and in Bechuanaland.

Gospel Doctor, The, *v*. Doctor Evangelicus.

Gotha, Almanach de, *v*. Almanach de Gotha.

Gothaer.

A political party which favoured constitutional government, and a confederation of states under Prussia. Originally applied to certain members of the Frankfort Parliament who assembled at Gotha, June, 1849.

Gotham.

A name given to the city of New York.

Gothamite.

A humorous epithet for a New-Yorker, first used by Washington Irving in his " Salmagundi " (1807).

Gotland Sea Laws, *v.* **Laws of Wisby.**

Götz with the Iron Hand.

A surname given to Götz or Gottfried von Berlichingen, a German feudal knight (1480–1562). His right hand having been lost in battle, it was replaced by an artificial iron one. He is the hero of a play by Goethe, " Götz von Berlichingen." Cf. **Bras de Fer.**

Government of July.

A name applied to the Government (1830–48) of Louis Phillippe, who was called to the throne in consequence of the revolution of July (q.v.).

Gowrie Conspiracy.

A conspiracy against the life or personal freedom of James VI of Scotland, by John Ruthven (earl of Gowrie), Alexander Ruthven, and others. It resulted in the death of the leaders in a struggle with the king's followers at Perth, Aug. 5, 1600.

Grace Contract, The.

An arrangement made be-

tween the government of Peru and the foreign holders of bonds of that nation, represented by Mr. Michael Grace. It was ratified by the Peruvian Congress, Oct. 25, 1889, and provided that the bonds, amounting to about $250,000,000 should be cancelled. The bondholders received in return all the state railroads for 66 years, and important privileges connected with them, together with all the guano in Peru up to 3,000,000 tons, except that on the Chincha Islands. The government also promised to pay the bondholders £80,000 sterling annually for 30 years. The " Peruvian Corporation " formed to take charge of the railroads, etc., also took possession of the Cerro de Pasco silver mines, transferred to it by Mr. Grace, who had received the concession.

Grace Darling of America, The.

A surname given to Ida Lewis Wilson (b. 1841), the keeper of Lime Rock lighthouse, Newport, Rhode Island. She has been the means of saving several lives from shipwreck.

Graceless Florins, *v.* **Godless Florins.**

Grammaticorum   Princeps.
(Latin, " The Prince of Grammarians").

A surname given by Priscian to Apollonius Dyscolus, a celebrated Alexandrian grammarian (fl. in the reigns of Hadrian and Antoninus Pius).

Grammaticus.

Surname of Pope Benedict V (d. 965 in confinement).

Granary of Europe, The.

In ancient times a surname given to the island of Sicily. Its fertile soil produced a large quantity of wheat, on which the population of Rome relied to a great extent for its subsistence.

Granary of Portugal, The.

A surname given to the province of Alemtejo, in Portugal.

Granary of Spain, *v*. Garden of Spain, The.

Gran Capitan, *v*. Great Captain, The.

Grand, Le (French, " The Great ").

A surname of Louis XIV, king of France (1638–1715); also called " Le Roi Soleil."

Grand Alliance.

An alliance against France formed in 1689 between the Emperor Leopold I, Holland, England and Bavaria, and joined later by Spain, Savoy and Saxony. Also an alliance formed at the Hague in 1701 between the Emperor Leopold I, England and Holland, and joined later by Prussia, Portugal and Savoy, directed against France and Spain.

Grand Army of the Republic.

A secret society composed of veterans who served in the army or navy of the United States during the Civil War. Its objects are preservation of fraternal feeling, strengthening of loyal sentiment, and aid to needy families of veterans. Its first " post " was organized at Decatur, Illinois, in 1866, and

D.N.

its annual meetings are known as " encampments."

Grand Bâtard, Le (French, "The Great Bastard ").

A surname given to Antoine de Bourgogne (1421–1504), a natural son of Philip the Good, duke of Burgundy, celebrated for his bravery.

Grand Corneille, Le.

Pierre Corneille, a celebrated French dramatist (1606–84), is often so styled.

Grand Corrupter, The.

A name given to Sir Robert Walpole, Earl of Orford (1676–1745), on account of his use of corrupt means to secure his ascendancy in the House of Commons.

Grande Armée, La.

The French army which Napoleon led against Russia in 1812.

Grande Chartreuse, La, *v*. Chartreuse, La Grande.

Grande Mademoiselle, La.

A name given to Anne Marie Louise d'Orléans, duchesse de Montpensier (1627–93).

Grande Semaine, La (French, " The Great Week ").

A name given by the Parisians to the week ending with the Grand Prix (q.v.) race.

Grandison Cromwell.

A nickname given to Marie Jean Paul Roch Yves Gilbert Motier, marquis de Lafayette, a celebrated French general and statesman (1757–1834).

Grand Monarque, Le.

A surname of Louis XIV

K

(1638–1715), also called "Le Grand" (The Great).

Grandmother's (or Grandmamma's) Review, My.

A nickname given by Lord Byron to "the British Review."

Grand Old Man, *v.* **Great Commoner, The.**

Grand Panjandrum, The.

A fictitious personage invented by the dramatist, Samuel Foote (1720–77.)

Grand Prix, Le.

The great horse-race at Longchamps established by Napoleon III (prize 20,000 francs), run by three-year-olds. Distance 1 mile 7 furlongs. Longchamps is situated in the Bois de Boulogne, and the course was first used for racing in the reign of Louis XVI, and races have been run here since 1859. The Grand Prix is run on the Sunday of Ascot week. Often called the **French Derby.**

Grand Prix de Rome.

A prize given by the Academy of Fine Arts to the most successful competitor in painting, sculpture, engraving, architecture or music. The examinations are held annually, and the successful candidates become pensioners of the government for four years. They are sent to reside at Rome, where Louis XIV founded the Académie de France in 1666. Transferred to the Villa Medici in 1801.

Grand Remonstrance, The.

A protest passed by the House of Commons, November 22, 1641. It rehearsed the unconstitutional and unwise acts of the reign of Charles I, and demanded remedies.

Grand Trianon, *v.* **Trianon, Grand.**

Grangers.

Members of certain secret societies ("granges") organized in the United States for the advancement of the interests of agriculture, by the removal of restraints and burdens on it, and otherwise.

Granite State, The.

New Hampshire is sometimes so called on account of the granite there occurring in abundance.

Gran Reunion Americana.

The name of a secret political society founded in London by Francisco Miranda about the end of the eighteenth century. It had for its object the emancipation of the American colonies from Spain, and had great influence in fomenting the revolutionary spirit. Among its members were Bolivar, San Martin, O'Higgins, Nariño, Montufar and others, who became conspicuous in the war for independence. *v.* **Lautaro Society, The.**

Grauer Bund, *v.* **Gray League.**

Graybacks.

A name given during the American Civil War, by the Federal soldiers to the Confederates, in allusion to their gray uniforms. *v.* **Bluebellies.**

Gray League (German, "Grauer Bund").

A German league in the present canton of Grisons, Switzerland, formed in 1424. In 1497–8, in company with the Gotteshausbund, it became allied with the Swiss cantons.

Gray's Inn, *v.* **Inns of Court.**

Gray-skin (Norwegian, " Graafeld ").

A surname of Harold II, King of the Norwegians from 950–63.

Great, The,

A surname given to the following :—

Affonso de Albuquerque, a celebrated Portuguese navigator (1452 or 3–1515), the founder of the Portuguese empire in the East. Also called the **Portuguese Mars.**

Albertus Magnus. *v.* **Magnus.**

Alfonso III (or Alphonso), King of Asturias and Leon (848–912).

Alexander III (356–323 B.C.), a famous conqueror, King of Macedon, son of Philip of Macedon. Also called the **Conqueror of the World.**

Alfred, King of the West Saxons (849–901).

Amadeus V, Count of Savoy (1249–1323).

Bruno (925–65), brother of Otto I, of Germany, made archbishop of Cologne, and duke of Lorraine in 953.

Canute (Cnut or Knut), King of England, Denmark and Norway (c. 994–1035).

Casimir III, King of Poland (1309–70).

Charles I (or Charlemagne), King of the Franks and Emperor of the Romans (c. 742 or 7–814).

Charles II (or III), Duke of Lorraine, 1604–75).

Great, The (*continued*).—

Charles Emmanuel I, Duke of Savoy (1562–1630).

Constantine I (Flavius Valerius Aurelius Constantinus), Roman Emperor, (272–337).

Cosmo (or Cosimo) de' Medici, Grand Duke of Tuscany (1519–74).

Cyrus, the founder of the Persian Empire (d. 529 B.C.).

Donatus, bishop of Carthage in 315, elected by the rigorists or opponents of the moderate party or " traditors " (*v.* **Donatists).**

Emanuel I (Manoel), King of Portugal, (1469–1521). Also called " The Happy."

Ferdinand I, King of Castile and Leon (d. 1065). He assumed the title of emperor of Spain in 1056.

Frederick II, King of Prussia, (1712–86).

Prince Vasili Galitzin, a Russian commander and politician (1633–1713).

Gustavus (II) Adolphus of Sweden (1594–1632). *v.* **Lion of the North.**

Hanno, a leader of the aristocratic party at Carthage, (fl. c. 3rd century B.C.), an opponent of Hamilcar Barca and Hannibal.

Herod I, King (40–4 B.C.) of Judea.

Hugues (or Hugh), Count of Paris and Duke of France (d. 956); also called " the White."

Ivan III, Grand Duke of Moscow (d. 1505).

John (João) I, King of Portugal (1357 – 1433). Married Philippa, daughter of John, Duke of Lancaster.

Great, The (*continued*).—

Justinian I (Flavius Anicius Justinianus), Byzantine emperor, (probably 483–565) (*v.* **Justinian Code**).

Khusrau (or Chosroes) I, King of Persia (r. 531–79). Also called the Just or the Generous (Nouschirvan).

Leo I, Byzantine emperor (c. 400–74), also surnamed " the Thracian."

Louis XIV, King of France, 1638–1715), also called **Old Bona fide**, and **le Roi Soleil** (*v.* **Grand, Le**).

Louis I, King of Hungary and Poland (1326–82).

Mahmud of Ghazni, Sultan of Ghazni (c. 971–1030).

Matteo Visconti, Lord of Milan, (1250–1323).

Maximilian I, Duke of Bavaria (1573–1651).

Matthias I, Corvinus, King of Hungary (1442–90).

Mohammed II, Sultan of Turkey (c. 1430–81). Also **the Father of Good Works** and **the Conqueror**,

Napoleon I, Emperor of the French (1769–1821).

Pedro III, King of Aragon (1239–85).

Nicholas I (pope, 858–67).

Otto (or Otho) I, Emperor of the Holy Roman Empire (912–73).

Peter I, Alexeievitch, Czar of Russia (1672–1725).

Pompey (Cneius Pompeius Magnus) a famous Roman general (106–48 B.C.).

Procopius, Andrew, a noted Hussite leader (d. 1434).

Roger Bernard, Comte de Foix, (fl. 1223–41).

Sigismund, King of Poland (1467–1548).

Great, The (*continued*).—

Sancho III, King of Navarre from 1001–35.

Sapor II, King of Persia from c. 310–c. 380.

St. Dionysius, a theologian, bishop of Alexandria, c. 247 (b. towards the end of 2nd century—d. 265).

St. Gertrude, a German mystic (1256–1311).

St. Gregory I, pope of Rome (c. 540–604). He it was who sent Augustine to Ethelbert, King of Kent, in 597.

St. Leo I (d. 461), pope from 440–61.

St. Vladimir, Grand Prince of Russia from 980–1015) (d. 1015). He extended the Russian dominions and promoted Christianity.

Theodoric, King of the East Goths (c. 454–526).

Theodosius I, Roman emperor (c. 346–95).

Waldemar, King of Denmark from 1157–82.

Waldemar, Margrave of Brandenburg from 1308–19.

Great American Traveller, The.

A self-bestowed surname of Daniel Pratt (1809–87), an eccentric person, who spent a large part of his time in lecturing through the United States. He lived upon charity.

Great Banbury Case, The, *v.* under **Tichborne Trial, The.**

Great Bell of Moscow, *v.* **Czar Kolokol.**

Great Captain, The (Spanish "El Gran Capitano").

A surname of Gonsalvo Hernandez de Cordova, a celebrated Spanish general (1453–1515).

Great Cham of Literature, The, v. Great Moralist, The.

Great Charter, The, v. Magna Charta.

Great Commoner, The.

William Pitt (afterwards Earl of Chatham), (1708–78), was so called as being a commoner and not a peer. Also called the British Cicero. A name also applied to William Ewart Gladstone (1809–98), in allusion to his having on more than one occasion declined the offer of a peerage. Also called the Grand Old Man, the People's William (or Will), and the Napoleon of Oratory. In American history the name has been applied to Henry Clay (1777–1852) and Thaddeus Stevens (1773–1868), American statesmen.

Great Condé, The (French, "le grand Condé").

A name given to Louis II de Bourbon, Prince de Condé, a celebrated French general, called during the lifetime of his father (Henri II) the duc d'Enghien (1621–86); also called le Héros de l'Histoire (the hero of history).

Great Dauphin, The.

The son of Louis XIV (1661–1711). His father Louis XIV died in 1715. v. Second Dauphin, The.

Great Dismal Swamp.

Name applied to a morass in south-eastern Virginia and north-eastern North Carolina, extending 30 to 40 miles southward from near Norfolk. Contains Lake Drummond, and is traversed by the Dismal Swamp Canal, connecting Chesapeake Bay and Albemarle Sound. A portion of the swamp has been reclaimed. Cf. "Dred: a Tale of the Dismal Swamp," by Mrs. H. B. Stowe (1856).

Great Duke, The.

The first Duke of Wellington (1769–1852). Also called the "Iron Duke."

Great Eagle, The, v. Light of the West, The.

Great Earl, The, v. Bell-the-Cat.

Great Earl of Cork, The.

Richard Boyle, an English politician (1707–62), created first earl of Cork in 1620, is commonly so called. He became lord treasurer of Ireland in 1631.

Great Eastern.

A steamship, the largest vessel ever constructed. Designed by I. K. Brunel, and launched at Millwall in 1858; made its first voyage across the Atlantic, June 1860; frequently used from 1865 in cable-laying; made a coal-hulk in 1884, and in 1886 was sold to be broken up for old iron. Length 680 feet, width 83 feet, depth 58 feet; registered tonnage about 19,000 tons. Since exceeded in length, but not in tonnage, by the "Deutschland," (685 feet), and the "Oceanic" (704 feet).

Great Elector, The.

A surname of Frederick William, Elector of Brandenburg (1620–88).

Great Harry.

The first warship of the British Navy, built in 1488, in the reign of Henry VII. It was a three-masted vessel, and said to have cost £14,000. Supposed to have been accidentally burned at Woolwich in 1533.

Great Latin War, The.

A war between Rome and Latium (340–338, B.C.), ending in the subjugation of the latter. Cf. Latin War, The.

Great Letter-writer of France, The, *v.* Solon of French Prose, The.

Great Magician of the North.

A surname given to Sir Walter Scott by Professor John Wilson (" Christopher North "). *v.* Wizard of the North, and cf. Magician of the North, The.

Great Marquis, The.

A surname popularly given to the Marquis of Pombal (Sebastião José de Carvalho e Mello), a famous Portuguese statesman (1699–1782) ; also to the first Marquis of Montrose (James Graham), a noted Scottish nobleman and soldier (1612–50).

Great Master of Love, The (Italian, " Gran maestro d'amore ").

A name given by Petrarch to the troubadour Arnaud Daniel. (Hueffer, "Troubadours," p. 45.)

Great Minstrel, The,

A surname given to Sir Walter Scott (1771–1832) by the "Edinburgh Review."

Great Mogul.

An extinct title borne by the chief of the Moguls or the empire founded in Hindustan by Baber, fifteenth century. After the death of Aurung-Zeb (Aurang-Zebe or Aureng-Zebe) in 1707, the empire was split up and the power passed to the Mahrattas and British. The last (nominal) emperor was deposed in 1857.

Great Mogul Diamond.

A Indian diamond said to have been seen at the court of Aurung-Zeb in 1665, and to have weighed 280 carats. By some it is identified with the Koh-i-noor (q.v.), and by others with the Orloff Diamond (q.v.).

Great Moralist, The.

A surname often given to Dr. Samuel Johnson, an English lexicographer, essayist and poet, (1709–84). Also called the Great Seer, the Literary Colossus, the Great Cham of Literature, the Leviathan of Literature, Ursa Major, the Giant of Literature, the Polyphemus of Literature, the English Socrates.

Great Mother of the Gods, The.

Cybele, or Rhea, the wife of Cronos (Saturnus) and mother of the Olympian Gods.

Great Pacificator, The.

A surname given to Henry Clay, an American statesman, (1777–1852), alluding to his success in reconciling sectional differences resulting from the Missouri Compromise (q.v.).

Great Pan, The, *v.* Patriarch of Ferney, The.

Great Paul.

A famous bell hung in St. Paul's Cathedral, London, in

1882. Weight about 17½ tons, height 8 feet 10 inches, and cost £3,000. It is only used on the occasion of the death or funeral of one of the members of the royal family, the bishop and lord mayor of London, or the dean of the cathedral.

Great Rebellion, The.

In English history, the war waged by the Parliamentarian army against Charles I, from 1642 to his execution in 1649, and the subsequent maintenance by force of a government opposed to the excluded sovereign, Charles II, until the Restoration in 1660.

Great Seer, The, v. Great Moralist, The.

Great Sow, The.

A surname given to Isabella of Bavaria, wife of Charles VI of France, in allusion to her dissolute life.

Great Storm, The.

A name given to the memorable storm of November 26–7, 1703. It destroyed the first Eddystone lighthouse, many vessels were wrecked, large numbers of people drowned, and the damage to property was enormous.

Great Table Diamond, The.

A famous royal Indian diamond, ranked by Tavernier, who saw it in Golconda in 1642, as the third in size and quality seen by him. It weighed about 242$\frac{5}{16}$ carats. It has disappeared, and it has been suggested that the Russian Table Diamond may be a part of it. The latter diamond weighs 68 carats.

Great Trek, The.

A name given to the great emigration of Dutch settlers from Cape Colony in 1836–7. This brought about the first colonization of the country beyond the Orange River. What is called the Second Trek, took place in 1844–5, and was an emigration from the country between the Orange and Vaal rivers. These trekkers founded the South African Republic.

Great Tom.

A bell, weighing about 17,000 lbs., in the tower of the Tom Gate of Christ Church, Oxford. It is tolled every night at ten minutes past nine (closing time).

Great Triumvirate of Italian Literature.

A collective name given to Dante Alighieri (1265–1321), Petrarch (Francesco Petrarca) (1304–74), and Giovanni Boccaccio (1313–75). Cf. **Immortal Four of Italy, The.**

Great Unknown, The.

One of the surnames given to Sir Walter Scott (1771–1832), in allusion to the authorship of the Waverley Novels, which was not divulged publicly until February 23, 1827. Cf. Hood's " Ode to the Great Unknown " (1825), ed. 1871, Moxon, vol v. p. 44. *v.* **Ariosto of the North** and **Wizard of the North.**

Great Unwashed, The.

A phrase alluding to the working-class, first used by Edmund Burke (1729–97) and afterwards by Sir Walter Scott (1771–1832).

Great Wall of China.

A wall begun by the Emperor Tsin Chihwangti 214 B.C., (finished 204 B.C.) as a defence against northern tribes. Extends from Shanhai-kwan, lat. 40° N., long. 119°50′ E., along the northern frontiers of Chihli, Shansi, Shensi and Kansu, to about lat. 39° 50′ N., long. 99° E. Length about 1500 miles.

Great Western, The.

A famous steamship, built by I. K. Brunel and launched at Bristol in July, 1837. Length 212 feet, breadth 35 feet 4 inches. Her engines were of 1,440 h.p., and she was of 1,340 tons register. She started from Bristol April 8, 1838, and reached New York in fourteen days.

Great Witch of Balwery, The.

A popular surname for one Margaret Aiken, a Scotchwoman of the latter part of the sixteenth century, accused of witchcraft, and who, to save her life, informed upon others.

Grecian Coffee House.

A noted London coffee-house in Devereux Court, on the left of Essex Street. The resort of the wits of the eighteenth century.

Greek Commentator, The.

A surname given to Fernando Nunez de Guzman (Nonnius Pincianus), a Spanish savant (1473–1553).

Greenbacks *v.* Bluebacks and Greenback Party.

Greenbackers, *v.* Greenback Party.

Greenback Party.

In American politics, a political party, formed in 1874, which urged the suppression of banks of issue, and the payment, in whole or in part, of the United States debt in greenbacks. It nominated as candidates for the presidency Peter Cooper in 1879, General James B. Weaver in 1880, and General Benjamin F. Butler in 1884. Since that time it has disappeared as a distinctive party, though the Populist or People's Party (q.v.) may perhaps be regarded as its successor.

Green-bag Inquiry, The.

The name given to an investigation into the nature of the contents of a green-bag containing reports (alleged to be seditious) on the state of the country, laid before Parliament, February 3, 1817, by the Prince Regent. The Habeas Corpus Act (q.v.) was suspended (March 3) in connection with this inquiry.

Green Count, The.

A surname given to Amadeus VI, a count of Savoy (1334–83), a grandson of Amadeus V.

Green-eyed Monster, The.

A synonym for jealousy used by Shakspere. (Cf. "Othello," act 3, sc. 3.)

Green Horse, The.

A nickname given to the 5th Dragoon Guards, from their green velvet facings. Also called "The Princess Charlotte of Wales's." Cf. White Horse, The.

Green Howards, The.

A nickname given to the nineteenth regiment of foot, from the Hon. Charles Howard, who was their colonel from 1738–48.

Green Isle.

A name sometimes given to Ireland, *v.* Emerald Isle, The.

Green Mountain Boys.

The soldiers from Vermont in the American Revolution, first organized under this name by Ethan Allen in 1775.

Green Mountain State.

A popular name of Vermont, which is traversed by the Green Mountains.

Green Vault, The (German, "Das grüne Gewölbe").

A series of eight rooms in the royal palace at Dresden, containing an unrivalled collection of precious stones, works of art, etc. So called from the colour of its original decorations.

Gregorian Calendar.

The present reformed calendar is so called from Pope Gregory XIII (1502–85), who introduced it in 1582 to correct an error which had accumulated to such an extent that the civil year (Julian Calendar) was then ten days behind the solar year. France, Italy, Spain, Denmark, Holland, Portugal and Flanders adopted the New Style in 1582, Germany in 1584, Switzerland at about the same time (1583–4), Hungary in 1587, Scotland in 1600 and England in 1752, Russia being the last to make the correction, at all events officially. In England the rectifica-tion was made by reckoning the day after September 2, 1752, as the 14th (the error had then amounted to eleven days).

Gretna Green.

A farmsteading near the village of Springfield, Dumfries-shire, Scotland, eight miles north-west of Carlisle. The name was afterwards applied to the village, which became notorious for the celebration of irregular marriages contracted by runaway parties from England. These marriages were rendered invalid (unless one of the parties has resided for some weeks in Scotland) by an Act passed in 1856.

Grolier Club.

A New York club, founded in 1884 and incorporated in 1888. Its object is the encouragement and promotion of book-making as an art, and the occasional publication of works designed to advance and illustrate that art. From a noted French bibliophile, Jean Grolier de Servières, vicomte d'Aguisy, known as Jean Grolier.

Gros, Le.

A surname of Charles III, King of France (839–88), and Emperor of the Romans (as King of France Charles II); also of Louis VI, King of France (c.1078–1137).

Grotta del Cane (Italian, "Grotto of the Dog").

A grotto near Pozzuoli, six miles west of Naples, so named from the carbonic acid gas collecting near the floor of the cave which will kill a dog, while a man, being taller and above the gas, escapes. A dog is often taken into the grotto until nearly asphyxiated and brought out again when it revives, to show visitors.

Grub Street.

A London street, now known as Milton Street. It is in the parish of St. Giles, Cripplegate, and runs from Fore Street to Chiswell Street. Formerly noted " as the abode of small authors, who as writers of trashy pamphlets and broadsides become the butts for the wits of their time . . . The name ' Grub Street,' as opprobrious, seems, however, to have been first applied by their opponents to the writings of Foxe, the martyrologist, who resided in the street." (Hare, "London," i. 273).

Grumbletonians.

A nickname in the latter part of the seventeenth century for members of the Country party (q.v.) as opposed to the Court party (q.v.) in Great Britain.

Grundy, Mrs., *v.* Mrs. Grundy.

Guardian, The.

A periodical published in London in 1713, and edited by Steele. It comprised 176 numbers (51 of them by Addison). It followed, but was inferior to the "Spectator" (q.v.).

Guelfic Order.

A Hanoverian order of knighthood founded in 1815 by George IV (then prince regent) and entitled the Royal Hanoverian Guelfic Order.

Guelfs (or Guelphs).

The papal and popular party of Italy in the middle ages, opposed to the Ghibellines, the imperial and aristocratic party. The Welfs (Guelfs) were a powerful family of Germany, so called from Welf I, in the time of Charlemagne. His descendants founded the princely house of Brunswick and Hanover, to which the present royal family of England belongs.

Guerre des Amoureux, La (French, " The Lovers' War ").

A name given to a civil war in 1580 during Henry V's reign. So called from the jealousies and rivalries of the leaders.

Guerrière, La.

A British warship captured by the United States ship " Constitution " during the war of 1812. *v.* Constitution.

Gueux (French, " Beggars, ragamuffins.")

The league of Flemish nobles organized in 1566 to resist the introduction of the Inquisition into the Low Counties by Philip II. The name was previously given them in contempt, and borne by their followers in the succeeding war.

Guinea Pig.

A popular name for a company director (with or without ability), whose name on the prospectus is a " draw " to the public, but who merely goes on the board for the sake of the director's fees (guineas).

Gulf States.

A collective name often applied to those of the United States of American bordering on the Gulf of Mexico, viz., Florida, Alabama, Mississippi, Louisiana and Texas.

Gullians.

A name sometimes given to the followers of William III of England (1650–1702).

Gunpowder Plot.

A conspiracy of certain Roman Catholics having for its object the destruction of James I, and the Lords and Commons in Parliament House, London. The leaders were Catesby, Percy, Digby, Winter, Guy Fawkes and others. It was foiled by the arrest of Fawkes on the night of November 4–5, 1605, as he was entering the cellar under Parliament House, previously filled with barrels of gunpowder by the conspirators.

Guy Fawkes' Day.

November 5, the anniversary of the discovery of the Gunpowder Plot (q.v.).

Habeas Corpus Act.

An Act of Parliament passed in the reign of Charles II (May 27, 1679), by virtue of which no one can be imprisoned without being brought to trial to determine whether his committal be just. Parliament may, however, in a great emergency, suspend the Act for a specified time if necessary.

Hadrian's Wall, *v.* Picts' Wall.

Hail, Columbia.

A patriotic American song, written by Joseph Hopkinson in 1798, for the benefit of an a ctor. The tune was then called " The President's March." Under the political excitement of the time the song became very popular, and, though possessing little poetical merit, is still kept in vogue by the force of patriotic sentiment.

Hakluyt Society.

A society established in London in 1846, with the object of printing annotated English editions of rare works on early geography, travels and history. Named in honour of Richard Hakluyt, an English geographer (c. 1552–1616).

Half-Breeds.

A nickname given in derision to the Stalwarts (q.v.) by the supporters of President Garfield's administration. Also called **Feather-Heads**.

Half Moon.

The vessel in which Henry Hudson sailed from Holland for America in 1609. He explored the coast in her, and went up the river named after him, the Hudson. Also an old house standing in Aldersgate, London, formerly the " Half Moon Tavern." It was much frequented by literary men, and is now also called, for no particular reason, " Shakspere's House."

Hallelujah Victory, The.

A victory said to have been gained by the Britons over the Picts and Scots at Mold, Flintshire, March, 30, 430, so named from the war-cry adopted by the Britons at the suggestion of St. Germain, Bishop of Auxerre, who was present **at** the battle.

Hammer, The.

A popular surname of Judas Maccabæus (d. 160 B.C.), the second of the five sons of Matthias the Hasmonean.

Hammer and Scourge of England, The.

A surname of Sir William Wallace, a Scottish patriot and national hero (c. 1274–1305).

Hammer of Heretics, The (Latin, " Malleus Hereticorum ").

A surname of Pierre d'Ailly (1350–c. 1420), president of the Council of Constance 1414–8. Also called the **Eagle of the Doctors of France.** Also a surname of St. Augustine (354–430) and Johann Faber, a German controversialist and opponent of the Reformation (1478–1541), from the title of one of his works.

Hammer of the Scots, The.

A surname given to Edward I, King of England (1239–1307). His son caused the words " Edwardus Longus Scotorum Malleus hic est," to be inscribed on his tomb in Westminster Abbey.   Also called **Longshanks** and the **English Justinian.**

Hampton Court Conference.

A conference appointed by James I at Hampton Court in 1604, to settle the disputes between the Puritan and High-Church parties in the Church of England. It was conducted on three days, January 14, 16 and 18, and resulted in a few alterations of the liturgy, but entirely failed to secure the objects sought by the Puritans. An important indirect result was the revision of the Bible, called King James's or authorized version, which was suggested at the time.

Handel and Haydn Society.

An American musical society, founded at Boston in 1815.

Handel Festival.

A triennial musical festival, held at the Crystal Palace, Sydenham.   So called in commemoration of the celebrated musical composer, G. F. Handel (1685–1759).

Handel Society.

An English society for the publication of Handel's works, formed in 1843, and dissolved in 1848.   A German society (Händel-Gesellschaft), with a similar object, was formed in 1856.

Handsome, The.

A surname of Frederick III, King of Germany (1286–1330); of Philip I, King of Castile (1478–1506).

Handsome Englishman, The (French, " Le bel Anglais ").

A surname given by the French troops under Marshal Turenne to John Churchill, Duke of Marlborough (1650–1722), alluding to his graceful manners and bearing.   *v.* also **Silly Duke, The.**   Arbuthnot, in his " History of John Bull," calls Churchill **Humphrey Hocus.**

Handsome Feilding, *v.* Beau Feilding.

Handsome Swordsman, The, *v.* Dandy King, The.

Hanging Judge, The.

A surname given to the Earl of Norbury (d. 1831), who was Chief Justice of the Common Pleas in Ireland 1820–7. He is said to have been in the habit of jesting with criminals when passing sentence of death upon them.

Hanover, House of, *v.* House of Hanover.

Hanover, Treaty of, *v.* Treaty of Hanover.

Hanseatic League.

A medieval confederation of cities of northern Germany and adjacent countries, called the Hanse towns, at one time numbering about ninety, with affiliated cities in nearly all parts of Europe, for the promotion of commerce by sea and land, and for its protection against pirates, robbers and hostile governments. Its origin is commonly dated from a compact between Hamburg and Lübeck in 1241, and the last general assembly, representing six cities, was held in 1669. The name, however, was retained by the union of the free cities of Lübeck, Hamburg and Bremen, which are now members of the German Empire.

Hansom Cab (or Hansom).

A two-wheeled patent safety cab was so named from its inventor, Joseph Aloysius Hansom, an English architect (1803–82). The principal feature of the original vehicle was the " suspended " axle. It had no outside seat.

Happy, The, *v.* Great, The. Emanuel I.

Happy Islands, *v.* Fortunate Islands, The.

Hardi, Le (French, " The Bold ").

A surname of Philip III, King of France (1245–85); also of Philip, Duke of Burgundy (1342–1404).

Hardshell Baptists, *v.* Softshell Baptists.

Hardshell Democrats, *v.* Softshell Democrats.

Harefoot.

A surname of Harold I, King of the English (d. 1040), who reigned from 1035–40.

Harmonists.

A communistic religious body organized by George Rapp in Würtemberg on the model of the primitive church, and conducted by him to Pennsylvania in 1803. Their settlement there was called Harmony (whence the name). Also called " Rappists " and " Economites."

Harmony Society, *v.* Harmonists.

Harness Prize, The.

A triennial prize for the study of Shaksperian literature (consisting of three years' interest on a sum of £500), awarded at the University of Cambridge (first time in 1874), founded in memory of the Rev. William Harness (1790–1869).

Harry of the West.

A nickname given to Henry Clay, an American statesman (1777–1852), who for many years represented Kentucky in the Senate of the United States.

Harry Twitcher.

A nickname given to Henry Peter Brougham, Baron Brougham and Vaux, a celebrated English statesman, orator, jurist and scientist (1778–1868), in allusion to an involuntary twitching of his facial muscles.

Hartford Convention.

A political assembly which met at Hartford December 15, 1814–Jan 5, 1815. It published a report protesting against the war with England, and against the action of the United States Government in refusing to pay the expenses of defending Massachusetts and Connecticut, because those states refused to place their militias under the control of the Federal Government. Its proceedings were carried on in secret, and the convention was suspected at the time of treason.

Harvest Moon, The.

The name given to the moon at the autumn equinox, c. September 23, when it rises at nearly the same time for seven successive days.

Hasmonean, The.

A surname of Mattathias, the father of the Maccabees.

Hassler Expedition.

A scientific expedition made in the United States Coast Survey steamer " Hassler," P. C. Johnson commanding, between December 4, 1871, and August, 1872. Starting from Philadelphia, the route embraced the West Indies, Brazilian coast, Strait of Magellan, and the Pacific Coast and islands to San Francisco, California Deep-sea dredgings were made at all favourable points.

Hatches, Matches and Dispatches.

A jocular name for the column of " Births," " Marriages " and " Deaths " in the newspapers.

Hawkabites (or Hawcubites).

A club of dissolute young men, associated in London, after the Restoration, for the pleasure of fighting. " A class of ruffians whose favourite amusement was to swagger by night about town, breaking windows, upsetting sedans, beating quiet men," etc. (" Old and New London," iv. 166).

Hawkeye State, The.

A popular surname for the State of Iowa, in allusion to a famous Indian chief (Hawkeye), who was at one time a terror to the early settlers there.

Haymarket, The.

A London market, established in 1644, on the site now partly covered by the Criterion Restaurant and Theatre, and Lower Regent Street. Abolished in 1830.

Heart of England, The.

A surname given to Warwickshire, from its central position (Cf. Michael Drayton's " Polyolbion," xiii.).

Heart of Midlothian, The.

A popular surname for the old jail in Edinburgh (capital of the county of Midlothian), taken down in 1817. The title of one of Sir Walter Scott's novels.

Heaven-sent Minister, The, *v.* **Bottomless Pit, The.**

Hecla, *v.* **Fury.**

Hector of Germany, The.

A surname of Joachim II, Elector of Brandenburg (1514–71).

Hectors, *v.* **Tityre Tus.**

Heilbronn, Union of, *v.* **Union of Heilbronn.**

Heir of the Republic, The.

A surname given to Napoleon Bonaparte (1769–1821), who assumed the title of Emperor after being First Consul of the Republic for nearly five years.

Hell Fire Clubs.

Clubs consisting of reckless and unscrupulous men and women. A number of these have existed. Three such associations were suppressed in London in 1721.

Hellmuth the Taciturn.

A surname of Hellmuth Karl Bernhard von Moltke, a celebrated Prussian field-marshal (1800–91), who, it is said, although master of several languages, never betrayed himself in any of them.

Helvetia.

The ancient Latin, and modern poetic name for Switzerland.

Henricians.

A sect of religious reformers in Switzerland and southern France in the twelfth century, followers of Henry of Lausanne. Also the followers or adherents of the Emperor Henry IV, who opposed Gregory VII in favour of the anti-Pope Clement III.

Henry Beauclerc (or Beauclerk), *v.* **Beauclerc.**

Henry Clay.

An American trotting stallion, the founder of the Clay family of trotters. By Andrew Jackson, by Grand Bashaw, a supposed Arabian imported from Algiers.

Henry the Minstrel, *v.* **Blind Harry.**

Hercules.

A British armoured war-ship, launched in 1867. Length, 325 feet, breadth 59 feet, displacement 8,840 tons.

Hercules, Pillars of, *v.* **Pillars of Hercules.**

Hercules of Music, The.

A surname given to Christopher Willibald Gluck, a celebrated German operatic composer (1714–87). Also the **Michelangelo of Music.**

Hermits of St. Paul, *v.* **Paulists.**

Herne the Hunter.

A traditionary personage, supposed to haunt Windsor Forest near an old oak known as Herne's Oak. It was blown down in 1863, and was supposed to be about 650 years old. Queen Victoria planted a young oak on the spot. (Cf. W. H. Ainsworth's novel, "Windsor Castle." Herne the Hunter is mentioned and Herne's Oak figures in Shakspere's "Merry Wives of Windsor," acts 4 and 5).

Hero of a Hundred Fights, The.

A surname given to Horatio, Viscount Nelson (1758–1805). *v.* Hero of the Nile, The. Also applied to the Duke of Wellington (1769–1852). *v.* Europe's Liberator.

Hero of Modern Italy, The.

A surname given to Giuseppe Garibaldi, a celebrated Italian patriot (1807–82), in allusion to his services in the cause of Italian independence. Also called the People's Captain ("el Capitano des Popolo") and the Liberator of Italy.

Hero of the Nile, The.

A surname given to Admiral Horatio (afterwards Viscount) Nelson (1758–1805), from his victory over the French fleet, August 1, 1798. Also called the Hero of a Hundred Fights.

Héros de la Fable, Le (French, " The Hero of Fable ").

A surname given to Henri II de Lorraine, duc de Guise (1614–64).

Héros de l'Histoire, Le, *v.* Great Condé, The.

Herring Pond, The.

A popular nickname for the Atlantic Ocean. In England, the other side of the Herring Pond refers to America.

Herrings, Battle of the, *v.* Battle of the Herrings.

Hesiod Cooke.

Name given to Thomas Cooke, an English writer (1703–56), from his translation of Hesiod.

Hetæria Philike (ἑταιρία φιλική).

A secret political society, founded at Odessa in 1814, for the purpose of liberating Greece from the Turkish dominion. In 1820 it chose as its leader Prince Alexander Hypsilanti, who in 1821 inaugurated the Greek war for independence.

Hibbert Lectures.

A foundation instituted by the trustees of Robert Hibbert, a West India merchant, who died in 1849. For many years the trustees applied the funds mainly to the higher culture of students for the Unitarian ministry, but in 1878 resolved to institute Hibbert Lectures, with a view to capable and really honest treatment of unsettled problems in theology apart from the interest of any particular church or system. Amongst the lecturers have been Max Müller, Page Renouf, Renan, Rhys Davids, Kuenen, Beard, Réville, Pfleiderer, Rhys, Sayce and Hatch. (" Chambers' Encyclopædia," v. 702).

Hibernia.

Ireland. Also called " Erin," the " Emerald Isle," and " Insula Sanctorum." *v.* Island of Saints.

Hickory Pole Canvass.

The presidential canvass of 1828 on behalf of Jackson. *v.* Old Hickory.

Hicksites.

A seceding body of Friends or Quakers, followers of Elias Hicks, formed in the United States in 1827, and holding Socinian doctrines.

Hicks' Hall.

The Sessions House of the

county of Middlesex, built in 1612, and taken down in 1782.

High-born Demosthenes, The, v. Silent, The.

Highbury Barn.

The name of a former place of amusement and public gardens at Highbury, London.

Highflyer.

A bay racehorse by Herod, foaled in 1774. He was the property of Richard Tattersall, founder of "Tattersall's" (q.v.) in London, who made £25,000 by his purchase. "Tattersall's" has always attributed the establishment of its fortune to the success of this horse. Highflyer is in the direct male line from the Byerly Turk (q.v.), the third great family of English thoroughbred stallions. *Rice.*

Highland Laddie, The.

A surname given by his Scottish admirers to Prince Charles Edward Stuart, the Young Pretender (q.v.).

Highland Mary.

The name given to Mary Campbell and Mary Morison, sweethearts of the poet Burns.

Hilary Term, v. St. Hilary's Day.

Hispania.

The ancient Latin and modern poetic name for Spain. The Greek name *Iberia* is also used in modern poetry.

Hodge.

A name given to the typical English peasant.

Hogarth Club.

A London club for artists,

established in 1870. It has a life class, sketching club and reading-room.

Hogarth of Novelists, The.

A surname given to Henry Fielding, a celebrated English novelist and playwright (1707–54). Also called the Prose Homer of Human Nature (by Byron).

Hohenzollern.

A German princely family. It ruled over Brandenburg from 1415, and has furnished the kings of Prussia since 1701, and the German emperors since 1871.

Holy, The, v. Prince, The.

Holy Alliance, The.

A league formed by the sovereigns of Russia, Austria and Prussia, in person, after the fall of Napoleon, signed at Paris, September 26, 1815, and afterwards joined by all the other European sovereigns except those of Rome and England. Its professed object was to unite their respective governments in a Christian brotherhood, but its real one was to perpetuate existing dynasties by their joint opposition to all attempts at change. A special clause debarred any member of the Bonaparte family from ascending a European throne. The league came to an end after the French Revolution of 1830.

Holy City, The.

A name indicating various cities according to the religion of the persons using it. Applied to Allahabad, by the Indian Mohammedans ; Benares, by the Hindus; Cuzco, by the Incas; Jerusalem, by Jews and Christians; Mecca, Medina and Damascus, by Mohammedans generally; Moscow and Kieff (or Kiev), by the Russians; and Rome, by Roman Catholics. *v.* also **Eternal City, The.**

Holy Grail, The.

A legendary cup or chalice supposed to have been of emerald, used by Christ at the Last Supper. In this vessel Joseph of Arimathea caught the last drops of Christ's blood as He was taken from the Cross. According to one account, it was carried by Joseph to Britain. The grail, according to another account, having been lost, it became the object of search or quest to knights-errant of all nations, none but a knight, perfectly chaste in thought and act, being qualified to discover it. The stories and poems concerning Arthur and the Knights of the Round Table are founded on this legend.

Holy Island, The, *v.* Island of Saints, The.

Holy League, The.

A league between Pope Julius II, Ferdinand of Aragon, and the States of Venice and Switzerland, formed in 1511 for the purpose of expelling Louis XII of France from Italy. A league between the Emperor Charles V, the Archbishops of Mainz and Salzburg, and the Dukes William and Louis of Bavaria, George of Saxony, and Eric and Henry of Brunswick, formed at Nuremberg July 10, 1538, for the support of the Roman Catholic faith in Germany, in opposition to the Smalkaldic League (q.v.). A league formed by the Roman Catholics in France in 1576, for the purpose of annihilating the Huguenot party, and elevating the Guises to the throne. It was supported by Philip II of Spain, and was finally overthrown by Henry IV in 1596.

Holy League of Cognac.

A league concluded May 22, 1656, between Pope Clement VII, Francis I of France, Milan and Venice, against the Emperor Charles V. Henry VIII was also in sympathy with the league. Also styled the "Clementine League."

Holy Maid of Kent, *v.* Nun of Kent.

Holy Mother of the Russians.

A name sometimes given to Moscow.

Holy Roman Empire.

The realm ruled by the emperor who claimed to be the representative of the ancient Roman emperors, and who asserted (in theory) authority over the nations of western and central Europe. Called "holy" from the interdependence of the empire and the church. It began with Charles the Great, King of the Franks, who was crowned Emperor of the West 800, and was succeeded by various Carolingian emperors. After Maximilian I and Charles V, the empire degenerated through the seventeenth and eighteenth centuries, and Francis II (Francis I of Austria) abdicated as the last emperor in

1806. The emperors were elected.

Holy Thorn, *v.* **Glastonbury Thorn.**

Holy Thursday.

Ascension Day is often so called. The name is sometimes (erroneously) applied to Maundy Thursday (q.v.).

Holy Week.

The week immediately preceding Easter.

Holywell Street.

A London street (now pulled down for the widening of the Strand), parallel to the Strand from Newcastle Street to St. Clement Danes Church, so named from a "holy well" in the locality. Formerly notorious as a place of sale for obscene literature.

Home Counties.

Middlesex, Surrey, Kent, Essex and Hertford (containing London and in its immediate neighbourhood) are known by this inclusive term.

Homer of Ferrara, The (Italian, "Omero Ferrarese").

A surname given (by Tasso) to Ludovico Ariosto. *v.* **Southern Scott, The.**

Homer of his Age, The.

A surname given to St. Angilbert, a Frankish poet (c. 740-814).

Homer of Orators, The, *v.* **Glorious Preacher, The.**

Homer of our Dramatic Poets, The.

A surname given (by Dryden) to William Shakspere, the greatest of dramatists (1564-1616). *v.* **Swan of Avon, Sweet.**

Homer of Philosophers, The.

A surname given to Plato, a famous Greek philosopher (429 or 7-347 B.C.).

Homer of Portugal, The.

A surname given to Luiz de Camoens (or Camoes), a celebrated Portuguese poet (c. 1524-80).

Homer of the French Drama, The.

A surname given (by Sir Walter Scott) to Pierre Corneille (le Grand Corneille), a celebrated French dramatist (1606-84), the **Father of French Tragedy.** Cf. **Virgil of the French Drama, The.**

Home Rule, *v.* **Home Rule Bills.**

Home Rule Bills.

Two Bills introduced into the British Parliament by Mr. Gladstone, with the object of providing a separate legislature for Ireland. The first, introduced in 1886, was defeated on the second reading (June 7); the second, introduced in 1893, passed the House of Commons (September 1), but was thrown out by the House of Lords (September 8) by 419 against 41 votes.

Home, Sweet Home.

A favourite English song. The music is in Bishop's opera "Clari, or the Maid of Milan." It is called a Sicilian air, but is probably Bishop's. Words by John Howard Payne.

Honest George.

A nickname of George Monk, Lord Albemarle (1608–70).

Honest John (or **Jack**).

A nickname of Lord Althorp (1782–1845).

Honest King, *v.* Re Galantuomo.

Honeyed Teacher, The, *v.* Mellifluous Doctor, The.

Hookey Walker.

A slang expression used to express incredulity. Sometimes abbreviated to " Walker."

Hoosiers, *v.* Hoosier State, The.

Hoosier State, The.

A popular surname of the State of Indiana, whose inhabitants are also frequently termed **Hoosiers.** By some said to be a corruption of husher, a common term for a bully in the Western States.

Hope Diamond, The.

A superb blue diamond, weighing, cut, 44⅜ carats, owned by the Hope family, and valued at from £20,000 to £30,000.

Hope Theatre, The.

A playhouse opened c. 1581 on Bankside, Southwark, London. Originally a bear-garden.

Hopkinsians.

Adherents of a theological system founded by Samuel Hopkins (1721-1803), and developed by Emmons and others.

Horace of France, The, *v.* French Horace, The.

Horatius Cocles of the Tyrol.

A surname given (for his defence of a bridge at Brixen, Tyrol, in 1798) by Napoleon I to General Alexandre Davy de la Pailleterie Dumas (1762–1806), father of Alexandre Dumas père the celebrated French novelist and playwright.

Hornet.

An American war-ship of 480 tons (18 guns rating). On February 12, 1813, near the mouth of the Demerara River, she fell in with the British war brigs " Espingle " (18 guns rating) and " Peacock," and captured the " Peacock."

Hospitalers of St. John of Jerusalem, Order of the, *v.* Order of the Hospitalers, etc.

Hospital Saturday.

A Saturday annually set apart in the streets, and elsewhere, for a collection on behalf of hospitals generally. Usually a Saturday in July.

Hospital Sunday.

A Sunday annually set apart for a - collection in churches, and elsewhere, on behalf of hospitals generally. The Sunday fixed upon for the purpose is, in England, that nearest June 15; in the United States it is the last Sunday in the year. *v.* Hospital Saturday.

Hotspur.

A surname of Henry Percy, son of Henry Percy, first Earl of Northumberland. Killed at the Battle of Shrewsbury, 1403.

Hotspur of Debate, The, *v.* Rupert of Debate, The.

House, The.

A name by which the London Stock Exchange is familiarly known. Also applied to either of the English Houses of Parliament.

House Beautiful.

The name of a place of rest mentioned in Bunyan's "Pilgrim's Progress."

House of Hanover.

The present reigning family of the United Kingdom of Great Britain and 'Ireland.

House of Nassau.

A princely European family, the reigning house in the Netherlands, descended from the line of Count Otto of Nassau (thirteenth century). The first prominent member was William the Silent, of Orange. Members of the house succeeded as stadholders, and from 1815 reigned as kings.

House of Orleans, *v.* Orleanists.

House of Plantagenet (or Anjou).

A line of English kings (1154–1399), founded by Henry II, son of Geoffrey, Count of Anjou, and Matilda, daughter of Henry I of England. In the direct line it became extinct on the death of Richard II in 1399.

House of Valois.

A French dynasty, a branch of the Capetian family. Reigned 1328–1589.

Hub of the Universe, The.

A surname given jokingly by O. W. Holmes (1809–95) to the State House of Boston, Mass., and afterwards extended to the city itself.

Huckster, The.

A surname given to Darius (r. 521–486 B.C.), son of Hystaspes, on account of his attention to trade and industry.

Huguenots.

The Reformed or Calvinistic communion of France in the sixteenth and seventeenth centuries. The Huguenots were the Puritans of France, noted in general for their austere virtues and the singular purity of their lives. They were frequently at war with the Catholics, but in spite of this and the massacre of St. Bartholomew (August 24, 1572), they continued numerous and powerful, and the Edict of Nantes (q.v.) secured to them full political and civil rights. Their political power was broken with the surrender of La Rochelle in 1628, and the revocation of the Edict of Nantes by Louis (1685); and the subsequent persecutions forced hundreds of thousands into exile to Prussia, the Netherlands, Switzerland, England, etc. Many settled in the colonies of New York, Virginia, etc., but especially in South Carolina. The name is sometimes applied at the present day to the descendants of the original Huguenots.

Hulsean Lectures.

A series of lectures, at Cambridge, on the Christian evidences, etc., paid for out of a fund bequeathed to the University by John Hulse, an English clergyman (1708–90).

Humphrey Hocus, *v.* Handsome Englishman, The.

Hundred Days, The (French, "Les Cent Jours").

The period of about 100 days (the middle of March to June 22, 1815), during which Napoleon I, after his escape from Elba, made his final effort to re-establish his empire. It ended in the crushing defeat at Waterloo and his abdication.

Hundred Towers, City of a (the), v. City of a Hundred Towers.

Hundred Years' War, The.

The series of wars between England and France, c. 1338–1453. The English, generally victors down to c. 1430, and rulers of a great part of France, were finally expelled entirely, except from Calais, which they held for about a century longer.

Hunter's Moon, The.

The name given to the moon when near the full next after the Harvest Moon (q.v.).

Huntingdonians.

A denomination of Calvinistic Methodists in England and Wales, adherents of George Whitefield and Selina, Countess of Huntingdon, after their separation from the Wesleys.

Hurricane, The, v. Modern Gracchus, The.

Hutin, Le (French, "The Quarreller").

A surname of Louis X, King of France (1289–1316).

Hyena, The Austrian, v. Austrian Hyena, The.

Hyksos, v. Shepherd Kings, The.

Iberia, v. Hispania.

Iconoclast Emperors.

Those Byzantine emperors who were noted for their opposition to image-worship in the Eastern Church. The contro-versy began with the edict of Leo the Isaurian in 726, and continued until the middle of the ninth century.

Iconoclasts.

A sect or party in the Eastern Empire in the eighth and ninth centuries, which opposed all use and honour or worship of icons or images, and destroyed them when in power. The party of Iconoclasts was originated by the Emperor Leo the Isaurian, and afterwards continued or revived by Constantine Copronymus and other emperors, especially Leo the Armenian and Theophilus. The emperors named treated those who honoured icons with great cruelty, and after the death of the last of them the party of Iconoclasts soon became extinct.

Idler, The.

A periodical established by Dr. Samuel Johnson (1709–84) in 1758. It extended to 103 numbers.

Idole du Temple, L' (French, "The Idol of the Temple").

A surname given to Marie Charlotte, Comtesse de Boufflers-Rouveret (1724-1800).

Îles Normandes (French, "Norman Isles").

The Channel Islands.

Illuminati (Latin, "The Enlightened").

A name given to different religious societies or sects because of their claim to perfection or enlightenment in religious matters. The most noted among them were the Alumbrados ("The Enlightened") of Spain in the sixteenth century; an ephemeral society of Belgium and northern France (also called Guérinets) in the seventeenth century; and an association of mystics in southern France in the eighteenth century, combining the doctrines of Swedenborg with the methods of the Freemasons.

Illuminator, The.

A surname of St. Gregory, the founder and patron saint of the Armenian Church (c. 257 –332). Consecrated patriarch of Armenia, c. 302.

Illustrious, The.

A surname of Hesychius, a Greek historical and biographical writer (fl. early in the sixth century).

Illustrious Doctor, The (Latin, " Doctor Solennis ").

A surname of Henry of Ghent, a scholastic philosopher (c. 1217–93).

Illustrious Infidel, The.

A surname given to Robert Green Ingersoll, an American lawyer, lecturer and politician (1833–99).

Immortal Dreamer, The.

A surname given to John Bunyan, the author of " Pilgrim's Progress " (1628–88). Also called the **Immortal Tinker** (he was a tinker by trade) and **Bishop Bunyan.**

Immortal Four of Italy, The.

A collective surname (given by H. W. Longfellow) to Italy's four greatest poets, viz.: Dante Alighieri (1265–1321), Petrarch (Francesco Petrarca), (1304–74), Ludovico Ariosto (1474–1533), and Bernardo Tasso (1544–95).

Immortals, The.

A joking nickname given to the members (forty in number) of the French Academy (q.v.). The Academy's motto is " À l'immortalité." Hence the nickname. Sometimes alluded to as the **Forty.**

Immortal Tinker, The, *v.* **Immortal Dreamer, The.**

Imperial City, The.

A name sometimes applied to the city of Rome. Also called the **Eternal City.**

Importants, The.

A French political clique formed after the death of Louis XIII, 1643. It intrigued against the Government unsuccessfully.

Impotent, The.

A surname of Henry IV, King of Castile (1425–74). The legitimacy of his daughter Joanna was questioned by the Cortès.

Incorruptible, The.

A surname of François-Joseph Maximilien Isidore de Robespierre, a celebrated French revolutionist (1759–94). Also called the **Sea-Green Incorruptible.**

Independence Day.

The anniversary of the Declaration of Independence (q.v.) of the United States of America, July 4, 1776. Also called the **Glorious 4th of July.**

Independent Order of Oddfellows, The, *v.* **Odd-fellows.**

Indian Æsop, The.

A surname given to Pilpay (or Bidpai), the supposed author of Indian fables. La Fontaine has made use of some of them.

Indian (or Sepoy) Mutiny.

The revolt against British authority in India, 1857–8. Its immediate cause was the introduction into the Sepoy Army of a new rifle, whose use required the touching of grease (on the cartridge); this offended the religious prejudices of the soldiers. The mutiny began at Meerut, May 10. The centres of activity were Delhi, Cawnpore (where in July a massacre of Europeans was ordered by Nana Sahib), and Lucknow. Lucknow's garrison was relieved by Havelock in September, and again by Campbell in November;Delhi was besieged and taken in 1857; Lucknow was finally conquered in March, 1858, and the last resistance overcome in the same year. The last Mogul (titular emperor) was banished.

Indian Summer, *v.* St. Martin's Summer.

Indolent King, The, *v.* Roi Panade, Le.

Inexpiable War, The.

A war between Carthage and her mercenaries (241–238 B.C.). The latter were unsuccessful.

Infâme Catin du Nord, L' (French, "The Infamous Harlot of the North ").

A surname given to Elizabeth Petrovna, Empress of Russia (1709–62), from her sensuality.

Infamous Harlot of the North, The, *v.* Infâme Catin du Nord, L'.

Infant Roscius, The, *v.* Young Roscius, The.

Infanta Maria Teresa.

An armoured cruiser of 7,000 tons, the flagship of Admiral Cervera in the Spanish-American War (q.v.). She was sunk in the Battle of Santiago, July 3, 1898; was raised under the direction of Naval Constructor Hobson; and was abandoned in a gale north of San Salvador, November 1, 1898.

Inflexible.

An ironclad British twin-screw double-turreted battle-ship, launched April, 1876. Length, 320 feet; breadth, 75 feet; displacement, 11,400 tons. Carries four 80-ton guns in the turrets.

Inghamites.

An English denomination, founded by Benjamin Ingham, a Yorkshire Evangelist (1712–72), which combines the ele ments of Methodism and Moravianism. The conversion of Ingham to Sandemanian views led to the disruption and nearly total extinction of the denomination.

Inner Temple, *v.* Inns of Court.

Innisfail, *v.* Emerald Isle, The.

Inns of Chancery.

Inns subordinate to the Inns of Court (q.v.), Clifford's Inn, Clement's Inn and Lyons Inn (pulled down in 1868), were attached to the Inner Temple; New Inn and Strand Inn (which have disappeared) to the Middle Temple; Barnard's Inn and Staple's Inn to Gray's Inn; Thavie's Inn and Furnival's Inn to Lincoln's Inn. Serjeant's Inn, in Chancery Lane, was formerly used by the Society of Serjeants-at-law, but this ceased to exist in 1877.

Inns of Court.

Legal societies in London, having the exclusive privilege of calling candidates to the Bar, and maintaining instruction and examination for that purpose; also the precincts or premises occupied by these societies respectively. They are the Inner Temple, Middle Temple, Lincoln's Inn and Gray's Inn. The first two originally belonged to the Knights Templars (whence the name **Temple**). These inns had their origin about the end of the thirteenth century (*v.* also **Temple, The**). *Hare*, " London," i. 59.

Inspired Idiot, The.

A surname given by Horace Walpole to Oliver Goldsmith (1728-74), in allusion to his ungainly person, frequent blunders and absurdities. *v.* **Goldy**.

Institut, *v.* Institute of France.

Institute of France (French, " Institut de France," or "L'Institut ").

An association of the members of five French Academies — L'Académie française, L'Académie des Inscriptions et Belles-Lettres, L'Académie des Sciences, L'Académie des Beaux Arts, and L'Académie des Sciences Morales et Politiques. Established by the Republican Convention in 1795, and is supported by the Government. Originally called L'Institut National, and the name has changed with the various changes in the Government.

Insula Sanctorum, *v.* Island of Saints.

Interim.

A provisional arrangement for the settlement of religious differences between Protestants and Roman Catholics in Germany during the Reformation epoch, pending a definite settlement by a Church Council. There were three interims: the **Ratisbon Interim,** promulgated by the Emperor Charles V, July 29, 1541, but ineffective; the **Augsburg Interim,** proclaimed also by Charles V, May 15, 1548, but not carried out by many Protestants; and the **Leipsig Interim,** carried through the Diet of Saxony, December 22, 1548, by the efforts of the Elector Maurice, and enlarged and published as the **Greater Interim** in March, 1549. It met with strenuous opposition. Religious toleration was secured for the Lutherans by the Peace of Passau, 1552.

International Working-men's Association, The (or The International).

A society formed in London in 1864, to unite the working-classes of all countries in promoting social and industrial reform by political means. By 1867 the association had become a powerful organization, though strenuously opposed by the continental European governments; but its manifestation in 1872 of sympathy with the doings of the Paris Commune in the preceding year, and internal dissensions, caused a great loss of reputation and strength.

International African Association.

An international commission provided for at the Brussels Conference of 1876, with the object of exploring and civilizing Central Africa. National committees were formed in France, Germany, Italy and elsewhere, to co-operate in the work. Out of it grew the Congo Committee, the International Association of the Congo, and the Congo Free State.

Intransigentists.

A Radical party in Spain, which in 1873-4 fomented an unsuccessful insurrection. A faction in France whose parliamentary programme includes various radical reforms and socialistic changes.

Intrepid.

A Tripolitan vessel, captured and so named by Americans, in which Stephen Decatur sailed into the Port of Tripoli on the night of February 16, 1804, and recaptured and burned the United States frigate "Philadelphia," which had fallen into the enemy's hands. The vessel was afterwards blown up in the harbour to destroy Tripolitan cruisers. An Arctic exploring vessel, which sailed from England in 1850 (Commander Austin).

Invincible Armada, The, *v*. Armada, The Invincible.

Invincible Doctor, The (Latin, "Doctor Invincibilis").

A surname given to the English scholastic philosopher, William of Occam (or Ockham), the reviver of Nominalism (c. 1270-1347). Also called "the Singular Doctor," "Princeps nominalium," and, in later times, "the Venerable Initiator" ("Venerabilis Inceptor"), as if he had not actually taken his degree.

Invincibles, *v*. Phoenix Park Murders.

Irish Agitator, The, *v*. Liberator, The.

Irish Atticus, The.

A surname given to George Faulkner (1700-75) by the Earl of Chesterfield in a series of letters addressed to him.

Irish Land League.

A league formed October, 1879, by the Irish Nationalist Party, under which organized resistance was made to the payment of rent. It was "proclaimed" by the Liberal Government as "an illegal and criminal association," October 20, 1881.

Irish Night, The.

A name given to a night of agitation and terror in London (after James II's flight) occasioned by an unfounded report that the Irish Catholics of Feversham's army had been let loose to murder the Protestant population, men, women and children.

Irish Roscius, The.

A surname given to Spranger Barry, an Irish actor (1719-77), a rival of Garrick, the Silvertongued.

Iron Arm, *v*. Bras de Fer.

Iron Chancellor, The.

A surname given to Prince von Bismarck (Otto Eduard Leopold), Chancellor of the German Empire, in allusion to his inflexible character

Iron City, The.

A name given to Pittsburg, Pennsylvania, on account of its iron manufactures.

Iron Duke.

A British warship, launched in 1871. Length, 280 feet; breadth, 54 feet; displacement, 6,010 tons. The " Iron Duke " ran into and sank her sister ship, the " Vanguard," off the coast of Ireland, September, 1875.

Iron Duke, The.

A popular surname of the Duke of Wellington (1769–1852). *v.* **Great Duke, The.**

Iron Emperor, The.

A surname given to Nicholas I, Czar of Russia (1796–1855).

Iron Gate of France, The

A surname given to Longwy (Meurthe-et-Moselle), a fortified town 34 miles north-west of Metz.

Iron Gates, The (of the Danube).

A celebrated defile, 1½ miles long, in the Danube, at the confines of Hungary, Servia and Roumania.

Iron Hand, Götz with the, *v.* **Götz with the Iron Hand.**

Iron Mask, The Man with the, *v.* **Man with the Iron Mask, The.**

Ironsides.

A surname of Edmund (or Eadmund) II, King of the West Saxons (c. 989–c. 1016).

Ironsides, The.

The famous regiment led by Cromwell in the English Civil War. The name was afterwards applied to the entire army under his control.

Iron Tooth.

A surname given to Frederick II, Elector of Brandenburg (d. 1471).

Iron Virgin, The.

The name of an instrument of torture used during the Middle Ages. A hollow wooden figure resembling a maiden of the fifteenth century, opening like a cupboard and lined with sharp iron spikes. The victim was forced into it, and the spikes pierced his body, causing a frightful death.

Irredentists.

An Italian political party, formed in 1878, for bringing about the " redemption " or the incorporation into the kingdom of Italy of all regions situated near Italy, where an important part of the population was Italian, but which were still subject to other governments, and hence called **Italia irredenta** (" unredeemed Italy ").

Irrefragable Doctor, The (Latin, " Doctor Irrefragabilis ").

A surname of Alexander of Hales, a noted English theologian and philosopher (b. at Hales, Gloucestershire; d. 1245). Also called the **Fountain of Life.**

Irvingites.

A religious denomination named after Edward Irving (1792–1834), although he was not its founder. Its proper name is the Catholic Apostolic Church, and it has an elaborate organization derived from its twelve " apostles," the first body of whom was completed in 1835. The adherents are not numerous, and are found chiefly in Great Britain. There are some on the continent of Europe and in the United States.

Isaurian, The.

A surname of Leo III, Byzantine emperor (d. 741).

Isis.

A name sometimes given to the upper course of the Thames.

Island City.

A name sometimes given to Montreal.

Island of Saints, The (Latin, " Insula Sanctorum ").

A medieval name given to Ireland as an early stronghold of Christianity. Also **Holy Island, Sacred Island.**

Islands of the Blest, v. Fortunate Islands, The.

Italian Molière, The.

A surname sometimes given to Carlo Goldoni, a noted Italian dramatist (1707–93).

Italian Nightingale, The.

A surname given to Angelica Catalani, a famous Italian singer (1779–1849). Also called the **Queen of Song.**

Italian Pindar, The.

A surname sometimes given to Gabriello Chiabrera, an Italian lyric poet (1552–1637).

Italiens, Les, v. Théâtre Italien.

Ivan Ivanovitch.

An imaginary personage, typifying the Russian people, in the same way that John Bull represents the English.

Jack, Captain, v. Captain Jack.

Jack Amend-all, v. Captain of Kent, The.

Jack Bray, Sir, v. Sir Jack Bray.

Jack Frost.

A familiar nursery name, the personification of frost or cold.

Jack-in-the-Green.

A puppet character in the English May-day games.

Jack Ketch.

John Ketch, a famous English executioner (d. November, 1686). The name has become a synonym for a hangman, and the executioner in the puppet-play of Punch and Judy is also so called. " Punchinello " being introduced into England from Italy at about the time of Jack Ketch's death, this was but natural.

Jack of Clubs.

A nickname given to Philip Henry Sheridan, a famous American general (1831–88) by his soldiers during the Civil War. v. also **Sheridan's Ride.**

Jack of Newbury.

A surname given to John Winchcomb, the greatest clothier in England in the time of Henry VIII. He armed and clothed one hundred of his men to march in the expedition against the Scots at Flodden Field.

Jack of Spades.

A nickname given to John Alexander Logan, an American general and statesman (1826–86) by his troops during the Civil War.

Jack Tar.

A nickname for a sailor.

Jack the Ripper, *v*. Whitechapel Murders. Cf. Monster, The.

Jacobins.

In France, the black or Dominican friars are so called, from the Church of St. Jacques (Jacobus), in which they were first established in Paris. Also the members of a club or society of French revolutionists organized in 1789 under the name of the Society of Friends of the Constitution, and called Jacobins from the Jacobin convent in Paris in which they met. Many of its members were executed with Robespierre in July, 1794, and the club was suppressed in November.

Jacobites.

In English history, the partizans or adherents of James II after he abdicated the throne, or of his descendants. The Jacobites engaged in fruitless rebellions in 1715 and 1745, on behalf of James Francis Edward and of Charles Edward, son and grandson of James II, called the Old and Young Pretender respectively (*v*. these headings). The name was also given to a sect of Christians in Syria, Mesopotamia, etc., originally an offshoot of the Monophysites, from Jacobus Baradæus, a Syrian, consecrated Bishop of Edessa c. 541. The head of the church is called the Patriarch of Antioch.

Jacquerie.

A revolt of the peasants against the nobles in northern France in 1358, attended by great devastation and slaughter. (From Jacques, a common name for a peasant.)

Jacques Bonhomme.

Name assumed by a French peasant, Guillaume Caillet, leader of the Jacquerie in 1358. Used as a general name for a French peasant. Cf. Hodge.

Jagersfontein, Excelsior, The.

The largest known diamond in the world, found in the Orange Free State, South Africa, June 2, 1893, in the mine of the Jagersfontein Company. Weight 971 carats; colour blue-white, and almost perfect.

Jansenists.

A body or school in the Roman Catholic Church, prominent in the seventeenth and eighteenth centuries, holding the doctrines of Cornelius Jansen (1585–1638). Jansenism is described by Catholic authorities as "a heresy which consisted in denying the freedom of the will and the possibility of resisting divine grace," under "a professed attempt to restore the ancient doctrine and discipline of the Church" ("Cath. Dict.").

Jason.

The name of a Norwegian sealer which, under Captain Larsen, visited the Antarctic regions in 1892–3 and 1893–4, reaching on the latter journey 68° 10′ S. lat. *v.* also **Stella Polare.**

Jay's Treaty.

A name given to the treaty between Great Britain and the United States concluded by John Jay, November 19, 1794, and ratified by the United States, August 18, 1795. Contained provisions for the surrender to the United States of the north-western military posts; the settlement of the eastern boundary; the payment of British debts and American claims; the restriction of American trade in the West Indies; and for neutrality at sea.

Jeames.

A nickname for a footman, flunkey or lackey. An old English form of James, so pronounced, and even spelt, in the best society till the end of the eighteenth century. Its use as a nickname dates from Thackeray's " Jeames's Diary." Has also been applied to " The Morning Post " newspaper.

Jean Baptiste.

A name applied to a French Canadian, from the frequency of these Christian names among French Canadians.

Jean-Jacques.

Rousseau, the Swiss-French philosopher (1712–78) is often alluded to by English writers by these, his Christian, names.

Jeannette, The.

A ship fitted out by James Gordon Bennett, junr., for Arctic exploration under George Washington De Long in 1879.

Crushed by the ice June 13, 1881. De Long and fourteen others reached the mouth of the Lena, Siberia, where all pershed from cold and starvation, except two men sent forward to obtain relief. The bodies of De Long and his companions were discovered March 23, 1882, by Chief Engineer George W. Melville.

Jean Paul.

The name under which Jean Paul Friedrich Richter, a celebrated German humorist (1763–1825) wrote, and by which he is familiarly known. Sometimes called **Jean Paul der Einzige** (Jean Paul the Only).

Jedbury Justice, *v.* Cupar Justice.

Jeffreys' Campaign, *v.* Bloody Assizes, The.

Jehu.

A common name for a coachman or cabman, especially a reckless one. Cf. 2 Kings, ix. 20: ". . . and the driving is like the driving of Jehu, the son of Nimshi ; for he driveth furiously."

Jemmy Twitcher.

A nickname given to John Montagu, fourth Earl of Sandwich (1718–92). His mistress, Martha Ray, was murdered April 7, 1779.

Jenkins's Ear, War of, *v.* War of Jenkins's Ear.

Jersey Lily, The.

A surname given to Mrs. Langtry (Lily Le Breton) (b. in Jersey, 1852), a noted English beauty and actress.

Jerusalem Coffee House.

An old house in Cornhill, London. It is one of the oldest of the City news-rooms, and is frequented by merchants and captains connected with the commerce of China, India and Australia. *Timbs.*

Jesuits.

The members of the " Society of Jesus " (or " Company of Jesus "), founded by Ignatius Loyola in 1534, and confirmed by the Pope in 1540. So called (first, it is said, by Calvin, c. 1550) from the name given to the order by its founder, Societas Jesu, the Company (or Society) of Jesus. Expelled from France in 1594; restored in 1603; again expelled in 1764, and for the last time in 1880. In 1773 the order was suppressed by Pope Clement XIV, but it was revived in 1814.

Jeunesse Dorée, La (French, " Gilded Youth ").

A band of young men who formed a reactionary faction against the Jacobins (q.v.) after the ninth Thermidor, year 2 (July 27, 1794).

Jewels of Cornelia, v. Cornelia's Jewels.

Jewish Plato, The.

A surname given to Philo Judæus, a Hellenistic Jewish philosopher of Alexandria (c. 20 B.C.–after 40 A.D.).

Jim Crow.

A dramatic song and negro dance brought out by Thomas D. Rice, the first " negro minstrel," in Washington in 1835. Joseph Jefferson, when only four years old, appeared with him in this dance.

Joachimites.

The followers or believers in the doctrines of an Italian mystic, Joachim, abbot of Floris (d.c. 1200). The most important feature of his doctrines was the belief that the history of man will be covered by three reigns : the first that of the Father, from the creation to the birth of Christ ; the second, that of the Son, from the birth of Christ to 1260 ; and the third, that of the Holy Spirit, from 1260 onwards.

Joan of the Tower.

A surname given to Joan, Queen of Scotland (c. July 1321–62). She was born in the Tower of London. Called by the Scots " Joan Makepeace," her marriage (to David II) being included among the conditions of the peace concluded at Northampton, July 12, 1328.

Joannites.

The adherents of St. John Chrysostom (c. 347–407), who supported him after his deposition from the patriarchate of Constantinople in 404.

Jockey of Norfolk.

A nickname given to Sir John Howard, an adherent of the House of York. Slain in the battle of Bosworth Field (Aug. 22, 1485). Cf. Shakspere's "Richard III," act 5, sc. 3.

Joe Miller, v. Father of Jests, The

John Barleycorn.

Name used to personify malt liquor as being made from

barley. Sometimes called Sir John Barleycorn. In one ballad he appears as a person.

John Bull.

The English nation personified. Used also as a synonym for a typical Englishman. Cf. Dr. John Arbuthnot's satire, "Law is a Bottomless Pit, or the History of John Bull" (1713).

John Company.

A nickname for the East India Company, originating in India.

John Doe.

The name of the fictitious plaintiff in ejectment actions. The custom of using the name was abolished in 1852. *v.* **Richard Roe.** Cf. **John Noakes** and **Tom Styles.**

John Finality.

A nickname given to Lord John Russell, English statesman, orator, and author (1792–1878), who always spoke of the Reform Bill of 1831 as a "finality." Created Earl Russell in 1861.

John Noakes (or Nokes).

A fictitious person or name formerly made use of by lawyers in actions of ejectment, generally coupled with that of **Tom Styles.** Cf. **John Doe** and **Richard Roe.**

Johnny (or Jean) Crapaud (French, "Toad").

A nickname for a Frenchman.

Johny Newcome.

A nickname given to any raw, unpractised youth or newcomer, and especially a very young officer in the British army or navy.

Johnny Rebs.

A nickname given during the American Civil War to the Confederate soldiers by the Federals.

John o' Groat's House.

A locality in the county of Caithness, Scotland ; N. lat. 58° 38' ; and W. long. 3° 4', near the north-eastern extremity of the island of Great Britain.

Jonathan's.

A noted coffee-house in Change Alley, formerly the "general mart for stock jobbers," according to "The Tatler."

Journée des Dupes (French, "Day of Dupes").

November 11, 1630, was so named when the enemies of Richelieu were foiled in their intrigues against him with the king.

Journée des Farines, La (French, "The Day of Flours").

A name given to January 3, 1591, from an attempt made by Henry IV to take Paris by surprise. Some of his officers, disguised as corn-dealers, with sacks on their shoulders, endeavoured to obtain possession of the St. Honoré gate, but were compelled to retreat.

Journées des Barricades.

Name applied to several insurrections in Paris (May 12, 1588 ; August 26–7, 1648 ; also in 1830, 1848, etc.).

Joyeuse.

The sword of Charlemagne (742 or 7–814).

Judgment of God, The, *v.* Battle of the Brothers.

Judgments of Oléron.

A code of maritime laws in use in Western Europe in the middle ages. It is the oldest collection of modern maritime laws, and is supposed to have been promulgated by Eleanor, duchess of Guienne, mother of Richard I of England, at Oléron, about the middle of the 12th century, and to have been introduced into England, with some additions, in the reign of Richard I.

Judicious Hooker, The.

A surname given to Richard Hooker, an eminent English divine (c. 1553–1600), from his wisdom and judgment.

Juggernaut Car.

A huge car used in the Jagannath annual festival (June or July) at Puri, India. It is 45 feet high, 35 ft. square, and supported on sixteen wheels 7 ft. in diameter. It is said that the number of instances of self-immolation by pilgrims throwing themselves under the car in its progress has been grossly exaggerated, that such instances have always been rare, and are now unknown. (Sir W. W. Hunter, "Statistical Account of Bengal," xix. 59 ff).

Julian Calendar.

The calendar (also called Old Style, to distinguish it from the Gregorian Calendar, or New Style), introduced by Julius Cæsar in 46 B.C.

Julianists.

A sect of Monophysites, which held the body of Christ to be incorruptible. So called from

D.N,

Julian, bishop of Halicarnassus early in the sixth century.

July, Government of, *v.* Government of July.

July, Revolution of, *v.* Revolution of July.

Junkers.

The members of the aristocratic party in Prussia, which came into power under Bismarck, when he was made prime minister in 1862.

Junta.

A group of Whig politicians very influential in the reigns (1689–1714) of William III and Anne. Its chief members were Somers, Russell, Wharton, and Montague, and they were the chief leaders of the party in Parliament.

Jupiter Carlyle.

A surname given to the Rev. Alexander Carlyle, a Scotch clergyman (1722–1805), minister at Inveresk 1748–1805. His head was considered worthy of being a model for a Jupiter Tonans.

Jupiter Scapin.

A nickname given to Napoleon Bonaparte (1769–1821) by the Abbé (Dominique Dufour) de Pradt, alluding to the mixture of greatness and littleness in his character. Cf. Emerson's "Representative Men (Napoleon)." The abbé was a bitter enemy of Napoleon.

Just, The.

Surname of Casimir II, King of Poland (1138–94) ; of Ferdinand I, King of Aragon (1379-1416) ; of Frederick Augustus I,

M

King of Saxony (1750–1827) ;
of James II, King of Aragon
(d. 1327) ; *v.* **Great, The**
(Khusrau) ; of Louis XIII,
King of France (1601–43).

Justiciary, The.

A surname given to Pedro I,
King of Portugal (1320–67).

Justinian Code.

The body of Roman law compiled and annotated at the command of the Emperor Justinian
I. This consists of the " Pan-
dects," or the condensed
opinions of the jurists, in fifty
books ; the " Institutiones " ;
and the " Novellæ " or "Novellæ Constitutiones," a collection
of ordinances—the whole forming the " Corpus Juris Civilis,"
or body of civil law, the most
important of all monuments of
jurisprudence.

Juvenal of Painters, The.

A surname given to William
Hogarth, a celebrated English
painter and engraver (1697–
1764).

Juvenal of the Provençals.

Surname of Pierre Cardinal,
a French troubadour, especially
noted for his satirical powers
(b. early in the thirteenth century–d.c. 1305).

Kaffir Circus, *v.* Kaffir King.

Kaffir King.

A nickname given, particularly
in financial circles, to Barnett
Isaacs Barnato (Barney Barnato), a Jewish speculator and
capitalist (1852–97). He made
a large fortune in the Kimberley
diamond mines and the gold
mines around Johannesburg,
and in 1895 was the centre of
the speculation in mining stocks
and shares known as the "Kaffir
Circus." He committed suicide
by jumping into the sea from
the steamer "Scot," near Fun-
chal.

Kansas-Nebraska Bill.

An Act passed by Congress in
1854, which provided for the
organization of the Territories
of Kansas and Nebraska. It
introduced the principle of
" squatter sovereignty," or local
option on the slavery question,
for the people of the Territories,
thus abrogating the Missouri
Compromise of 1820. It dis-
rupted finally the Whig party,
led to the rise of the Republican
party, and was an important
link in the chain of events leading to the Civil War.

Karlings, *v.* Carolingians.

Karlsbad, Congress of.

A congress of ministers representing Austria, Prussia, and a
number of minor German States,
held at Karlsbad in August,
1819, to discuss the democratic
movement in Germany. The
congress resolved to recommend
to their respective governments
and to the Diet of the German
Confederation, the so-called
" Karlsbad Decrees," the most
important of which were that
the press should be subjected to
a rigorous censorship ; that a
central commission should be
established at Mainz for the
investigation of demagogical
intrigues ; that the Burschen-
schaft, a secret organization
among the students, should be
suppressed ; and that the universities should be placed under

government inspection. These resolutions were adopted by the Diet, September 20, 1819.

Kearsage, The.

A wooden corvette (of 1,031 tons register) launched at Portsmouth, New Hampshire, September, 1861. She carried 163 men, including officers, and was commanded by Captain John A. Winslow. On June 19, 1864, off Cherbourg, she sank the Confederate cruiser "Alabama" (q.v.), and, on February 2, 1894, she was wrecked on the Roncador Reef in the Caribbean Sea.

Kentish Man.

A native of West Kent is often so called, as distinguished from a **Man of Kent**, a native of East Kent.

Kentucky Resolutions.

Nine resolutions prepared by Thomas Jefferson and passed by the legislature of Kentucky in 1798. A tenth was passed in 1799. They declared the "alien and sedition laws" void, and emphasized the rights of the several states.

Key of Christendom.

A name once given to Buda, Hungary, from its strategically important position between Germany and Turkey.

Key of India.

Herat is so named.

Key of Russia.

A name sometimes given to Smolensk.

Key of the Gulf.

Cuba is sometimes so called, on account of its position at the entrance of the Gulf of Mexico.

Key of the Mediterranean.

Gibraltar is so named from its position. Sometimes familiarly called "**Old Gib.**"

Keystone State.

A popular designation of Pennsylvania, the central state of the original thirteen.

Kilhamites.

The members of the "New Connexion of Wesleyan Methodists," so called from Alexander Kilham (1762–98), the founder of the organization.

King Bomba (Italian, **Bomba**, "Bomb").

A nickname given in Italy to Ferdinand II, of the Two Sicilies (1810–59), from his bombardment of Messina and other cities during the revolutionary troubles of 1849.

King Cotton.

A popular name used to personify the great staple production of the Southern States.

King Franconi, *v.* Dandy King, The.

King George's War.

The war waged between Great Britain and its American colonies against France and its Indian allies, being the American phase of the War of the Austrian Succession, 1741–8. So named from George II.

King Log.

In Esop's Fables, a worthless and heavy log sent by Jove to the frogs who prayed for a king.

On their complaining to him of such an inert monarch, he sent them a stork, who devoured them.

King-maker, The.

A popular designation of Richard Nevil (or Neville), Earl of Warwick (c. 1428–71), on account of his influence in securing the accession of Edward IV and the restoration of Henry VI. Sometimes also called the **Last of the Barons.** (Cf. Lord Lytton's novel bearing this title).

King of Bark, The.

A nickname given by the Swedish peasants to Christopher III, King of Sweden and Denmark (d. 1448), owing to their having, in time of scarcity, to use birch-bark mixed with meal for food. The king himself had to do likewise. Hence the nickname.

King of Bath.

A surname of Richard ("Beau") Nash. *v.* **Beau Nash.**

King of Beasts, The, *v.* **King of the Desert.**

King of Birds, The.

The eagle is often so called.

King of Brave Men, The, *v.* **Roi des Braves, Le.**

King of Cotswold, The.

A surname given to Grey Brydges, Lord Chandos (d. 1621), owing to his luxurious style of living and numerous attendants.

King of Dunces.

A name given in the "Dunciad," a satirical poem by Alexander Pope, to Colley Cibber, an English actor and dramatist (1671–1757).

King of England's Viceroy.

A surname given, in derision, by the French to Louis XVIII, king of France (1755–1824), owing to his expressions of gratitude to the British government for helping him to regain his throne.

King of Feuilletons, The, *v.* **Roi des Feuilletons, Le.**

King of Men.

A title given to Zeus (Jupiter), Odin, and to Agamemnon.

King of Painters, The.

A surname (self-bestowed) of Parrhasius, a celebrated Greek painter, one of the greatest of antiquity (fl. c. 400 B.C.).

King of Preachers, The, *v.* **Roi des Prédicateurs, Le.**

King of Reptiles, The, *v.* **Roi des Reptiles, Le.**

King of Roads (Rhodes).

A joking nickname given to John Loudon Macadam, a Scottish engineer, inventor of the system of macadamizing roads (1756–1836).

King of Rome, The.

A title given at his birth to Napoleon II (François Charles Joseph Napoléon Bonaparte, Duc de Reichstadt), son of Napoleon I and Marie Louise (1811–32).

King of Terrors.

One of the many expressions used to refer to death. The word **Smallback** is sometimes used in Scotland, in allusion to a skeleton.

King of the Barricades, The, *v.* **Roi Citoyen, Le.**

King of the Beggars.

A surname given to Bamfylde Moore Carew, a noted English vagabond (1693–probably c. 1770).

King of the Border (or of Thieves).

A nickname of Adam Scott, of Tushielaw, a noted robber (beheaded 1529), who infested the borderland of England and Scotland.

King of the Commons, The, *v.* **Goodman (or Gudeman) of Ballengeigh (or Ballinbreich), The.**

King of the Desert.

A surname sometimes given to the lion ; also called **The King of Beasts.**

King of the Feds, The.

A nickname given to Alexander Hamilton, a celebrated American statesman (1757–1804), chief author of "The Federalist," a collection of essays in favour of the United States Constitution.

King of the Markets, The, *v.* **Roi des Halles, Le.**

King of Waters, The, *v.* **Father of Waters, The.**

King Philip's War.

The war between the New England colonists and the confederated Indians (1675–6), under the leadership of Philip, an Indian chief. King Philip was killed at Mount Hope, R.I.

King Pym.

A nickname given to John Pym (1584–1643) from his influence as a Parliamentary leader.

King's Evidence.

A prisoner giving evidence against a fellow-prisoner is said to turn **King's evidence.**

King's Shilling, The, *v.* **Queen's Shilling, The.**

King Stork, *v.* **King Log.**

King William's War.

The war waged by Great Britain and its colonies against France and its Indian allies, being the American phase of the contest between various European powers and Louis XIV of France (1689–97). Also called the "War of William and Mary."

Kirke's Lambs.

A name ironically given to the English infantry regiment (Tangier regiment) commanded by Colonel Percy Kirke, infamous for its cruelty in the Monmouth insurrection, 1685.

Kirk of Field.

A solitary house near Edinburgh, to which Lord Darnley was removed while convalescent from an attack of small-pox. The house was blown up with gunpowder by the Earl of Bothwell, it is said with the queen's knowledge, on the night of February 9, 1567.

Kit Carson.

Christopher Carson, a noted American trapper, guide, soldier, and Indian agent in New Mexico (1809–68).

Kit-Cat Club, The.

A London club which flourished, according to the generally received account, from 1703 to 1733. Its meetings were held at the "Cat and Fiddle," kept by Christopher Cat, a noted mutton-pieman, near Temple Bar. It was founded by members of the Whig party, and among its frequenters were Steele, Addison, Lord Orford and others. The name is thought to be derived from the name of the landlord of the tavern, though "The Spectator" (No. 9) says it was from the name of the pies, which were called "kit-cats." The club occasionally met at Jacob Tonson's house, at Barn Elms, where a room was built for it, the walls of which were adorned with portraits of its members. As the ceiling was low, Sir Godfrey Kneller, who painted them, used a small canvas (36 by 28 in.), which has since been known as "kit-cat" size.

Kitchen Cabinet, The.

A group of politicians very influential with Andrew Jackson during his administration (1829–37). Its chief members were Major Lewis and Amos Kendall (Schouler, "Hist. of U.S.," iii. 495).

Kit's Coity (or Coty) House.

A noted cromlech or dolman near Aylesford, Kent, formed of three supports, with a capstone measuring 11 ft. by 8 ft.

Kloster-Zeven, Convention of, v. Convention of Closter-Seven.

Knecht Ruprecht (German, "Knight Rupert").

The German genius of Christmas, corresponding to St. Nicholas, or Santa Claus. In some parts of Germany he is supposed to appear just before Christmas, with a bag on his back and a rod in his hand, to inquire into the conduct of the children, rewarding or punishing them according to their deserts. The actual dispenser of gifts on Christmas Eve is, however, the Christ-child.

Knight of Liddesdale, The.

A surname given to Sir William Douglas, a Scottish nobleman (d. 1353). He sided with David II against Edward Baliol, obtaining as a reward the lordship of Liddesdale; hence the surname. Also called the **Flower of Chivalry.**

Knight Rupert, v. Knecht Ruprecht.

Knights of Alcantara.

A Spanish religious and military order, created about 1156 by the brothers Don Suarez and Don Gomez de Barrientos to fight the Moors. Name taken from the fortified town of Alcantara. The order ceased to exist as a spiritual body in 1835, but still exists civilly.

Knights of Labour.

One of the largest labour organizations in the United States, established in Philadelphia (1869) by Uriah S. Stevens for the protection of working people and the development of skilled labour throughout the States. Its head is called the General Master Workman.

Knights of Malta, v. Order of the Hospitalers, etc.

Knights of Rhodes, v. Order of the Hospitalers, etc.

Knights of the Golden Circle.

A former secret order in the United States, in sympathy with the Secessionists.

Knights of the Holy Sepulchre.

A military order established by Godfrey de Bouillon in 1099, to watch the sepulchre of Christ.

Knights Templars, or Knights of the Temple, *v.* **Templars.**

Knight without Fear and without Reproach, *v.* **Chevalier sans peur, etc.**

Knight without Reproach.

Surname of Arnauld Guilhelm de Barbazan, a French general (d. 1432) under Charles VII.

Know-nothing Party, *v.* **Anti-Masonic Party.**

Koh - i - noor ("Mountain of Light").

The largest diamond belonging to the British crown. Acquired by Nadir Shah in 1739, and by Queen Victoria in 1850. It then weighed $186\frac{1}{16}$ carats, but has been re-cut and is now $106\frac{1}{16}$ carats. Also written **Koh-i-nur.**

Kolokol ("The Bell ").

A journal founded in London by Alexander Hertzen (or Herzen), published in Russia, and demanding the emancipation of the serfs and other reforms. It acquired great influence, and many copies were smuggled into Russia, though prohibited by the Government. It was published until 1865. In 1868 it reappeared in Geneva, published in French, but without much success.

Ku-Klux Klan.

A former secret organization in the Southern United States, of which the object was to intimidate the negroes, carpet-baggers and "scalawags," and to prevent them from political action. It arose probably in 1867 ; was guilty of numerous outrages ; and was suppressed in consequence of an Act of Congress (the " Force Bill ") passed in 1871. Also called the **White League.**

Labadists.

The followers of Jean de Labadie, a French mystic and separatist (1610–74), originally a Jesuit. The Labadists were Christian communists, and among their tenets were denial of the obligation of Sabbath observance, on the ground that life is a perpetual sabbath ; belief in the direct influence of the Holy Spirit ; and belief in marriage as a holy ordinance valid only among believers. The sect disappeared about the middle of the eighteenth century

Lackland (or Sans Terre).

A surname of John, king of England (c. 1167–1216), from his having received from his father no fiefs, like his other brothers.

Lack-learning Parliament, *v.* **Parliament of Dunces.**

Lad, The, *v.* **Youth, The.**

Ladies' Mile, The.

A drive in Hyde Park, London, on the north side of the Serpentine. The Coaching and Four-in-Hand Clubs meet there.

Ladies' Peace, The, *v.* **Paix des Dames, La.**

Lady Bountiful.

A synonym for a charitable woman, derived from a character in G. Farquhar's comedy "The Beaux' Stratagem" (1707).

Lady of England, The ("Domina Anglorum").

A title conferred upon Matilda (1102–67), daughter of Henry I, wife of Geoffrey V of Anjou and mother of Henry II.

Lady of the Mercians, The.

A name applied to Æthelflæd (d. c. 918), daughter of Alfred the Great, and wife of Æthelred, ealdorman of Mercia.

Lady of the Sun, The.

A surname given to Alice Perers (Perrers, Pierce, or Perren), a mistress of Edward III of England, and a married woman of great beauty. Notorious for her influence in English affairs about the time of the Good Parliament (q.v.).

La Force.

An ancient Parisian prison, now suppressed. It was situated in the rue Pavée, au Marais, and the rue du Roi-de-Sicile. Built in 1265 by Charles, king of Naples and Sicily, and was the residence of the dukes of La Force in the sixteenth century. It became a prison in the reign of Louis XV, and was the scene of the massacre of September, 1792, of the murder of the Princesse de Lamballe, and other atrocities of the Reign of Terror (q.v.).

Lagabœter (Reformer of the Laws).

A surname of Magnus VII, king (1262–80) of Norway (d.

1280). He collected and published a new code of laws.

La Gloire.

A French warship, the first fully equipped ironclad ship, launched in 1858. Length 254 ft., breadth 55 ft., depth 25 ft.

Lake of the Four (Forest) Cantons.

Lucerne is so called from its bordering on the four cantons, Lucerne, Schwyz, Uri, and Unterwalden. v. Forest Cantons.

Lake of the Thousand Lakes.

A name given to Lake Saima, in Finland.

Lake Poets, v. Lake School.

Lake School.

A name given to a group of poets, including Wordsworth, Coleridge, and Southey, from their residence in or connection with the Lake District of England (Cumberland, Westmoreland, and Lancashire). First given in derision in the "Edinburgh Review." The name was afterwards extended to Lamb, Lloyd, and Wilson. Also called Lake Poets and Lakists.

Lake State, The.

A popular surname for the State of Michigan, it bordering on Lakes Superior, Michigan, Huron, and Erie.

Lakists, v. Lake School.

Lambeth Articles.

Nine articles drawn up at Lambeth in 1595, intended to embody the Calvinistic doctrine respecting predestination, justification, etc. They were never approved by the Church in any regular synod, and therefore possess no ecclesiastical authority.

Lame, The.

A surname given to Charles I of Anjou, king of Naples (1246–1309); to Hermann (Latin, "Hermannus Contractus"), a German historian (1013–54); St. Henry II, emperor of the Holy Roman Empire (c. 972–1024).

Lame and Unstable Peace, The, v. Paix Boiteuse et Malassise, La.

Lame Duck.

A Stock Exchange term for a member of the House (q.v.) who is in difficulties.

Land League, Irish, v. Irish Land League.

Land of Beulah.

A land of rest, "where the sun shineth night and day," in Bunyan's "Pilgrim's Progress." The pilgrims stay here until the time comes for them to go across the river of Death to the Celestial City. (Cf. Isa. lxii, 4.)

Land of Cakes.

A name given to Scotland, famous for its oatmeal cakes.

Land of Nod.

The unknown land, on the east of Eden, to which Cain fled (see Genesis iv.). Colloquially the phrase, in humorous allusion to this, is used to mean a state of sleep (nodding).

Land of Steady Habits.

A popular nickname for Connecticut.

Land of the White Elephant.

A name given to Siam.

Land of Wisdom, v. Pays de Sapience, Le.

Land o' the Leal.

A mythical land of happiness. Used as meaning heaven in Lady Nairne's poem, "The Land o' the Leal."

Lap-King, The.

A surname of Olaf, the first Christian king of Sweden (r. 993–1024).

Last Astrologer, The.

A surname given to William Lilly, a noted English astrologer and prophet (1602–81).

Last Battle, The.

A name sometimes given to the battle of Culloden Moor, near Inverness, April 16, 1746, it having been the last battle fought on British soil.

Last Man, The.

A surname given to Charles I of England (1600–49) by the Parliamentarians, meaning that he was the last man who should ever occupy the throne of England. (Cf. Son of the Last Man, The.)

Last Minstrel of the English Stage, The.

A surname given to James Shirley, an English dramatist (1596–1666).

Last of the Barons, The, v. Kingmaker, The.

Last of the Fathers, The.

A name applied to St. Bernard (1091–1153). Also called the Oracle of the Church.

Last of the Goths, The.

A name applied to Roderick, the last monarch of the West-Gothic kingdom of Spain (fl. c. 710). Southey has written a poem entitled " Roderick, the Last of the Goths" (published in 1814).

Last of the Greeks, The.

A name applied to Philopœmen, a general of the Achæan League (c. 252-183 B.C.).

Last of the Incas, The.

A surname given to Atahualpa (or Atahuallpa), an Inca sovereign of Peru (c. 1495-1533).

Last of the Knights, The.

A name applied to Maximilian I, emperor of the Holy Roman Empire (1459-1519).

Last of the Puritans, The.

A surname given to Samuel Adams, an American patriot and statesman (1722-1803).

Last of the Romans, The, *v.* Last of the Tribunes, The.

Last of the Saxons, The.

A surname given to Harold II, king of the English (c. 1022-66), the last of the Saxon kings.

Last of the Schoolmen.

A surname wrongly applied to Gabriel Biel (or Byll), a German scholastic philosopher (d. 1495). Also given to Francisco Suarez, a noted Spanish Jesuit theologian and scholastic philosopher (1548-1617).

Last of the Tribunes, The.

A surname given to Cola di Rienzi, an Italian patriot (c. 1313-54). Sometimes the Last of the Romans. (Cf. Bulwer Lytton's novel, " Rienzi " (1835.)

Last of the Troubadours, The.

A name applied to Jacques Jasmin, a Provençal poet (1798-1864). Also known as " the Barber Poet," having been employed in a barber's shop. Sometimes called the **Burns of France.**

Lateran Council.

The name of a number of ecclesiastical councils held at various times in the Lateran Church at Rome.

Latin Empire, The.

The empire established by the Crusaders of western and south-western Europe at Constantinople in 1204. It was overthrown and succeeded by the (restored) Byzantine Empire in 1261.

Latin League.

A confederation of the cities of Latium, existing in Italy in the earliest historic times and continuing until 338 B.C., when the Latin towns were finally incorporated in the dominion of Rome. According to the earliest tradition, the league included thirty cities, among which Alba Longa held the foremost place.

Latin Quarter, *v.* Quartier Latin.

Latin Union, The.

A monetary alliance of France, Belgium, Italy, and Switzerland, formed by convention December 23, 1865, and joined by Greece in 1868. Its object was the maintenance and regulation of a uniform interchangeable gold and silver coinage, based on the French franc. Its limited term was continued by two renewals (1878 and 1885), Belgium withdrawing on the latter occasion and adopting the single gold standard.

Latin War, The.

In German history, a revolt of the peasantry in Salzburg in 1523, owing to the unpopularity of an archbishop. It was soon suppressed. (Cf. **Great Latin War, The.**)

Latin War, The Great, *v.* Great Latin War, The.

Latter-Day Saints.

A name given to the Mormons by themselves.

Laughing Philosopher, The.

A surname given to Democritus, a Greek philosopher (c. 460-c. 357 B.C.) He is said to have been of a cheerful disposition, which prompted him to laugh at men's follies. Also called "The Abderite," from Abdera, Thrace, where he was born. Cf. **Weeping Philosopher, The.**

Laureate of the Gentle Craft, The.

A surname given to Hans Sachs, a German poet, the most celebrated of the *minnesingers.* He was a shoemaker by trade.

Lautaro Society.

A secret political society, originally established in various Spanish cities, during the first years of the nineteenth century. It was affiliated with the Gran Reunion Americana (q.v.), and had for its aim the emancipation of Spanish South America. The first American branch (called the Lautaro Lodge) was formed at Buenos Ayres by San Martin and others about July, 1812.

L'Autre (French, the "other one").

An expression by which Napoleon was often alluded to by his partisans during his stay at Elba.

Lawgiver of Parnassus, The.

A surname given to Nicholas Boileau-Despréaux, a famous French critic and poet (1636–1711), owing principally to his "Art poétique." Also called the **Solon of Parnassus** and the **Poet of Reason.**

Law's Bubble, *v.* Mississippi Scheme.

Laws of Wisby.

A code or compilation of maritime customs and adjudications adopted by the town of Wisby, in the island of Gotland, in the Baltic Sea. It has been claimed that these laws are older than the laws of Oléron (*v.* Judgments of Oléron) but the better opinion seems to be that they are later, and in some respects an improvement upon them. Sometimes called the **Gotland Sea Laws.**

League, The, *v.* Ligue, La.

League of Rhine Cities.

A union of German cities (Mainz, Worms, Oppenheim, and others near the Rhine), formed in 1254 for the purpose of preserving the public peace. It was revived in the fourteenth century, but its influence diminished after its defeat at Worms by the Elector Palatine in 1388.

League of the German Princes, The, v. Fürstenbund, Der.

League of the Public Weal, The, v. Ligue du Bien Public, La.

Leaning Tower (of Pisa), The.

The cylindrical campanile at Pisa (begun in 1174). It is 181 ft. high, 51½ ft. in diameter at the base, and inclines 13 ft. 8 in. towards the south. About half of the sinkage took place during the construction, and the efforts made to correct it by diminishing the height of the stages on the north side resulted in a convexity of ten inches on the south. The spire originally designed was, on account of the continued sinking of the foundation, not built.

Learned Blacksmith, The.

A surname given to Elihu Burritt, a social reformer and linguist (1811–79), who was a blacksmith by trade.

Learned Painter, The.

A surname given to Charles Lebrun, a noted French historical painter (1619–90) and author of several works.

Learned Tailor, The.

A surname given to Henry Wild, a native of Norwich, England, where he was born c. 1684. He was in early life a tailor, and while working at his trade mastered the Latin, Greek, Hebrew, Chaldaic, Syrian, Arabic, and Persian languages. Also called the **Arabian Tailor.**

Leather Wedding, v. Wedding Anniversaries.

Lebel Rifle.

A breech-loading magazine rifle adopted by the French army in 1887, replacing the Gras rifle.

Lecompton Constitution.

A pro-slavery constitution, framed during the agitation for the admission of Kansas to the Union by a constitutional convention at Lecompton, September 5-November 7, 1857, and rejected as a whole, by the people January 4, 1858. The clause sanctioning slavery was separately submitted December 21, 1857, and adopted.

Lee-Metford Rifle.

A breech-loading magazine rifle introduced into the British army in 1888, superseding the Martini-Henry.

Leges Corneliæ, v. Cornelian Laws.

Légion d'Honneur, La.

An order of distinction and reward for civil and military services, instituted May, 1802, during the consulate, by Napoleon Bonaparte, but since modified from time to time in important particulars.

Legion of Honour, v. Légion d'Honneur, La.

Leg-of-Mutton School, The.

A nickname given to parasite poetasters, a leg of mutton being supposed to typify the source of their inspiration. First used by J. G. Lockhart in " Blackwood's Magazine."

Leipsic Colloquy.

A conference between Lutheran and Reformed theologians, held at Leipsic in 1631.

Leipsic Disputation.

A theological controversy between Luther and Karlstadt on one side and Eck on the other, held at Leipsic, June 27– July 15, 1519.

Leipsic Interim.

A statement of belief drawn up by Melancthon and other German Protestant theologians, making important concessions to the Roman Catholics. It was formally adopted in December, 1548.

Leonidas of Modern Greece, The.

A surname given to Markos Bozzaris (or Botzaris), a Greek patriot and soldier (c. 1788–1823). He is the subject of a poem by Fitz-Greene Halleck, " Marco Bozzaris."

Leonidas Wedell.

A surname given by Frederick the Great to General H. C. Wedell (1712–82), an officer in the Prussian service, in allusion to his heroic defence of the Elbe, at Teinitz, November 19, 1744.

Leonine City.

That part of the city of Rome which is west of the Tiber and north of Trastevere. First fortified by Pope Leo IV (hence its name).

Leonists.

A name sometimes used for the members of the religious body known as the Waldenses or Waldensians (q.v.)

Leper, The.

Surname of Baldwin IV, king of Jerusalem from 1173–83. Was victorious over Saladin in 1177 and 1182.

Leviathan of Literature, The, *v.* **Great Moralist, The.**

Lewis Baboon.

A nickname given to Louis XIV, king of France (1638–1715) in Arbuthnot's " History of John Bull" (Cf. **Philip Baboon**).

L'homme de Décembre (French, " The Man of December").

A name given to Napoleon III in 1870, when he was deposed, in allusion to his *coup d'état* in December, 1851.

Libby Prison, The.

A notorious Confederate military prison in Richmond, Virginia, during the Civil War, originally a tobacco warehouse. It was afterwards taken down, carried to Chicago, and there set up as a war museum.

Liberal Party.

The name by which the Whig party has been known since about the time of the first Reform Bill (q.v.). It has generally advocated reforms in government and extension of power for the people, has favoured free trade, and, during the last few years, has advocated Home Rule for Ireland (*v.* **Home Rule Bills**). It has been in office under Grey, Melbourne, Russell, Aberdeen, Palmerston, Gladstone and Rosebery as prime ministers.

Liberal Unionists.

A political party formed in 1886 by the secession from the Liberal party of those who objected to Gladstone's Home Rule proposals. They acted generally with the Conservatives, their recognized leader being the Marquis of Hartington, now Duke of Devonshire.

Liberator, The.

An anti-slavery paper published at Boston 1831–65, edited by Garrison.

Liberator, The.

A surname given to Daniel O'Connell, a celebrated Irish political agitator (1775–1847), in allusion to his efforts (unsuccessful, however, after all) to bring about a repeal of the Articles of Union between Great Britain and Ireland. Also called the **Irish Agitator** and the **Big Beggarman.**

Liberator, The, *v.* **Libertador, El, Liberator of Europe,** and **Europe's Liberator.**

Liberator of Genoa, *v.* **Father of Peace, The.**

Liberator of Italy, The, *v.* **Hero of Modern Italy, The.**

Liberator of the New World, The.

A surname given to Benjamin Franklin, a celebrated American philosopher, statesman, diplomatist and author (1706–90).

Libertador, El (Spanish, " The Liberator ").

A title given to Simon Bolivar, a famous Venezuelan general and statesman (1783–1830) for his victories in 1813, 1819, and 1824 over the Spaniards. Also called the **Washington of South America** and the **Washington of Colombia.**

Liberty Bell, The.

A famous bell cast in London in 1752. It bore the motto,

" Proclaim liberty throughout the land unto all the inhabitants thereof." Afterwards recast at Philadelphia, with the same inscription, and it was rung when the Declaration of Independence was adopted by Congress. It is now in Independence Hall in Philadelphia.

Liberty Enlightening the World.

A colossal figure formed of plates of bronze on an iron framework, supported on a high granite pedestal, on Bedloe's Island in New York Bay. The figure represents a robustly-formed woman, fully draped in Greek tunic and mantle, and diademed, holding a torch in her uplifted right hand. The height of the statue is 151 ft. ; of the pedestal 155 ft. Sculptor, Bartholdi. A gift to the United States by popular subscription by the people of France. The pedestal was designed by Richard M. Hunt, and paid for by popular subscription in the United States. The statue was inaugurated in 1886.

Liberty Party.

In United States politics, an anti-slavery party, founded 1839–40. It opposed the annexation of Texas, and nominated James G. Birney for President of the United States in 1840, and again in 1844.

Liberty Tree, The.

An elm-tree formerly standing in Washington Street, Boston. Effigies of objectionable persons were hung upon it during the Stamp Act (q.v.) excitement. A building now covers its site.

Light-Horse Harry.

A surname of the American

cavalry commander, Henry Lee (1756–1818), commander of "Lee's Legion."

Lighthouse of San Salvador, The.

The Izaleo volcano, in the San Salvador Republic, is so named because the light from its almost constant eruptions is visible far at sea.

Light of the West, The.

A surname given to Maimonides (Moses ben Maimun or Maimuni), the most celebrated Jewish scholar, philosopher and writer of the middle ages (1135–1204). Also called the **Great Eagle.**

Light of the World, The.

A surname given to Sigismund, Emperor of the Holy Roman Empire (1361–1437), in allusion to his intelligence and enlightenment.

Ligue, La (French, "The League").

A name by which the Holy League (q.v.) of 1576 is known in French history.

Ligue du Bien Public, La (French, "The League of the Public Weal").

A union of powerful French nobles, formed against Louis XI, c. 1465.

Ligurian Republic.

The name assumed by the Republic of Genoa, formed on the model of France, in 1797. Annexed by France 1805.

Ligurian Sage, The.

A surname given to Aulus Persius Flaccus, a Roman satirist (34–62).

Lillibullero (or Lilliburlero).

A political song satirizing James II of England, who had made an unwelcome nomination to the lord-lieutenancy of Ireland, written by Lord Wharton c. 1686. The music, originally a march or quick-step, was by Henry Purcell. Although the merest doggerel, the song gave a great impetus to the revolution of 1688, and the whole army and the people sang it constantly. The refrain, "Lilliburlero bullen a la," is said to have been a watchword of the Irish Roman Catholics in their massacre of the Protestants in 1641.

Limbo (or Limbus).

A region, supposed to lie on the edge or confines of hell, in which the souls of just men not admitted into heaven or purgatory remained to await the resurrection. Such were the patriarchs and other pious people who died before the birth of Christ. The limbo was, therefore, called **Limbus Patrum.** There was also a Limbus Pueroorum (or Infantum) for infants dying unbaptized. To these were added a **Limbus Fatuorum,** or Fools' Paradise, the receptacle of all vanity and nonsense. (Cf. Milton's "Paradise Lost," bk. III, ll. 440–97.) The word **limbo** is often used familiarly in the sense of a prison or durance vile.

Lincoln's Inn, *v.* Inns of Court.

The name is derived from the Earl of Lincoln, who built his town house here in the fourteenth century on property originally belonging to the Black Friars.

Lincoln's Inn Fields Theatre.

A theatre formerly standing on the south side of Lincoln's Inn Fields, built by Christopher Rich, and opened by John Rich in 1714. In 1734 Italian operas were given there. In 1756 it was converted into barracks and used for other purposes until 1848, when it was demolished to make room for an addition to the College of Surgeons. There were two other theatres near its site, viz., the Duke's Theatre (q.v.) and the theatre in Little Lincoln's Inn Fields (1695–1705).

Lion, Le.

A surname given to Louis VIII of France (1187–1226) for his valour.

Lion, The.

A surname of Henry, Duke of Saxony and Bavaria (1129–95) : of William, king of Scotland (1142–1214).

Lion-hearted, The, *v.* Cœur de Lion.

Lion-hunter, The.

A surname given to Roualeyn George Gordon Cumming a Scottish traveller and sportsman (1820–66), who lived and hunted in South Africa 1843–8.

Lion of God.

A surname of the Caliph Ali (c. 600–61), son of Abu Taleb, Mahomet's uncle.

Lion of Lucerne.

A famous piece of sculpture (by Thorwaldsen), commemorating the heroism and devotion of nearly 800 Swiss guards who died to save Louis XVI in the attack on the Tuileries, August 10, 1792. The colossal figure of the crouching lion, transfixed and dying, but still faithfully defending the lilied shield of France is carved in the round in a recess in the face of an upright, vine-draped rock, in a little park at Lucerne. An inscription, with the names of the officers killed, is cut in the rock.

Lion of St. Mark.

A symbolical lion, represented as winged and holding an open book, on which is written *Pax tibi, Marce, Evangelista meus,* or a part of this. It is the characteristic device of Venice. *v.* Columns of St. Mark and St. Theodore.

Lion of Sweden, The.

A surname given to Johan Banér (or Banier or Banner), a Swedish general (1596–1641) in the Thirty Years' War (q.v.)

Lion of the North.

A surname of Gustavus (II) Adolphus the Great of Sweden (1594–1632). Also called the Star of the North by the Protestants of Germany, and sometimes the Swedish Maccabæus.

Lion of the Sea, The, *v.* Cape of Storms (Portuguese, Leão do Mar).

Lion Sermon, The.

An annual sermon preached in St. Katharine Cree Church, Leadenhall Street, London, in memory of Sir John Gayer, who was Lord Mayor of London in 1646. He was travelling in the Turkish dominions when a " king of the desert " threatened to swallow him up. The knight knelt down and prayed, and the animal fled.

Lion's Mouth, *v.* Bocca di Leone.

Literary Club, The.

A club founded by Sir Joshua Reynolds, Dr. Samuel Johnson, and others, meeting originally at the Turk's Head in Gerrard Street (*v.* Club, The), and continuing to meet there until 1783. After several removals they settled in the Thatched House in St. James's Street. " So originated and was formed," says Forster, " that famous club which had made itself a name in literary history long before it received, at Garrick's funeral, the name of the Literary Club." The name was changed to " the Johnson Club," and on the Thatched House being taken down the club removed to the Clarendon Hotel in Bond Street, where it celebrated its centennial in 1864. It is still in existence. *Chambers, Timbs.*

Literary Colossus, The, *v.* Great Moralist, The.

Little, The (Latin, Parvus).

A surname of John of Salisbury, a noted English ecclesiastic, scholar and author, bishop of Chartres (c. 1115–80). He was present at the murder of Thomas à Becket.

Little Corporal, The, *v.* Caporal, Le Petit.

Little Duke, The, *v.* Protestant Duke, The.

Little England.

A popular surname given to Barbadoes by the inhabitants.

Little Giant, The.

A popular surname of Stephen Arnold Douglas, an American democratic politician (1813–61).

Little Italy.

A popular name given to the colony of Italians at Saffron Hill, London.

Little Mac.

A nickname of George Brinton McClellan, a celebrated American general and politician (1826–85). *v.* Little Napoleon, The.

Little Magician, The.

A popular name for Martin Van Buren, eighth President of the United States (1782–1862).

Little Marlborough, The.

A surname of Count Kurt Christoph Schwerin, a German general (1684–1757).

Little Master, The.

A surname given to Hans Sebald Beham, a celebrated painter and engraver (c. 1500–50), in allusion to the extreme smallness of his prints. Also to other artists of the same period.

Little Napoleon, The.

A surname given to George Brinton McClellan, a celebrated American general and politician (1826–85) by his troops during the Civil War. Also **Little Mac.** Also to Pierre Gustave Toutant Beauregard, another American general (1818–93) in a similar manner. *v.* **Old Bory.**

Little Paris.

A name sometimes given to Brussels. Also to Milan, Italy.

Little Parliament.

The Parliament convened by Cromwell, July 4, 1653, so

D.N.   N

called from the small number—
about 140—of its members.
By it Cromwell was constituted
Lord Protector. Also called
" Barebones' Parliament " (q.v).

Little Phil.

A nickname of Philip Henry
Sheridan, a famous American
general (1831–88).

Little Queen, The.

A surname given to Isabella
of Valois (or of France) (1389–
1409), who married Richard II
of England. The marriage contract was signed March 9, 1396,
when she was but seven years
old. In June, 1404 (after
Richard's death), she married
Charles, Count of Angoulême,
the poet.

**Little Red Fox, The, *v*. Peaceful,
The.**

Little Rhody.

A popular name for Rhode
Island, the smallest of the
United States.

Little Venice.

A name sometimes given to
Arendal, Norway, on account of
its situation.

Little Whig, The.

A nickname given to Anne,
Countess of Sutherland (d. 1716),
second daughter of the great
Duke of Marlborough.

Live-Oak State.

The State of Florida.

Liverpool Landseer, The.

A surname given to William
Huggins, a noted animal painter
(1821–84).

**Living Anatomy, The, *v*. Patri-
arch of Ferney, The.**

Living Dictionary.

A surname given (by George I)
to Baron Gottfried Wilhelm von
Leibnitz (or Leibniz), a celebrated German philosopher and
mathematician (1646 – 1716).
Cf. **Walking Library**.

**Living Pentecost, The, *v*. Pente-
côte Vivante, La.**

Livy of Portugal, The.

A surname given to João de
Barros, a Portuguese historian
(1496–1570).

Livy of Spain, The.

A surname given to Juan de
Mariana, a Spanish Jesuit historian (1537–1624).

**Lloyd, North German, *v*. Nord-
deutscher Lloyd.**

Lloyd's Coffee-house.

A noted coffee-house in Lombard Street, which became the
centre of ship-broking and
marine insurance, kept by
Edward Lloyd (fl. c. beginning
of eighteenth century). He
previously kept a coffee-house
in Tower Street. " Lloyd's
News " (September, 1696–
February, 1697), was published
by him, revived as " Lloyd's
List " (1726), and containing
shipping and commercial news.
The corporation known as
" Lloyd's," Royal Exchange,
takes its name from him.

Lloyd's, *v*. Lloyd's Coffee-house.

Lloyd's List.

A periodical containing shipping intelligence issued by
" Lloyd's," Royal Exchange,
since 1716, and as a daily since
1800.

Local Option.

A name referring to proposed legislation, empowering local municipalities to regulate the number of public-houses in their districts.

Locksmith King, The.

Nickname of Louis XVI, king of France (1754–93), alluding to his hobby of lock-making.

Locofocos.

A nickname given by the Whig newspapers in New York (1835) to the Democratic Party (q.v.), alluding to an incident occurring at a stormy political meeting at Tammany Hall (q.v.). The chairman of the meeting left his seat and the lights were extinguished, but the opposing faction produced candles and *loco-foco* matches and re-lighted the hall.

Log-Cabin and Hard-Cider Campaign, The, *v.* Log-Cabin Harrison.

Log-Cabin Harrison.

A nickname given to Harrison, 9th President of the United States (1773–1841). His electoral campaign in 1840 was called the Log-Cabin and Hard-Cider Campaign.

Loi Bérenger (French, " Bérenger Law ").

The name by which a French law passed in 1891 is popularly known, from its introducer. A kind of First Offenders' Act.

Loi Naquet (French, "Naquet Law."

The name given to the law introduced by Alfred Joseph Naquet (b. 1834), re-establishing divorce in France.

Lollards.

A semi-monastic society for the care of the sick and the burial of the dead, originating at Antwerp c. 1300. Also the English followers of Wycliffe, adherents of a wide-spread movement, partly political and socialistic, and in some respects anticipating Protestantism and Puritanism, in the fourteenth and fifteenth centuries. They were also called Bible-men, from their reverence for the Bible. Lollards were very numerous at the close of the fourteenth century, and perhaps formed later part of the Lancastrian party in the Wars of the Roses. Also called **Wickliffites** or **Wyckliffites.**

Lombard League.

An association between Brescia, Bergamo, Mantua, Verona, Cremona, Treviso, and other cities of Lombardy and Northern Italy, founded in 1167 for protection against Barbarossa. It rebuilt Milan, defeated Frederick at Legnano in 1176, and secured liberties by the Peace of Constance in 1183. It was renewed against Frederick II in 1226.

Lombard Street.

The name of a street in the City of London, often used figuratively to mean the banking or financial world. Cf. **Wall Street.**

Lying Dick Talbot.

A nickname given to the Irish Jacobite, Richard Talbot, Duke of Tyrconnel, Lord-Lieutenant of Ireland, 1686–9 (d. 1691).

London.

A steamship that foundered in the Bay of Biscay, January 10, 1866. Gustavus Vaughan Brooke, the tragedian (b. 1818), lost his life in this ship.

London Company.

A company of merchants and others dwelling in and near London, formed for the purpose of planting colonies in America. It was chartered in 1606, founded a colony at Jamestown in 1607, and was dissolved in 1624.

London Protocol.

The protocol of May 8, 1852, by which the Great Powers recognized Prince Christian of Glücksburg and his male descendants as heirs to Denmark, including Schleswig and Holstein. It was not ratified by the German Diet or the states of Schleswig and Holstein. Also the protocol of March 31, 1877, by which the Great Powers called upon Turkey to make peace with Montenegro and to carry out certain reforms affecting the Christian population in the Sultan's dominions. It was rejected by the Porte, and Russia alone took up arms against Turkey.

London Wall.

A Roman wall built round London between 350 and 369. It enclosed 380 acres. There were two gates in it—the western gate (Newgate) for the Pretorian Way, or Watling Street, and the northern gate (Bishopsgate) for the road to York, or Ermine Street. There was also a gate at the bridge at Dowgate, and possibly one at Billingsgate. The wall was broken down during the Danish invasion, but restored by Alfred (886). Posterns were then opened at Ludgate, Cripplegate, and probably at what was later Moorgate. Fragments of it are still discernible, the most notable portion being in London Wall, between Wood Street and Aldermanbury.

Lone-Star State, The.

A popular surname for the State of Texas, from the single star on its coat-of-arms.

Longchamps.

A race-course at the end of the Bois de Boulogne, west of Paris.

Long Friday.

A name given to Good Friday by the Anglo-Saxons.

Long Meg.

A column of red freestone near Penrith, England, 15 ft. in circumference and 18 ft. high. Supposed to be part of a Druidical temple.

Long Meg of Westminster.

A nickname given to a " lusty, bouncing romp," and procuress in the time of King Henry VIII, whose " Life and Pranks " were printed in 1582.

Long Parliament.

The Parliament which assembled November 3, 1640, and carried on the Civil War. On its showing a disposition to come to terms with the party of Charles I, it was " purged " (*v.* **Pride's Purge**) December 6, 1648, by the expulsion of a large number of its members. The Parliament was forcibly dissolved by Cromwell, April 20, 1653, but was twice restored in 1659, being finally dissolved in March, 1660, after providing for the summoning of a free Parliament. In its later history it was known as the " Rump Parliament " (q.v.).

Long Peter.

A surname given to Peter Aartsen, an eminent Flemish painter (1507–73), in allusion to his tall stature.

Long Scribe.

A nickname given to Vincent Dowling (d. 1852), a British sportsman and authority on all matters connected with field and other sports. He was very tall.

Longshanks.

A surname of Edward I, king of England (1239–1307). *v.* English Justinian, The.

Long Sword.

A surname given to William, a natural son of Henry II of England (and probably a child of the " Fair Rosamond") afterwards Earl of Shrewsbury (d. 1226). (Cf. Michael Drayton's "Polyolbion," xxiii.) Also to William I, Duke of Normandy (r. 927–42).

Long Tom.

A forty-two pound gun originally part of the armament of the French line-of-battleship Hoche, captured in 1798 by the English and sold to the Americans. Brought to New York, from Fayal, on the steamship "Vega," April 18, 1893. Thomas Jefferson, third President of the United States (1743–1826), was also nicknamed " Long Tom," in allusion to his stature.

Long Walk, The.

A straight avenue, about three miles long, in Windsor Park.

Lord Fanny.

A nickname given to Vice-chancellor Lord Hervey (Baron Hervey of Ickworth)(1694–1743), on account of the effeminacy of his habits. Also called (by Pope) Sporus.

Lord Gawkey, *v.* **Tiddy-doll.**

Lord Harry, *v.* **Old Harry.**

Lord of the Age.

A title given to Soliman (or Solyman) the Magnificent, Sultan of Turkey (c. 1490–1566).

Lord of the Isles.

A title assumed intermittently from the twelfth to the sixteenth century by various Scottish chieftains who maintained a practical independence among the islands west of Scotland. Some of the most notable were John Macdonald (d. 1388) and Alexander Macdonald, and the eleventh Earl of Ross. (" The Lord of the Isles " is the title of one of Sir Walter Scott's poems.)

Lord Peter.

A nickname given to the Pope in Arbuthnot's " History of John Bull."

Lords of Little Egypt, The.

A title assumed by the leaders of a horde of gypsies who invaded Hungary and Bohemia from the East, and calling themselves Christian pilgrims.

Lord Strutt.

A nickname given to Charles II of Spain (1661–1700) in Arbuthnot's " History of John Bull."

Losantiville, *v.* **Queen City, The.**

Losecoat Field.

The battle of Stamford (1470)

is sometimes so called because the defeated rebels threw away their coats in their flight.

Lost Cause, The.

A name often used to mean the cause of the Southern States in the American Civil War ; i.e., of negro-slavery and State-sovereignty.

Louisa.

A nickname given to Lewis Wallace, an American general, diplomatist, lawyer, and author (b. 1827) by his soldiers during the Civil War.

Louisiana Purchase.

The territory which the United States acquired, under Jefferson's administration, in 1803, by purchase from France, then under the government of Bonaparte as first consul. The price was $15,000,000. It consisted of New Orleans and a vast tract extending westward from the Mississippi River to the Rocky Mountains, and from the Gulf of Mexico to British America.

Lovers' War, The, v. Guerre des Amoureux, La.

Low Countries.

A name given (a) to the Netherlands ; (b) to the low region near the North Sea comprised in the modern Netherlands and Flanders (Belgium).

Lower Empire, v. Bas-Empire, Le.

Loyal Legion, v. Military Order of the Loyal Legion of the United States.

Lubberland, v. Cocaigne, The Land of.

Lucianists.

The followers of Lucian, or Lucan, a Marcionite leader in the second century, who taught that the actual soul and body of a man would not come forth in the resurrection, but some representative of them.

Lucifer.

The morning star ; the planet Venus when it appears in the morning before sunrise. (When it follows the sun, or appears in the evening, it is called Hesperus, or the evening star.) From a passage in Isaiah (xiv. 12) the name, Lucifer, was, by mistake, also given to Satan—

Pandæmonium, city and proud seat
Of Lucifer ; so by allusion call'd
Of that bright star to Satan paragon'd.
Milton, " Paradise Lost," x, 425.

Luddites.

A name given to the rioters who attempted to destroy machinery at Nottingham and elsewhere in England, 1811–2 and 6 ; from a man named Lud. v. General Lud.

Ludgate.

An old gate of the City of London. In the earlier history of the City, the whole region between it and Westminster was a marsh or fen, and the only western egress was by Watling Street at Newgate. Later the fen was filled up, the "Straunde" road made, and Ludgate built some time in the twelfth century. Ludgate was destroyed in 1760, except the statue of Elizabeth.

Ludlow's Code, *v.* **Code of 1650.**

Ludwig der Springer (German, " Ludwig the Leaper ").

A popular surname given to a margrave of Thuringia (b. 1042), who escaped from the castle of Giebichenstein, near Halle, by boldly leaping into the Saale.

Lumber State, The.

A popular surname for the State of Maine, alluding to its extensive lumber trade.

Lun, *v.* **Father of Harlequins, The.**

Lusitania.

The ancient Latin and modern poetic name for Portugal.

Lutetia.

The ancient Latin and modern poetic name for Paris.

Lydford Law, *v.* **Cupar Justice.**

Lynch Law.

A term used to express summary punishment without trial, generally carried out by a mob. The phrase is said to have been derived from Charles Lynch, a Virginian planter and colonel (1736–96), who set himself, with two neighbours, the task of securing order by punishing offenders with stripes or banishment without legal process. There are other versions.

Lyonesse (or **Leonnoys**).

A mythical region near Cornwall, in the Arthurian cycle of romance. It was the land from which Arthur came, and of which Meliadus was king. It is said to be more than 40 fathoms under water between the Land's End and the Scilly Isles, the sea having gradually encroached upon the land.

Mabille (or **Jardin Mabille**).

A famous open-air garden formerly existing in Paris in the neighbourhood of the Champs Elysées, a resort of the " demimonde."

Macaire, Robert.

A typical villain in French comedy, originally an assassin.

Macedonian, *v.* **United States.**

Macedonian, The.

A surname given to Basil I (Basilius), a Byzantine emperor (c. 813 or 826–86), and founder of the Macedonian dynasty.

Macedonia's Madman, *v.* **Madman of Macedonia, The.**

Madame Déficit, *v.* **Madame Véto.**

Madame Etiquette.

A nickname given to the Duchesse de Noailles, mistress of the ceremonies at the court of Marie Antoinette.

Madame Sans Gêne (French, without constraint, free-and-easy).

A nickname of the wife of Marshal (François Joseph) Lefebvre, duke of Dantzic (1755–1820), who was raised from the ranks by Napoleon I. She was originally a washerman, and followed her husband to the wars as a " vivandière." She was rude, kind-hearted and without knowledge of social etiquette, and became the butt of the court, but her natural shrewdness gave her the advantage in the long run. The heroine of a play by Victorien Sardou (produced 1893) so named.

Madame Véto.

A nickname given to Marie

Antoinette during the French Revolution. She is mentioned by this name in " La Carmagnole " (q.v.). Also called **Madame Déficit** by the Parisians, in allusion to Budget deficiencies. Her husband, Louis XVI (1754–93), was called **Monsieur Véto**.

Mad Anthony.

A nickname given to Anthony Wayne, an American general (1745–96) on account of his reckless bravery.

Mad Cavalier, The.

A surname of Prince Rupert (1619–82), nephew of Charles I of England.

Madman, The.

A surname given to Sebastian, King of Portugal (1554–78).

Madman of Macedonia, The.

A surname sometimes given to Alexander (III) the Great, King of Macedonia (356–323 B.C.).

Madman of the North.

A surname given to Charles XII of Sweden (1682–1718). Sometimes called the **Brilliant Madman** and the **Quixote of the North**.

Mad Parliament.

(So named by the partizans of Henry III in derision.) A great council held at Oxford in 1258 in order to settle the differences between the king and the barons which had arisen owing to the persistent evasion by the former of the provisions of Magna Charta. It enacted the Provisions of Oxford (q.v.), requiring the king's faithful observance of the Great Charter, and providing for the assembling of a parliament three times a year and regular control over the chief justiciar, chancellor and other high officers.

Mad Poet, The.

A surname sometimes given to Nathaniel Lee, an English dramatist (c. 1653–92). He became insane in 1684 and was confined in an asylum for five years. Also applied to MacDonald Clarke, an American poet (1798–1842) on account of his eccentricities. He died in the Insane Asylum at Bloomingdale, New York.

Mad Priest, The.

Surname given to John Ball, an English priest (d. 1381). He it was who preached at Blackheath on the text—

" When Adam dalf, and Eve span,
    Who was thenne a gentilman ? "

Madrid, Treaty of, v. Treaty of Madrid.

Mæonian Swan, v. Father of Epic Poetry.

Maffia (or Mafia).

A formidable secret society in Sicily, organized for the purpose of promoting smuggling and protecting its members against the police.

Magician of the North, The (German, " Magus aus Norden ").

A surname of Johann Georg Hamann, a noted German *littérateur* and philosophical writer (1730–88).

Magister Sententiarum, *v.* **Master of Sentences.**

Magna Charta (or **Carta**).

The great charter of the liberties (Magna Charta Libertatum) of England, granted and sealed by King John in a conference between him and his barons at Runnymede, June 15, 1215. Its most important articles are those which provide that no freeman shall be taken, or imprisoned, or proceeded against, except by the lawful judgment of his peers or in accordance with the law of the land, and that no scutage or aid shall be imposed in the kingdom (except certain feudal dues from tenants of the Crown), unless by the common council of the kingdom. The remaining and greater part of the charter is directed against abuses of the king's power as feudal superior. The charter granted by Henry III is only a confirmation of that of his father, King John.

Magnanimous, The.

A surname given to Alfonso V (or Alphonso), King of Aragon and, as Alfonso I, King of Sicily and Sardinia and of Naples (1385–1458); to John Frederick (Johann Friedrich), Elector of Saxony (1503–54); to Philip, Landgrave of Hesse (1504–67); to Albert V, Duke of Austria (Emperor of Germany as Albert II) (1397–1439).

Magnificent, The.

A surname given to Alfonso III (or Alphonso), King of Aragon (1265–91); Edmund (or Eadmund) I, King of the West Saxons and Mercians (c. 922–46); *v.* **Devil, The;** Solyman I,

Sultan of Turkey (c. 1490–1566). Also called the **Lord of the Age;** *v.* **Magnifico, Il.**

Magnifico, Il (Italian, "The Magnificent").

A surname of Lorenzo de' Medici, a celebrated Florentine statesman and patron of letters (c. 1449–92), grandson of Cosmo the Elder. Also called the **Father of Letters.**

Magnus.

A surname given to Albertus, a scholastic philosopher and member of the Dominican order (1193, or 1205–80). Also surnamed **Doctor Universalis.**

Magog, *v.* **Gog and Magog;** also Ezekiel xxviii, 2.

Maiden, The.

A surname given to Malcolm IV, King of Scotland (1141–65).

Maiden, The.

A name given to a sort of guillotine which the Regent Morton introduced into Scotland. He was himself beheaded by it in 1581.

Maiden Queen, The.

Queen Elizabeth of England (1533–1603), who never married. Also called the **Virgin Queen** and the **World's Wonder.**

Maiden Town, The.

A surname given to Edinburgh, from a tradition that it was at one time the residence of the daughters of the Pictish kings who were sent to that stronghold for protection in war time. Also called the **Castle of Maidens** or the **Mountain of Sorrow.**

Maid of Athens.

The daughter of Theodore Macri, a consul at Athens. She made Byron's acquaintance, and he is said to have addressed the song beginning "Maid of Athens, ere we part," to her.

Maid of Bath, The.

A surname given to Miss Eliza Ann Linley, an English soprano singer (1754–92), who married Richard Brinsley Sheridan, the dramatist, under romantic circumstances. Cf. Foote's play, " The Maid of Bath."

Maid of Kent, *v.* Nun of Kent.

Maid of Norway, *v.* Fair Maid of Norway.

Maid of Orleans, The.

A surname given to Joan of Arc (Jeanne d'Arc or Darc), the French national heroine (1412–31). Also called La Pucelle and the Wondrous Maid.

Maid of Saragossa.

A surname given to Agustina (d. June, 1857), noted for her bravery in the defence of Saragossa, 1808–9. Cf. Lord Byron's "Childe Harold," canto 1.

Maine Liquor Law.

A stringent law against the sale of intoxicating liquors as a beverage, enacted in Maine in 1851. The first prohibitory law in the United States.

Main Plot, The.

A conspiracy in 1603 in favour of Arabella Stuart against James I of England. Raleigh was implicated in it and was imprisoned. The principal or " main " plot of two organized against James on his accession. *v.* Bye, or Surprise, Plot.

Maison Dorée, La.

A noted restaurant in Paris, situated in the Boulevard des Italiens. Built by Lemaire in 1839.

Maître Adam (French, "Master Adam").

A name by which the French poet, Adam Billaut (1602–62) is familiarly known.

Malbrough or Malbrook.

A celebrated French song, beginning " Malbrough s'en vat-en guerre," probably dating from c. 1709. Marie Antoinette took a fancy to it in 1781, after which Beaumarchais introduced it in " Le Mariage de Figaro " in 1784, and Beethoven repeated it in his " Battle Symphony " (1813), as the symbol of the French army. The air is that to which " We won't go home till morning " is sung. *Grove.*

Malignants, The.

The adherents of Charles I and Charles II (Royalists and Cavaliers) during the Civil War ; so called by the opposite party, the Roundheads (q.v.).

Malleus Monachorum (Latin, "The Maul of Monks").

A surname given to Thomas Cromwell, Earl of Essex (c. 1485–1540), an English statesman, the son of a blacksmith. In 1535 he was appointed vicar-general of Henry VIII to carry into effect the Act of Supremacy (q.v.), in which capacity he began (1536) the suppression of the monasteries.

Malthusian Doctrine.

The doctrine set forth in Thomas Robert Malthus's essay on the "Principle of Population" (published 1798), which he defines to be that population increases in a geometrical and means of subsistence in an arithmetical ratio, and that vice and crime are necessary checks of this increase in numbers.

Mamelukes.

A corps of cavalry formerly existing in Egypt, whose chiefs were long the sovereign rulers of the country. About 1251 they established their government in Egypt by making one of their own number sultan. Their government was overthrown by Selim I of Turkey in 1517, but they formed part of the Egyptian army until 1811, when Mehemet Ali destroyed most of them by a general massacre.

Mammoth Cave.

The largest known cave, situated in Edmonson county, near Green River, Kentucky, seventy-five miles south-southwest of Louisville. It extends over an area of eight or ten miles in diameter, and consists of numerous chambers connected by avenues which are said to be in the aggregate 150 miles in length. The stalactite formations are of great beauty and the animal inhabitants very interesting. The cave was discovered in 1809.

Manchester Martyrs, The.

A name given, by the Irish, to three men (Allan, Larkin and O'Brien), who were executed for murdering a policeman in an attempted rescue of Fenian prisoners at Manchester in 1867.

Manchester of America, The.

A surname given to Lowell, Massachusetts, noted for its manufactures of cotton and woollen goods. Also called the Spindle City.

Manchester of Belgium, The.

A surname given to Ghent, Belgium, noted for its manufactures of linen, cotton, lace, leather goods and engines.

Manchester of Prussia, The.

A surname given to Elberfeld, an important manufacturing town in the Rhine Province, Prussia.

Manchester Poet, The.

A surname given to Charles Swain, an English poet (1803–74), born at Manchester.

Manchester School, The.

A name applied to a party of English Radicals organized at Manchester c. 1848. An offshoot of the Anti-Corn Law League. Richard Cobden and John Bright were its chief representatives.

Manicheans (or Manichæans).

The followers of Mani (or Manes, or Manichæus) (b. c. 215–6 A.D.), according to whom a realm of light and a realm of darkness have always been opposed to each other. In the visible world both are mingled, and the object of the world is to free the light from the intermingled darkness. Valentinian III punished the Manicheans with banishment, Justinian with death. Vandal persecution destroyed them in North Africa.

Man Milliner, The.

A surname of Henry III, King of France (1551–89), who spent his time in devising new fashions in dress instead of attending to State affairs. His favourites and companions in his debauchery were called **Mignons.**

Man of Bath, The.

A surname given to Ralph Allen (1694–1764), a friend of Pope, an English philanthropist. Cf. Pope's "Epilogue to the Satires of Horace," Dialogue i. ll. 135–6.

Man of Blood, The.

A name given by the English Puritans to Charles I (1600–49). Also applied to Thomas Simmons, an English murderer, executed at Hertford, March 7, 1808.

Man of Blood and Iron, The.

A name given to Prince von Bismarck (Otto Eduard Leopold), a Prussian statesman (1815–98).

Man of Chios, The, *v.* Father of Epic Poetry, The.

Man of December, The, *v.* L'homme de Décembre.

Man of Destiny, The.

A name given to Napoleon I (1769–1821).

Man of Kent, *v.* Kentish Man.

Man of Ross, The.

A surname given to John Kyrle, a benevolent and public-spirited man (1637–1724, at Ross), a general mediator in the neighbourhood of the estates he inherited from his father. Immortalized by Pope in his "Moral Essays" (iii. 250).

Man of Sedan, The.

A name given to Napoleon III (1808–73). He was taken prisoner at Sedan, September 2, 1870, during the Franco-Prussian War. Also called the **Man of Silence.**

Man of Silence, The, *v.* Man of Sedan, The.

Man of Sin, The, *v.* Noll.

Man of Steel, The, *v.* Adamantius.

Man of the People, The.

A name given to Charles James Fox, an English statesman and orator (1749–1806) on account of a satire by George Colman the younger. *v.* **Young Cub, The.**

Man on Horseback, The.

A popular surname of Georges Ernest Jean Marie Boulanger, a French general and politician (1837–91), from his habit of appearing in public on his favourite black horse.

Mantuan Swan (or Bard).

A surname of Virgil, a famous Roman poet (70–19 B.C.), as a native of Mantua. Also **Swan of Mantua.**

Man without a Skin, The.

A name given to Richard Cumberland, an English dramatist (1732–1811), by David Garrick. His extreme sensitiveness made him incapable of enduring the slightest adverse criticism. Also called the English **Terence**, or **Terence of England.** Cf. Sir Fretful Plagiary, in "The Critic," by R. B. Sheridan.

Man with the Iron Mask, The.

A French State prisoner confined in the Bastille (where he

died, November 19, 1703), Pigne-rol, and other prisons in the reign of Louis XIV. His name was never mentioned, but he was buried under that of Marchiali, and he always wore a mask of iron covered with black velvet. He has been supposed to be (1) the Duke of Vermandois, a natural son of Louis XIV and Mademoiselle de la Vallière ; (2) an elder brother of Louis XIV, the son of Anne of Austria and the Duke of Buckingham ; (3) a twin brother of Louis XIV ; (4) Count Matthioli, a minister of the Duke of Mantua, im-prisoned for treachery ; (5) a soldier of fortune named Mare-chiel, the head of a conspiracy to assassinate the king and his ministers. This last conjecture was considered the most reason-able until 1891, when Captain Bazeries, of the garrison of Nantes, published in the " Progrès de Nantes " (re-published in " Le Temps," August 7, 1891), a translation of some cypher despatches of Louis XIV and of Louvois, apparently showing that the prisoner was Général de Bulonde, who raised the siege of Cuneo unnecessarily, and compromised the success of the campaign. Opinions still differ as to the identity of the prisoner. (This personage is introduced into A. Dumas' novel, " Le Vicomte de Bragelonne.")

Maple City, The.

A surname given to Ogdens-burg, St. Lawrence county, New York, from the number of its shade-trees.

Marabouts.

The members of a Moorish priestly order or race of Northern Africa, successors of the Mora-bits or Almoravides, a Moham-medan sect or tribe who ruled Morocco and part of Spain in the eleventh and twelfth centuries. They exercise great influence over the Berbers and Moslem negroes.

Marais, Le (French, " The Marsh ").

A name given to the group of members who sat in the lower part of the Assembly during the first French Revolution. Cf. " La Montagne " (*v.* Montagne, La). The name specially applied to the region of Paris lying east of the Rue St.-Denis and north of the Rue St.-Antoine. It was subject to inundations. A large part of it was held in the middle ages by the knights of the Temple. Also a swampy region in the western part of France, near La Rochelle. In ancient times it was an arm of the sea.

Marandaise.

The sword of Ryance, a legendary king of Ireland and Wales in the Arthurian legends.

Marburg Conference.

A fruitless conference held at Marburg, Prussia, October, 1529, between Luther and others on one side, and Zwingli and other Swiss reformers on the other.

Marcellians.

The professed followers of Marcellus, Bishop of Ancyra, in the fourth century. The Mar-cellains held the doctrine that the Holy Spirit and the Word, or Logos, are merely impersonal agencies and qualities of God, and that the incarnation of the Logos is temporary only.

Marcellinists.

The adherents of Marcellina, a female gnostic of the second century, and a teacher of Gnosticism in Rome.

Marches.

The border regions of England and Wales.

Marcionites.

The followers of Marcion of Sinope, a Gnostic religious teacher of the second century, and the founder at Rome of the Marcionite sect, which lasted until the seventh century or later. Marcion taught that there were three primal forces: the good God, the evil matter, and the Demiurge, the finite and imperfect God of the Jews.

Mardi Gras. (French, literally, " Fat Tuesday.")

Shrove Tuesday, the day before Ash Wednesday and last day of carnival. Derived from the French practice of parading a fat ox (" bœuf gras ") during the celebration of the day.

Mariana.

The name given by John Mason to the territory granted to him (1622) between the Salem River and the Merrimac.

Marianne, La.

A French republican secret society formed to overturn the government instituted by the " coup d'état " of 1851. It received orders from the society in London, of which Ledru-Rollin and Mazzini were members. One of its passwords was, " Connaissez-vous Marianne ? " and the answer was " De la montagne." In 1854 the government arrested many members of the society, and punished them by longer or shorter terms of imprisonment. Also called in English, **Mary Ann.**

Maria Wood.

The name of a civic pleasure-barge, once the property of the lord mayors of London. Built in 1816 by Sir Matthew Wood, and named after his eldest daughter. Sold in 1859 for £410 to Alderman Humphrey.

Maroons.

The name formerly given in Jamaica to bands of fugitive slaves and their descendants. They formed villages in the mountains in the seventeenth century. Under their leader, Cudjoe, they became formidable early in the eighteenth century, attacking plantations and openly opposing government troops. In 1738 Governor Trelawney made a treaty of peace with them, securing their freedom and granting them lands. They rebelled in 1795, were partially reduced in 1796, and many of them were sent to Nova Scotia and Sierra Leone. The last outbreak of the survivors was in 1798.

Marseillaise, La.

A popular French patriotic song. Words and music by Claude Joseph Rouget de Lisle, a captain of engineers, and were composed at Strasburg in a fit of enthusiasm on the night of April 24, 1792. It was first called " Chant de guerre pour l'armée du Rhin." *Grove,* "Dict. of Music," ii, 220.

Marshal Forward (or "Vorwarts.")

A nickname of Field Marshal Gebhard Leberecht von Blücher, Prince of Wahlstadt (1742–1819). He commanded the Prussians at Waterloo, June 18, 1815.

Marshalsea Prison.

A prison in Southwark, London, used latterly for debtors, and abolished in 1849.—See *Hare,* "London" i, 465 ; also *Dickens,* "Little Dorrit."

Mars of Portugal, The, *v.* Portuguese Mars, The.

Martinists.

The members of the school of religionists formed originally by the Chevalier St.-Martin (1743–1803) a few years before the beginning of the French Revolution. The Martinists were transplanted to Russia during the reign of Catherine II. *Blunt,* "Dict. of Sects."

Martinus Scriblerus Club, *v.* Scriblerus Club.

Martyr, The, *v.* Royal Martyr, The.

Also a surname of Edward, King of the West Saxons (c. 963–79). Murdered by order of his stepmother Elfrida ; of St. Justin, a celebrated Greek church father (d. probably c. 163 A.D.). He is said to have been scourged and beheaded at Rome. Also called the Philosopher.

Martyr King, The.

A surname given to Louis XVI, King of France (1754–93) ;

also to Henry VI, King of England (1421–71).

Marvellous Boy, The.

A name given to Thomas Chatterton, an English poet (1752–70). He committed suicide.

Marylebone Gardens.

A formerly celebrated place of entertainment in London. It consisted principally of a garden at the back of "The Rose" tavern in High Street, Marylebone, and was in existence in the middle of the seventeenth century. Its popularity gradually died out and the site was built over c. 1778. Beaumont Street and part of Devonshire Place now cover it. The tavern was rebuilt in 1855, and the Marylebone Music Hall was built behind it. *Grove.*

Mary Stuart of Italy, The.

A surname given to Jane I, Queen of Naples (1325–82). (Cf. "Jeanne de Naples," a tragedy by J. F. de La Harpe.)

Mason and Dixon's Line.

A boundary line between Maryland and Pennsylvania, fixed by Charles Mason and Jeremiah Dixon, employed by Lord Baltimore and William Penn. The line fixed (1763–7) ran to a point 244 miles west from the Delaware River, N. lat. 39° 43'. It is famous as (in part) the boundary between the free and the former slave states. *v.* also **Dixie's Land.**

Masque de Fer, *v.* Man with the Iron Mask, The.

Massachusetts Bay Company.

A colonizing company chartered in 1629 and growing out of the Dorchester Company. Its immediate cause was the danger to political and religious freedom in England under Charles I. Endicott was the first local governor. In 1630 Winthrop, as the new governor, conducted a large expedition which founded Boston.

Massacre of Glencoe.

A name given to the massacre (Feb., 1692) of about forty Macdonalds by royal troops at Glencoe at the instigation of the Master (afterwards Earl) of Stair.

Massacre of St. Bartholomew.

A massacre of the Huguenots, commencing in Paris on the night of August 23-4 (St. Bartholomew's Day), 1572. The anti-Huguenot leaders were the Duke of Guise, the queen mother (Catherine de Medici) and Charles IX. Coligny was the principal victim, and the total number in France is estimated at from 20,000 to 30,000. The occasion was the wedding festivities of Henry of Navarre. Sometimes called the **Bloody Wedding**.

Massacres of September.

A series of murders perpetrated by the extreme revolutionists at Paris, September 2-6, 1792, the victims being royalists and constitutionalists confined in prison. The massacres were undertaken by the Commune of Paris, and were occasioned by the consternation felt over the approach of the Prussians, whose avowed abject was to restore the king. (See Duruy, " Hist. of France.")

Master, The, *v.* **Meister, Der.**

Master Adam, *v.* **Maître Adam.**

Master Betty, *v.* **Young Roscius.**

Master of Sentences (Latin, "Magister Sententiarum").

A surname given to Peter Lombard (Petrus Lombardus), an Italian theologian (c. 1100–60) appointed bishop of Paris, 1159. From his work " Sententiarum libri IV."

Maud S.

An American trotting mare, by Harold, dam Miss Russell. At Cleveland in 1885 she made the record of one mile in 2:08¾, but lost it to Sunol (2·08¼) in 1891.

Maul of Monks, The, *v.* **Malleus Monachorum.**

Maundy Thursday.

The Thursday preceding Good Friday. Sometimes (erroneously) called **Holy Thursday.**

Mauser Rifle.

A breech-loading magazine rifle adopted in 1871 for the German army.

Mauvais, Le (French, "The Bad ").

A surname given to Charles II, King of Navarre (1332–87).

May-day.

The first day of May. A day on which the opening of the season of flowers and fruit was formerly celebrated throughout Europe, and it is still marked in some places by various festive observances, such as the crowning of the May-queen, dancing round the May-pole, etc. Cf.

Tennyson's poem, "The May Queen." Sometimes jokingly called Chummies' Day (Chimney Sweeps' Day), from the custom of that trade to perambulate the streets with a Jack-in-the-Green (q.v.).

Mayflower.

A ship, of about 180 tons burthen, in which the English Pilgrims sailed from Southampton to Plymouth, Massachusetts, in 1620. Some of them had left Leyden for Delfshaven and embarked there in the "Speedwell" (q.v.) some weeks before, joining the others at Southampton. Also an American wooden centre-board sloop yacht, designed by Edward Burgess, launched May 6, 1886. Dimensions : length, over all, 100 feet ; length load water line, 85·7 feet ; beam, 23·6 feet ; beam, load water-line, 22·3 feet ; draught, ten feet ; displacement, 128 tons. She was selected to defend America's cup against the "Galatea" in 1886 on September 7 and 9, and won both races.

May Laws.

A series of Prussian laws passed 1873-4, and modified in 1887, regulating ecclesiastical matters, and restricting the power of the church over individuals and property. So named from having been first promulgated in May, 1873 ; also called **Falk Laws,** from the name of the minister who furthered them. The term is also applied to an order which received the Czar's assent May 3, 1882, concerning the Jews in Russia, resulting in unparalleled cruelty to them, and causing horror and indig-

D.N.

nation throughout western Europe.

May Meetings.

A collective name given to the annual meetings in London (generally held at Exeter Hall in April and May) of various religious and philanthropic societies.

Maynooth Grant, The.

The name given to a grant made by the government under Sir Robert Peel's administration in 1845 to the Roman Catholic College at Maynooth, Ireland, fourteen miles from Dublin. Abolished when the Irish Church was disestablished in 1869.

Maypole, The.

A nickname given by the people to the Duchess of Kendal (d. 1743), George I's mistress, in allusion to her height and leanness. She was German, and named Erangard Melrose de Schulemberg.

Mazarin Bible.

An edition of the Bible printed by Gutenberg at Mainz in 1450-5, being the first book ever printed with movable types. So named from the first known copy of it being discovered in the Mazarin library at Paris in 1760.

Mazas.

A prison in Paris, situated in the Boulevard Mazas, opened in 1850. Officially named the "Maison d'Arrêt Cellulaire," the name it had hitherto borne having been renounced in 1858, at the request of the family of Mazas. It is still, however,

o

popularly called the Prison Mazas.

McKinley Act.

A tariff Act, so named from the chairman (William McKinley) of the Ways and Means Committee, which became law October, 1890. Some of its leading provisions are increased duties on tin-plates and on barley, and some other agricultural products ; a general increase in the duties on wool and woollen and cotton manufactures ; and the remission of the duty on raw sugar (with a bounty to domestic sugar producers). Another important part was the reciprocity feature, which provided for the remission of duties on sugar, molasses, tea, coffee, and hides, from countries which should remove duties on American imported products. Repealed 1894.

Meal-Tub Plot.

A pretended conspiracy against the Protestants, fabricated in 1679 by Dangerfield. So named from the papers having been kept in a meal-tub. Dangerfield subsequently confessed, and was whipped and pilloried.

Medjidi (Turkish, "Glorious").

A Turkish order of knighthood, instituted in 1852 by the Sultan Abdul-Medjid, and conferred upon many foreign officers who took part with Turkey in the Crimean War.

Meek, The.

A surname of Frederick II, Elector and Duke of Saxony (1411–64).

Meister, Der (German, "The Master").

A surname given to Johann Wolfgang von Goethe, poet, dramatist and prose-writer (1749–1832), by his admirers. The greatest name in German literature. Also called the Coryphæus of German Literature and the Voltaire of Germany.

Mekhitarists.

An order of Armenian monks in communion with the Church of Rome, under a rule resembling the Benedictine, founded by Peter Mekhitar at Constantinople in 1701, confirmed in 1712 by the Pope, and finally settled on the island of San Lazzaro, near Venice, in 1717. The Mekhitarists are devoted to the religious and literary interests of the Armenian race wherever found. Also written Mechitarists.

Melchites (from the Armenian, "Melek," king).

The orthodox Eastern Christians, as distinguished from the Monophysites or Nestorians. The name Melchites is sometimes also given to members of communities of Christians in Syria and Egypt, formerly in communion with the Orthodox Greek Church, who have submitted to the Roman See.

Meletians.

A sect of the fourth and fifth centuries, followers of Meletius, a schismatic bishop of Lycopolis, in Egypt. After his death they adopted Aryan views. Also the followers of Meletius, made bishop of Antioch about 360.

Mellifluous Doctor, The.

A surname of St. Bernard, a celebrated French ecclesiastic (1091–1153). Also **Honeyed Teacher.**

Mennonites.

A Christian denomination, originating in Friesland early in the sixteenth century, and holding doctrines of which Menno Simons (1492–1559) was the chief exponent. The leading features of the Mennonite bodies have been baptism on profession of faith, refusal of oaths, of civic offices, and of the support of the state in war, and a tendency to asceticism. Many of these beliefs and practices have been modified, and in the seventeenth century the sect became divided into the Upland (Obere) Mennonites, or Ammanites, and the Lowland (Untere) Mennonites, the former being the more conservative and rigorous. Members of the sect are found in the Netherlands, Germany, Russia, etc., and especially in the United States.

Mercator's Projection.

The name given to a map of the world showing all the meridians of longitude as perpendicular to the equator, in other words, the surface of the globe as if it were flat. Consequently the shapes of countries in proportion to their distance from the equator, and especially near the poles, are exaggerated. The system was invented by Mercator (Gerhard Kremer), a Flemish geographer (1512–94).

Merciless Parliament, The.

An English parliament of 1388, so named on account of the cruelty exercised by it towards the adherents of Richard II. Also called the "Wonderful (or Wonder-making) Parliament."

Mercurius.

A surname (on account of his eloquence) of Pope John II, pope 532–5.

Mercurius Aulicius.

A journal in the royal interest, written and published by Sir John Birkenhead at Oxford while the king and court were there. The first number was issued in January, 1642, and it appeared continuously until 1645, after which it was issued occasionally as a weekly. *Dict. Nat. Biog.*

Mercutio of Actors, The.

A surname given to William Thomas Lewis, a noted English comedian (c. 1748–1811).

Mère des Peuples, La (French, "The Mother of Peoples").

A surname given to Marguerite of France (1523–74), daughter of Francis I, King of France, by the people of Savoy. She married Emmanuel Philibert, Duke of Savoy, in 1559.

Merinthians, *v.* **Cerinthians.**

Mermaid Club.

A celebrated club, said to have been established by Sir Walter Raleigh in 1603. It met at the Mermaid Tavern, and Jonson, Beaumont, Fletcher, Selden, and probably Shakspere, were among its members. The Mermaid Tavern was long said to have stood in Friday Street, Cheapside, London, but Ben Jonson has, in his own verse, settled it in Bread Street—

" At Bread Street's Mermaid
having dined and merry,
Proposed to go to Holborn in a
wherry."—Gifford.

It appears, however (see Timbs, " Clubs," pp. 7–8), that the tavern had a way to it from ' Cheap,' Friday and Bread streets, it lying behind these thoroughfares.

Mermaid Tavern, The, *v.* Mermaid Club, The.

Merovingians.

A dynasty of Frankish kings, whose eponymic a n c e s t o r, Merwig, or Merovæus, lived in the fifth century. Violent family feuds caused the power of the Merovingians to wane, until they were finally deposed by Pepin le Bref (the Short), who caused himself to be crowned king of the Franks in 751.

Merrie England, *v.* Merry England.

Merrimac.

A forty-gun screw frigate built for the United States government in 1855. Her hull having been cut down and altered, she was re-named the " Virginia," and commanded by Commodore Franklin Buchanan. On March 8, 1862, she destroyed the " Congress " and the " Cumberland " (sailing ships) at Newport News. The next day she attacked the "Minnesota," and was met by the " Monitor," which had arrived the night before. The engagement lasted from 8 a.m. till noon, and resulted in favour of the " Monitor " (q.v.).

Also a collier sunk by Assistant Naval Constructor Hobson, June 3, 1898, in an attempt to block the entrance to the harbour of Santiago de Cuba.

Merry Andrew.

A surname given originally to Andrew Borde, a learned but eccentric physician (1500–49), who (Hearne says) frequented " markets and fairs," " where he would make humorous speeches, couched in such language as caused mirth," etc. The name has since become a synonym for a buffoon or clown.

Merry England.

An ancient surname given to England, the word " merry " being used in the sense of pleasant or agreeable, e.g. the " merry month of May." (Cf. Belle France, La.)

Merry Monarch, The.

Charles II of England (1630–85) has been so surnamed.

Merveilleuse (French, "Marvellous").

The sword of Doolin (or Doon) of Mayence, ancestor of Ogier the Dane.

Messenger.

A grey thoroughbred horse, by Mambrino, imported into the United States from England, c. 1788. All the main lines of trotting horses, except the Morgans and Clays, are descended from him.

Meteor, *v.* Thistle.

Methodists.

The followers of Charles

Wesley, an English clergyman (1703–91), who founded the Methodist church or sect. He and his followers at Oxford were derisively called Methodists, from the regularity and strict method of their lives and studies.

Methuen Treaty.

A commercial treaty between England and Portugal, negotiated in 1703 by Paul Methuen. Portuguese wines imported into England were admitted for one-third less duty than French wines.

Michael.

A twenty-five-ton barque, one of the ships of Frobisher's first expedition. It early abandoned the other ship, the " Gabriel," and returned to England.

Michel - Ange français, Le (French, " The French Michel Angelo ").

A surname given to Pierre Puget, a famous French painter, sculptor, engineer, and architect (1622–94). Also to Jean Cousin, a French painter, engraver, and sculptor (c. 1500–90).

Michelangelo of Music, The, *v.* Hercules of Music, The.

Michelangelo of the Lyre, The, *v.* Father of Music, The.

Middle Ages.

A name given to a period of about 1,000 years, beginning, according to some, with the invasion of France by Clovis (486), and ending with that of Naples in 1494, or, according to others, with the fall of the Western Empire (q.v.) (476),

and ending with that of the Eastern Empire (q.v.) in 1453.

Middle Flowery Kingdom.

A native appellation for China.

Middle Kingdom, *v.* Middle Flowery Kingdom.

Middle States.

A collective name for the States of New York, New Jersey, Pennsylvania, Delaware, and (sometimes) Maryland.

Middle Temple, *v.* Inns of Court.

Midlothian Campaign, The.

The name given to an electoral campaign in Midlothian by Mr. Gladstone in 1880.

Mignons, *v.* Man Milliner, The.

Milan Decree.

A decree issued December 17, 1807, at Milan, by Napoleon. It declared the forfeiture of all vessels bound to or from British ports, and of all which paid licenses or duties to Great Britain, or had submitted to search by British cruisers.

Milanese Bach, The, *v.* English Bach, The.

Milesians.

The natives of Ireland or the Irish race are so called, from the tradition of an ancient conquest and re-organization of the country by two sons of Milesius, a fabulous king of Spain.

Military Knights of Windsor.

A body of military pensioners having their residence within the precincts of Windsor Castle. Called also " Windsor Knights," and sometimes the " Poor Knights of Windsor."

Military Order of Savoy.

An order founded by King Victor Emmanuel I of Sardinia in 1815, adopted by the kingdom of Italy, and still in existence.

Military Order of the Loyal Legion of the United States.

A society organized at Philadelphia, April 15, 1865, to commemorate the services and perpetuate the memory of those who served in the Union army, and to afford relief to soldiers who survived the war.

Mill-Boy of the Slashes.

A name sometimes given to Henry Clay (1777–1852), a celebrated American statesman and orator, on account of the circumstances of his boyhood.

Millenary Petition.

A petition presented by about a thousand Puritan ministers to James I on his progress to London in April, 1603, asking for certain changes in ceremonial, etc.

Mills Bill.

A tariff bill, named after the chairman (R. Q. Mills) of the Ways and Means Committee, passed by the Democratic House in 1888, and rejected by the Republican Senate. It placed wool, lumber, hemp, and flax on the free list, and reduced duties on pig-iron, woollen goods, etc.

Milton of Germany, The.

A surname given to Friedrich Gottlieb Klopstock, a noted German poet (1724–1803).

Minerva Press.

A printing house in Leadenhall Street, London, noted in the eighteenth century for the publication of sentimental novels.

Ming.

The ruling dynasty in China from 1368 to the accession of the present Manchu dynasty in 1644.

Minims (from Latin, " Minimus," least).

An order of monks, founded in the middle of the fifteenth century by St. Francis of Paula, confirmed by Pope Sixtus IV, and again confirmed by Pope Alexander VI under the name of " Ordo Minimorum Eremitarum S. Francisci de Paula " (Order of the Least Hermits of St. Francis of Paula). Members of this order, in addition to the usual Franciscan vows, were pledged to the observance of a perpetual Lent.

Minors.

The Franciscan friars, the Minorites, so-called from a name of the Franciscan order, **Fratres Minores,** or Lesser Brethren.

Minstrel of the Border, The, *v.* Wizard of the North, The.

Minute-Men.

A nickname given, during the American Revolutionary War, to the militia, consisting of 12,000 men, constituted November 23, 1774, by the Provincial Congress of Massachusetts, from the men being pledged to be ready for service at a minute's notice.

Mirabeau of the Mob, The.

A surname given to Georges

Jacques Danton, a celebrated French Revolutionist (1759–94).

Mirabeau-Tonneau (French, "Barrel-Mirabeau").

A nickname given to André Boniface Louis Riquetti, Vicomte de Mirabeau (1754–92), a brother of the great orator. So called from his rotundity of appearance and his drinking capacity.

Miracle of Nature, The.

A surname of Christina, Queen of Sweden (1626–89). She became a Roman Catholic and settled in Rome, where she died. Was a patroness of men of letters and science, and collected a library which, after her death, was purchased by Pope Alexander VIII.

Miracle of our Age, The.

A surname given to Sir Philip Sidney (or Sydney), an English author and general (1554–86).

Miracle-Plays, *v.* Passion Play.

Miraculous Child, The, *v.* Dieu-Donné.

Mise of Lewes (French, "Mise," arbitration, agreement.

An agreement between the English defeated party under Henry III and the barons under Simon de Montfort, in 1264, directly after the battle of Lewes. It provided for native councillors and the re-organization of Parliament.

Mising Link, The.

A term generally applied to some animal supposed to be intermediate, from the zoo-

logical point of view, between man and the ape.

Mississippi Scheme (or Bubble).

A speculative scheme (also known as "The System") formed under the leadership of John Law (1671–1729) for paying off the national debt of France. He acquired from the French government control of the territory then called "Louisiana" for colonization and trade, the "Compagnie d'Occident" being incorporated for this purpose in 1717. The enterprise became famous under the name of "The Mississippi Scheme." For a while "the System" prospered, fortunes were made in speculation, and Law possessed great power, but the over-issue of paper money and the hostile action of the government brought about a catastrophe, and in May, 1720, "the System" collapsed. Law was driven from France and his estates confiscated.

Missouri Compromise.

An agreement relative to the extinction of slavery, embodied in a bill passed by Congress, March 2, 1820, and in the Act of Congress admitting Missouri into the Union, passed in 1821. It enacted that in all the territory ceded by France, known as Louisiana, north of 36° 30′ N. lat., excepting Missouri, slavery should be for ever prohibited ; and on this concession by the pro-slavery party in Congress, Missouri was admitted as a slave State. It was abrogated by the passage of the Kansas-Nebraska Bill (q.v.) in 1854.

Mistress of the Adriatic, The.

Venice. Also called the Queen of the Adriatic.

Mistress of the Seas, The.

A surname sometimes given to Great Britain in allusion to her naval supremacy.

Mistress of the World, The.

A surname given to ancient Rome.

Mitre, The.

A noted London tavern (formerly No. 39, Fleet Street), the favourite resort of Dr. Johnson. Site now occupied by Hoare's Bank. *Timbs.*

Modern Antigone, The, *v.* **Filia Dolorosa.**

Modern Aristophanes, The, *v.* **English Aristophanes, The.**

Modern Athens, The, *v.* **Athens of America.**

Also applied to Edinburgh, sometimes called the " Queen of the North " (q.v.).

Modern Babylon, The.

London.

Modern Gracchus, The.

A surname given to the Comte de Mirabeau (Gabriel Honoré Riquetti), the greatest orator of the French Revolution (1749–91). Also called the **Hurricane**, in allusion to his fiery eloquence.

Modern Messalina, The.

A name sometimes given to Catherine II of Russia (1729–96) ; also called " the Semiramis of the North."

Modern Pliny, The.

A surname given to Konrad von Gesner, a celebrated Swiss naturalist and scholar (1516–65). His " Historia Animalium " was the most learned and exhaustive work on the subject down to that time.

Modern Rabelais, The.

A surname given to William Maginn, an Irish author (1793–1842), in allusion to his learning, wit, eloquence and humour.

Modern Sesostris, The, *v.* **Armed Soldier of Democracy, The.**

Modern Wagner, The.

A surname given to Engelbert Humperdink, a noted German composer (b. 1854).

Mohammedan Athens, The.

A surname given to Bagdad, Mesopotamia.

Mohocks.

Ruffians who infested the streets of London about the beginning of the eighteenth century, so called from the Indian tribe Mohawks or Mohocks. Cf. Lecky, " England in the Eighteenth Century," i. 522–3.

Molinists.

Those who hold the opinions of Luis Molina, a Spanish Jesuit theologian (1535–1600), in respect to grace, free will and predestination. Also the Quietists, or followers of Miguel Molinos, a Spanish mystic (1640–96), who taught the direct relationship between the soul and God.

Moll Cutpurse.

The nickname of a notorious woman, whose real name was Mary Frith (b. c. 1584 or 9). She nearly always wore a man's dress, and is said to have been the first woman who used tobacco. Introduced by Middleton and Dekker in " The Roaring Girl," also by Fielding in " Amends for Ladies."

Molly Maguires.

A lawless secret association in Ireland, organized with the object of defeating and terrorizing agents and process-servers and others engaged in the business of evicting tenants. The name was assumed from **Molly** (=Mary) and **Maguire** (a common Irish surname), in allusion to the woman's dress they wore as a disguise. Also a secret organization in the mining regions of Pennsylvania, notorious for the commission of various crimes and outrages, until its suppression by the execution in 1877 of several of their leaders.

Mona.

The Latin name of Anglesea ; used also for the Isle of Man.

Monarch of Mont Blanc, The.

A popular surname for Albert Richard Smith, an English novelist, humorist and miscellaneous writer (1816–60). He used to lecture at the Egyptian Hall, London (1852–8) on his ascent of Mont Blanc, etc.

Monarchy in Stone, The.

A name given to the tower of Westminster Palace, from its containing the sculptured history of British sovereigns.

Money Market.

A name generally applied to the portion in a newspaper dealing with Stock Exchange business, rates of exchange, financial news, etc.

Moniteur.

The official journal of the French government (1799–1868). It first appeared under the name of the " Gazette Nationale," and from 1799 was known as the " Moniteur Universel."

Monitor.

An ironclad steam battery, consisting of an iron hull covered by a projecting deck, and surmounted by a revolving turret protecting the guns, designed by John Ericsson. Launched at Greenpoint, New York, January 30, 1862. On March 9, 1862, occurred the battle between the "Monitor " and the " Merrimac " (q.v.), resulting in a draw that was equivalent to a victory for the former. She was sunk off Cape Hatteras, December 29, 1862, when on her way to Beaufort, South Carolina. Dimensions : Length of hull, 124 feet ; beam of hull, 34 feet ; length of deck, 172 feet ; width of deck, 41 feet ; draught, 11 feet ; height of turret, 9 feet. Armament, two 11-inch Dahlgren guns, throwing 180℔ shot.

Monk, The.

A surname given to Alfonso IV (or Alphonso), King of Leon (d. c. 933) ; *v.* **Peaceful, The.**

Monk Lewis.

A nickname given to Matthew Gregory Lewis, an English poet, dramatist and romance writer (1775–1818), in allusion to his " Ambrosio ; or, the Monk " (1795).

Monk of Westminster, The.

A surname given to Richard

of Cirencester, an English Benedictine monk and historian, who died at Westminster c. 1401.

Monroe Doctrine.

In American politics the doctrine of the non-intervention of European powers in matters relating to the American continents. It received its name from statements contained in President Monroe's annual message to Congress, December, 1823, at the period of a suspected concert of the powers in the Holy Alliance to interfere in Spanish America on behalf of Spain. Richard Olney, appointed secretary of state in 1895 under President Cleveland, promulgated an extension of this doctrine, called the Olney Doctrine, to the effect that " no European power has the right to intervene forcibly in the affairs of the New World (q.v.) ; that the United States, owing to its superior size and power, is the natural protector and champion of *all* American nations ; and that permanent political union between a European and American State is unnatural and inexpedient."

Monsieur.

A title formerly applied to the eldest brother of the King of France.

Monsieur Véto, *v.* Madame Véto.

Mons Meg.

An old cannon in the castle at Edinburgh. It was made at Mons, in Flanders.

Mon Soldat (French, "My Soldier ").

A pet name given by his mistress, Gabrielle d'Estrées, to Henry IV. King of France (1553–1610).

Monster, The.

A popular surname given to one Renwick Williams, tried and convicted July 8, 1790, of shockingly wounding numbers of women with a sharp, double-edged knife. Cf. **Jack the Ripper.**

Montagnards, *v.* Montagne, La.

Montagne, La (French, "The Mountain").

A name given to the extreme Revolutionary party in the legislatures of the first French Revolution. Derived from the fact that they occupied the higher part of the hall. Cf. " Le Marais " (*v.* **Marais, Le**). Among the chief " Montagnards " were Robespierre and Danton. The name was temporarily revived in the legislatures following the Revolution of 1848.

Montagu House.

A mansion erected by Hooke for Ralph Montagu, first Duke of Montagu, " after the French manner," in the (then) suburb of Bloomsbury, London. It was burned down in 1686. It was rebuilt, but only partially inhabited, and sold to the nation in 1753 for £10,000, for the reception of the Sloanè collection. The last remnants of the old house were removed in 1845 and replaced by the present British Museum.

Mont Cenis Tunnel.

A railway tunnel, built 1861–70, passing under the Col de Fréjus, fourteen miles from the Mont Cenis road. It is the second longest[1] tunnel in the world (7¾ miles), and reaches the height of 4,245 feet. The Mont Cenis road was made by Napoleon I (1803–10) to connect the valley of the Isère, France, with Susa, Italy.

Montgomery Charter, The.

A charter granted to the city of New York by John Montgomery (" Captain General and Governor in Chief of the province of New York, and the province of New Jersey and territories depending thereon in America, and Vice Admiral of the same ") under George II, dated January 15, 1730. It extended the Dongan Charter (q.v.), and was in force until 1830.

Monumental City, The.

A surname given to the city of Baltimore, Maryland, in allusion to its numerous monuments.

Moonlighters.

A name given to the members of a secret society in Ireland, who committed numerous outrages in 1881.

Moorgate.

A postern gate in the old London city wall, built on the moor side of the city in the time of Henry V (c. 1415). It was rebuilt in 1472, and pulled down c. 1750.

Moral Gower.

A surname given by Chaucer to John Gower, a celebrated English poet (c. 1325–1408) in allusion to his poem " Confessio Amantis."

Moravians.

The members of the Christian denomination entitled the Unitas Fratrum, or United Brethren, which traces its origin to John Huss. Its members were expelled from Bohemia and Moravia in 1627, but in 1722 a remnant settled in Herrnhut, Saxony (hence the brethren are sometimes, in Germany, called "Herrnhuter"). The members of the denomination believe in the Scriptures as the only rule of faith and practice, and maintain the doctrines of the total depravity of human nature, the love of God the Father, the actual humanity and godhead of Jesus Christ, the atonement, the work of the Holy Spirit, good works as the fruit of the Spirit, the second coming of Christ, and the resurrection of the dead.

Mordure.

King Arthur's enchanted sword ; also called Excalibur (q.v.) or Caliburn.

Morey Letter, The.

A letter forged in the name of J. A. Garfield, favouring Chinese cheap labour. It was published in New York, October, 1880 (shortly before the presidential election), addressed to a fictitious H. L. Morey.

Morglay (same as Claymore).

The sword of Sir Bevis of Hampton, a knight of the Arthurian romances.

Morley, Mrs., *v.* Queen Sarah.

Mormons.

The adherents of a religious body in the United States,

---

[1] The longest is the St. Gothard Tunnel (q.v.).

which calls itself " The Church of Jesus Christ of Latter-day Saints." This denomination was founded in 1830 by Joseph Smith, a native of Sharon, Vermont. The Mormons accept the Bible, the Book of Mormon, and the Book of Doctrine and Covenants as authoritative, and regard the head of their church as invested with divine authority, receiving his revelations as the word of God, the Lord. They maintain the doctrines of repentance and faith, a literal resurrection of the dead, the second coming of Christ, and His reign upon earth (having the seat of His power in their territory), baptism by immersion, baptism for the dead, and polygamy as a sacred duty for those who are capable of entering into such marriage. The Mormons removed to Utah in 1847-8, and have since spread into Idaho, Arizona, Wyoming, etc. They have frequently defied the United States government. Also called **Mormonists** and **Mormonites**. There is also a comparatively small branch of the Mormon Church, calling itself " The Re-organized Church of Jesus Christ of Latter-day Saints," which is opposed to polygamy, and is ecclesiastically independent of the original organization.

Morning Star of Song, The, *v.* **Father of English Poetry, The.**

Morning Star of the Reformation, The, *v.* **Doctor Evangelicus.**

Morocco, *v.* **Banks's Horse.**

Morus Multicaulis Mania.

A speculative mania, c. 1835,

in the United States, causing people to purchase mulberry-trees at fabulous prices with the view of rearing silkworms. It was of short duration, but resulted in heavy losses by its dupes.

Mossbacks.

A nickname most common in Ohio, applied to old-fashioned members of the Democratic Party (q.v.), derived from the popular name of an old snapping-turtle, called a " mossback " on account of its shell being covered with a moss-like growth.

Most Christian Doctor, The, *v.* **Doctor Christianissimus.**

Most Christian King.

A title conferred upon various French kings, particularly Louis XI (1423-83).

Most Learned of the Romans, The.

A surname given to Marcus Terentius Varro, a famous Roman scholar and author (116-c. 27 B.C.).

Most Methodical Doctor, The.

A surname given to John Bassol (d. 1347), a noted Scotch theologian.

Most Profound Doctor, The, *v.* **Doctor Fundatissimus.**

Most Resolute Doctor, The, *v.* **Doctor Resolutissimus.**

Mother Ann, *v.* **Shakers.**

Mother Douglas.

A notorious procuress of the eighteenth century (d. 1761) " at the north-east corner of Covent Garden," where she

resided. Figures in Foote's play
" The Minor " as Mrs. Cole.

Mother of Believers, The (Um-mu-l-Mu' minin).

A surname given to Ayesha
(c. 611–c. 678), the favourite wife
of Mohammed.

Mother of Books, The.

A surname given to the city
of Alexandria, Egypt, in allusion
to its immense library.

Mother of Cities, The.

The ancient city of Balkh,
Central Asia.

Mother of Diets.

A name sometimes given to the
city of Worms, in Germany.

Mother of Peoples, The, v. Mère des Peuples, La.

Mother of Presidents, The.

A name sometimes given to
Virginia, the native State of
Washington, Jefferson, Madison,
Monroe, W. H. Harrison, Tyler,
and Taylor. v. Old Dominion,
The.

Mother of States.

A name occasionally applied
to Virginia, from whose territory
several other States were formed.

Mother of the Camps, The (Latin, Mater Castrorum).

A surname given by the
Roman legions in Gaul to
Victoria or Victorina, after the
death of her son Victorinus (268),
one of the Thirty Tyrants (q.v.).

Mother of the Gods, The, v. Great Mother of the Gods, The.

Mother of the Gracchi, v. Cornelia's Jewels.

Mother Shipton's Prophecies.

Various pretended prophecies
published in England in the
fifteenth, seventeenth and
eighteenth centuries. Charles
Hindley, an English bookseller
(d. 1893) wrote some of them.
Many of them are attributed to
T. Evan Preece, a prophetess of
South Wales.

Mound City, The.

A surname sometimes given
to the city of St. Louis, Missouri, in allusion to the ancient
artificial mounds in its neighbourhood.

Mountain, The, v. Montagne, La.

Mountain Brutus, The.

A surname given to William
Tell, a legendary hero of
Switzerland in the beginning
of the fourteenth century.

Mountain Dew.

A name frequently jokingly
given to whisky, especially
Scotch. In former times there
were many illicit stills in the
mountainous districts.

Mouse Tower.

A mediaeval watch-tower on a
rock in the middle of the Rhine,
near Bingen noted from its
legendary connection with the
fate of Hatto II, Archbishop of
Maing (d. 969 or 970). He is
said to have been eaten alive
by mice as a punishment for
having burned to the ground a
barn full of people caught
stealing grain during a famine,
he having likened their dying
shrieks to the piping of mice.
He is also said to have built the
Mouse Tower in a vain endeavour
to escape from his assailants.

Mrs. Bull, *v.* **Brandy Nan.**

Mrs. Grundy.

One of two rival farmers' wives in Morton's comedy "Speed the Plough." She is constantly alluded to by Mrs. Ashfield, the other farmer's wife, in the phrase, "What will Mrs. Grundy say?" but never appears on the scene. Her name has become proverbial for conventional propriety and morality.

Muggletonians.

A sect founded in England by Lodowick Muggleton and John Reeve, c. 1651. The members of the sect believed in the prophetic inspiration of its founders, as being the two witnesses mentioned in Rev. xi, 3–6, and held that there is no real distinction between the persons of the Trinity, that God has a human body, and that Elijah was his representative in heaven when he descended to die on the Cross. The last member of the sect is said to have died in 1868.

Mug-house Club.

A club which met in Long Acre, London, in the early part of the eighteenth century. Its name was derived from the fact that each member drank his ale out of his own mug. After this a number of mug-houses were established by the partisans of the Hanover succession, in order that the Protestants might rally in them against the Jacobite mobs. It was at one of these, in Salisbury Court, Fleet Street, London, that the most serious of the "Mug-house riots" took place (July 23, 1716). The mob attacked the Hanoverians assembled there; the fighting continued all night, and the ring-leader of the mob was killed.

Mugwumps (From Algonquian "mugquomp," a chief or leader).

The independent members of the Republican party who, in 1884, openly refused to support the nominee (Blaine) of that party for the presidency of the United States, and either voted for the Democratic or the Prohibitionist candidate, or did not vote at all. The word took the popular fancy, and was at once accepted by the Independents themselves as an honourable title.

Mulberry Garden.

A place of refreshment in London, much frequented by persons of quality in the seventeenth century. Sir Charles Sedley produced a comedy with this title in 1668, partly taken from Molière's "L'Ecole des Maris."

Mumbo Jumbo.

Originally a bugbear common to Mandingo towns, used by the natives to keep their women in subjection. Mungo Park describes it. The words are now used to denote various idols or fetishes fantastically clothed, worshipped by certain negro tribes.

Munchausen of the West, The.

A surname given to David Crockett, an American pioneer, hunter and politician (1786–1836), in allusion to his "tall" stories.

Muns, *v.* Tityre Tus.

Muscovy.

A name often given formerly to Russia.

Muse de la Patrie, La (The Country's Muse).

A surname given to Delphine Gay (Mme. de Girardin), a celebrated French writer of novels, comedies, and poems.

Muse Limonadière, La. (French, the coffee-house muse).

A nickname given to Charlotte Bourette, a French poetess (1714–84), who kept a café frequented by all the Paris wits of the time.

Muse of Greece, *v.* Attic Muse, The.

Music of the Future, The.

A term (often used derisively) applied to the Wagnerian ideal of music, and derived from the title of one of Wagner's essays. (Wilhelm Richard Wagner, the celebrated German operatic composer and poet was b. 1813, d. 1883.)

Mutiny Act.

An Act passed annually by the British Parliament from 1689 to 1879. It provided for the punishment of cases of mutiny and desertion, and for the maintenance of a standing army (without violation of the Bill of Rights).

Mutiny at the Nore.

A mutiny of the British fleet at the Nore (May–June, 1797), forcibly suppressed.

Mutiny of the Bounty, *v.* Bounty, The.

Nachen, The.

A ship of 200 tons burthen, commanded by Edward Brawnde, which sailed from Dartmouth, England, March 8, 1615, to make "further tryall" of the New England coast. Brawnde also went to Cape Cod to search for pearls.

Nag's Head Tavern.

An old London tavern at the corner of Friday Street, not far from the Mermaid (*v.* Mermaid Club), and the Mitre (q.v.), where the consecration of the first Protestant bishop in 1559 was alleged by the Romanists to have taken place ; hence derisively called "The Nag's Head Consecration." The ceremony was really performed at the Church of St. Mary-le-Bow. *Chambers.*

Nail City, The.

A nickname of Wheeling, capital of Ohio County, West Virginia, from its nail factories.

Namby Pamby.

A nickname of Ambrose, an English writer (1671–1749), given to him by Henry Carey and adopted by Pope.

Nameless City, The.

A surname sometimes applied to ancient Rome, from its having, it is said, a mysterious appellation, which it was death to utter.

Nancy Hanks.

A fast American trotting mare. In 1892 she broke the trotting record of Sunol (2.08¼) by a mile in 2.05¼, and this she herself lowered to 2.04 in October, 1892. By Happy Medium by Hambletonian (10), dam by Dictator, brother to Dexter.

Napoleonic Wars.

A general name for the wars 1796–1815, in which Napoleon Bonaparte was the leading figure.

Napoleon of Mexico, The.

A surname given to Agustin de Iturbide, a Mexican revolutionist, afterwards emperor (1783–1824).

Napoleon of Oratory, The, v. Great Commoner, The.

Napoleon of Peace, The, v. Roi Citoyen, Le.

Napoleon of the Drama, The.

A surname given to Alfred Bunn, lessee of Drury Lane Theatre from 1819–26 ; also to his predecessor, Robert William Elliston, a celebrated English actor and manager (1774–1831).

Narses.

A name sometimes used to mean a eunuch, from Narses, a general of the Byzantine empire (c. 478–c. 573), who was a eunuch.

Nassac Diamond, The.

A famous diamond, at one time in the possession of the East India Company. It formerly weighed 89¾ carats, but has been re-cut and now weighs 78⅝ carats. Present owner, the Duke of Westminster, and value about £30,000.

National Assembly.

The first of the revolutionary assemblies in France (1789–91). The States General were elected in 1789, and in June of that year the third estate assumed the title of National Assembly, absorbing the two remaining estates. Also called the Constituent Assembly, its chief work being the foundation of a Constitution. The legislatures organized in France in 1848 (after the February revolution) and in 1871 (after the overthrow of the second empire) are also known as National Assemblies.

National Convention.

The sovereign assembly which sat from September 21, 1792, to October 26, 1795, and governed France after abolishing royalty.

National Covenant.

In Scottish history, the bond or engagement, subscribed in 1638, based upon the covenant or oath for the observance of the Confession of Faith drawn up in 1581 (preceded by a similar one in 1557) which was signed and enjoined upon all his subjects by James VI (afterwards James I of England), and renewed in 1590 and 1596. Its object was the maintenance of the Presbyterian or Reformed religion against Romanism, and its immediate cause was the attempt of Charles I to force a liturgy upon Scotland. At the restoration of the episcopacy in 1662, the National Covenant and the Solemn League and Covenant (q.v.) were proscribed, and liberty of conscience was not regained until after the revolution of 1688.

National Institute, v. Institute of France.

Nationalist Party.

The Irish party formed for

the advocacy of Home Rule, *v.* Parnellite Party.

National Liberals.

In German politics, a party which, before the creation of the German Empire in 1871, advocated, along with progressive measures of reform, the completion of governmental unity in Germany. After that time and until 1879 it embraced those persons who, though of liberal antecedents, continued in support of Bismarck's later policy. Since 1880 the party's strength in the Reichstag has been greatly diminished.

National Party.

A name of the Greenback-Labour party in the United States.

Nation of Gentlemen.

A surname given to Scotland by George IV (1762–1830), referring to the treatment he received on his visit there in 1822.

Nation of Shopkeepers, A.

A surname given to England by Napoleon Bonaparte, but not originated by him.

Nations, Battle of the, *v.* Battle of the Nations.

Navigator, The.

A surname of Henry, Prince of Portugal (1394–1460), distinguished for his encouragement of science and geographical discovery.

Neri, The (or Blacks).

An Italian political faction dating from about 1300. Their opponents were called the Bianchi (or Whites).

D.*N.*

Nero of Germany, The, *v.* Sardanapalus of Germany, The.

Nero of the North.

A name given to Christian II (1481–1569) King of Denmark and Norway (and, in his early years, of Sweden). Also called " The Cruel."

Nestorians.

The followers of Nestorius, patriarch of Constantinople (d. after 439). They denied the hypostatic union of two natures in one person in Christ, holding that he possessed two distinct personalities, the union between which is merely moral. After the Council of Ephesus (431) the Nestorians were driven into Persia, where they firmly established themselves. Later they spread to India, Bactria, and as far as China. About 1400 the greater part of their churches perished under the persecutions of Timur, and in the sixteenth century a large part of the remainder joined the Roman Catholics. These are called **Chaldeans.**

Nestor of Europe, The.

A surname given to Leopold I, King of the Belgians (1790–1865).

Nestor of the Chemical Revolution, The.

A surname given (by Lavoisier) to James Black, a noted chemist born at Bordeaux of Scotch parents (1728–99).

Neutral Ground.

During the Revolutionary War, that part of New York (in Westchester County) which lay

P

between the British lines (at New York city and elsewhere) on the south and the American lines on the north. The scene of J. Fenimore Cooper's novel of "The Spy." Also a small tract of ground near Gibraltar, lying between the English and the Spanish lines.

New Albion.

The name given by Drake to the Pacific coast now included in northern California, Oregon, and the region northward.

New Amsterdam (Dutch, "Nieuw Amsterdam").

The name originally given to the present city of New York by the first Dutch settlers. Similarly, what is now the State of New York was called the New Netherlands.

Newbury Addresses.

Two anonymous letters to the American army, written from Newbury, New York, by John Armstrong, in 1783, setting forth the grievances of the soldiers, chief among which was the arrears of pay.

New England.

A collective name given to the north-eastern section of the United States, comprising the States of Maine, New Hampshire, Vermont, Massachusetts, Connecticut, and Rhode Island. It formed part of "North Virginia," granted to the Plymouth Company by James I in 1606. The name was given to it by Captain John Smith.

New England Confederation.

The union effected by the colonies of Massachusetts Bay,

Plymouth, Connecticut, and New Haven in 1643, suggested by the need of a common defence against the Dutch and the Indians. Discontinued in 1684.

New France.

The region in North America, claimed and in part settled by France. By 1650 it included the basins of the St. Lawrence and of the Great Lakes, with Labrador and the present Nova Scotia, New Brunswick, and part of Maine. Contests with England arose, and four wars ensued—King William's (q.v.), Queen Anne's (q.v.), King George's (q.v.), and the French and Indian (q.v.), Quebec and Montreal were the chief settlements. By 1750 New France, with Louisiana added, comprised the St. Lawrence and Great Lakes basins, with the Mississippi basin, though settlements were confined to a few points on the lakes and rivers. The result of the treaty of 1763 was the cession of all the region east of the Mississippi to England, and that west of the Mississippi to Spain.

Newgate.

The western gate of London Wall by which the Watling Street left the city. It was at first called Westgate, but later Chancellor's gate. In the reign of Henry I, Chancellor's gate was rebuilt and called Newgate. The prison was burned during the Gordon riots in 1780, and was rebuilt in 1782. Executions have taken place there since Tyburn. Now (1903) being pulled down.

Newgate Calendar.

A biographical record of the

most notorious criminals confined in Newgate.

New Hampshire Grants.

A name given to Vermont in its earlier history.

New Holland.

A former name of Australia.

New Israelites, *v.* **Southcottians.**

New Jerusalem Church, *v.* **Swedenborgians.**

New Leinster.

A name formerly given to what is now Stewart Island, New Zealand. Cf. **New Munster.**

New Lights, *v.* **Campbellites.**

New Model, The.

The name given to the Parliamentary army from the time of its re-organization in 1645. It was commanded by Sir Thomas Fairfax, and later by Cromwell.

New Munster.

A name formerly given to what is now the South Island of New Zealand. Cf. **New Leinster.**

New Netherlands, *v.* **New Amsterdam.**

New Roof, The.

A nickname of the Federal Constitution about the time of its adoption. *Fiske.*

New Sarum.

Salisbury, Wiltshire.

New Spain.

The colonial name (Spanish, Nueva España) of Mexico.

New Style, *v.* **Gregorian Calendar.**

New Sweden.

A Swedish colony in Delaware,

founded in 1638. Conquered by the Dutch in 1655.

Newtown.

A name given in its earliest history to what is now Cambridge, Massachusetts.

New Ulster.

A name formerly given to what is now the North Island of New Zealand. Cf. **New Munster.**

New World, The.

North and South America ; the western hemisphere.

Niblo's Garden.

A theatre in Broadway, near Prince Street, New York city. It was one of the oldest in the city, having been opened in 1828 as the Sans Souci ; in 1829 it was a concert saloon. Niblo's garden and theatre, owned by William Niblo, were opened in 1839, burned in 1846 and in 1872, and re-opened in the latter year. Taken down in 1895.

Nicene Councils.

Two general councils which met at Nicæa, in Asia Minor. The first met in 325, condemned Arianism, and promulgated the Nicene Creed (q.v.), in its earlier form. The second was held in 787, and condemned the Iconoclasts (q.v.).

Nicene Creed or **Symbol.**

A summary of the chief tenets of the Christian faith, first set forth as of ecumenical authority by the first Nicene Council (325). Its wording closely resembles the ancient creeds of Oriental churches, and it is specially founded upon the baptismal creed of the Church of Cæserea in Palestine. *v.* also **Athanasian Creed** and **Apostles' Creed.**

Nic Frog.

A nickname given to a Dutchman in Arbuthnot's " History of John Bull."

Nickers, *v.* **Tityre Tus.**

Nightmare of Europe, The, *v.* **Armed Soldier,** etc.

Nigritia.

A name formerly given to the Soudan.

Nihilists.

The adherents of nihilism. Nihilism was originally a social (not political) movement in Russia, in opposition to the customary forms of matrimony, the parental authority, and the tyranny of custom, but became later a more or less organized secret effort on the part of a large body of malcontents to overturn the established order of things, both social and political. In the former sense the word was introduced by Turgenieff in 1862.

Nikolsburg, Truce of.

A preliminary peace between Prussia and Austria, concluded at Nikolsburg, July 26, 1866. Confirmed by the peace of Prague, August 23, 1866.

Nine Worthies.

A collective name for the following famous persons :—

Three Gentiles.
Hector.
Alexander the Great.
Julius Cæsar.
Three Jews.
Joshua.
David.
Judas Maccabæus.

Three Christians.
Arthur.
Charlemagne.
Godfrey of Bouillon.

Also applied to nine privy councillors of William III of England's reign (1689–1702), viz. :—

Devonshire	
Dorset	
Monmouth	Whigs
Edward Russell	
Carmarthen	
Pembroke	
Nottingham	Tories
Marlborough	
Lowther	

Niobe of Nations, The, *v.* **Eternal City, The.**

Niobites.

A branch of the Monophysites, founded by Stephanus Niobes in the sixth century, who opposed the views of the Severians (q.v.). Niobes taught that, according to strict Monophysite doctrine, the qualities of Christ's human nature were lost by its absorption into his divine nature. The Niobites gradually modified their views, and returned to the orthodox church.

Nitrate King, The.

A surname given to Colonel John Thomas North (1844–96).

Noble, The.

A surname given to Alfonso IX (or Alphonso), King of Castile (1155–1214). Also called the **Good.**

Noche Triste (Spanish, disastrous night).

The name given by the Spanish conquerors of Mexico to the night of June 30, 1520, memorable for a struggle in which their forces were nearly annihilated. After the death of Montezuma, Cortes resolved to leave Tenochtitlan (Mexico City) secretly, but the movement was detected by the natives, and a terrible battle ensued. The Spaniards finally escaped with the loss of about 450 of their small force, besides 4,000, Indian allies. Much of the plunder they had acquired was sunk in the lake, and was never recovered.

Noetians.

The followers of Noetus, a heretic of Asia Minor (d. probably c. 200) who is said to have taught that " Christ was the Father, and that the Father was born and suffered and died."

Noll [i.e. Oliver] or Old Noll.

A nickname for Oliver Cromwell (1599–1658). Also called by the **Fifth-Monarchy Men** (q.v.) the **Man of Sin.**

Nomansland.

A name formerly given to a district in South Africa, now comprised within Griqualand East.

No Man's Land, or Public Land Strip.

A district ceded by Texas to the United States in 1850, lying between 100° and 103° W. long., north of Texas. It was not included under any government, though often wrongly represented as in the Indian Territory. It constitutes Beaver County in Oklahoma.

Nombre de Dios (Spanish, name of God).

A Spanish port and settlement on the Caribbean coast of the Isthmus of Panama. Owing to its unhealthy situation it was abandoned in 1597, on the foundation of Porto Bello.

Nonconformists, *v.* **Puritans.**

No-Popery Riots, *v.* **Gordon Riots.**

Norddeutscher Bund (German, North German Confederation).

The German union formed after the dissolution of the Germanic Confederation in 1866, under the presidency of Prussia. It was the model for the German Empire, which took its place in 1871.

Norddeutscher Lloyd (German, North German Lloyd).

A Bremen company, founded in 1857, for maintaining regular steamship lines between Bremen and New York, Baltimore, and other ports ; also between New York and various Mediterranean ports.

Norfolk Boy, The.

A nickname given to Richard Porson, an English classical scholar (1759–1808) famous for his knowledge of Greek, alluding to his birthplace.

Norman, The, *v.* **Conqueror, The.**

Norman Isles, *v.* **Îles Normandes.**

Northamptonshire Peasant Poet.

A surname given to John Clare, an English poet (1793–1864).

North-East Passage.

A passage for ships along the

northern coast of Europe and Asia to the Pacific Ocean. The first to make the complete voyage by this passage was the Swedish explorer Nordenskjold in 1878–9, after it had been from time to time attempted in vain for upwards of three centuries.

Northern Apostle, The, *v.* **Apostle of the North, The.**

Northern Athens, *v.* **Athens of the North, The.**

Northern Bear, The.

A popular surname for Russia. Also called the **Northern Giant,** in allusion to the size, power and growth of the Russian empire.

Northern Herodotus, The.

A surname given to Snorre (or Snorri or Snorro) Sturleson (or Sturluson), an Icelandic historian (1179–1241).

Northern Liberties.

A former district now included in the city of Philadelphia.

Northern Semiramis, The, *v.* **Semiramis of the North, The.**

Northern War, The.

A war between Sweden (under Charles XII) on one side and Russia (under Peter the Great), Denmark, Saxony, Poland, and finally Prussia and Hanover on the other. It began in 1700, and ended by treaties (1719–21) in which Sweden ceded Bremen and Verden to Hanover, Stettin and part of western Pomerania to Prussia, and Livonia, Esthonia, Ingria, and part of Karelia to Russia, and lost the supremacy in northern Europe. Russia restored Finland.

North German Confederation, *v.* **Norddeutscher Bund.**

North German Lloyd, *v.* **Norddeutscher Lloyd.**

North River.

A name given to the Hudson River near its mouth, in distinction from the Delaware or " South River."

Northumberland.

The ship in which Napoleon Bonaparte was conveyed to St. Helena. He was transferred to the Northumberland from the Bellerophon (q.v.), August 7, 1815.

Northumberland House.

An historic house, formerly situated in the Strand, on the south-east side of Trafalgar Square. Built in the beginning of the seventeenth century, and was bought and removed (in 1873–4) by the Metropolitan Board of Works, to make room for Northumberland Avenue.

North-West Passage.

A passage for ships from the Atlantic to the Pacific Ocean by the northern coasts of the American continent, long sought for and in part found by Parry and others. Sir Robert M'Clure, in his expedition of 1850–4, was the first to achieve the passage, although his ship was abandoned, and the journey completed partly on ice and partly on the relieving vessel.

Norwich Festival.

A triennial musical festival held at Norwich, Norfolk. Established in 1824.

Nostradamus of Portugal, The, v. Portuguese Nostradamus, The.

Nottingham Poet, The.

A surname given to Philip James Bailey, an English poet (1816–1903), born in Nottinghamshire.

Novara Expedition.

An Austrian scientific expedition around the world in the frigate Novara, 1857–9.

Novatians.

A sect founded in the third century by Novatianus or Novatus, a Roman Presbyter, and by Novatus of Carthage. The sect continued to the sixth century.

Noyades (French, drownings).

Executions practised during the Reign of Terror by the Revolutionary agent Carrier at Nantes towards the close of 1793 and the beginning of 1794. The prisoners, having been bound, were embarked in a vessel with a movable bottom, which was suddenly opened when the vessel reached the middle of the Loire, the condemned persons being thus precipitated into the water.

Nun of Kent.

A surname given to Elizabeth Barton, a religious impostor (c. 1506–34). She was admitted to the priory of St. Sepulchre, Canterbury, in 1527, with the monk Edward Bocking as her confessor, and began to prophesy about political questions and denounce the enemies of the Catholic church. She was arrested in 1533 and executed at Tyburn with Bocking and several other priests and friars implicated in the imposture and convicted of treasonable conspiracy. Also called the (Holy) Maid of Kent.

Nu-pieds (French, bare feet).

A name given to Norman peasants who in 1639 revolted at Avranches against heavy and unjust taxation. The rising was put down by Richelieu with relentless cruelty.

Nurse Nokes.

A name given to James Nokes, an English actor (d. c. 1692), from the success of his Nurse in Otway's "Caius Marius," a curious amalgamation of Shakspere's "Romeo and Juliet" and another play.

Nutmeg State.

A name sometimes given to Connecticut owing to its alleged manufacture of wooden nutmegs.

Oakboys.

A body of insurgents in the north of Ireland in the year 1763. They are said to have risen in resistance to an Act which required householders to give personal labour on the roads. Another of their grievances was the resumption by some of the clergy of a stricter exaction of tithes. The movement was soon suppressed. The Oakboys received their name from oak sprays which they wore in their hats.

Oaks, The.

A race for three-year-old fillies, run annually at Epsom, Surrey, on the Friday after the

Derby (q.v.). The distance is 1½ miles, and the race was established in 1779 by the Earl of Derby. The first Oaks was won by the Earl of Derby's Bridget. Often called " the Ladies' race."

Obelisk of Luxor.

An obelisk, brought from Egypt under Louis Philippe, and set up in the Place de la Concorde, Paris (1833). It is a monolith of pink Syene granite 76 feet high, to which the pedestal adds 16½ feet. The shaft is inscribed on all four sides with hieroglyphs which refer to Rameses II and III.

O'Connell's Tail.

A nickname given to the parliamentary following of Daniel O'Connell, an Irish agitator and orator (1775–1847), about the years 1830–47.

Octavian Library.

A public library at Rome, the first library open to the public, founded by the emperor Augustus in honour of his sister Octavia, and housed in the Portico of Octavia. It perished in the fire which raged at Rome for three days in the reign (79–81) of Titus.

October Club.

In English politics, a club composed of extreme Tories, first formed about 1690, and influential in the reign of Queen Anne. So named from the October ale for which the club was celebrated. Swift's influence was the principal factor in its dispersal.

October States.

In recent American political history, those States (Ohio, Indiana, etc.), which held elections in October instead of in November. In presidential campaigns extreme interest centred in the action of such states, on account of the bearing on the ensuing November elections. The elections are now held in November.

Odd-Fellows (a fanciful name assumed by the original founders of the society).

A secret benevolent and social society, called the Independent Order of Odd-Fellows. The order arose in the eighteenth century, and various lodges were, c. 1814, consolidated into the Manchester Unity, which is now the principal body in Great Britain. There are also lodges in the United States, Germany, Switzerland, Australia, South America, etc.

Odrysian Bard, The.
Orpheus.

Offa's Dyke.

An intrenchment extending from near the mouth of the Wye northward near the border of England and Wales to the mouth of the Dee. It was built for defence against the Welsh by Offa, King of Mercia, in the eighth century.

O'Gorman Mahon, The.

A name given to Charles James Patrick Mahon, an Irish politician and adventurer (1800–91).

Ohio Company, The.

A company of Virginia and Maryland colonists to whom the British crown granted, in 1749, 500,000 acres in the Ohio

Valley for the purpose of settlement.

Ohio Idea.

In American politics the advocacy of greenbacks in payment for United States bonds and of greenbacks in place of national-bank notes. This project was pushed especially in Ohio by the Democratic leaders Allen, Pendleton and Ewing, c. 1868–70. *v.* **Greenback Party.**

Old, The.

A surname of Gorm, the first king of United Denmark (fl. c. 860–935) ; and of Hakon or Haco V, king of Norway, from 1217 till c. 1263.

Old Abe.

A nickname of Abraham Lincoln (1809–65) the sixteenth President of the United States.

Old Bags.

A nickname given to John Scott, first Earl of Eldon (1751–1838), for twenty-five years lord chancellor of England. There are several versions of the origin of the name, but one is that he was so called from the large and richly embroidered bag in which the great seal of England is carried before the lord chancellor when he goes to take his seat on the judicial bench or the woolsack.

Old Beeswax.

A nickname given to Raphael Semmes (1809–77) commander of the Alabama (q.v.), from his habit of waxing his formidable moustache.

Old Bona Fide, *v.* **Great, The.**
(Louis XIV).

Old Bory.

A nickname given to Pierre Gustave Toutant Beauregard, an American general (1818–93). Also called the **Little Napoleon.**

Old Bullion.

A nickname of J. H. Benton, an American Democratic statesman (1782–1858).

Old Buck, *v.* **Old Public Functionary, The.**

Old Buena Vista.

A nickname given to Zachary Taylor, twelfth President of the United States, alluding to his victory at Buena Vista, Mexico (February 23, 1847). Also called **Old Rough and Ready** (q.v.).

Old Chapultepec.

A nickname given to Winfield Scott, an American general (1786–1866) from his victory at Chapultepec (September 13, 1847) terminating the Mexican War.

Old Chickamauga.

A nickname given during the American Civil War to James Barrett Steedman, an American general (1818–83), in allusion to the battle of Chickamauga, in which he distinguished himself (1863).

Old Chief.

A surname given to Henry Clay, a celebrated American statesman and orator (1777–1852)

Old Colony, The.

The territory in eastern Massachusetts occupied by the Plymouth Colony.

Old Country, The.

A name often used in Australia and the United States when referring to Great Britain or, sometimes, Ireland

Old Dessauer, The, *v.* Alte Dessauer, Der.

Old Dominion, The.

A name popularly given to the State of Virginia. Origin variously explained, but perhaps the best account is that Captain John Smith called Virginia " Old Virginia " to distinguish it from " New Virginia," as the New England colony was called. The colony of Virginia was alluded to in documents as " the colony and dominion of Virginia ; " hence the phrase " the Old Dominion." Also called the "Mother of Presidents."

Old Douro.

A nickname given to the Duke of Wellington (1769-1852) in allusion to his passage of the river Douro (May 11, 1809).

Old Ebony, *v.* Ebony.

Old Fox, The (French, le vieux renard).

A nickname of Marshal (Nicolas Jean de Dieu) Soult, duc de Dalmatie (1769-1851).

Old French War, The (or The Old French and Indian War), *v.* French and Indian War.

Old Fritz (German, Der Alte Fritz).

A nickname given to Frederick the Great (1712-86) by his soldiers.

Old George.

A nickname of George Monk,

Duke of Albemarle, a celebrated English general (1608-70), the restorer of Charles II to the throne of England.

Old Gib., *v.* Key of the Mediterranean, The.

Old Glorious.

A nickname given to William III of England (1650-1702).

Old Glory.

A popular name for the United States flag, the Stars and Stripes. *v.* also England's Pride and Westminster's Glory.

Old Grog.

A nickname given to Admiral Edward Vernon (1684-1757), who introduced the beverage grog (c. 1745). The name is said to be due to his grogram breeches, or, according to another account, the grogram cloak he wore in foul weather.

Old Guard, The.

A noted body of troops in the army of Napoleon I. It made the last French charge at the battle of Waterloo (June 18, 1815).

Old Harry.

Satan. Also nicknamed Old Scratch, Old Nick, Lord Harry. Sometimes called the Prince of Darkness.

Old Hickory.

A nickname given to General Andrew Jackson (1767-1845), from the toughness and strength of his character.

Old Hunkers, *v.* Barnburners.

Old Ironsides, *v.* Constitution.

Old Jack, *v.* Stonewall Jackson.

Old Lady of Threadneedle Street.

A name given to the Bank of England, from its location in Threadneedle Street, London.

Old Line State.

A popular surname of the State of Maryland, in allusion to the boundary line (*v.* **Mason and Dixon's Line**) between it and Pennsylvania.

Old Man Eloquent, The.

A surname applied to Isocrates (436–338 B.C.), S. T. Coleridge (1772–1834), J. Q. Adams (1767–1848) and others. Cf. Milton's Sonnet IX.

Old Man of the Mountain, The, *v.* Assassins, The.

Old Man of the Sea, The.

A name often used to indicate a person who cannot be shaken off, in allusion to the monster (in appearance a decrepit old man) in the story of Sinbad the Sailor (Arabian Nights' Entertainments) who leaped upon Sinbad's back and refused to dismount.

Old Morality.

A nickname given to William Henry Smith, a prominent English Conservative politician (1825–91). He was First Lord of the Admiralty 1877–80, Secretary for War 1885–6 and 1886–7.

Old Nick, *v.* Old Harry.

Old Noll, *v.* Noll.

Old North State, The.

A name sometimes given to North Carolina.

Old Parr.

Thomas Parr, a reputed centenarian, who died in 1635 at London. He was said to have been born in 1483, but the evidence was found to be untrustworthy when inquired into by Mr. Thoms, the editor of "Notes and Queries."

Old Pretender, The, *v.* Chevalier de St. George.

Old Probabilities.

A nickname for the chief signal-officer of the Signal-service Bureau (United States). Sometimes abbreviated to **Old Probs.**

Old Public Functionary, The.

A nickname given to James Buchanan, fifteenth President of the United States (1791–1868). Also called **Old Buck** and **Old Zach.**

Old Put.

A nickname of Israel Putnam, an American Revolutionary general (1718–90).

Old Reliable.

A nickname of George Henry Thomas, a distinguished American general (1816–70).

Old Rosey.

A nickname given during the Civil War to William Starke Rosecrans, an American general (1819–98).

Old Rough and Ready.

A nickname often given to General Zachary Taylor, twelfth President of the United States (1784–1850). Also called **Old Buena Vista** (q.v.).

Old Rowley.

A nickname given to Charles II of England (1630–85).

Derived by some from the name of a stallion in the royal stud, and by others from Roland in the expression " a Roland for an Oliver," the King being likened to Roland, and Oliver representing the Lord Protector. A part of Newmarket race-course is called the **Rowley Mile.**

Old Scratch, *v.* **Old Harry.**

Old Stars.

A nickname given to Ormsby McKnight Mitchel, an American general & astronomer (1810–62).

Old Style, *v.* **Julian Calendar.**

Old Tecumseh.

A familiar name given by his troops to Wm. Tecumseh Sherman, the American general (1820–91).

Old Three Stars.

A nickname given to Ulysses Simpson Grant, American general, 18th President of the U.S. (1822–85), alluding to the three stars indicating his rank as lieutenant-general.

Old Tip.

A nickname given to General William Henry Harrison, ninth President of the United States (1773–1841) in allusion to his victory of Tippecanoe (November 6, 1811). Sometimes called **Tippecanoe.** Also called the **Washington of the West.**

Old Tom.

A popular name for a kind of gin. Said to be derived from " Tom " Chamberlain (one of the firm of Hodges' gin distillery) who first manufactured it.

Old To-morrow:

A nickname given to Sir John A. Macdonald (1815-91).

Old Waggon, *v.* **United States.**

Old World, The.

A name often applied to Europe, or to the eastern hemisphere, since the discovery of America.

Old Zach, *v.* **Old Public Functionary, The.**

Olifant.

The name of Roland's horn, the sound of which might be heard at a distance of twenty miles. Roland was the most celebrated of Charlemagne's paladins, and is said to have died at the battle of Roncesvalles in 778. Cf. the " Chanson de Roland."

Olmütz Conference.

A conference between Prussia (represented by von Manteuffel) and Austria (represented by Schwarzenberg) under the mediation of Russia, November 28–29, 1850, respecting affairs in Germany, particularly in Hesse and Schleswig–Holstein, whose populations were in revolt against their respective rulers, the electors of Hesse and the King of Denmark. Schleswig-Holstein was abandoned to Denmark, and the elector of Hesse re-instated in power.

Olney Doctrine, The, *v.* **Monroe Doctrine, The.**

Olympia.

An American armoured cruiser of 5,870 tons displacement, launched in 1892. She has been the flag-ship of the Asiatic squadron during the Spanish-American war and later troubles in the Philippines.

Omnibus Bill, The.

A series of compromise measures passed through Congress in 1850, largely through the influence of Henry Clay. The chief provisions were the admission of California to the Union as a free State, organization of the territories of Utah and New Mexico (without restrictions on slavery), abolition of the slave-trade in the District of Columbia, and a fugitive-slave law.

One-Armed Devil, The, *v.* One-Armed Phil.

One-Armed Phil.

A nickname given to Philip Kearny, an American general (1815–62) who lost his arm in the Mexican War. Also called the **One-Armed Devil**.

One Thousand Guineas.

An annual horse-race run in the spring at Newmarket.

Only, The, *v.* Jean Paul.

Oom Paul.

A nickname of Stephanus Johannes Paulus Kruger (b. 1825), ex-President of the South African Republic.

Open Door.

A name given to the English policy in China, defined in the Anglo-German agreement (1900) as the free access of all nations to the ports, rivers and littorals of China.

Opium War.

A war between Great Britain and China, due to the attempt of the Chinese government to prevent the importation of opium. It began in 1840, and ended with the treaty of Nanking (q.v.) in 1842.

Opportunists.

In recent French history, the republican party represented by Léon Gambetta, Jules Ferry and others, who adapted their course to the exigencies of the time (hence the name). Opposed to the radicals and doctrinaires.

O.P. Riots.

The " old-price riots " which took place in 1809 at Covent Garden Theatre, London, commencing September 18. The cost of the new theatre then just built was so great that the proprietors raised the price of admission, and the public resolved to resist. The excitement continued for weeks, and many of the rioters were arrested. At a banquet to celebrate the triumph of the cause in the acquittal of the leading rioters, Mr. Kemble himself appeared, and terms were agreed upon ; and on the sixty-seventh night a banner in the house, with " We are satisfied " inscribed upon it, proclaimed that all was over. The 4s. rate of admission to the pit was diminished by 6d., but the half-price remained at 2s. *Doran*, " English Stage," ii. 362–6.

Oracle of Denmark, The.

Count Johann Hartwig Ernst von Bernstorff (1712–72), a Danish statesman, was so called by Frederick the Great.

Oracle of the Church, The, *v.* Last of the Fathers, The.

Orange Free State.

A republic in southern Africa to the south of the Vaal River, bounded on the east by Natal, Basutoland on the south-east, the Orange River on the south, and Griqualand West on the west. Now called the Orange River Colony.

Orangemen.

Irish Protestants. The name was given to them about the end of the seventeenth century by Roman Catholics on account of their support to William III of England, Prince of Orange. Also a secret politico-religious society, instituted in Ireland in 1795, for the purpose of upholding the Protestant religion and ascendency, and of opposing Romanism and the Roman Catholic influence in the government of the country. Orangemen are especially prominent in Ulster, Ireland.

Orange-Peel.

A nickname given to Sir Robert Peel, a noted English statesman (1788–1850) when Chief Secretary for Ireland (1812–8) alluding to his strong anti-Catholic spirit.

Orator Henley.

A surname given to John Henley, an English preacher celebrated for his eccentricities (1692–1756 or 9).

Orator Hunt.

A surname given to Henry Hunt (1773–1835), a political demagogue and member of Parliament during the Wellington and Peel administrations.

Orator of the Human Race, v. Anacharsis.

Orcades.

The ancient name of the Orkney Islands.

Orchard of Ireland.

A name given to County Armagh, Ireland.

Order for Merit.

A Prussian order, composed of two classes, military and civil. The first class was founded by Frederick the Great in 1740 (Cf. **Order of Generosity**). Since 1840 it has been given exclusively for distinction in the field. The second-class (or second order) was founded by Frederick William IV in 1842 for distinction in science and art.

Order of Alcantara.

A Spanish military order said to be a revival of a very ancient order of St. Julian, and to have received its name from the city of Alcantara, given by Alfonso IX of Castile in 1213 to the Knights of Calatrava, and transferred by the latter.

Order of Alexander Nevski.

A Russian order founded in 1722 by Peter the Great, but first conferred by the empress Catharine I in 1725.

Order of Calatrava.

A Spanish military order founded in the middle of the twelfth century, and taking its name from the fortress of Calatrava, which had been captured from the Moors in 1147, and was confided to the new order. It is still in existence.

Order of Charles III.

A Spanish order, founded by Charles III in 1771.

Order of Charles XIII.

A Swedish order founded by Charles XIII in 1811, for Freemasons of the higher degrees.

Order of Christ.

A Portuguese order, founded by King Dionysius and confirmed c. 1318. It contains three degrees, of which the highest is limited to six persons.

Order of Civil Merit.

The name of several orders, the most prominent of which is that of Prussia. *v.* **Order for Merit.**

Order of Fidelity.

An order of the duchy of Baden, founded by the margrave Charles William in 1715. It is still in existence, and consists of two classes only, that of grand cross and that of commander. Also an order of Portugal, founded by John VI in 1823 for the supporters of the monarchy during the insurrectionary movements in that country.

Order of Generosity.

A Prussian order of distinction founded in 1665, but not organized until 1685, and superseded in 1740 by the Order for Merit (q.v.).

Order of Glory ("Nishan Iftikar").

An order of the Ottoman empire, instituted by Mahmoud II in 1831.

Order of Isabella the Catholic.

An order (known as the **Royal American Order**) instituted in 1815 to reward loyalty among the American colonists and dependents of Spain. The order still exists.

Order of Jesus, of Jesus Christ, etc.

The name of several orders of more or less religious character, in Spain, Sweden, etc.

Order of Leopold.

An Austrian order founded by Francis I, emperor of Austria, in memory of the emperor Leopold II. It dates from 1808, and is still in existence.

Order of Louisa.

A Prussian order founded by Frederick William III in 1814, for women only.

Order of Maria Louisa.

A Spanish order for women, founded in 1792, and still in existence.

Order of Maria Theresa.

An Austrian order founded by the empress of that name in 1757, but modified by the emperor Joseph II.

Order of Maximilian.

An order for the encouragement of art and science, founded in 1853 by Maximilian II of Bavaria.

Order of Medjidi, *v.* Medjidi.

Order of Military Merit.

An order instituted in 1759 by Louis XV of France for Protestant officers, as the Order of St. Louis (q.v.) was limited to Catholics. In 1814 it was reorganized for officers of the army and navy. It has not been conferred since 1830. Also an order founded by Duke Charles Eugene of Würtemberg in 1759.

Order of Odd-fellows, *v.* **Odd-fellows.**

Order of Our Lady of Montesa.

A Spanish order, founded in the fourteenth century by the King of Aragon, afterwards attached to the crown of Spain.

Order of Our Lady of Mount Carmel.

An order founded by Henry IV of France on the occasion of his embracing Catholicism, and in a measure replacing the Order of St. Lazarus (q.v.).

Order of Sincerity, *v.* **Order of the Red Eagle.**

Order of SS. Cosmo and Damian.

A religious order in Palestine in the middle ages, especially charged with the care of pilgrims.

Order of St. Andrew.

A Russian order founded by Peter the Great in 1698.

Order of St. Andrew (in Scotland), *v.* **Order of the Thistle.**

Order of St. Benedict of Aviz.

A Portuguese order of knighthood, originating in a military order founded by Alfonso I, 1143–7, to suppress the Moors. Aviz became the seat of the order in 1187. Transformed in 1789 into an honorary order for the reward of military merit.

Order of St. Gall, *v.* **Order of the Bear.**

Order of St. George.

A Bavarian order founded or, as is asserted, restored by the Elector Charles Albert in 1729. It is still in existence, and is divided into three classes. Also a Russian order founded in 1769 by the empress Catherine II. This is conferred only upon a commanding general who has defeated an army of 50,000 men, or captured the enemy's capital, or brought about an honourable peace. There is now no person living who has gained this distinction regularly, though it has been given to a foreign sovereign.

Order of St. James of the Sword.

Also called **St. James of Compostela.** A Spanish order of great antiquity, asserted to have been approved by the Pope in 1175, and still existing. In the middle ages this order had great military power, and administered a large income.

Order of St. Lazarus.

An order which had its origin in the Holy Land, and was afterwards transplanted into France, where it retained independent existence until, under Henry IV, it was in a measure replaced by the Order of Our Lady of Mount Carmel (q.v.). It disappeared during the Revolution.

Order of St. Louis.

A French order founded by Louis XIV in 1693 for military service, and confirmed by Louis XV in 1719. After the restoration of the Bourbons in 1814 this order was re-instated. No knights have been created since 1830. *v.* **Order of Military Merit.**

Order of St. Michael.

A French order instituted August 1, 1469, by Louis XI and modified by Henry III and

Louis XIV. It has not been conferred since 1830.

Order of St. Michael and St. George.

A British order instituted in 1818, originally for natives of the Ionian and Maltese islands and for other British subjects in the Mediterranean, but it has since been greatly extended.

Order of St. Patrick.

An order of knighthood instituted by George III of England in 1783. It consists of the sovereign, the lord lieutenant of Ireland, and twenty-two knights.

Order of St. Stanislaus.

A Polish order, dating from 1765, and adapted by the czars of Russia.

Order of the Annunciation.

The highest order of knighthood (**Ordine supremo dell' Annunziata**) of the ducal house of Savoy, now the royal house of Italy, dating under its present name from 1518, when it superseded the Order of the Collar, said to have been founded by Count Amadeus VI of Savoy in 1362, but probably older. Also an order of nuns founded c. 1500 at Bourges, France, by Queen Jeanne of Valois after her divorce from Louis XII. Also an order of nuns, founded c. 1604 at Genoa, Italy, by Maria Vittoria Fornari.

Order of the Bath.

An order supposed to have been instituted at the coronation of Henry IV of England in 1399. It received this name from the fact that the candidates for the honour were put into a bath

the preceding evening to denote a purification or absolution from all former stain, and that they were now to begin a new life. The present Order of the Bath, however, was instituted by George I in 1725, as a military order, consisting, exclusive of the sovereign, of a grand master and thirty-six companions. In 1815 the order was greatly extended, and in 1847 it was opened to civilians. It is now composed of three classes, viz : Military and civil knights grand crosses, G.C.B. ; knights commanders, K.C.B. and knights companions, C.B.

Order of the Bear.

An order of knights instituted by the emperor Frederick II, and having its centre at the abbey of St. Gall, in Switzerland. It ceased to exist when St. Gall became independent of the house of Austria.

Order of the Black Eagle.

A Prussian order, founded by Frederick I, January 17, 1701, on his accession as King of Prussia. The number of knights is limited to thirty, exclusive of the princes of the blood royal, and all must be of unquestioned nobility.

Order of the Burgundian Cross.

An order founded by the emperor Charles V, which did not survive.

Order of the Chrysanthemum.

An order founded by the Mikado of Japan in 1876.

Order of the Conception.

An order founded in the seventeenth century by some

of the nobles of the Holy Roman Empire, and common to Germany and Italy.

Order of the Cordon Jaune.

A French order, now extinct, for Protestant and Roman Catholic knights, founded in the sixteenth century by the Duke of Nevers for the protection of widows and orphans.

Order of the Crescent.

A Turkish order, instituted in 1799, and awarded only for distinguished bravery in the naval or military service. Abolished in 1851. An Order of the Crescent was founded by Charles of Anjou in Sicily in 1268, but had a short existence. René the Good, of Anjou, count of Provence and titular king of Naples, founded another short-lived Order of the Crescent in the fifteenth century.

Order of the Crown.

The title of several honorary orders founded by sovereigns in the nineteenth century, each including as part of its name that of the country to which it belongs. (1) The Order of the Crown of Bavaria, founded by King Maximilian (I) Joseph in 1808. Granted to persons who have attained distinction in the civil service of the state. (2) The Imperial Order of the Crown of India, founded in 1878 for women, at the time of the assumption by Queen Victoria of the title of Empress of India. It includes a number of Indian women of the highest rank. (3) The Order of the Crown of Italy, founded by King Victor Emmanuel in 1868. (4) The Order of the Crown of Prussia, founded by King William I on his coronation in 1861. (5) The Order of the Crown of Roumania, founded by King Charles on assuming the royal title in 1881. (6) The Order of the Crown of Saxony, founded by King Frederick Augustus in 1807, soon after his assumption of the kingly title. It is of but one class, and limited to persons of high rank. (7) The Order of the Crown of Siam, founded in 1869. (8) The Order of the Crown of Würtemberg, founded by King William I in 1818.

Order of the Danebrog.

The second in importance of the Danish orders of knighthood, originally instituted in 1219, revived in 1671, regulated by royal statutes in 1693 and 1808, and several times modified since. The order may be conferred on foreigners.

Order of the Fan.

A Swedish order founded in 1744, and now extinct.

Order of the Fish.

A decoration founded by the Mogul emperors in India, and conferred upon certain English statesmen in the early part of the nineteenth century. The insignia are of the nature of standards borne before the person upon whom the order is conferred.

Order of the Garter.

The highest order of knighthood in Great Britain, consisting of the sovereign, the Prince of Wales, and twenty-five knights companions, and open, in addition, to such English princes and foreign sovereigns as may be chosen, and sometimes to extra companions chosen for special reasons, so that the whole order usually numbers about 50. Formerly the knights companions were elected by the body itself. But since the reign of George III appointments have been made by the sovereign. The order, at first (and still sometimes) called the Order of St. George, was instituted by Edward III some time between 1344 and 1350, the uncertainty arising from the early loss of all its original records. The foundation, motto (" Honi soit qui mal y pense "), and name of the order are usually ascribed to the following incident, probably fictitious. King Edward III picked up a garter dropped by the Countess of Salisbury at a ball, and placed it on his own knee, using the above words in response to the notice taken of the occurrence by the courtiers. The sovereign, when a woman, wears the ribbon on the left arm.

Order of the Golden Fleece.

An order founded by Philip the Good, duke of Burgundy, in 1430, on the occasion of his marriage with the infanta Isabella of Portugal. After the cession of the Spanish Netherlands to Austria, the latter power in 1713-4 claimed the office of grand master previously exercised by the Spanish kings, and as the dispute remains undecided, the order, therefore, exists independently in Austria and in Spain.

Order of the Griffin.

An order of the grand duchy of Mecklenburg-Schwerin, founded in 1884.

Order of the Holy Ghost (Saint Esprit).

The leading order of the later French monarchy, founded by King Henry III of France in 1578, replacing the Order of St. Michael (q.v.). The king was the grand master, and there were 100 members, not including foreigners. The members were required to adhere to the Roman Catholic Church and to be of a high grade of nobility. The order has been in abeyance since the revolution of 1830. Also an order founded at Montpellier, France, about the end of the twelfth century, and united to the order of St. Lazarus by Pope Clement XIII. Also a Neapolitan order. *v.* **Order of the Knot.**

Order of the Hospitalers of St. John of Jerusalem.

A body of military monks, which took its origin from an earlier, non-military community, under whose auspices a hospital and a church had been founded at Jerusalem. Its military organization was perfected in the twelfth century. After the retaking of Jerusalem by the Moslems, these knights defended Acre in vain, took shelter in Cyprus, and in the fourteenth century occupied the island of Rhodes. In 1522 Rhodes was seized by the Turks, and the knights, after some wanderings, had possession given them of Malta, the government of which they administered until it was occupied by Napoleon in 1798. At different times the order has been officially called **Knights of Rhodes** and **Knights of Malta.** It maintains a certain independent existence to the present day. The dormant " langue " of England was revived 1827–31, and is again located at St. John's Gate, Clerkenwell, London.

Order of the Illuminati.

A celebrated secret society founded by Professor Adam Weishaupt at Ingolstadt, in Bavaria, in 1776 ; originally called the **Society of the Perfectibilists.** It was deistic and republican in principle ; aimed at general enlightenment and emancipation from superstition and tyranny ; was to some extent associated with freemasonry, and spread widely through Europe, though the Illuminati were never very numerous. The order excited much antagonism, and was suppressed in Bavaria in 1785, but lingered for some time elsewhere.

Order of the Indian Empire.

An order instituted in 1878 for British subjects in India, to commemorate the assumption by Queen Victoria of the title of Empress of India, and open to natives as well as to persons of European extraction.

Order of the Iron Cross.

A Prussian order founded in 1813 for military services in the wars against Napoleon. In 1870 the order was re-organized. It consists of the great cross (conferred only on a few princes and generals), and two classes comprising several thousand Germans.

Order of the Iron Crown.

An order founded by Napoleon I as King of Italy, and adopted by Francis I of Austria after the fall of Napoleon. It consists of three classes.

Order of the Knights of Malta. *v.* Order of the Hospitalers, etc.

Order of the Knot.

A military order of short duration, founded at Naples in the fourteenth century.

Order of the Legion of Honour, *v* Légion d'Honneur, La.

Order of the Lion.

The name of several orders in Germany, etc., especially an order founded in 1815 by William I, first king of the Netherlands, and continued by the later kings. It is an order for civil merit.

Order of the Martyrs, *v.* Order of SS. Cosmo and Damian.

Order of the Palm.

A German society founded at Weimar in 1617 for the preservation and culture of the German language. It disappeared after 1680. Also called **Fruit-bringing Society.**

Order of the Red Eagle.

An order founded by the Margrave of Bayreuth in 1705, and adopted in 1792 by Frederick William II of Prussia on his accession to the principality. Formerly **Order of the Red Eagle of Bayreuth** ; also called **Order of Sincerity.**

Order of the Saint Esprit, *v.* Order of the Holy Ghost.

Order of the Star of India (Full title, **The Most Exalted Order of the Star of India**).

An order for the British possessions in India, founded in 1861. The motto is " Heaven's light our guide."

Order of the Thistle (Full title, **The Most Ancient and Most Noble Order of the Thistle**).

A very old Scottish order which has been renewed and remodelled, and is still in existence. Motto is " Nemo me impune lacessit."

Order of the White Eagle.

An order founded at the beginning of the eighteenth century by Augustus II of Poland and Saxony, or, as is alleged, revived by him. It has been adopted by the Czar of Russia, and is composed of one class only.

Order of the White Elephant.

A Danish order alleged to be of great antiquity. Its foundation, however, is specifically ascribed to Christian I (1462), and its re-organization to Christian V (1693). Limited to thirty knights besides the members of the royal family, and no person can be a knight who is not already a member of the Order of the Danebrog.

Order of the White Falcon.

An order founded by the Duke of Saxe-Weimar in 1732, and renewed in 1815. It is still in existence, and consists of three classes, numbering, exclusive of the family of the reigning grand duke, twelve grand crosses, twenty-five command-ers, and fifty knights. Also called **Order of Vigilance.**

Order of the Yellow String, *v.* **Order of the Cordon Jaune.**

Order of Vigilance, *v.* **Order of the White Falcon.**

Orders in Council.

Orders promulgated by the British sovereign with the advice of the Privy Council. Specifically the orders of 1807, which prohibited neutral trade directly with France or the allies of France. All goods had to be landed in England, pay duties there, and be re-exported under English regulations.

Ordinance of Nullification.

An ordinance passed by a State convention of South Carolina, November 19, 1832, declaring void certain Acts of the United States Congress levying duties and imposts on imports, and threatening that any attempt to enforce those Acts, except through the courts in that State, would be followed by the secession of South Carolina from the Union. It was repealed by the State convention which met on March 16, 1833, Andrew Jackson having in the meantime (December 11, 1832) published a proclamation in which he announced his intention of enforcing the Federal laws, and ordered United States troops to Charleston and Augusta.

Ordinance of 1784.

An Act of the United States under the Confederation, passed April 23, 1784, for the temporary government of the North-west

Territory, which comprised tracts ceded to the United States by the several States.

Ordinance of 1787.

An Act of Congress, passed in 1787, securing to the Northwest Territory freedom from slavery, religious freedom, education, etc., and provided for its future subdivision.

Ordinances of Secession.

Ordinances passed by conventions of eleven Southern States in 1860-1, declaring their withdrawal from the Union.

Oregon.

An American battleship, built in San Francisco, launched in 1893. She is of 10,288 tons' displacement, and on her trial trip maintained for four hours a speed of 16·79 knots. She took a prominent part in the battle of Santiago, July 3, 1898, with the " Brooklyn " forcing the surrender of the " Cristóbal Colón " (q.v.).

Organic Statute.

A Russian edict of 1832 by which Poland lost its constitution.

Organizer of Victory, The.

A surname given to Lazare-Nicolas - Marguerite Carnot, a celebrated French statesman, strategist and man of science (1753—1823).

Orient, L'.

The name of the French flagship at the battle of the Nile (August 1, 1798). She was blown up during the engagement, and Commodore Louis Casabianca, with his son, a boy

of ten, were killed in it. Mrs. Hemans has made the incident (although slightly departing from the historical facts) the subject of a poem.

Oriental Catullus, The.

A surname given to the Persian poet, Sadi, who lived, it is said, from 1190-1291.

Origenists.

The followers of Origen (Origenes) of Alexandria, one of the Greek fathers of the church (probably c. 185-probably 253); those who professed to hold the doctrines held by or attributed to Origen.

The members of a sect mentioned by Epiphanius as followers of some unknown person named Origen.

Orleanists.

The adherents of the princes of the Orleans family. The family is descended from a younger brother (Philip) of Louis XIV, and has furnished one sovereign, Louis Philippe, who reigned from 1830-48.

Orloff Diamond, The.

A famous gem, the chief ornament of the Russian imperial sceptre ; sometimes called the sceptre diamond. Purchased at Amsterdam by Count Grigori Orloff, and was given by him to Catherine II. It weighs 193 carats. Also called " Koh-i-nur."

Ormonde.

A bay thoroughbred horse foaled in 1883. In 1886 he won the Derby, St. Leger and Two Thousand Guineas. He became a ' roarer,' and was sent to Buenos

Ayres. In 1892 he was bought by Mr. McDonough, of California, for $150,000, the largest price ever paid for a horse. Ormonde is considered the greatest racer ever bred in England.

Orphan of the Temple, The, *v*. Filia Dolorosa.

Orpheus of Highwaymen, The.

A popular surname for John Gay, an English poet (c. 1685–1732) in allusion to his " Beggar's Opera " (1728), called " A Newgate Pastoral."

Orpheus of the Green Isle, The.

A surname given to Turloch O'Carolan, a famous Irish minstrel (1670–1738), who travelled with a harp from door to door. The last of the improvising wandering bards.

Ostend Manifesto.

A despatch drawn up in 1854 by three diplomatic representatives of the United States, after a conference at Ostend, Belgium, urging that the United States should acquire Cuba.

Our Fritz (" Unser Fritz").

A nickname given by the Germans to Frederick William, crown prince (afterwards emperor) of Germany (1831–88). Also called **Frederick the Noble.**

Our only General.

A nickname given to Viscount Wolseley (b. 1833), made a general in 1882.

Overland Route, The.

The route from England to India through France and Italy to Brindisi, and thence by steamer by the Suez Canal, Red Sea and Indian Ocean. The time required for the journey is from three to four weeks. Formerly, the principal land route (viâ Utah) to California.

Ovid of France, The, *v*. French Ovid, The.

Oxford Movement.

A name sometimes given to a movement in the Church of England towards High Church principles, as against the tendency towards liberalism and rationalism. So called from the fact that it originated in the University of Oxford, 1833–41.

Oxford School.

A name given to that party of the Church of England which adopted the principles promulgated in the " Tracts for the Times." The members of the party were also called **Tractarians** (q.v.). and **Puseyites** (q.v.)

Pacific, The.

A surname given to Frederick III, Emperor of the Holy Roman Empire (1415–93). The last German emperor crowned at Rome (1452).

Pacification of Ghent.

A union between Holland, Zealand, and the southern provinces of the Low Countries, formed against Spanish supremacy, concluded at Ghent, Nov. 8, 1576.

Pacification of Pinerolo.

A treaty concluded by the English Commonwealth, under Cromwell, with France in 1655, providing for the cessation of the Waldensian persecution by the Duke of Savoy.

Pacte de Famille (French, " Family Compact ").

A name given to three treaties in the eighteenth century between the French and Spanish Bourbon dynasties, especially the last of the three (1761), in consequence of which Spain joined with France in the war against Great Britain. The branch house of Bourbon ruling in Italy was also included in this alliance.

Pacte de Famine (French, " Famine compact ").

A monopoly formed by certain rich men in France, at the end of the reign of Louis XV, for the purpose of raising the price of corn by causing a factitious scarcity of it.

Paddy.

A nickname for an Irishman.

Painter of Nature, The.

A surname given (by Ronsard) to Remi Belleau, one of the Pleiad poets (1528–77). Also called **le gentil Belleau**.

Painter of the Graces, The.

A surname given to Andrea Appiani, a noted Italian fresco-painter (1754–1817).

Paix Boiteuse et Mal-assise, La (French, " The lame and unstable peace ").

A name given to a treaty of peace, of short duration, concluded at St. Germain-en-Laye between the Catholics and the Protestants, in 1570, by Henri de Mesmes (1531-96). *v.* also **Paix Fourrée, La.**

Paix de Monsieur, La (French, " The Peace of Monsieur ").

A peace forced upon Henry III of France in 1576 by a combination of Huguenots, the Politiques, and the Duc d'Alençon (" Monsieur "). *v.* **Monsieur.** Great concessions were made to the Huguenots and to the Duc d'Alençon.

Paix des Dames, La (French, " The ladies' peace ").

A name given to the Peace of Cambray (negotiated August 5, 1529), because the preliminaries were conducted by Louise, mother of Francis I, and Margaret, aunt of Charles V.

Paix Fourrée (French, " Patched-up Peace ").

A name given to the peace concluded at Longjumeau in 1568 (preparing the way for that of 1570. *v.* **Paix Boiteuse et Mal-assise, La**) between the Catholics and Calvinists. Also called **La Petite Paix.** The reconciliation at Chartres, May 9, 1409, between the children of the Duke of Orleans (assassinated not long before) and Jean sans Peur, Duke of Burgundy (his murderer) is also called **la paix fourrée.** The murder of the Duke of Orleans (November 23, 1407) by Jean sans Peur was the beginning of the struggle between the **Armagnacs** (q.v.) and the **Burgundians** (q.v.).

Palamites.

The followers of Gregorius Palamas, a monk of Mount Athos, in the fourteenth century, who taught that there exists a divine light, eternal and uncreated, which is not the substance or essence of deity, but God's activity or operation. The Palamites were favoured by the emperor, Joannes Cantacuzenus, and their doctrine was confirmed by a council at Constantinople in 1351. They were called by their opponents **Euchites** and **Massalians ;** also **Hesychasts** and **Umbilicanimi.**

Palmetto City, The.

A popular surname for the city of Charleston, South Carolina, alluding to the number of palmetto trees in its streets. *v.* also **Palmetto State, The.**

Palmetto State, The.

South Carolina ; so named from the palmetto on its coat of arms.

Palmyra of the Deccan, The.

A name given to Bijapur, a town in Southern India.

Palmyra of the North.

A name sometimes given to St. Petersburg, Russia.

Palo Alto.

A bay trotting stallion by Electioneer, dam Winnie (thoroughbred). He won the stallion record in 2.08¾, and held it until he died. His record was lowered by Stamboul.

Pam.

A nickname familiarly applied to Viscount Palmerston, a British statesman (1784–1865).

Panama Canal.

A projected ship-canal across the Isthmus of Panama. Ferdinand de Lesseps supported the scheme, and a company was formed after an " international scientific congress " had met in Paris in May, 1879. The shares were rapidly taken, and active work was commenced in 1881. Work was continued, with some interruptions, until March, 1889, when the company went into liquidation. Of the total length of the canal (54 miles), 12 miles had been so far finished as to be navigable, but this did not include the more difficult portions. In December, 1892, De Lesseps and his son, the contractor Eiffel and others were arrested on charges of fraud in connection with the canal ; and at their trial it was shown that a large portion of the funds had been used in subsidizing the French press and in bribing members of the French legislature, etc.

Pan-American Congress.

A congress of representatives from the United States, Mexico, Haiti, and all the States of Central America and South America, held at Washington, 1889–90, for the purpose of consultation on matters common to the various States, and for the furtherance of international commerce and comity.

Pandects of Justinian.

A collection of Roman civil law made by the emperor Justinian in the sixth century, containing decisions or judgments of lawyers, to which the emperor gave the force and authority of law. This compilation, the most important of the body of Roman civil law, consists of fifty books. Also called the **Digest.**

Pandies.

The Hindus ; the Sepoys. Name specially applied by the British troops to the Sepoys in the Indian mutiny of 1857-8. Derived from the Hindoo word " panda," a Brahman.

Pan-handle, The.

A familiar nickname (alluding to its form) given to the most northerly portion of the State of West Virginia.

Pantheon of the British, The.
Westminster Abbey, London.

Papa la Violette, *v.* **Caporal la Violette.**

Papa Violet, *v.* **Caporal la Violette.**

Paper King, The.

A surname given to John Law (1671-1729), from his financial schemes. *v.* Mississippi Scheme.

Paper-Saving Pope.

A nickname given by Dean Swift to Alexander Pope, a famous English poet (1688-1744), alluding to his translation of the " Iliad " and " Odyssey " having been written on odd scraps of paper.

Paper Wedding, v. Wedding Anniversaries.

Paphlagonian, The.

A surname of Michael IV, Byzantine emperor from 1034-41.

Pappenheimer Regiment.

A regiment of cuirassiers in the Imperialist service in the Thirty Years' War.

Paradise of Bohemia, The, *v.* **Bohemian Paradise, The.**

Paradise of Central Africa. The.

A name given to Fatiko by Sir Samuel White Baker.

Paradise of Fools, *v.* **Limbo.**

Parc-aux-Cerfs.

A house in Versailles, France, which was notorious as a harem of Louis XV (r. 1715-74). Cf. **Well-beloved, The.**

Paris Garden.

A circus for bull-and-bear-baiting, at Bankside, near the Globe Theatre, London. It is said to have derived its name from one De Paris, who built a house there in the reign of Richard II. It was in use at the beginning of Henry VIII's reign, and was afterwards fitted up and used for a playhouse also.

Parish Priest of Meudon, The, *v.* **Curé de Meudon, The.**

Paris of Japan, The.

A name given to Osaka (or Ozaka), a city in the main island of Japan.

Parliament of Bats (Bludgeons).

A parliament under Henry VI, 1426. Orders had been sent to the members that they should not wear swords, so they came, like modern butchers, with long staves. *Gurdon,* " Hist. of Parliament."

Parliament of Dunces, The (Latin, " Parliamentum Indoctorum ").

A parliament convened at Coventry by Henry IV in 1404, so named because all lawyers were excluded from it. Also called the **Unlearned Parliament** and the **Lack-learning Parliament.**

Parliamentum Vanum (Latin, " The Useless Parliament ").

A name given to Charles I's

first parliament. It met June 18, 1625, adjourned to Oxford, August 1, on account of the plague, and, offending the King, was dissolved August 12, 1625.

Parnassus of Japan, The.

A name given to Fusi-yama or Fuji-san, the highest mountain of Japan, seventy miles south-west of Tokio. A resort of pilgrims.

Parnellite Party.

The Irish Nationalist party as it came under the leadership of Parnell c. 1879. Its only important aim was the securing of home rule for Ireland. After the judgment against Charles Stewart Parnell in the O'Shea divorce case, the party divided, a small fraction of it, called now distinctively the Parnellites, being led by John Redmond, while the great majority of the Nationalists (often called Anti-Parnellites) chose Justin McCarthy as leader.

Parricide, The.

A surname (Parricida) of Johannes (John of Swabia), a German prince (1290–1368). He murdered his uncle, King Albert I, May 1, 1308, for withholding his hereditary dominions.

Parsley Peel.

A nickname given to the first Sir Robert Peel, a calico printer (1750–1830). So called from the quantity of calico made by him with a parsley-leaf pattern on it.

Parson Brownlow, *v.* **Fighting Parson, The.**

Parson's Emperor (German " Pfaffen-Kaiser ").

A name given to the emperor Charles IV. (1316–78), who owed his elevation to the Pope.

Parthenopean Republic, The.

A name given to the republic established at Naples by the French in January, 1799.

Parthenope of Naples, The, *v.* **Christian Virgil, The.**

Partition Treaties.

Two treaties made between France, England and the Netherlands in 1698 and 1700 (the latter on the death of the Bavarian electoral prince), for the settlement of the Spanish succession. By the first, Spain, the Indies, and the Netherlands were given to the Bavarian electoral prince, Joseph Ferdinand ; Guipúzcoa and the Sicilies to France ; and Milan to the Archduke Charles. By the second, Spain, the Indies, and the Netherlands went to the Archduke Charles, and France was to receive the two Sicilies, Milan (or its equivalent, Lorraine), and Guipúzcoa.

Parvus, *v.* **Little, The.**

Passion Play.

A mystery-, or miracle-play representing the different scenes in the passion of Christ. The passion play is still extant in the periodic representations (every ten years) at Oberammergau, a village in Upper Bavaria, on the Ammer, forty-five miles south-west of Munich, perhaps the only example to be found at the present time.

Patched-up Peace, The, *v.* **Paix Fourrée, La.**

Pathfinder, or Pathfinder of the Rocky Mountains.

A surname given to John Charles Frémont (1813–90), a noted American general, explorer and politician.

Patriarch of Dorchester.

John White, an English preacher (1574–1648), is sometimes so called.

Patriarch of Ferney, The.

Voltaire (François Marie Arouet), is often so called (1694–1778). The last twenty years of his life were spent at Ferney, near Geneva, but early in 1778 he visited Paris, and died there (May 30). Also called the **Philosopher of Ferney**, the **Dictator of Letters**, the **Apostle of Infidelity**, the **Great Pan**, the **Plato of the Eighteenth Century** (by Carlyle), **l'Anatomie Vivante** (the living anatomy).

Patriarch of New England, The.

A surname sometimes given to John Cotton, a Puritan clergyman (1585–1652). He imigrated from England and settled in Boston in 1633.

Patriot King, The.

A surname given to Henry St. John, Viscount Bolingbroke, an English statesman and political writer (1678–1751). He wrote (1749), "Idea of a Patriot King."

Patriot of Humanity, The.

A surname given (by Byron) to Henry Grattan, an Irish orator and statesman (1746–1820). He procured the repeal of "Poynings' Law" in 1782 (*v.* Statute of Drogheda).

Patriots.

A faction of the Whig party in the reigns of George I and George II opposed to Sir Robert Walpole.

Patron Saints, *v.* Seven Champions of Christendom ; also under the headings of Apostle of, etc.

Paulicians.

A sect probably founded by Constantine of Syria during the latter half of the seventh century. They held the dualistic doctrine that all matter is evil, believed that Christ, having a purely ethereal body, suffered only in appearance ; and rejected the authority of the Old Testament and religious ordinances and ceremonies. Said to have become extinct in the thirteenth century. The name is probably derived from their high regard for the apostle Paul.

Paulists.

A body of Roman Catholic monks professing to follow the example of the Apostle Paul. Specifically in the United States, the congregation of the Missionary Priests of St. Paul, a Roman Catholic organization founded in New York city in 1858 for parochial, missionary and educational work. Also called **Paulites**, or **Hermits of St. Paul**.

Paulites, *v.* Paulists.

Paul Pry.

A synonym for a meddlesome, inquisitive person, derived from the principal character in a comedy (both so named) by John Poole, produced in 1853.

Paul's Cross Sermons.

Sermons still preached on Sunday mornings in St. Paul's. Paul's Cross was a cross situated near the north-eastern angle of old St. Paul's in the churchyard, originally the place of assembly of the folksmote. From it great public assemblies were addressed and sermons preached.

Paul's Walk, *v.* Duke Humphrey's Walk.

Pavement of Martyrs.

A name given to a spot on the battlefield near Tours where Charles Martel defeated the Saracens in 732. It was in this battle that he gained the surname of Martel (the hammer), cutting through the ranks of the Moslems with irresistible might, dealing ponderous blows right and left. The whole array of the Saracens broke and fled in utter rout.

Poole, "Story of the Moors," p. 30.

Paysan du Danube, Le (French, "The Peasant of the Danube ").

A surname given to Louis Legendre, a member of the French National Convention (1756–97), in allusion to the eloquence of the peasant in La Fontaine's fable, " Le Paysan du Danube."

Pays de Sapience, Le (French, " The land of Wisdom ").

A name given to Normandy by the French.

Peaceful, The.

A surname given to Alexander II, King of Scotland (1198–1249). Also called the **Little**

Red Fox. To Casimir I, King of Poland (d. 1058 ; r. 1040–58). Also called the **Monk**, and the **Restorer of Poland.** To Edgar (or Eadgar), King of England (944–75), from his quiet reign.

Peaceful Prelate, The.

A surname given to Jean Baptiste Massillon, bishop of Clermont, a noted French pulpit-orator (1663–1742). Cf. **Fighting Prelate, The.**

Peace of Amiens.

A treaty between England, France, Spain and Holland, signed March 27, 1802. England restored all conquests except Ceylon and Trinidad, the Ionian Republic was acknowledged, the French were to abandon Rome and Naples, and Malta was to be restored to the Knights of St. John.

Peace of Monsieur, *v.* Paix de Monsieur, La.

Peace of Nuremberg.

A religious truce concluded in 1532 between the Emperor Charles V and the Protestants.

Peace of Nystad.

A peace negotiated in 1721 between Russia and Sweden, ending the **Northern War** (q.v.).

Peace of Oliva.

A peace concluded in 1660 at Oliva, Prussia, between Sweden, Poland, the Empire, and Brandenburg. Sweden received important concessions from Poland and renounced Courland.

Peace of Peking.

A treaty negotiated at Peking in October, 1860, between China on one side and Great Britain and France on the other. China ratified the treaty of Tientsin, paid indemnities, and made other concessions.

Peace of Prague.

A treaty concluded in 1635 between the emperor Ferdinand II and the elector of Saxony, by which the latter received Lusatia. Also a treaty between Prussia and Austria, concluded August 23, 1866, by which the Lombardo-Venetian kingdom was annexed to Italy, the Germanic Confederation dissolved, and a new arrangement of Germany provided for, excluding Austria. Austria ceded her rights in Schleswig-Holstein to Prussia, and paid Prussia a war indemnity of £3,000,000.

Peace of Presburg.

A treaty concluded between France and Austria, December 26, 1805. Austria ceded her Venetian possessions to the kingdom of Italy, Tyrol, Vorarlberg, Passau, etc., to Bavaria, and her Swabian possessions to the South German States. Bavaria and Würtemberg were made kingdoms. Austria received the principality of Salzburg and some smaller possessions.

Peace of Rastatt.

A treaty concluded between France and Austria, March 6, 1714. Supplemented by the Treaty of Baden (q.v.).

Peace of Ryswick (or Ryswijk).

A treaty signed at Ryswijk, a village in the province of South Holland, Netherlands, September 21, 1697, between France on one side and England, the Netherlands and Spain on the other. France acknowledged William III as King of England; the Dutch restored Pondicherry to the French; and England and France mutually restored conquests in America.

Peace of Sistova.

A treaty concluded between Turkey and Austria, August 4, 1791. It fixed as the boundaries practically those established by the peace of Belgrade in 1739.

Peace of the Pruth.

A treaty concluded at Hush between Russia and Turkey, July 23, 1711. Peter the Great and his army (which had been blockaded at Hush, near the Pruth) were relieved; Azof and other possessions were ceded to Turkey; and it was stipulated that Charles XII of Sweden should be permitted to return home unmolested. Called also the Treaty of Falczi.

Peace of the Pyrenees.

A treaty between France and Spain, concluded in November, 1659, on an island of the Bidassoa (near the Pyrenees). Spain ceded to France a great part of Artois, parts of Flanders, Hainault and Luxemburg, most of Roussillon and part of Cerdagne; a marriage was arranged between Louis XIV and the Infanta of Spain, Maria Theresa, daughter of Philip IV.

Peace of Tilsit.

A treaty between France, Russia and Prussia signed at Tilsit, east Prussia (between France and Russia), July 7, 1807, and between France and Prussia two days later. (Napoleon and Alexander met June 25, 1807). ⸙Under its provisions, part of Prussia was ceded to Russia, the region west of the Elbe was ceded to Napoleon, the Confederation of the Rhine and Joseph, Louis and Jérôme Bonaparte recognized, Prussian harbours closed to British trade, the Prussian army reduced to 42,000 men, etc.

Peace of Tolentino.

A treaty concluded at Tolentino, February, 1797, between Pope Pius VI and Napoleon Bonaparte. The Pope ceded Avignon, the Comtat-Venaissin, Bologna, Ferrara, the Romagna, and Ancona to the French.

Peace of Utrecht.

The peace concluded in 1713, through several separate treaties between France on one side and Great Britain, Holland, Prussia, Savoy and Portugal on the other, and acceded to by Spain. With the subsequent treaties of Rastatt and Baden (*v.* **Peace of Rastatt** and **Treaty of Baden**), it put an end to the **War of the Spanish Succession** (q.v.).

Peace of Westphalia.

The treaties signed at Münster and Osnabruck in 1648 (general peace signed at Münster, October 24, 1648), which ended the **Thirty Years' War** (q.v.).

Peace of Zurich.

A treaty which terminated hostilities between France and Sardinia on one side and Austria on the other, November 10, 1859.

Peaces.

In addition to above, *v.* also under **Treaty of**, etc.

Pearl of Ireland, The.

A surname given to St. Bridget (Brigit or Bride), a patron saint of Ireland (d. 523).

Pearl of the Antilles, The, *v.* Queen of the Antilles, The.

Pearl Wedding, *v.* Wedding Anniversaries.

Peasant Bard, The.

A name given to Robert Burns, a famous Scottish lyric poet (1759–96).

Peasant-Boy Philosopher, The.

A surname given to James Ferguson, a Scottish astronomer and lecturer (1710–76).

Peasant of the Danube, The, *v.* Paysan du Danube, Le.

Peasant Poet, Northamptonshire, *v.* Northamptonshire Peasant Poet.

Peasant Pope, The.

A surname given to Guiseppe Sarto, Pope Pius X (b. 1835). Elected Pope August 4, 1903.

Peasants' War, The.

An insurrection of the peasantry against the nobles and clergy in southern Germany. It broke out in 1524, and spread through Franconia, Swabia, Thuringia and Alsace, being suppressed with great cruelty in May and June, 1525.

Peculiar People, The.

A small sect of Faith-Healers, founded in London in 1838. In cases of illness not requiring surgical aid they refuse medical assistance, and rely upon prayer, anointing, etc., for recovery. The sects of Faith-Healers and Christian Scientists in the United States hold similar views.

Peelers.

A nickname given to the uniformed constabulary appointed under the " Peace Preservation Act " of 1814, introduced by Sir Robert Peel. Afterwards extended to the new police of England, also called **Bobbies,** from Sir Robert Peel's Christian name.

Peelites.

A political party existing after the repeal of the corn-laws in 1846. Originally (in large part) Tories, but free-traders and adherents of Sir Robert Peel (hence the name), they formed for several years a group intermediate between the Protectionist Tories and the Liberals. Several took office in the Aberdeen administration (1852–5), and Gladstone, Sidney Herbert and others eventually joined the Liberal party.

Peep o' Day Boys.

A Presbyterian faction in the north of Ireland, c. 1785–90, opposed to the Roman Catholic " Defenders." Closely allied to the **Orangemen** (q.v.).

Pelagians.

The followers of Pelagius (d. probably c. 420), who is said to have been a British monk named Morgan (of which **Pelagius** is the Latin rendering), taking up his residence at Rome before 405. They held that there was no original sin through Adam, and consequently no hereditary guilt ; that every soul is created sinless by God ; that the will is absolutely free ; that the grace of God is universal, but not indispensable ; and they rejected infant baptism. Pelagius, however, held to the belief in the Trinity and in the personality of Christ.

Pelican.

The ship in which Drake sailed round the world. He left Plymouth November 15, 1577, with four other ships, which were either lost or deserted him, and he completed his famous voyage September 26, 1580. The " Pelican " was carefully preserved by order of Queen Elizabeth, but was finally broken up, and a chair caused to be made from her timbers by John Davis, the arctic navigator, is now in the Bodleian Library.

Pelican State.

The State of Lousiana is sometimes so named, from the pelican on its coat of arms.

Pendleton Act.

An Act of Congress (approved Jan. 16, 1883) regulating the civil service of the United States, so called from its promoter, Senator George H. Pendleton, of Ohio. Cf. Appleton's " Annual Cyclopædia," 1884.

Peninsular Campaign.

The campaign of the Federal Army of the Potomac under McClellan, March–August, 1862, for the capture of Richmond by way of the peninsula between the York and James rivers.

Peninsular State.

A name sometimes given to

Florida. Also called the **Everglade State.**

Peninsular War.

The military operations carried on in Portugal, Spain and southern France by the British, Spanish and Portuguese forces (largely under Wellington), against the French, in 1808–14. The French were driven out of the Peninsula.

Penniless, The, *v.* **Pochi Danari.**

Penny Dreadfuls.

A jocular name for a class of weekly penny periodicals devoted chiefly to stories of a blood-curdling or sensational character. Cf. **Shilling Shockers.**

Pennsylvania Farmer, The.

A surname given to John Dickinson, an American statesman (1732–1808), and president of Pennsylvania 1782–5. Derived from the "Letters from a Pennsylvania Farmer to the Inhabitants of the British Colonies," which he published in 1768.

Penruddock's Rebellion.

An unsuccessful rising on behalf of Charles II in 1655, so called from its leader, Colonel Penruddock, who was captured and executed.

Pensioned (or Pension) or Cavalier Parliament.

A name given to the English Parliament of 1661–79, which was favourable to the Cavalier or Royalist cause.

Pentarchy.

A name given to the five great European powers— Austria, France, Great Britain,

Prussia and Russia. For about half a century after the Congress of Vienna (1814–5) they were of nearly equal strength, each being far superior to any of the other European nations.

Also, in recent Italian politics, a parliamentary group under the leadership of the five politicians, Cairoli, Crispi, Zanardelli, Nicotera and Baccarini.

Pentecôte Vivante, La (French, "The Living Pentecost ").

A surname given to Cardinal Guiseppe Mezzofanti, an Italian linguist (1774–1849), who is said to have spoken fifty or fifty-eight languages. Called by Byron "a walking polyglot."

People's Captain, The, *v.* **Hero of Modern Italy, The.**

People's Friend, The.

A surname given to William Gordon, an English philanthropist (1801–49).

People's Party, or Populists.

A party formed in 1891 in the United States, in which were merged the Farmers' Alliance and other kindred organizations. Among their aims are an increase of the circulating medium, free coinage of silver, free trade, an income tax, suppression of monopolies, etc.

People's William (or Will), The, *v.* **Great Commoner.**

Père aux Rondeaux, Le (French, "Father Rondo ").

A surname given to J.-B. Davaux, a celebrated French composer (d. 1822).

Père de la Pensée, Le (French, "The father of thought ").

A surname given by his soldiers to Nicolas Catinat, a marshal of France (1637-1712).

Père des Lettres, Le (French, " The father of letters ").

Francis I of France (1494-1547), a patron of literature, has been so named.

Père Duchesne, Le.

A surname given to Jacques René Hébert, a notorious French Revolutionist (1755-94), from his being chosen to edit a Revolutionary paper having that title.

Père du Peuple, Le (French, " The father of the people ").

A surname given to Louis XII, king of France (1462-1515).

Père Hyacinthe.

The name by which Charles Loyson, a French pulpit orator, is often called (b. 1827).

Père Joyeux du Vaudeville, Le (French, " The joyous father of the vaudeville ").

A surname given to Oliver Basselin, a Norman poet and artisan (fl. fifteenth century). His songs were called **Vaux-de-Vire**, from their place of origin (he was born in the Val-de-Vire, Normandy), whence **vaude-ville**.

Perfect, The.

A surname of John II, king of Portugal (d. 1495). During his reign (1481-95) Bartholomew Dias discovered the Cape of Good Hope (1486).

Perfidious Albion, *v.* **Albion perfide.**

Perilous Siege, The, *v.* **Round Table, The.**

Perpetual Peace, The.

A name given to the treaty concluded at Fribourg between France and the Swiss Confederation in 1516.

Persian Anacreon, The, *v.* **Anacreon of Persia, The.**

Peruvian Corporation, *v.* **Grace Contract, The.**

Peter Funk.

A name given to a bogus bidder at auctions. He is employed to bid against an intending purchaser, to raise the price.

Peterloo Massacre.

A riot at St. Peter's Field, Manchester, England, August 16, 1819. A large assembly, mainly of the labouring classes, had met on behalf of reform, under the leadership of Hunt. They were charged by the military, and many killed and wounded. (The name Peterloo is formed in imitation of **Waterloo**.)

Peter Porcupine.

A nickname given to William Cobbett, a noted English political writer (1762-1835). He published (at Philadelphia) " Porcupine's Gazette," a Federalist daily newspaper, also " Porcupine's Works."

Peter's Pence.

The name usually given to a tribute formerly paid to the pope by the people of England. Said to have originated in an undertaking by Offa (c. 792) to find funds to support a Saxon college at Rome, for which purpose the tax was imposed. It was paid annually at the festival of St. Peter, one penny being demanded from every family possessed of thirty pence yearly from land. Abolished in 1534 by Henry VIII. Sometimes called **Rome-Scot.**

Peter the Great of Egypt, The.

A surname given to Mehemet (or Mohammed) Ali, Viceroy of Egypt (c. 1769-1849).

Petite Paix, La, *v.* **Paix Fourrée, La.**

Petition of Right.

An Act of Parliament passed in 1628, one of the chief documents of the English Constitution. It provided that "no freeman be required to give any gift, loan, benevolence, or tax without common consent by Act of Parliament ; that no freeman be imprisoned or detained contrary to the law of the land ; that soldiers or mariners be not billeted in private houses ; and that commissions to punish soldiers and sailors by martial law be revoked and no more issued." *Acland and Ransome,* " Eng. Polit. Hist.," p. 88.

Petit Trianon, *v.* **Trianon, Petit.**

Petrarch of Spain, The, *v.* **Prince of Spanish Poetry, The.**

Petrified City, The.

A surname given to Ishmonie, in Upper Egypt, in allusion to the great number of statues of men, women, children and animals there, which, according to popular superstition, were once living and miraculously changed into stone.

Petticoat Lane.

A London street in Whitechapel (now called Middlesex Street), so named from the second-hand clothes market held there, especially on Sundays.

Philidor.

The name by which François André Danican, a noted French musical composer and chessplayer (1726-95) is generally known. Author of " Analyse du jeu des échecs " (1749).

Philip Baboon.

A nickname given to Philip, duke of Anjou, afterwards king of Spain (1683-1746), Louis XIV's grandson, in Arbuthnot's " History of John Bull." Cf. **Lewis Baboon.**

Philippe Égalité.

A name given during the French Revolution to Louis Philippe Joseph, duc d'Orléans (1747-93).

Philosophe Inconnu, Le (French, " The unknown philosopher ").

A name given to Louis-Claude de St.-Martin, a French mystical philosopher (1743-1805). Also called the **French Böhme,** having translated several of the works of Jakob Böhme (or Böhm, or Behmen), a celebrated German mystic.

Philosopher, The, *v.* **Martyr, The.**

Philosopher, The.

A surname of Leo VI, Byzantine emperor. *v.* **Wise, The.** Also of Marcus Aurelius Antoninus (originally Marcus Annius Verus, usually known as Marcus Aurelius), a celebrated Roman emperor (121-180), and of Porphyry, a Neoplatonic philosopher and teacher of philosophy at Rome (c. 233–c. 305).

Philosopher of China, The.

A surname given to Confucius, a celebrated Chinese philosopher (c. 550–478 B.C.).

Philosopher of Ferney, v. Patriarch of Ferney, The.

Philosopher of Malmesbury, The.

A surname given to Thomas Hobbes, a celebrated English philosopher (1588–1679), who was born at Malmesbury, Wilts. Cf. Lord Byron's " Don Juan," xv. 96.

Philosopher of Sans Souci, The.

A surname (self-bestowed) of Frederick (II) the Great, king of Prussia (1712–86). He died at Sans Souci, near Potsdam. Voltaire called him the **Philosopher Prince.** Also called (by the English) the **Protestant Hero.**

Philosopher of Wimbledon, The.

A surname of Horne Tooke (the assumed name of John Horne), an English politician and philologist (1736–1812). Died at Wimbledon. His chief work is the philological treatise, " Epea Pteroenta, or Diversions of Purley."

Philosopher Prince, The, v. Philosopher of Sans Souci, The.

Philosophical Club, v. Royal Society Club.

Phœbe, v. Essex.

Phœbus.

A surname of Gaston, Comte de Foix (1331–93), derived either from the beauty of his person or from a golden sun in his escutcheon.

Phœnix, v. Volunteer.

Phœnix, The.

An old London theatre in St. Giles-in-the-Fields. It was altered from a cockpit (v. **Cockpit, The**), and was sometimes called by that name. One of the chief places of amusement in 1583 ; destroyed in 1649.

Phœnix Park Murders.

The assassination of Lord Frederick Charles Cavendish (b. 1836), chief secretary to the lord lieutenant of Ireland, and undersecretary, Thomas H. Burke, while they were walking in Phœnix Park, Dublin, May 6, 1882. The murderers belonged to a secret society or gang known as " Invincibles."

Phosphorists.

A poetic school, of romantic tendency, in Sweden, in the first part of the nineteenth century, so named from their organ, " Phosphoros." The leading writer of the school was Atterbom.

Phrygian Cap, v. Red Cap of Liberty.

Physical-Force Party.

A name sometimes given to the Young Ireland party (q.v.), after O'Connell's repudiation of the use of force, c. 1843.

Piasts.

The first dynasty of Polish rulers. In Poland it ended with the death of Casimir III in 1370, but continued some centuries longer in Mazovia and Silesia.

Picards.

A sect in Bohemia about the beginning of the fifteenth century, suppressed by Ziska in 1421. They are accused of an attempt, under the guise of restoring man's primitive innocence, to renew the practices of the Adamites, in going absolutely unclothed and in maintaining the community of women, etc.

Pichegru's Conspiracy, *v.* Georges's Conspiracy.

Picts' Wall.

Another name for Hadrian's Wall, a wall of defence for the Roman province of Britain, constructed by Hadrian between the Solway Firth and the mouth of the Tyne. Ruins of it still extend for miles between Tynemouth and the estuary of the Solway.

Pierrot.

A typical character in French pantomime. He dresses in loose white clothes with enormous white buttons, and his face is whitened. He is a gourmand and thief, capable of every crime, incapable of a good action, and absolutely without moral sense. The present type was created by Gaspard Deburau under the Restoration ; previously he had been a gayer and more insignificant personage, a cross between a fool and an *ingénu. Larousse.*

Pieux, Le (French, " The pious ").

A surname of Louis I (also called " Le Débonnaire "), emperor of the Holy Roman Empire (778–840) ; of Louis VII,

king of France (c. 1120–80), also called " Le Jeune " ; of Robert II, king of France from 996–1031.

Pigott Diamond, The.

A famous diamond brought to England by Earl Pigott. It weighed 49 carats, and was thought to be worth about £40,000.

Pilate's Staircase, *v.* Scala Santa.

Pilgrimage of Grace.

An insurrection in Yorkshire and Lincolnshire (1536–7), headed by Robert Aske. It was occasioned by the ecclesiastical and political reforms of Henry VIII. The rebels occupied York, where they were joined by the Archbishop. Their number having increased to 30,000, they proceeded to Doncaster, where they were induced to disband by the representations of the royal commissioners. Finding themselves deceived, they rose again under Sir Francis Bigod. Martial law was declared in the north, and the rising was suppressed with great severity.

Pilgrim Fathers, The.

The founders of Plymouth Colony, Massachusetts, in 1620. *v.* Forefathers' Day.

Pillar of the Doctors, The, *v.* Doctor Venerabilis.

Pillars of Hercules.

In ancient geography, the two opposite promontories — Calpe (Gibraltar) in Europe and Abyla in Africa—situated at the eastern extremity of the Strait of Gibraltar, sentinels, as it were, at the outlet from the Mediterranean into the unknown Atlantic. According to one of several explanations of the name, they were supposed to have been torn asunder by Hercules.

Pillnitz, Convention of.

A meeting at Pillnitz, in August, 1791, between the emperor Leopold II, Frederick William II of Prussia, and the Comte d'Artois (later Charles X of France). They issued a declaration hostile to the French Revolution, which formed the basis of the first coalition against France.

Pilot that weathered the Storm, The, v. Bottomless Pit, The.

Pine-Tree Flag, The.

A flag carried by the first war vessels commissioned by Washington at the beginning of the Revolution. It originated with Massachusetts Colony, and consisted of a pine tree in the centre of a white field, and the motto, " Appeal to heaven."

Pine-Tree Money.

A name given to silver money coined in Boston, Mass., during the seventeenth century, from the figure of a pine tree on the obverse side.

Pine-Tree State.

The State of Maine is so called from the pine tree in its coat of arms.

Pious, The.

A surname given to Albert IV, duke of Austria (1379–1414) ; Edward VI, king of England (1537–53) ; Frederick III, Elector Palatine (1515–76) : v. Pieux, Le.

Pirate of the Gulf, The.

A surname given to Jean Lafitte, a French privateer and smuggler (c. 1780–c. 1826).

Pitt Bridge.

The name originally given (but not accepted by the public) to Blackfriars Bridge by its architect, Robert Mylne (1734–1811).

Pitt Diamond, The.

A celebrated diamond purchased by Thomas Pitt, grandfather of William Pitt, first earl of Chatham, and sold by him to the Regent of Orleans in 1717 for about £135,000. It came originally from India (the Parteal mines, on the Kistna), was one of the crown jewels of France, and was set in the handle of the first Napoleon's sword. It weighs about 137 carats. Also known as the **Regent Diamond.**

Plain, The (French, " La plaine ").

In the legislatures of the first French Revolution, the floor of the house, occupied by the more moderate party ; hence that party itself as distinguished from **La Montagne** (q.v.), and **Le Marais** (q.v.).

Plain and Perspicuous Doctor, The, v. Doctor Planus et Perspicuus (or Conspicuus).

Platonic Puritan, The.

A surname given to John Howe, an English Puritan clergyman (1630–1705). Domestic chaplain to Cromwell. Or the Puritan Plato.

Plato of the Eighteenth Century, The, *v.* **Patriarch of Ferney, The.**

Players, The.

A New York Club founded by Edwin Booth, incorporated in 1888. Its objects are "the promotion of social intercourse between the representatives of the dramatic profession and of the kindred professions of literature, painting, sculpture and music and the patrons of the arts," etc.

Plimsoll's Act.

A popular name for the Merchant Shipping Act of 1876, passed mainly through the efforts of Samuel Plimsoll in the interests of merchant seamen. Its main object is to prevent unseaworthy ships leaving English ports. It also regulates the loadline and deck cargoes.

Plon-Plon.

A nickname of Prince Napoleon Bonaparte (1822–91), given to him on account of his supposed cowardice in the Crimean War. (A corruption of *plomb-plomb*, alluding to running away from bullets).

Plotter, The.

Surname of Robert Ferguson, a Scottish conspirator and political pamphleteer (d. 1714). He removed to England c. 1655, and was appointed to the living of Godmersham, Kent, from which he was expelled in 1662 by the Act of Uniformity. He was concerned in the Rye House Plot (q.v.), also in a similar conspiracy against William III.

Ploughman of Madrid.

A surname of St. Isidore (San Isidro). It is said that the angels came down and ploughed his grounds for him, the holy man having neglected them in order to devote his time to religious duties. *Ticknor*, "Span. Lit.," ii. 165.

Plough Monday.

A name given to the Monday following Twelfth Day, when ploughmen drew a plough from door to door asking for money.

Plumed Knight, The.

An epithet frequently applied to James Gillespie Blaine (1830–93), first by R. G. Ingersoll at Cincinnati in 1876, in a speech supporting Blaine's nomination for the presidency.

Plutarch of France, The.

A surname given to François de la Mothe Le Vayer, a French philosopher and writer (1583–1672).

Plymouth Brethren, or Plymouthites.

A sect of Christians who first attracted notice at Plymouth, England, in 1830, but have since extended over Great Britain, the United States, and among the Protestants of France, Switzerland, Italy, etc. They recognize all as brethren who believe in Christ and the Holy Spirit as his vicar, but they have no formal creed, ecclesiastical organization, or official ministry, condemning these as the causes of sectarian divisions. Also called **Darbyites**, after John Nelson Darby (1800–82), to whose efforts their origin and the diffusion of their principles are to be ascribed.

Pochi Danari (Italian, " The penniless ").

A surname given by the Italians to Maximilian I, Emperor of the Holy Roman Empire (1459–1519).

Poet of Poets, The.

A surname given to Percy Bysshe Shelley, a famous English poet (1792–1822).

Poet of Reason, The, *v.* **Lawgiver of Parnassus, The.**

Poet of the Excursion, The, *v.* **Bard of Rydal Mount.**

Poet of the Poor, The.

A surname given to George Crabbe, an English poet (1754–1832).

Poets' Corner.

A space on the east side of the south transept in Westminster Abbey, London, containing the tablets, statues, busts or monuments of Shakespere, Ben Jonson, Chaucer, Milton, Spenser, and other British poets.

Poet Sire of Italy, The.

A surname given to Dante Alighieri, a celebrated Italian poet (1265–1321), author of the " Divina Commedia."

Poet Squab.

A nickname given by Lord Rochester to John Dryden, a celebrated English poet and dramatist (1631–1700), in allusion to his corpulence in later life. Also called **Glorious John** (cf. Sir Walter Scott's " The Pirate," ch. xii.).

Poictiers, *v.* **Wasp.**

Polaris.

The vessel in which Captain Charles Francis Hall, an American Arctic explorer (1821–71), sailed July 3, 1871, on an expedition to the North Pole. On August 30 it reached 82° 11 N. lat., the highest point until then attained. *v.* **Fram.**

Polar Star, *v.* **Stella Polare.**

Polish Bayard, The.

A surname given to Prince Jozef Anton Poniatowski, a Polish general (1762–1813).

Polish Byron, The.

A surname given to Adam Mickiewiez, a noted Polish poet (1798–1855).

Polish Franklin, The.

A surname given to Tadeusz Czacki, a Polish writer and promoter of education in Poland (1765–1813).

Polish Voltaire, The.

A surname given to Ignatius Krasicki, a Polish poet and man of letters (1735–1801).

Polyphemus of Literature, The, *v.* **Great Moralist, The.**

Pompey's Pillar.

A Corinthian column of beautifully polished red granite at Alexandria, standing on a pedestal or foundation of masonry. The total height is about 99 ft., of which the shaft measures 73 and the capital 16½ ft. An inscription shows that it was erected in 302 A.D. in honour of Diocletian, whose statue stood on the summit. There is no reason for the name.

Pons Asinorum (Latin, " Asses' bridge ").

A name applied to the fifth proposition of the first book of Euclid, so named from the difficulty in understanding it often experienced by beginners. Sometimes also applied to the forty-seventh proposition in the same book.

Pontiac's War (or Conspiracy).

An Indian war in 1763, between the settlers and garrisons on the western frontier and the Indians from the tribes of the Delawares, Wyandottes, Shawnees, Mingoes, Chippewas, etc. Pontiac was the leader of the Indians. They captured Mackinaw, Presque Isle, and other forts, and unsuccessfully besieged Detroit.

Pool, The.

A part of the Thames immediately below London Bridge is so called.

Poor Man's Priest.

A surname given to (Father) Richard Radclyffe Dolling (1851–1902), a clergyman working among poor people in the East End of London.

Poor Priest, The.

Surname of Bernard, a French monk (1588–1640), who devoted his fortune and his life to the service of the poor.

Pope of Geneva, The.

A surname given to John Calvin, a celebrated Protestant reformer and theologian (1509–64), who died at Geneva.

Pope of Philosophy, The.

A surname given to Aristotle, the most famous and influential of Greek philosophers (384–322 B.C.). Also called the **Stagirite**, from his birthplace, Stagira.

Pope of the Huguenots, The.

A surname given to Cardinal Richelieu (1585–1642), who, although he destroyed the Huguenots as a political party, yet allowed them freedom of worship. Also applied to Philippe de Mornay (Duplessis-Mornay), a French diplomatist and Huguenot leader (1549–1623).

Popish Plot.

An alleged conspiracy of the Roman Catholics in 1678 to murder Charles II and control the government in the interest of the Romish Church ; chiefly contrived by Titus Oates, an English impostor.

Populists, v. People's Party, or Populists.

Porkopolis.

A nickname often given to Cincinnati, also Chicago, both noted pork-packing centres.

Porphyrogenitus (Latin, " Born in the purple ").

Surname given to Constantine VII, Byzantine emperor (905–59).

Porte, The, v. Sublime Porte.

Porteous Riots, The.

The name given to an outbreak in 1736 in Edinburgh. The mob broke into the Tolbooth prison and hanged an officer of the city guard, Captain John Porteous. (Cf. Sir Walter Scott's novel, " The Heart of Midlothian ").

Portland Vase, The.

A famous urn of blue transparent cameo-cut glass, ten inches high. Discovered c. 1630 in a sarcophagus in a tomb in the Monte del Grano, near Rome. So called from its possessors, the Portland family, who bought it in 1787 from Sir William Hamilton (its original purchaser in 1770), and placed it in the British Museum. Also called the **Barberini Vase**, because it was first deposited in the Barberini Palace. The vase was smashed by a stone thrown at it by a young man in February, 1845, but was subsequently mended. Cf. " Chambers's Journal," April, 1903.

Port-Royal.

A Cistercian abbey for nuns, situated about seventeen miles south-west of Paris, founded in 1204. Reformed under the abbess Jacqueline Marie Angélique Arnauld in 1608 ; was called Port-Royal des Champs, after the establishment (1266) of a branch house at Paris (called Port-Royal de Paris) ; and became noted as a centre of Jansenism. The older establishment became famous for its schools and as a centre of learning. Suppressed in 1709. Port-Royal de Paris continued until 1790.

Port Royal.

A name formerly given to Annapolis, Nova Scotia.

Portuguese Apollo, The.

A surname given to Luiz de Camoens, a celebrated Portuguese poet (c. 1524–80).

Portuguese Cid, The.

A surname given to D. Nuno Alvarez Pereira, first constable of Portugal (1360–1431). He retired to a convent in 1421.

Portuguese Horace, The.

A surname given to Antonio Ferreira, a noted Portuguese poet (1528–69).

Portuguese Livy, The.

A surname given to João de Barros, a noted Portuguese historian (1496–1570).

Portuguese Mars, The. v. Great, The (Affonso de Albuquerque).

Portuguese Nostradamus, The.

A surname given to Gonçalo Annes Bandarra, a Portuguese cobbler and rimer (b. early in the sixteenth century-1556), on account of his prophecies and thaumaturgical character. He was condemned by the Inquisition in 1541, but escaped with his life.

Portuguese Nun, The.

A surname given to Mariana Alcaforada, a Portuguese lady who addressed a series of letters to the Chevalier de Chamilly with whom she was deeply in love, although her passion was not reciprocated. So called on account of her supposed connection with a convent.

Portuguese Paradise, The.

A name given to Cintra, fifteen miles north-west of Lisbon, Portugal.

Portuguese Theocritus, The.

A surname given to Francisco da Sá de Miranda, a Portuguese poet (1495–1558).

Portuguese Titian, The.

A surname given to Alonso

Sanchez Coello, a Spanish painter, especially noted for his portraits (c. 1520–90).

Postman Poet, The.

Surname given to Edward Capern (1819–94), a rural letter-carrier at Bideford, who wrote verses (cf. " Dict. Nat. Biog."). Also called the **Bideford Postman.**

Potteries, The.

A district in Staffordshire, England, famous for the manufacture of earthenware, porcelain, etc. It includes Stoke-upon-Trent, Newcastle-under-Lyme, Etruria, etc.

Poughkeepsie Seer, The.

A surname given to Andrew Jackson Davis, an American spiritualist (b. 1826).

Poynings's Law.

Two Acts of the Irish Parliament in 1494, named from Sir Edward Poynings. *v.* **Statute of Drogheda.**

Pragmatic Sanction.

A term first applied to certain decrees of the Byzantine emperors, regulating the interests of their subject provinces and towns ; then to a system of limitations set to the spiritual power of the Pope in France in 1438, which laid the foundations of the so-called Gallican Church. Lastly, it became the name for an arrangement or family compact, made by different potentates, regarding succession to sovereignty — the most noted being that of Charles VI. It provided (1) that the lands belonging to the house of Austria should be indivisible ;

(2) that in the absence of male heirs these lands should devolve upon Charles's daughters (the eldest of whom was Maria Theresa), according to the law of primogeniture ; and (3) that in case of the extinction of this line the inheritance should pass to the daughters of Joseph I and their descendants.

Praguerie.

An unsuccessful insurrection in France (1440) in opposition to the establishment of a standing army. (From **Prague,** referring to the Russian insurrection there).

Prairial Insurrection.

An unsuccessful insurrection of the Paris populace against the Convention, on the first Prairial, year 3 (May 20, 1795).

Prairie State, The.

A name given to Illinois.

Praise God Barebones. *v.* **Barebones' Parliament.**

Premier Grenadier de France, Le, *v.* **Premier Grenadier de la République, Le.**

Premier Grenadier de la République, Le.

A French soldier, Théophile Malo Corret de la Tour d'Auvergne (1743–1800), was so named by Napoleon. He refused the rank of general. Distinguished himself in the wars of 1792–1800, and was commander of the " Infernal Column." From his death until 1814 his name was retained on the roll of his company as a mark of honour, the colour-sergeant answering " Mort au champ d'honneur " (Dead on the field of honour), when la Tour d'Auvergne's name was called. Also known as " le Premier Grenadier de France."

President.

An American frigate, built at New York in 1794, a sister ship to Constitution and United States (q.v.). On January 15, 1815, it defeated the British ship " Endymion," but surrendered to her consorts. Also an American steamship which left New York for Liverpool, March 21, 1841. It was sighted on the 24th, but was never seen again. Tyrone Power, the Irish comedian (b. 1797) was on board.

Pretender, The, *v.* Chevalier de St. George.

Pride's Purge.

The forcible exclusion from the House of Commons, December 6, 1648, of all the members who were favourable to compromise with the royal party. This was effected by a military force commanded by Thomas Pride (hence the name), in execution of orders of a council of Parliamentary officers.

Priest, The.

A surname of Konrad, a Middle High German epic poet (date of birth and death unknown) ; also of Lamprecht, another Middle High German epic poet (the date of whose birth and death are also unknown).

Priest of Nature, The.

A surname given (by Campbell) to Sir Isaac Newton, a famous English mathematician and natural philosopher (1642–1727).

Primrose Day, *v.* Primrose League.

Primrose League.

A league or combination of persons pledged to principles of Conservatism as represented by Benjamin Disraeli, earl of Beaconsfield (1804–81), and opposed to the " revolutionary tendencies of Radicalism." The object of the league is declared to be " the maintenance of religion, of the constitution of the realm, and of the imperial ascendancy of Great Britain." The scheme of the organization was first discussed at the Carlton Club in October, 1883. The name and symbol of the league are derived from Beaconsfield's favourite flower, which it has been fashionable to wear on April 19, the anniversary of his death, generally called Primrose Day.

Prince, The.

A surname of Judah I (fl. 190–220), the seventh patriarch and president of the Sanhedrim in succession from Hillel. Also called " the Holy."

Prince John.

A nickname of John van Buren, an American lawyer (1810–66), Attorney-General of New York, from his figure and manners.

Prince of Alchemy, The.

A surname given to Rudolf (or Rudolph) II, emperor of the Holy Roman Empire (1552–1612). Also the German Trismegistus.

Prince of Ancient Comedy, The, *v.* Father of Comedy.

Prince of Artists, The.

A surname given to Albrecht

Durer, a famous German painter and engraver (1471–1528).

Prince of Coxcombs, The.

A surname given to Charles Joseph, Prince de Ligne, an Austrian field-marshal (1735–1814).

Prince of Darkness, The, *v.* **Old Harry.**

Prince of Destruction, The, *v.* **Firebrand of the Universe, The.**

Prince of Diplomatists, The.

A surname given to Charles Maurice de Talleyrand-Périgord, prince de Bénévent (1754–1838), a famous French statesman and diplomatist.

Prince of Gossips, The.

A surname given to Samuel Pepys, an English politician and diarist (1633–1703) in allusion to the gossipy nature of his famous "Diary" (January, 1660–May, 1669).

Prince of Grammarians, The, *v.* **Grammaticorum Princeps.**

Prince of Liars, The.

A surname given by Cervantes to Fernão Mendes Pinto, a Portuguese adventurer and traveller in the East (c. 1509–83).

Prince of Music, *v.* **Father of Music, The.**

Prince of Orators, The

A surname given to Demosthenes, the greatest of Greek orators (384 or 5–322 B.C.).

Prince of Painters, The.

A (self-bestowed, it is said) surname of Parrhasius, a celebrated Greek painter (fl. c. 400 B.C.). Also applied to Apelles, another famous Greek painter (fl. c. 330 B.C.).

Prince of Philosophers, The.

A surname given to Plato, a famous Greek philosopher (429 or 7–347 B.C.).

Prince of Physicians, The.

A surname given to Avicenna (a corrupt form of Ibn Sina), the most celebrated Arabian physician and philosopher (980–1037).

Prince of Poets, The.

A surname given to Edmund Spenser, a celebrated English poet (c. 1552–99).

Prince of Princes, The.

A surname given (by Lord Byron, in "Don Juan") to George IV of England (1762–1830).

Prince of Showmen, The.

A surname given to Phineas Taylor Barnum, a famous American showman (1810–91).

Prince of Spanish Poetry, The.

A surname given to Garcilasso de la Vega, a celebrated Spanish poet (1503–36). Also called the **Spanish Petrarch** or the **Petrarch of Spain.**

Prince of Story-Tellers, The.

A surname given to Giovanni Boccaccio, a celebrated Italian novelist and poet (1313–75), author of the "Decamerone." Also called the **Father of Italian Prose** and the **Bard of Prose.**

Prince of the Ode, The.

A surname given to Pierre de Ronsard, a celebrated French poet (1524–85).

Prince of the Peace.

A title given to Manuel de Godoy, duke of Alcudia (1767–1851), who negotiated with France the peace of Bâle, 1795.

Prince of the Sonnet, v. French Ovid, The.

Prince of the Vegetable Kingdom, The.

A surname given by Linnæus to the palm-tree.

Princess Alice.

An iron saloon steamer belonging to the London Steamboat Co. with, it is estimated, over 900 persons on board, principally women and children, sunk in the Thames in a collision with the "Bywell Castle," a large iron screw steamer, September 3, 1878. About 200 persons were saved, and about 640 bodies were recovered. The courts afterwards decided that the "Princess Alice" was solely to blame.

Prince Titi.

A nickname given to Frederick Louis, prince of Wales (1707–51), eldest son of George II, from the pseudonym adopted by him in his memoirs.

Prisoner of Chillon, The.

A surname given to François de Bonnivard, a Genevan prelate and politician (1496–c. 1570), the hero of Lord Byron's poem, "The Prisoner of Chillon." He was confined for six years in a dungeon of the Castle of Chillon.

Prisoner of Ham, The.

A surname given to Napoleon III, emperor of the French (1808–73). He was imprisoned in the citadel of Ham, near St. Quentin, France, for six years (1840–6), but afterwards escaped and fled to England. v. **Badinguet.**

Prisoner of the Vatican, The.

A surname given to Pope Pius IX (1792–1878) by his adherents. In 1870 he was deprived of his temporal possessions, and the Vatican was assigned to him as a place of residence.

Prix de Rome, Grand, v. Grand Prix de Rome.

Proclamation of Schönbrunn.

A proclamation issued December 27, 1805, by Napoleon I at Schönbrunn, declaring that the Bourbon dynasty in Naples had ceased to reign.

Prodigy of France, The.

A surname given (by Erasmus) to Guillaume Budé (Budæus), a French savant (1467–1540) for his great erudition.

Prodigy of Learning, The.

A surname given (by Jean Paul Richter) to Christian Samuel Friedrick Hahnemann, a German physician, founder of homeopathy (1755–1843).

Profound Doctor, The (Latin, "Doctor Profundus").

A surname given to several schoolmen, particularly to Thomas Bradwardin(e), a celebrated English prelate, theologian and mathematician (c. 1290–1349). Also to Richard Middleton, an English scholastic divine (d. 1304). Or **Solid Doctor.**

Prophet of the Syrians, The.

A surname given to Ephraem

Syrus, a theologian and sacred poet of the Syrian Church (c. 308-c. 373).

Prose Homer of Human Nature, The, *v.* **Hogarth of Novelists, The.**

Prosperity Robinson.

Nickname given to Frederick Robinson (Viscount Goderich) owing to his eulogy of British prosperity shortly before the financial crisis of 1825. Cf. **Adversity Hume.**

Protector of the Indians (Spanish, " Protector Universal de los Indios ").

Bartolomé de las Casas, a Spanish Dominican (1474–1566), who received this official title in 1516. Later there were local protectors in the different colonies. Sometimes also called the **Apostle of the Indians.**

Protestant Duke, The.

A name given to James Fitzroy, Duke of Monmouth (1649–85), a (reputed) illegitimate son of Charles II of England and Lucy Walters. Also called the **Little Duke.**

Protestantenverein (German, Protestant union).

An association of German Protestants formed in 1863 at Frankfort-on-the-Main. Among its objects are toleration, freedom from ecclesiastical domination, union of different churches in a national church, and the development of Protestantism.

Protestant Hero, The, *v.* **Philosopher of Sans Souci, The.**

Protestant Livy, The.

A surname given to John

Philipson Sleidanus, historian (1506–56), for his " History of the Reformation."

Protestant Pope, The.

A name sometimes given to Pope Clement XIV (1705–74), who suppressed the Jesuits by the brief " Dominus ac Redemptor noster " (1773).

Proud, The.

A surname given to Albert Margrave of Meissen (1158–95).

Proud Duke, The.

A name given to Charles Seymour, sixth duke of Somerset (d. 1748).

Provisions of Oxford.

A set of articles passed by the " Mad Parliament " (q.v.) at Oxford in 1258. They provided for a committee of twenty-four to redress grievances in church and state ; for a standing body of fifteen, as a council to the king, who should hold three annual parliaments, and communicate with a body of twelve representing the barons ; and for a body of twenty-four members to negotiate financial aids.

Provisions of Westminster.

Ordinances passed through the influence of the barons in Parliament at Westminster, 1259. " They embodied the grievances of the barons stated at Oxford, and mainly concerned the administration of justice and local government by the sheriffs."

Prudhomme, Monsieur Joseph.

A self-satisfied character created by Henri Monnier in 1852, noted for his high-sound-ing but empty phrases. Frequently quoted and referred to in French literature. The name was taken from the Old French term, " Prud'homme," signifying a wise and honourable person selected as a member of a council to settle disputes between employers and employed.

Pucelle, La (French, "The Maid").

The surname given to Joan of Arc. *v.* **Maid of Orleans.**

Puffing Billy.

The name of an early locomotive engine (1813), so called from the great noise made by the two blast pipes in the chimney.

Pulpit Buffoon, The.

A surname given to Hugh Peters (or Peter), an English Puritan clergyman (c. 1598–1660), hanged at Charing Cross as an accomplice in the death of Charles I. So called by Sir William Dugdale.

Pure, The.

A surname given to Baffo, a Venetian lady (lived c. 1580–1600), sultana and councillor of the sultan Amurath III.

Puritan.

A wooden centre-board sloop designed by Edward Burgess, and launched in South Boston in 1885. Dimensions : length, over all, 94 feet ; beam, 22 feet 7 inches ; displacement, 105 tons. Winning two out of three of the trial races, she was selected to defend the America Cup in 1885. This she did successfully in two races with the Genesta (q.v.), September 14 and 16.

Puritan City, The.

A name sometimes given to Boston, Massachusetts.

Puritan Plato, The, *v.* **Platonic Puritan, The.**

Puritans.

A name originally given in 1564 to those clergymen of the Church of England who refused to conform to the liturgy and discipline as arranged by Archbishop Parker and others, and insisted on a return to a " purer " form of faith and worship. The name afterwards became more generalized, and has come to mean the whole Cromwellian party. *v.* **Roundheads.** Since the Restoration the name has been changed to **Nonconformists.**

Puseyites.

The followers of Edward Bouverie Pusey, an English theologian (1800–82). In 1835 he took part in the tractarian movement (*v.* **Tractarians**), and later was suspended for three years (1843–6) from the function of preaching, for publishing " The Holy Eucharist a Comfort to the Penitent." The movement thus started took the name of Puseyism.

Pushful Joe.

A nickname given to the Right Hon. Joseph Chamberlain. (b. 1836).

Putrid Sea.

Another name for Sivash, an arm of the Sea of Azof, northeast of the Crimea, separated from the main sea by the tongue of Arabat, and connected with it by the Strait of Genitchi. It is shallow, very salt, and largely occupied by lagoons and swamps. Length about 100 miles.

Pym of France, The.

A surname given to Mathieu Molé (1584–1656). Appointed "Garde des sceaux" in 1650.

Quadrilateral.

The four fortresses of Legnago, Mantua, Peschiera, and Verona, in Italy, famous for their strength and their strategic importance during the Austrian occupation of northern Italy.

Quadruple Alliance, The.

A league against Spain, formed in 1718 by Great Britain, France, Austria, and the Netherlands. *v.* **Triple Alliance.**

Quadruple Treaty, The.

A league formed against the usurper Dom Miguel of Portugal and Don Carlos of Spain in 1834. The signatory powers were Great Britain, France, Spain, and Portugal.

Quai d'Orsay.

The quay on the south bank of the Seine, Paris, where the department of foreign affairs and the building of the Corps Législatif are situated. The name is hence used figuratively for the French foreign office, or the government in general, like Downing Street (q.v.), for the English, and Dublin Castle (q.v.) for the Irish executive.

Quaker City.

Philadelphia, which was colonized by Quakers.

Quaker Poet, The.

Surname of Bernard Barton, an English poet, a member of D.N.

the Society of Friends (1784–1849). A friend of Charles Lamb. Also of John Greenleaf Whittier, an American poet and author (1807–92), member of the Society of Friends (q.v.).

Quakers, *v.* Society of Friends.

Quaker Soldier, The.

Surname of Clement Biddle, an American revolutionary officer (1740–1814). A personal friend and correspondent of Washington.

Quarreller, The, *v.* Hutin, Le.

Quartier Latin (French, Latin quarter).

The name given to the quarter of Paris, on the south side of the Seine, in the vicinity of the Sorbonne. It has been frequented by the student class for centuries.

Quasimodo Sunday.

In France and Germany, Low Sunday is generally known by this name, on account of the "Introit" in the mass used on that day beginning with the word **Quasimodo** (1 Peter ii. 2).

Queen Anne's Bounty.

The name of a fund established in 1703 (Queen Anne's reign) for the augmentation of the smaller church livings. Derived from the first fruits and tithes of all livings of the value, at that time, of over £50, also from private benefactions and sums formerly granted by Parliament. The office of the fund is in Queen's Yard, Westminster.

Queen Anne's War.

The name given in the United States to the war against the

s

French and Indians, 1702–13, part of the War of the Spanish Succession (q.v.).

Queen City, or Queen of the West.

A name given to Cincinnati, Hamilton County, Ohio. Original name **Losantiville**.

Queen City of the Lakes.

A name given to the city of Buffalo, Erie County, New York.

Queen City of the South.

A name given to Sydney, Australia.

Queen Dick.

A nickname given to Richard Cromwell (1626–1712), son of Oliver Cromwell, whom he succeeded as Lord Protector, September, 1658. He resigned in May, 1659, and his brief rule was characterized by timidity and incapacity.

Queen Elizabeth's Pocket-Pistol.

A brass gun, 24 feet long, in Dover Castle, is so called. It was a present from Charles V to Henry VIII.

Queen of Cities, The, v. Eternal City, The.

Queen of Hearts, The.

A name given to Elizabeth Stuart, queen of Bohemia (1596–1662), daughter of James VI of Scotland (James I of England), and wife of Frederick, elector palatine (later king of Bohemia).

Queen of Queens, The.

A surname given by Antony to Cleopatra, the last queen of Egypt (69–30 B.C.).

Queen of Song, The, v. Italian Nightingale, The.

Queen of Tears.

A name sometimes given to Mary of Modena (1658–1718), second wife of James II of England.

Queen of the Adriatic, The, v. Mistress of the Adriatic, The.

Queen of the Antilles.

A name given to Cuba. Also the **Pearl of the Antilles**.

Queen of the East.

A name given to Antioch, in Syria. A title of Zenobia, queen of Palmyra (d. after 274). A name given to Batavia in Java.

Queen of the Eastern Archipelago, The.

A popular surname for Java.

Queen of the Mississippi Valley, The.

A surname given to St. Louis, Missouri.

Queen of the North.

A name given to Edinburgh, Scotland. Also called the **Modern Athens**.

Queen of the Sea, The.

A surname given to ancient Tyre, next to Sidon the oldest and most important city of Phœnicia.

Queen of the West, The, v. Queen City, The.

Queen of Watering Places.

A surname sometimes given to Scarborough, Yorkshire.

Queen Sarah.

A nickname given to Sarah

Jennings, duchess of Marlborough](1660–1744). Also called Mrs. Freeman in her private intercourse with Queen Anne, who took the name of Mrs. Morley.

Queen's Evidence, *v.* **King's.**

Queen's Marys, The.

A collective name for four young ladies of quality who accompanied Mary, Queen of Scots, to France in 1548. Their names were Mary Bethune (Beaton), Mary Leuison (Livingstone), Mary Flemyng (Fleming) and Mary Seyton (Seton or Seaton). Cf. "The Queen's Marys," by Whyte-Melville.

Queen's Pipe, The.

A name given to the dock kiln in the London Docks winecellars where useless goods that have not paid duty are burnt.

Queen's Shilling.

The coin (usually a shilling) handed to a recruit on his declaring his intention and willingness to enter the British army. Its acceptance is considered as equivalent to signing a contract. Since the death of Queen Victoria it is called the **King's Shilling.**

Quixote of the North, The. *v.* **Madman of the North, The.**

Rabelais of Germany, The.

A surname given to Johann Fischart, a German satirist and Reformer (b. c. middle of sixteenth century–d. c. 1590).

Racine of Italy, The.

A surname given to Pietro Antonio Domenico Bonaventura Trapassi Metastasio, a noted Italian poet (1698–1782).

Racine of Music, The.

A surname given to Marie-Gaspard Sacchini, an Italian composer (1734–86).

Racine's Imitator, *v.* **Singe de Racine, Le.**

Ragman Roll.

A collection of parchments containing the record of the fealty of Scottish barons, clergy, and gentry to Edward I of England when in Scotland in 1296. " . . . called by the Scots 'ragman' because of the many seals hanging from it." . . . "In course of time, it is said, 'ragman's roll' became 'rigmarole.'" *Morley*, "English Writers," iv. 291.

Raid of Ruthven.

In Scottish history, a conspiracy at Castle Ruthven, near Perth, in 1582. The Earls of Gowrie, Mar and others, seized the person of James VI and took him out of the keeping of his guardians, the Duke of Lennox and the Earl of Arran.

Railroad City, The.

Indianapolis, the capital of Indiana and of Marion County, is sometimes so called.

Rail-Splitter, The.

A nickname of Abraham Lincoln, sixteenth President of the United States (1809–65), in allusion to his early life.

Railway King, The.

A surname given to George Hudson, an English speculator and railway promoter (1800–71). He lost the greater part of his large fortune in the railway panic of 1847–8.

Rainy-Day Smith.

A nickname given to John Thomas Smith, engraver, antiquary and art writer (1766–1833).

Ram Alley.

An alley leading from Fleet Street to the Temple, formerly securing immunity from arrest ; hence it was the resort of sharpers and persons of ill-fame of both sexes. It was full of cooks' shops, and is frequently referred to in this connection in contemporary literature. A comedy by Lodowick Barry, printed in 1611, bears the title of "Ram Alley ; or, Merry Tricks."

Rambler, The.

A periodical after the style of the "Spectator." published in London by Dr. Samuel Johnson, 1750–2.

Rambouillet Decree.

A decree issued by Napoleon I, March 23, 1810, providing for the seizure and sale of American vessels.

Rand, The.

A name by which Witwatersrand, a hilly region of the Transvaal, west of Johannesburg, containing extensive goldfields, is familiarly known.

Ranelagh Gardens.

Gardens formerly situated near the Thames, Chelsea, London. They were noted for concerts from 1704 to 1805, and famous as the scene of wild and extravagant entertainments, masquerades, etc. They were closed in 1805, and no trace now remains.

Ranz des Vaches (French, "Chime of the Cows").

A strain of an irregular description, which in some parts of Switzerland is sung or blown on the Alpine horn in June to call the cattle from the valleys to the higher pastures. *Grove.*

Raphael of Cats, The.

A surname of Gottfried Mind, a Swiss painter (1768–1814), especially famous for his pictures of cats. Also called "the Bernese Friedli."

Raphael of England, The.

A surname given to Sir Joshua Reynolds, a celebrated English portrait-painter (1723–92). He founded the Literary Club (q.v.).

Raphael of France, The, *v.* **French Raphael, The.**

Raphael of Holland, The.

A surname given to Martin von Heemskerk (or Hemskerk), a Dutch historical painter (1498–1574).

Raphael of Music, The.

A surname given to Wolfgang Amadeus Mozart, a celebrated Austrian composer (1756–91).

Rappists, *v.* **Harmonists.**

Rare Ben Jonson.

A surname given to Benjamin (usually known as Ben) Jonson, a celebrated English dramatist (c. 1573–1637). Buried in Westminster Abbey in the Poets' Corner (q.v.). A casual visitor, Sir John Young, caused the words "O rare Ben Jonson" to be cut on his tomb.

Called (by Dekker) the **English Horace**.

Ratisbon Interim.

A provisional arrangement devised by the emperor Charles V for the settlement of the points of dispute between the Catholics and Protestants. It was based on a conference held during the Diet at Ratisbon, in 1541, between leading theologians (Melanchthon, Bucer, Eck, etc.).

Rebel Brigadiers.

A nickname given by Northern politicians to the Southern Congressmen who had served in the Confederate army during the American Civil War.

Rebellion, The.

In United States history, the American Civil War. In Scottish history, the Jacobite insurrections.

Red, The.

A surname given to Amadeus VII, a count of Savoy (r. 1383–91), a son of Amadeus VI.

Red Cap of Liberty.

The red cap ("bonnet rouge") worn during the French Revolution. Supposed to be an imitation of the Phrygian cap, which among the Romans was an emblem of liberty, and worn by slaves when freed.

Red Cross Knight, The.

A name given to St. George, the patron saint of England.

Red Cross Knights, *v.* Templars.

Red Cross Society.

A philanthropic society founded to carry out the views of the Geneva Convention of 1864. Its objects are to care for the wounded in war and secure the neutrality of nurses, hospitals, etc., and to relieve suffering occasioned by pestilence, floods, fire, and other calamities. The society was established through the efforts of Henri Dunant. The president of the American National Red Cross Society is Clara Barton. The distinctive flag is a red cross on a white ground.

Redeemed Captive, The.

A surname given to the Rev. John Williams, a New England clergyman (1644–1729), who was made prisoner by the French and Indians in 1704, and obtained his freedom in 1706. He published a narrative of his experiences under the title of "The Redeemed Captive."

Red Lions, The.

An association formed in 1839 at the Red Lion in Church Street, Birmingham, England. "By degrees the ' Red Lions '—the name was assumed from the accident of the first meeting-place—became a very exclusive club. Forbes first drew round him the small circle of jovial philosophers which included Lankester, Thomson, Bell, Mitchell, and Strickland. Many were added afterwards, as the club was kept up in London in meetings at Anderton's in Fleet Street." *Timbs.*

Red Prince, The.

A surname given to Prince Frederick Charles of Prussia (1828–85), nephew of the Emperor William I, alluding to the colour of his favourite hussar uniform.

Red Republicans.

A nickname given by the French to those republicans who are in favour of maintaining extreme republican doctrines even at the cost of bloodshed. Also called " bonnets rouges," from the red caps worn by them at the time of the French Revolution.

Red River Expedition.

An unsuccessful Federal expedition (March–May, 1864) up the Red River valley, for the purpose of recovering western Louisiana. Also the expedition under Wolseley in 1870, which succeeded in quelling the insurrection under Louis Riel in the valley of the Red River of the North.

Reekie, Auld, *v*. Auld Reekie.

Reformation, The.

The great religious revolution in the sixteenth century, which led to the establishment of the Protestant churches. In Scotland it was introduced by John Knox c. 1560. In England it led, in the reign of Henry VIII, to the abolition of the papal supremacy and the liberation from papal control of the Church of England, which was firmly established under Elizabeth, after a short Roman Catholic reaction under Mary.

Reform Bill.

A Bill for the purpose of enlarging the number of voters in elections for members of the House of Commons, and of removing inequalities in representation. The first of these bills, passed in 1832, disfranchised many rotten boroughs, gave increased representation to the large towns, and enlarged the number of the holders of county and borough franchise. The effect of the second Reform Bill, passed in 1867, was in the direction of a more democratic representation, and the same tendency was further shewn in the Franchise Bill passed in 1884.

Reformer of the Laws, *v*. Lagabœter.

Reform War (Spanish, "Guerra de la Reforma").

A civil war in Mexico, 1857–61, ending with General Juarez's entry into Mexico, January 11, 1861, his opponent, General Miramon, having been finally defeated at Calpulalpa, December 22, 1860.

Re Galantuomo (Italian, "honest king").

A surname given to Victor Emmanuel II, king of Sardinia, king of Italy as Victor Emmanuel I (1820–78), alluding to the manner in which he redeemed his promises concerning the government.

Regent Diamond, *v*. Pitt Diamond, The.

Reign of Terror.

That period of the first revolution during which France was under the sway of a faction which made the execution of persons, regardless of age, sex, and condition, who were considered obnoxious to their measures, one of the cardinal principles of their government. This period may be said to have begun in March, 1793, when the Revolutionary tribunal was appointed, and to have ended in July, 1794, with the overthrow of Robespierre and his associates. Also called "the Terror."

Reindeer, *v.* **Wasp.**

Remonstrance, The Grand, *v.* **Grand Remonstrance, The.**

Remonstrants, *v.* **Arminians.**

Reptile Fund, The.

A name given in Germany to a Prussian fund held for the deposed Hanoverian dynasty, part of which it was alleged was diverted to the subsidizing of journals in the interest of the government.

Reptile Press, The.

A name, in Germany, given collectively to the journals believed to be subsidized by the Prussian government. It came into use in 1869. Cf. **Reptile Fund.**

Republican Party.

The usual name of the Democratic Party (in full, Democratic-Republican Party) during the years following 1792–3 ; it replaced the name Anti-Federal, and was replaced by the name Democratic. *v.* **Democratic Party.** Also a party formed in 1854, having as its original purpose opposition to the extension of slavery into the Territories. It was composed of Free-soilers, of anti-slavery Whigs, and of some Democrats (who unitedly formed the group known as Anti-Nebraska men), and was joined by the abolitionists, and eventually by many Know-nothings. The party favours generally a broad construction of the Constitution, liberal expenditures, extension of the powers of the national government, and a high protective tariff. Among the measures with which it has been identified in whole or in part are the suppression of the rebellion, the abolition of slavery, reconstruction, and the resumption of specie payments. Nicknamed by the pro-slavery, or conservative party, **Black Republicans.**

Republican Queen, The.

A surname given to Sophie Charlotte, queen of Prussia (1668–1705), wife of Frederick I. Charlottenburg was named after her.

Resolute.

An Arctic exploring ship which belonged to Sir Edward Belcher's squadron. Sailed with the "Assistance," "Pioneer," "Intrepid," and "North Star" in April, 1852, to search for Sir John Franklin. On May 15, 1854, at the command of Belcher, and against their will, Captain Kellett and Commander McClintock abandoned the "Resolute" and the "Intrepid" in the ice off Melville Island. On September 17, 1855, Captain Buddington, in the American whaler "George Henry," met the deserted "Resolute" in sound condition about forty miles from Cape Mercy. She must have drifted through Barrow Strait, Lancaster Sound and Baffin Bay. She was recovered, and the United States bought her and restored her in perfect condition to the British service, presenting her to the Queen through Captain Hartstein in 1856.

Resolute Doctor, The.

A surname given to John Baconthorpe (Bacon or Bacho), an English Carmelite monk and schoolman (d. 1346). Cf. **Doctor Resolutissimus.**

Resolution.

An exploring ship in which, with the "Discovery," Sir Thomas Button sailed from England in 1612. He wintered at the mouth of Nelson's River, and accomplished the exploration of Hudson Bay and of Southampton Island, returning to England in the autumn of the next year.

Restaurador del Parnaso (Spanish, "The Restorer of Parnassus").

A surname given to Juan Melendez Valdes, a Spanish poet (1754–1817).

Restoration, The.

In English history, the re-establishment of the English monarchy with the return of Charles II in 1660 ; often applied to the whole reign (1660–85) of Charles II.

Restorer of Parnassus, The, *v.* Restaurador del Parnaso.

Restorer of Poland, The, *v.* Peaceful, The.

Restorer of the Roman Empire.

A surname given by the senate to Aurelian (Claudius Lucius Valerius Domitius Aurelianus), Roman emperor (c. 212–75).

Reuter, *v.* Reuter's Telegraph Agency.

Reuter's Telegraph Agency.

An agency for the collection and transmission of news, developed by P. J. von Reuter in the decade 1850–60, and later, and now extending over nearly the entire world.

Revenge, The.

The name of a ship commanded by Sir Richard Grenville. One of six under Lord Thomas Howard that encountered a Spanish fleet of fifty-three vessels near the Azores. (Cf. Tennyson's poem, "The Revenge.")

Revised Version.

The version of the Bible completed as regards the New Testament in 1880, and published May 17, 1881 ; and as regards the Old Testament in 1884, and published May 19, 1885. It does not, however—at all events at present—seem likely to supersede the Authorised Version (q.v.).

Revocation of the Edict of Nantes.

A proclamation of Louis XIV of France, October 22, 1685, annulling the Edict of Nantes (q.v.).

Revolutionary Tribunal.

In French history, specifically, an extraordinary court of justice established by the Convention, in 1793, to take cognizance of all attacks directed against the Revolution, the republic and the public welfare. Suppressed in 1795.

Revolution of February, The.

The revolution in France of 1848. An outbreak in the evening of February 23 led to the abdication of King Louis

Philippe on the following day, and this was followed by the formation, on the same day, of a provisional government and the declaration of a republic.

Revolution of July.

The revolution of July 27, 28 and 29, 1830, by which the government of Charles X and the elder line of the Bourbons was overthrown. The younger line (Orleans) was soon called to the throne in the person of Louis Philippe.

Revolution of 1848.

The French revolution of February, 1848, which overthrew the government of Louis Philippe.

Rex Romanorum (Latin, " The King of the Romans ").

A title assumed by the Saint Henry II, emperor of the Holy Roman Empire, previous to his coronation in 1014, and for many years afterwards borne by the heirs of the emperors of Germany. Cf. **King of Rome, The.**

Rhenish Confederation, v. Confederation of the Rhine.

Ribbon Society, The.

In Irish history, a secret association formed c. 1808 in opposition to the Orange organization of the northern Irish counties, and so named from the green ribbon worn as a badge by the members. The members were bound together by an oath, had passwords and signs, and were divided locally into lodges. The primary object of the society was soon merged in a struggle against the landlords, with the purpose of securing to tenants fixity of tenure, or of inflicting retaliation for real or supposed agrarian oppression.

Richard Roe.

The name of the imaginary defendant in fictions formerly in use in cases of ejectment. *v.* **John Doe.**

Right, Captain, *v.* Captain Right.

Ringing Island, The.

A surname given to England, on account of the music of its many bells.

River of Light, *v.* Sea, or River, of Light.

River of Swans, The.

A name given to the Potomac, a river in the United States, length about 400 miles.

Roan Barbary.

The favourite horse of King Richard II (1366–1400). (Cf. Shakspere's " King Richard II," Act V, Sc. 5).

Roaring Forties.

The notably rough part of the North Atlantic crossed on the passage from Europe to North American ports between the 40th and 50th degrees of north latitude. The term is also applied to the region between the 40th and 50th degrees of south latitude in the South Atlantic, Pacific and Indian Oceans.

Robber, The.

A surname given (by the Scots) to Edward IV, King of England (1441–83).

Robert Macaire, *v.* Macaire, Robert.

Robin Bluestring.

A nickname of Sir Robert Walpole (1676–1745), referring to his blue ribbon as a Knight of the Garter.

Robin Redbreasts, *v.* **Bow Street Runners.**

Rob Roy (Gaelic, " Red Rob").

A nickname of Robert Macgregor (or Campbell), a Scottish freebooter (1671–1734). The hero of a novel by Sir Walter Scott so named.

Rock, Captain, *v.* **Captain Rock.**

Rock Day, *v.* **St. Distaff's Day.**

Rocket.

The name of an early railway locomotive engine, made by George Stephenson (1781–1848). During its trial trip in 1829 it attained a speed of twenty-nine miles an hour.

Rock Lizards.

A nickname for natives of Gibraltar born of British parents.

Rock of Chickamauga.

A name given to General George Henry Thomas (1816–70), commander of the Federal left wing at Chickamauga, for his stubborn defence in that battle (September 19, 20, 1863).

Roe, Richard, *v.* **Richard Roe.**

Roi Citoyen, Le (French, " The Citizen King ").

A surname of Louis Philippe, King of the French (1773–1850). Died at Claremont, Surrey. Sometimes called the **King of the Barricades,** and the **Napoleon of Peace.**

Roi des Braves, Le (French, " The King of Brave Men ").

A surname given by his troops to Henry IV, King of France (1553–1610).

Roi des Feuilletons, Le (French, " The King of ' Feuilletons ' ").

A surname given to Jules Gabriel Janin (1804–74), a clever and popular French journalist, and for many years a writer for the " feuilleton " portion of the " Journal des Débats."

Roi des Halles, Le (French, " The King of the Markets ").

A name given to the Duc de Beaufort (1616–69) from his popularity with the Parisian populace.

Roi des Prédicateurs, Le (French, " The King of Preachers ").

A surname given to Louis Bourdaloue (1632–1704), a noted French preacher. Also called the **Founder of Christian Eloquence.**

Roi des Reptiles, Le (French, " The King of Reptiles ").

A surname given to Bernard Germain Étienne de la Ville, Count Lacépède (1756–1825), in allusion to his natural history researches. The author of " Histoire Naturelle des Reptiles."

Roi Panade, Le (French, " The Indolent King ").

A nickname given to Louis XVIII, King of France (1755–1824), alluding to his listlessness and want of energy.

Rois Fainéants, Les (French, " The Do-nothing Kings ").

A name given to King Clovis II of Neustria (d. 656) and his ten successors. They were merely figure-heads, being entirely under the management of the mayor of the palace, or major domus. The empire of the Merovingians slowly declined in the hands of the " rois fainéants " until 751, when Pepin le Bref usurped the crown.

Roi Soleil, Le (French, " The Sun King "). *v.* **Great, The** (Louis XIV).

Roman Achilles, The.

A surname given to Sicinius Dentatus (d. 449 B.C.) on account of his bravery. Also the **Roman Roland.**

Roman Roland, The, *v.* **Roman Achilles, The.**

Roman Wall, *v.* **Picts' Wall.**

Rome of the North, The.

A name given to Cologne.

Rome-Scot, *v.* **Peter's Pence.**

Roof of the World, The.

A name given (by the natives) to a series of broad valleys that traverse the elevated and extensive plateau of Pamir in Central Asia. This lofty tableland has a mean elevation of 13,000 feet and an area of about 37,000 square miles.

Rookery, The.

A dense mass of houses, once the worst part of St. Giles's in London. It has been cleared away in the formation of New Oxford Street.

Root and Branch.

The extremists of the Parliamentary party who (c. 1641) favoured the overthrow of episcopacy; also the policy of these extremists.

Rosamond, Fair, *v.* **Fair Rosamond.**

Rosamond's Bower, *v.* **Fair Rosamond.**

Rosamond's Pond.

A sheet of water formerly in the south-west corner of St. James's Park, London. It was " long consecrated to disastrous love and elegiac poetry." Filled in in 1770.

Rosetta Stone.

The name given to a stone, now in the British Museum, originally found by French soldiers who were digging near the Rosetta mouth of the Nile. It is a piece of black basalt, containing part of three equivalent inscriptions, the first or highest in hieroglyphics, the second in demotic characters, and the third in Greek. According to these inscriptions the stone was erected in honour of Ptolemy Epiphanes, March 27, 196 B.C. The stone is famous as having furnished to Young and Champollion the first key for the interpretation of Egyptian hieroglyphics.

Rosicrucians.

A mystic secret society which became known in the seventeenth century, and was alleged to have been founded by Christian Rosenkreuz, a German noble, in 1388. Extinct in the eighteenth century. Its actual existence is, however, denied by some. Cf. Lord Lytton's "Zanoni," and works by Johann Valentin Andreä (1586–1654). v. also **Searcher, The.**

Rosinante.

Don Quixote's charger, all skin and bone.

Rota, or Coffee Club, The.

A London political club founded in 1659 as a kind of debating society for the dissemination of republican opinions. It met in New Palace Yard "at one Miles's, where was made purposely a large ovall table with a passage in the middle for Miles to deliver his coffee." The club was broken up after the Restoration. *Timbs.*

Rotten Row (From French, " Route du roi," the king's way).

A fashionable thoroughfare for equestrians in Hyde Park, London, extending west from Hyde Park Corner for one and a-half miles. "The old royal route from the palace of the Plantagenet kings at Westminster to the royal hunting forests was by what are now called ' Birdcage Walk,' ' Constitution Hill,' and ' Rotten Row ' ; and this road was kept sacred to royalty, the only other person allowed to use it being (from its association with the hunting-grounds) the Grand Falconer of England." *Hare,* " London," ii. 107.

Rough and Ready, Old, *v.* **Old Rough and Ready.**

Rough Riders.

The popular name of the First United States Volunteer Cavalry, organized by Theodore Roosevelt and Leonard Wood for service in the Spanish-American war (q.v.). It consisted of 1,000 men, recruited mainly from Western States.

Roundheads.

The members of the Parliamentarian or Puritan party during the civil war in England. So called opprobriously by the Royalists or Cavaliers, in allusion to the custom among the Puritans of wearing the hair closely cut, while the Cavaliers usually wore theirs in ringlets. The Roundheads were one of the two great parties in English politics first formed, c. 1641, and continued under the succeeding names of Whigs (q.v.), and Liberals (*v.* **Liberal Party**), as opposed to the Cavaliers (q.v.), Tories (q.v.), and Conservatives (*v.* **Conservative Party**) respectively.

Round Robin.

A name given to a petition or remonstrance signed by a number of persons, generally in a circular form so as to avoid giving prominence or precedence to any single name. A celebrated English one is that signed by Sir Joshua Reynolds, Burke, Gibbon and others, and sent to Dr. Samuel Johnson suggesting that Oliver Goldsmith's epitaph should be written in English. To this Johnson would not agree.

Round Table, The.

In the " Arthurian Legends " a table made by Merlin for Uther Pendragon, who gave it to the father of Guinevere, from whom Arthur received it, with

100 knights, as a wedding gift. The table would seat 150 knights. One seat was called the " siege," or " seat perilous," because it was death to any knight to sit upon it unless he were the knight whose achievement of the Holy Grail (q.v.) was certain.

Round Table Conference.

A resultless conference of representatives of the Gladstonian Liberals and Liberal-Unionists in 1887, the object of which was to effect a re-union of the Liberal party.

Rowley Mile, The, *v.* Old Rowley.

Roxburghe Club, The.

A club founded in 1812, at the time of the sale of the library of John, duke of Roxburghe. " The Rev. Thomas Frognall Dibdin claimed the title of founder. The avowed object of the club was the reprinting of rare pieces of ancient literature. . . . It still exists, and, with the Dilettanti Society, may be said to have suggested the publishing societies of the present day, at the head of which is the Camden " (*v.* Camden Society). *Timbs.*

Royal American Order, *v.* Order of Isabella the Catholic.

Royal George.

An English man-of-war of 108 guns. While being re-fitted at Spithead, August 29, 1782, she suddenly heeled over, under the strain caused by the shifting of her guns, filled, and went down with her commander, Admiral Kempenfelt, and nearly 1,000 sailors, marines and visitors on board, about 800 of whom were lost.

Royal Hanoverian Guelfic Order, *v.* Guelfic Order.

Royalist Butcher, The, *v.* Boucher Royaliste, Le.

Royalists.

The partisans of Charles I and of Charles II, during the civil war and the Commonwealth (q.v.) ; the Cavaliers (q.v.) as opposed to the Roundheads (q.v.). In American history, the adherents of the British government during the revolutionary period. In French history, the supporters of the Bourbons as against the revolutionary and subsequent governments.

Royal Martyr, The.

A surname given to Charles I of England (1600–49). Also the **Martyr** and (by Herbert) the **White King.**

Royal Oak.

A celebrated oak-tree, formerly standing on the borders of Staffordshire, England, near Shiffnal, in the branches of which Charles II of England (1630–85) is said to have remained concealed for twenty-four hours, when fleeing from his pursuers after the battle of Worcester (September 3, 1651).

Royal Society Club, The.

A London Club, which appears to have existed from 1709. It has consisted largely, but not exclusively, of fellows of the Royal Society. Its members were formerly known as " Royal Philosophers," and later as " Royals."

Royal Sovereign.

A British line-of-battle ship

of 100 guns and 2,175 tons register. She served in the Channel Fleet, 1793–5, and was the flagship of Vice-Admiral Cuthbert Collingwood at Trafalgar, October 21, 1805. Also a British line-of-battle ship of 120 guns and 3,144 tons register ; launched in 1864.

Ruby Wedding, *v.* **Wedding Anniversaries.**

Rufus (The Red).

A surname of William II of England (1056–1100), from his red hair.

Rule, Britannia.

An English national air, words by Thomson and Mallet, music by Arne : both were composed for the masque " Alfred," first performed at Cliefden House, Maidenhead, the residence of Frederick, Prince of Wales, in 1740.

Rummer Tavern.

An old London tavern, situated between Whitehall and Charing Cross, kept by Sam Prior, the uncle of Matthew Prior, the poet.

Rump Parliament.

The name given to the remnant of the Long Parliament (q.v.) after Pride's Purge (q.v.). In German history, the name given to the remnant of the National Assembly of Frankfort, which met at Stuttgart, June 6–18, 1849.

Rupert of Debate, The.

A surname applied (by Bulwer-Lytton) to Lord Stanley, afterwards 14th Earl of Derby (1799–1869). Also called the **Hotspur of Debate** (by Macau-

lay) and **Scorpion Stanley** (by Daniel O'Connell).

Russian Byron, The.

A surname sometimes given to Alexander Pushkin (or Poushkin), a celebrated Russian poet (1799–1837).

Russian Livy, The.

A surname given to Nicholas Mikhaelovitch Karamzin (or Karamsin), a Russian historian, novelist and poet (1765–1826).

Russian Murat, The.

A surname given to Count Mikhael Andrievitch Miloradovitch, a Russian general (1770–1825) distinguished in the Napoleonic Wars.

Russian Table Diamond, *v.* **Great Table Diamond. The,**

Russian Voltaire, The.

A surname (self-bestowed) of Alexandre Pétrovitch Soumarokov, a Russian poet (1718-77).

Rye House Plot.

A conspiracy by some extreme Whigs to kill Charles II and the Duke of York (James II), June, 1683. So called from Rye House, Hertfordshire, the meeting-place of the conspirators. Lord Russell (William), Algernon Sidney, and Robert Baillie were executed for alleged complicity.

Rysdyk's Hambletonian (10).

A bay trotting stallion, foaled c. 1849. From him has sprung most of the improved trotting stock of America.

Sabbatarians, *v.* **Southcottians.**

Sabbatians.

A Novatian sect of the fourth

century, followers of Sabbatius, who adopted the Quartodeciman rule. Also called **Sabathians, Sabbathaists, Sabbathians.**

Sacred Island, The, *v.* Island of Saints, The.

Sacred Nine, The.

The Muses.

Sadler's Wells.

A noted London theatre, at Islington (built 1764), of which Samuel Phelps (1804–78) was colessee from 1844 until 1862.

Sad Palm Sunday.

A name given to Palm Sunday, March 29, 1641, the date of the Battle of Towton, fought between the Yorkists and Lancastrians, in which the latter are said to have lost 28,000 men. (Cf. Michael Drayton's " Polyolbion," xxviii.)

Sage, Le (French, " The Wise ").

A surname given to Charles V, King of France (1337–80). Also called the **Solomon of France.**

Sage of Chelsea, The.

Surname given to Thomas Carlyle, a celebrated Scottish essayist and historian (1795–1881). He settled at Cheyne Row, Chelsea, in 1834, and died there. Sometimes also called the **Censor of the Age,** from the fault-finding or critical spirit of his style. Also called the **Chelsea Philosopher.**

Sage of Concord, The.

A surname given to Ralph Waldo Emerson, a celebrated American essayist, lecturer and poet (1803–82), who lived at Concord, Mass.

Sage of Crotona, The.

A surname given to Pythagoras, a famous Greek philosopher and mathematician (probably c. 582–c: 500 B.C.). He founded a philosophic school at Crotona.

Sage of Monticello, The.

A surname given to Thomas Jefferson, third President of the United States (1743–1826), from his country residence at Monticello, Virginia.

Sage of Princeton.

A surname given to Theodore Roosevelt (b. 1858), President of the United States, succeeding President McKinley in 1901.

Sage of Samos, The.

A surname given to Pythagoras, a famous Greek philosopher and mathematician (c. 582–c. 500 B.C.), born at Samos, Greece. Also the **Samian Sage.**

Sagest of Usurpers, The.

A surname given (by Lord Byron, in " Childe Harold ") to Oliver Cromwell, Lord Protector of the Commonwealth of England, Scotland and Ireland (1599–1658).

Sailor King, The.

A popular surname for William IV of England (1765–1837), who entered the navy as a midshipman in 1779, and in 1827 was created Lord High Admiral of England. He reigned 1830-7.

Saint, The.

Surname of Ferdinand III, King of Castile and Leon (c. 1200-52).

Saints, *v.* under St.

Salian, The.

A surname given to Conrad II, King of Germany and Roman Emperor (d. 1039), founder of the Franconian or Salian dynasty.

Salic Law.

A law excluding females from the throne of France, said to have been instituted by Pharamond in 421. Owing to this law Hanover was separated from the English Crown at the accession of Queen Victoria in 1837. Edward III's claim to the throne of France was barred by this law in 1338. This was the commencement of the Hundred Years' War (q.v.).

Salisbury Court Theatre.

An old London theatre. In 1583 it was one of the principal "playhouses." Destroyed 1649, the Duke's Theatre (q.v.) taking its place in 1660.

Salvator.

A famous American racehorse, chesnut with white legs and blaze, foaled in 1886. In 1890 he won the Suburban and the match against Tenny (by Rayon d'Or); and in a race against time on the straight course at Monmouth he made the record for one mile 1.35½.

Samian Sage, The, *v.* Sage of Samos, The.

Sancy Diamond, The.

A famous Indian diamond, weighing 53½ carats, originally purchased by M. de Sancy, French ambassador at Constantinople, and sold by him to Queen Elizabeth of England.

Sandemanians.

A religious denomination, followers of Robert Sandeman (1718–71), a native of Perth, Scotland, and a zealous disciple of John Glas. Among the distinctive practices of the body are community of goods, abstinence from blood and from things strangled, love-feasts, and weekly celebration of the communion. Called in Scotland Glassites.

Sand Lots Party.

An anti-Chinese workingmen's party in California, about 1877–80. So called from a place of meeting—the Sand Lots—an open space in the western part of San Francisco. Its leader was Denis Kearney.

Sandy, *v.* Sawney.

San Juan Question, The.

A dispute concerning the possession of the San Juan Islands in the Gulf of Georgia, south-east of Vancouver, which arose through different interpretations of the treaty of 1846. They were occupied jointly by British and American garrisons in 1859. By the Treaty of Washington the question was referred to the arbitration of the Emperor of Germany, who decided in favour of the United States, October 1872.

Sans Peur et Sans Reproche, *v.* Chevalier Sans Peur, etc.

Sans Terre, *v.* Lackland.

Santa Claus.

A corruption of Sant Nicolaus (or St. Nicholas), who lived c. 300 A.D. A prominent saint of the Greek Church, and the patron saint of Russia, seafaring men, thieves, virgins and children. The custom of placing gifts in children's shoes or stockings on the eve of St. Nicholas's day (December 6) is said to be derived from an incident in the life of the saint.

Santa Klaus, *v*. Santa Claus.

Santa Maria, La.

Columbus's largest vessel and flagship, in the voyage of 1492. She was a decked boat, of the type known as a carack, over 200 tons burthen, and about 63 feet long and 20 feet beam. Some accounts call her the "Marie Galante." She was a dull sailer, and was wrecked on the coast of Española, December 25, 1492.

Sappho of Toulouse, The.

A surname given to Clémence Isaure, a French lady (c. 1450–c. 1500), restorer of the floral games at Toulouse (1490), for an ode to Spring, composed by her.

Sardanapalus of Germany, The.

A surname given to Wenceslas VI (or IV), king of Bohemia and emperor of Germany (1359–1419). Also the **Nero of Germany** and the **Drunkard**.

Sardinian Convention.

A convention between Sardinia, France and Great Britain, January, 1855, by which Sardinia agreed to furnish a military contingent against Russia in the Crimean War.

Sarnia.

The Roman name of the island of Guernsey.

Satanic School.

A name first given by Southey

to a class of writers who were supposed to write in opposition to the received principles of morality and the Christian religion. Among the most prominent were Byron, Moore, Shelley Bulwer, Paul de Kock, Victor Hugo, etc.

Satyr, The.

A surname given (by Thomas Woolner) to Charles II, king of England (1630–85).

Savannah.

The name of the first steamship that crossed the Atlantic. About 350 tons burthen and 100 feet in length, built in New York in 1818 by Francis Pickett. The ocean voyage occupied twenty-six days, but she only used her paddles during sixteen. The vessel was finally wrecked off Long Island.

Saviour of Society.

A surname given to Napoleon III (1808–73).

Saviour of the Nations.

A surname given to the Duke of Wellington (1769–1852). *v*. **Iron Duke, The.**

Savoy Conference.

A conference held at the Savoy, London, after the restoration of Charles II (1661), between twenty-one Episcopalians and an equal number of Presbyterians, for the purpose of securing ecclesiastical unity. It utterly failed, leaving both parties more bitterly hostile than before.

Savoy Confession, *v*. Savoy Declaration.

Savoy Declaration.

A "declaration of the faith

and order, owned and practised in the Congregational churches in England," agreed upon at a meeting at the Savoy, London, in 1658. It is no longer regarded as authoritative among Congregational churches. Also called **Savoy Confession.**

Sawney.

A nickname for a Scotsman (a corruption of **Sandy**, a familiar contraction of **Alexander**). The word is also used to mean a simpleton.

Saxon, The.

A surname of Lothair II, emperor of the Holy Roman Empire (d. 1137). Made Duke of Saxony 1106.

Saxon Dynasty.

A line of German kings and emperors of the Holy Roman Empire, commencing with Henry the Fowler in 919, and ending with Henry II in 1024.

Saxon Switzerland, The (German, " Sächsische Schweitz ").

A name given to the mountainous region of Saxony, southeast of Dresden.

Saybrook Platform.

A declaration of principles adopted by a Congregational synod at Saybrook in 1708, substantially the same as the Cambridge Platform (q.v.).

Scala, La.

A theatre in Milan, Italy, one of the largest in the world. Inaugurated 1778.

Scala Santa (Italian, " Holy Staircase ").

A staircase on the north side of St. John Lateran, at Rome. It consists of twenty-eight marble steps, said to have come from the house of Pilate at Jerusalem, and leads to the mediaeval Papal chapel in ;the Lateran Palace. The stairs can be ascended only by penitents on their knees. Also called **Pilate's Staircase.**

Scarlet Woman, The.

A name sometimes given by Protestants to the Church of Rome in allusion to Revelation xvii.

Scavenger's Daughter.

A name given to an instrument of torture, invented by William Skeffington, a lieutenant of the Tower of London, in the reign (1509–47) of Henry VIII. It consisted of a spiked iron frame compressing the victim's body, so as to cause bleeding from the nostrils, etc.

Scholastic, The.

A surname given to Epiphanius (fl. c. 510 in Italy).

Scholastic Doctor, The.

A surname given to Anselm of Laon, a French theologian (1030–1117).

Schomburgk Line.

The boundary between British Guiana and Venezuela and Brazil, surveyed by Sir Robert Schomburgk, 1841–4. The settlement of the boundary dispute by arbitration has been urged by the United States government, most forcibly in 1895–6, and its attitude for a time threatened serious complications with England. Arbitration was agreed to by England in the latter year.

Schoolmaster of the Republic, The.

A surname given to Noah Webster, an American lexicographer and author (1758–1843).

Scian Muse, The.

A surname given (by Lord Byron) to Simonides, a noted Greek poet (556–c. 469 B.C.), born in the island of Ceos (or Kea, the modern Zea or Tzia).

Scio's Blind Old Bard, *v.* Father of Epic Poetry, The.

Scorpion Stanley, *v.* Rupert of Debate.

Scotch Hobbema, The.

A surname given to Patrick (or Peter) Nasmyth, a Scottish landscape painter (1787–1831), from his style having a certain resemblance to that of Hobbema. A brother of James Nasmyth, the inventor of the steam-hammer.

Scotch Sappho, The.

A surname given to Catherine Cockburn (*née* Trotter), dramatist and controversial writer (1679–1749).

Scotia.

A modern Latin and poetic name for Scotland (cf. Nova Scotia). Formerly **Caledonia** (q.v.).

Scotland's Scourge, *v.* Scourge of Scotland, The.

Scotland Yard.

A short street in London, near Trafalgar Square. The headquarters of the London police were formerly in this street, and the name has come to be used figuratively as synonymous with the police executive (in like manner to Downing Street for the government executive). The police headquarters are now removed to New Scotland Yard, on the Thames Embankment.

Scots Greys.

A regiment of British dragoons, first organized under Claverhouse, c. 1683.

Scottish Anacreon, The.

A surname given to Alexander Scot, a Scottish poet of the sixteenth century.

Scottish Boanerges, The.

A surname given to the brothers James Alexander and Robert Haldane, the former (1768–1851) a preacher, and the latter (1764–1842) a philanthropist and theological writer.

Scottish Hogarth, The.

A surname given to David Allan, a Scottish historical and portrait painter (1744–96).

Scottish Homer, The.

A surname given to William Wilkie, a Scottish poet (1721–72).

Scottish Solomon, The, *v.* British Solomon, The.

Scottish Teniers, The.

A surname given to Sir David Wilkie, a noted Scottish genre-painter (1775–1841).

Scottish Theocritus, The.

A surname given to Allan Ramsay, a Scottish poet (1686–1758), in allusion to his pastoral comedy, the "Gentle Shepherd," "the first genuine pastoral after Theocritus."

Scourers, *v.* **Mohocks.**

Scourge of God, The (Latin, " Flagellum Dei ").

A surname of Attila, a famous king of the Huns (d. 453) on account of the ruthless and widespread destruction wrought by his arms. Also called the **Terror of the World.**

Scourge of Grammar, The.

A surname given (in " The Dunciad ") to Giles Jacob, a lawyer and dramatic writer (1686–1744).

Scourge of Homer (Homeromastix).

A surname given to Zoilus, a Greek rhetorician (fl. fourth century B.C.), from his severe criticisms of Homer.

Scourge of Princes.

A surname given to Pietro Aretino, an Italian writer of satirical sonnets and comedies (1492–1556).

Scourge of Scotland (Latin, " Scotorum Malleus ").

A name sometimes given to Edward I of England (1239–1307), from his victories over the Scots. Also called **Longshanks** (q.v.).

Scrambling Committee, The.

A name given to the Irish " patriots " in the Irish Parliament, received into favour by the Duke of Devonshire (Viceroy in 1755), and signalized themselves by their rapacity in regard to the division of the surplus revenue.

Scriblerus Club.

A club of writers in London, founded by Swift in 1714, after the breaking up of " The Brothers " (q.v.) in 1713. Among the members were Pope, Arbuthnot, Bolingbroke, Gay, and others. The club was non-political, and was formed, at Pope's suggestion, for the purpose of satirizing broadly all literary incompetence. Also called the **Martinus Scriblerus Club.**

Scythe-Bearers or **Scythe-Men.**

A name given to bodies of revolutionists, mainly peasants, armed with scythes, in the Polish insurrections of 1794, 1831, 1846, and in the movement of the Prussian Poles in 1848.

Sea-Born City, The.

A name sometimes given to Venice.

Sea-Girt Isle.

A poetic name for Great Britain.

Sea-Green Incorruptible, *v.* **Incorruptible, The.**

Sea of Glory.

One of the principal gems of the Persian crown, a diamond weighing 66 carats.

Sea, or **River, of Light.**

The largest diamond belonging to the Shah of Persia, weighing 186 carats.

Sea of Stars.

A name given to the source of the Hoang-ho, or Yellow River, in Thibet, from its sparkling waters. (Cf. Southey's " Thalaba the Destroyer," vi, 12).

Searcher, The.

A surname given to Robert

Fludd (or Flud), an English physician and mystical philosopher (1574–1637). He wrote several treatises in defence of the Rosicrucians.

Seatonian Prize, The.

An annual prize of £40 at Cambridge University for the best English poem on a sacred subject, awarded from a fund bequeathed by the Rev. Thomas Seaton.

Second Aristotle, The.

Surname of Alessandro Achillini, an Italian physician and philosopher (1463–1512).

Second Augustine, The, v. Doctor Angelicus.

Second Charlemagne, The.

A surname given to Charles V, emperor of the Holy Roman Empire (1500–58).

Second Dauphin, The.

The eldest son, Louis, duc de Bourgoyne (1682–1712), of the Great Dauphin (q.v.). His grandfather, Louis XIV (d. 1715), survived both of them.

Second Shakspere, The.

A surname given (by Edward Phillips, in his " Theatrum Poetarum ") to Christopher Marlowe, an English poet and dramatist (1564–93).

Second Solomon, The, v. British Solomon, The.

Second Théâtre-Français, Le.

Name given to the Odéon theatre at Paris, near the Luxembourg. Opened in 1782 as the Théâtre-Français ; called the Théâtre de la Nation in 1789 ; and in 1796 the Odéon. Burned

in 1799, and rebuilt in 1807, when it was called the Théâtre de l'Impératrice. At the restoration it became " Le Second Théâtre-Français." It receives a subsidy from the State as an offshoot of the Comédie-Française (q.v.).

Second Trek, The, v. Great Trek, The.

Second Washington, The.

A surname given to Henry Clay, a celebrated American orator and statesman (1777–1852).

Seekers.

A name originally given to the Quakers or Society of Friends (q.v.), from their seeking the truth.

Self-denying Ordinance.

An ordinance passed by the English Parliament, April 3, 1645, requiring members of either house of Parliament holding military or civil office to vacate such positions at the expiration of forty days.

Semiramis of the North.

Surname given to Catherine (II) or Catharine, Empress of Russia (1729–96), (also called " the Modern Messalina "); also of Margaret, queen of Norway, Denmark and Sweden (1353–1412).

Sepoy Mutiny, v. Indian (or Sepoy) Mutiny.

September Convention.

A treaty concluded September 15, 1864, between France and Italy. France was to withdraw troops from Rome in two years, and Italy was to guarantee the retention of Rome by the Pope.

September Laws.

In French history, laws restricting the freedom of the Press, promulgated in September, 1835.

September Massacres, v. Massacres of September.

Septembriseurs, v. Septembrists.

Septembrists.

The instigators of the September massacres in Paris in 1792. In Portuguese history, the partisans of the liberal constitution of September, 1822.

Septennial Act.

An Act of Parliament passed in 1716, which superseded the Triennial Act (q.v.), and prolonged to seven years the possible life of Parliament. Parliament *must* be dissolved at the end of seven years.

Seraphic Doctor, v. Doctor Seraphicus.

Seraphic Saint, The.

A surname of St. Francis of Assisi (1182–1226), founder of the order of the Franciscans.

Serapis, v. Bonhomme Richard.

Serpent Column, The.

A bronze column in Constantinople. The base of the golden tripod set up in the sanctuary at Delphi from the spoils of the Persians at Platæa in 479 B.C. It was placed in the spina of the hippodrome by Constantine, and consists of three intertwined serpents, whose diverging heads are now broken. Height eighteen feet.

Servant of the Servants of God, The, v. Servus Servorum Dei.

Servita, v. Brother Paul.

Servus Servorum Dei (Latin, " The Servant of the Servants of God ").

A surname adopted by Pope Gregory I (544–604), and retained by his successors. By the Servants of God, he referred to the bishops.

Sette Comuni, v. Seven Communes.

Settlement (or Plantation) of Ulster.

The colonization of a large part of Ulster with English and Scottish settlers, c. 1609–11.

Seven Bishops, Case of the, v. Case of the Seven Bishops.

Seven Champions of Christendom.

In mediaeval tales the following seven national saints : St. Denis of France, St. Anthony of Italy, St. James of Spain, St. George of England, St. Andrew of Scotland, St. Patrick of Ireland, and St. David of Wales. Their exploits are celebrated in many ballads, plays, etc., notably in the " Famous History of the Seven Champions of Christendom," by Richard Johnston, a romance entered on the Stationers' Register in 1596.

Seven Chief Virtues, The.

These, according to the Roman Catholic Church, are : Faith, Hope, Charity, Prudence, Temperance, Justice and Fortitude. Cf. **Seven Deadly Sins.**

Seven Communes (Italian, " Sette Comuni ").

A district in the northern part

of the province of Vicenza, northern Italy, long noted as the seat of communities speaking a Germanic dialect, now nearly supplanted by Italian. Cf. **Thirteen Communes.**

Seven Days' Battles.

In the Peninsular campaign of the American Civil War, the series of battles between the Federal army under McClellan and the Confederate army under Lee, in the Chickahominy swamp region east of Richmond. The fighting began at Oak Grove, June 25, 1862, and the seven days' battle ended with the Federals being unsuccessfully assailed at Malvern Hill by Lee, July 1. A few weeks later the Army of the Potomac was withdrawn from the James, and the Peninsular campaign ended.

Seven Days' Campaign.

A name sometimes given to the series of battles in Bohemia between Austria and Prussia in 1866, ending with the decisive Prussian victory of Sadowa. July 3, 1866.

Seven Days' King, The.

A surname given to Masaniello (Tommaso Aniello or Anello), a Neapolitan insurrectionist (c. 1622–47), in allusion to his brief rule in Naples (1647).

Seven Deadly Sins.

These, according to the Roman Catholic Church, are : Pride, Anger, Envy, Sloth, Lust, Covetousness and Gluttony. Cf. **Seven Chief Virtues.**

Seven Great Hymns.

A collective name given to seven celebrated Latin hymns

of the Mediaeval Church Their names are:—

> The Celestial Country.
> Dies Iræ.
> Stabat Mater Dolorosa.
> Stabat Mater Speciosa.
> Veni, Creator Spiritus.
> Veni, Sancte Spiritus.
> Vexilla Regis.

Seven-hilled City, The, *v.* **Eternal City, The.**

Seven Liberal Arts.

A collective name given, during the Middle Ages, to the following subjects : arithmetic, geometry, astronomy, music, logic, rhetoric and grammar.

Seven Sacraments.

The following are recognized by the Roman Catholic Church, viz. : Baptism, Confirmation, The Eucharist, Penance, Holy Orders, Matrimony, and Extreme Unction.

Seven Sages (or Wise Men) of Greece.

These included Bias (fl. middle of sixth century B.C.); Chilo (or Chilon), (fl. early in the sixth century B.C.); Cleobulus (d. c. 560 B.C.); Periander (d. 585 B.C.) ; Pittacus (c. 651–c. 569 BC.); Solon (c. 638–c. 559 B.C.); Thales (c. 640–c. 546 B.C.).

Seven Sleepers of Ephesus, The.

Seven Christian youths, who are said to have concealed themselves in a cavern near Ephesus during the persecution under Decius (249–51), and to have fallen asleep there, not waking until two or three hundred years later, when Christianity had become the religion of the empire.

Seven Weeks' War.

The war of 1866 (sometimes called the Austro-Russian war), caused immediately by the Schleswig-Holstein question, and indirectly by the long rivalry between Austria and Prussia. The war was ended, after about seven weeks of fighting, by the preliminaries of Nikolsburg, July 26, confirmed by the peace of Prague (q.v.), etc.

Seven Wise Men of Greece, *v.* Seven Sages of Greece.

Seven Wonders of the Middle Ages, The.

These were:—

The Coliseum at Rome,
The Catacombs of Alexandria,
The Great Wall of China,
The Leaning Tower of Pisa,
The Porcelain Tower of Nanking,
The Mosque of St. Sophia at Constantinople,
The Ruins of Stonehenge.

Seven Wonders of the New World, The.

A collective name for the following natural objects in the United States of America, viz.: Niagara Falls, Yellowstone Park, Garden of the Gods, Mammoth Cave, Yosemite Valley, Giant Trees, Natural Bridge.

Seven Wonders of the World, The.

The seven most remarkable structures of ancient times. These were:—

1. The Egyptian Pyramids.
2. The Mausoleum erected by Artemisia at Halicarnassus.
3. The Temple of Artemis at Ephesus,
4. The Walls and Hanging Gardens at Babylon.
5. The Colossus at Rhodes.
6. The Statue of Zeus by Phidias, in the great Temple at Olympia, and
7. The Pharos or Lighthouse at Alexandria.

Seven Years' War.

One of the greatest wars of the eighteenth century, waged (1756–63) against Frederick the Great of Prussia by an alliance whose chief members were Austria, France and Russia. Frederick had the assistance of British subsidies and of the Hanoverian troops. Saxony and Sweden were against him. The war is sometimes known as the third Silesian war. Closely connected with the Seven Years' War was the struggle between the French and English, 1754–63, ending with the peace of Paris in 1763, and the triumph of England in America and India.

Severians.

An Eneratite sect of the second century. A Gnostic sect of the second century often identified with a Monophysite sect, followers of Severus, patriarch of Antioch 512–9. *v.* Niobites.

Shafiites.

The members of one of the four divisions or sects into which the orthodox Mohammedans, or Sunnites, are divided. So named from its founder, Shafi'i.

Shah Diamond, The.

A famous diamond, weighing 86 carats, presented to the Czar of Russia by Prince Chosroës, younger son of the Abbas Mirza.

Shaivas, *v.* Smartas.

Shakers.

Name of a sect—seceded from the Society of Friends (q.v.) or Quakers—whose official title is "The United Society of Believers in Christ's Second Appearing," founded by Ann Lee (1736–84), "Mother Ann," c. 1758. In 1774 she emigrated to America and founded (1776) the American society. They believe in spiritualism, practice celibacy and community of goods, are opposed to war, refrain from oaths, and denounce baptism and the Lord's Supper.

Shakspere-Bacon Controversy.

A discussion arising from an attempt (in 1857) on the part of Miss Delia Bacon (1811–59), to prove that Francis Bacon was the author of Shakspere's plays. Ignatius Donnelly, an American author (b. 1831), in 1887 published "The Great Cryptogram," in which he endeavoured to show that "Bacon's authorship is avowed under a cipher in the text of the plays in the folio of 1623." The theory has not, however, been favoured by Shaksperian scholars generally.

Shakspere of Divines, The.

A name given to Jeremy Taylor, an English bishop and celebrated theological writer (1613–67). Also the Spenser of English Prose Writers.

Shakspere of Germany, The.

A name sometimes given to August Frederick Ferdinand von Kotzebue, a German dramatist (1761–1819).

Shakspere of the Boulevard(s), The, *v.* Corneille of the Boulevard(s), The.

Shannon, The.

A British man-of-war which captured the American vessel of war, "Chesapeake" (q.v.), off Marblehead, Mass., June 1, 1813.

Sharp Knife.

A nickname given by the North-American Indians to Andrew Jackson, seventh President of the United States (1767–1845), alluding to his perspicacity and shrewdness.

Shays's Rebellion.

An insurrection in western Massachusetts against the State government, 1786–7, under the leadership of Daniel Shays and others, occasioned by the unsettled condition of affairs at the close of the Revolution, and the consequent popular discontent. The insurgents were finally dispersed February, 1787, at Petersham, where 150 of them were captured. Shays escaped.

Sheffield of Germany, The.

A surname given to Solingen, a town in the Rhine Province, Prussia, eighteen miles from Cologne, famous for its iron and steel manufactures (especially sword and foil blades).

Shepherd Kings, The.

A name given to a dynasty of kings, of a foreign race, who ruled Egypt for about 511 years, between the thirteenth and the eighteenth dynasty (c. 2000

B.C.). Also called **Hyksos.** They are believed to have sprung from a tribe of shepherds who invaded Lower Egypt.

Shepherd Lord, The.

A name given in legends to Henry de Clifford, fifteenth Baron Clifford (d. 1523).

Shepherd of the Ocean.

A name given to Sir Walter Raleigh (1552–1618) by Spenser.

Sheridan's Ride.

A famous incident of the Battle of Cedar Creek, Virginia, October 19, 1864. Sheridan's army was surprised before daybreak and defeated by the Confederates under General Early. Sheridan, who was at Winchester, twenty miles from the field, heard the sound of battle, and rode rapidly to the scene of action. As he galloped past the retreating soldiers he shouted, " Face the other way, boys ! We are going back ! " He re-formed his corps, and before the close of the day had gained a decisive victory. Cf. the poem by T. B. Read, " Sheridan's Ride " (1865).

Sherman Bill.

An Act of Congress approved July 14, 1890, supported by Senator Sherman and others, as a compromise measure. It directed the secretary of the treasury to purchase silver bullion to the amount of 4,500,000 oz. per month, issuing treasury notes in payment. The repeal of the Act was often urged, and in the summer of 1893, as the Act was believed to be the main cause of the business depression,

President Cleveland summoned Congress to meet in special session August 7. After a prolonged struggle the Vorhees Bill, which repealed the silver purchasing clause, but affirmed bi-metallism as a national policy, was passed October 30, and approved by the House and the President November 1.

She-Wolf of France, The.

A surname given to Isabella of France (1292–1358), wife of Edward II of England, and daughter of Philip the Fair, King of France.

Shiahs.

A division of the Mohammedans, which maintains that Ali, first cousin of Mohammed and husband of his daughter Fatima, was the first legitimate iman or successor of the prophet, and rejects the first three caliphs of the Sunnis (the other great division) as usurpers. They claim to be the orthodox Mohammedans, but are treated by the Sunnis (v. **Sunnites**) as heretics. The Shiahs comprise nearly the whole Persian nation, and are also found in Oude, a province of British India; but the Mohammedans of the other parts of India are for the most part Sunnis. Also called **Shiites.**

Shield of Rome, The, v. Cunctätor.

Shiites, v. Shiahs.

Shilling Shockers.

A jocular name for a class of novels, sold at a shilling, containing stories of a thrilling, sensational character. Cf **Penny Dreadfuls.**

Ship of the Desert, The.

A surname sometimes given to the camel, from its ability to go without water for a long time, a great advantage in crossing deserts. Cf. Lord Byron, " The Deformed Transformed," i, 1).

Short, The, *v.* Bref, Le.

Short-Lived Administration, The.

A name given to the administration under the premiership of William Pulteney in 1746, which lasted only two days.

Short Parliament.

The Parliament which sat from April 13 to May 5, 1640. It was followed in November by the Long Parliament (q.v.).

Siamese Twins, The.

Eng and Chang, twins born of a Chinese father and a Siamese mother (1811–74). They were joined to one another by a short tubular cartilage, in the centre of which was their common umbilicus. They married sisters in 1842. The one survived the other 2½ hours. Cf. **Biddenden Maids, The.**

Sicilian Theocritus, The.

A surname given to Giovanni Meli, a Sicilian poet (1740–1815).

Sicilian Vespers, *v.* Vêpres Siciliennes.

Sickly, The.

A surname of Henry III, King of Castille (1379–1406).

Sick Man, The, or Sick Man of the East.

A name given to the Turkish Empire, in allusion to its decaying condition. First used by the Czar Nicholas of Russia in a conversation with the British Ambassador, Seymour, January 11, 1854.

Silent, The.

A surname of William I, Prince of Orange and Count of Nassau (1533–84), the founder of the Republic of the United Provinces. Also called (by Motley) the **High-Born Demosthenes.**

Silent City, The.

A surname given to Venice, from the absence of the noise usually made by horses and vehicles.

Silent Sister, The.

A surname given to Trinity College, Dublin, in allusion to the little influence exerted by it in proportion to its resources.

Silesian Wars.

Three wars waged by Frederick the Great of Prussia against Austria for the possession of Silesia. In the first war (1740–2) Prussia was allied with Saxony, Bavaria and France, and Austria with Great Britain. In the war of 1744–5, Austria was aided by Saxony. The possession of Silesia by Prussia was confirmed by the peace of Dresden, December 25, 1745. The third of the Silesian wars is the Seven Years' War (q.v.).

Silk Wedding, *v.* Wedding Anniversaries.

Silly Billy.

A nickname of William IV, King of Great Britain (1765–1837). Also of William Frederick, Duke of Gloucester (1776–1834), nephew of George III of

England, in allusion to his feeble intellect.

Silly Duke, The.

A nickname given to John Churchill, Duke of Marlborough (1650–1722), in allusion to his habit of answering all questions of which he disapproved by remarking, " Oh, silly! silly! " *v.* also **Handsome Englishman, The.**

Silly Season, The.

A name often applied to that period of the year when Parliament is not sitting, and coinciding with the end of the London season, when everyone, who is anyone, is out of town, and there is a corresponding dearth of news—in other words, a dead or off season for the newspapers.

Silurist, The.

A surname given to Henry Vaughan, a Welsh poet and mystic (1621–93).

Silver-Fork School.

A name given to a group of novelists (Theodore Hook, Mrs. Trollope, Lady Blessington, etc.) who laid great stress on matters of etiquette.

Silver Grays.

The bolting Whigs, led by Francis Granger, who left the New York convention of 1848, is so called from the fact that several of them were grey-haired men.

Silver-tongued, The.

A surname given to Joshua Sylvester, the translator of Guillaume de Salluste Du Bartas's " Divine Weeks and Works " (" La première se-

maine," or " La Création "); to William Bates, an eminent Puritan divine (1625–99); to Anthony Hammond, miscellaneous writer (1668–1738). *v.* also **Irish Roscius, The.**

Silver Wedding, *v.* **Wedding Anniversaries.**

Simple, The (French, " le Simple " or " le Sot ").

A surname given to Charles III, king of France (879–929).

Singe de Racine, Le (French, " The Monkey," i.e. imitator, of Racine).

A surname given to Jean Galbert de Campistron, a French dramatic poet (1656–1723).

Single-Speech Hamilton.

A nickname given to William Gerard Hamilton, an English politician (1729–96), from his " maiden speech," which remained his most notable effort.

Single-Tax.

A name given to a theory of taxation promulgated by Henry George, an American writer and sociologist (1839–97) in 1887. The theory is that public revenue should be obtained by taxing land only, irrespective of improvements.

Sing Song, *v.* **Free-and-Easy.**

Singular Doctor, The, *v.* **Invincible Doctor, The.**

Sinner's Friend, The, *v.* **Apostle of Temperance, The.**

Sir Jack Brag.

A nickname given to John Burgoyne, an English lieutenant-general and dramatist (c. 1722–92). He figures in an old ballad with this title.

Sir John Barleycorn, *v.* **John Barleycorn.**

Sister of Shakspere, The.

A surname given to Joanna Baillie, a Scotch dramatist and poet (1762–1851).

Six Articles, Act of, *v.* **Act of Six Articles.**

Six Cities, The.

In German history, the cities of Bautzen, Zittau, Löbau, Kamenz, Görlitz and Lauban, which in 1346 formed a league against plundering knights, and received privileges. The last two were ceded to Prussia in 1815; the first four (under the name Four Cities), retain certain rights.

Six Months' War.

The Franco-German War, from July, 1870, to January, 1871.

Six Nations, The.

A confederation of Indian tribes of the Huron-Iroquois family. It was composed at first of the Mohawks, Senecas, Cayugas, Oneidas and Onondagas (the Five Nations), to which the Tuscaroras were afterwards added.

Sixteen-string Jack.

A popular nickname given to John Rann, a notorious English highwayman (hanged at Tyburn, November 30, 1744), from his wearing breeches with eight strings at each knee.

Skinners The, *v.* **Ecorcheurs.**

Also a body of marauders who pillaged Westchester County, New York, during Revolutionary times. *v.* **Cowboys.**

Slave States, The.

Those of the United States in which, in the period before the Civil War, slavery flourished. They were Virginia, North and South Carolina, Georgia, Florida, Alabama, Mississippi, Louisiana, Texas, Arkansas and Tennessee (all of which seceded), and Missouri, Kentucky, Maryland and Delaware.

Slayer of the Bulgarians, The.

A surname given to Basil II, a Byzantine Emperor (c. 958–1025). He began a war with Bulgaria in 987, resulting (1018) in its incorporation with the Byzantine empire.

Slough of Despond.

A bog described in the firs part of " The Pilgrim's Progress," by John Bunyan.

Sluggard, The, *v.* **Fainéant, Le.**

Smalkaldic Articles.

The articles of Protestant faith drawn up by Luther, and submitted to a meeting of electors, princes, and states at Smalkald (or Schmalkalden) in 1537, designed to show how far the Protestants were willing to go, in order to avoid a rupture with Rome.

Smalkaldic League.

A league entered into at Smalkald in 1531 by several Protestant princes and free cities, for the common defence of their faith and political independence against the Emperor Charles V.

Smalkaldic War.

The unsuccessful war waged (1546–7) by the Smalkaldic League against Charles V.

Smallback, *v.* **King of Terrors.**

Small-beer Poet, The.

A nickname given by Cobbett to William Thomas Fitzgerald, a British poet (c. 1759–1829), chiefly now known by a reference to him in Lord Byron's " English Bards and Scotch Reviewers."

Smartas or Smarta Brahmans.

One of the three principal classes into which the Hindus proper of the present day may be divided as to religion, the other two being the Shaivas and the Vaishnavas.

Smek.

A surname of Magnus II, king of Sweden (1316–74). He was deposed by the nobles (1363), and died at sea.

Smoky City, The.

A name frequently given to Pittsburg, Pennyslvania.

Smollett of the Stage, The, *v.*
Fielding of the Drama, The.

Smyrnean Poet, The.

A surname given to Mimnermus, a Greek elegiac poet of Colophon (fl. c. 630–600 B.C.)

Snow King, The.

An epithet given by the Austrians to Gustavus (II) Adolphus of Sweden (1594–1632). *v.* **Snow Queen, The.** Also given to Frederick V, Elector Palatine (1596–1632). *v.* **Winter King.** In 1619 he accepted the crown of Bohemia, but in 1620 lost both Bohemia and his hereditary dominions. *v.* **Snow Queen, The.**

Snow Queen, The.

A surname given to Elizabeth Stuart of England (1596–1662), wife of Frederick V, Elector Palatine (*v.* **Snow King, The**). Also given to Christina, Queen of Sweden (1626–89), daughter of Gustavus (II) Adolphus (*v.* **Snow King, The**).

Soapy Sam.

A nickname given to Samuel Wilberforce, bishop of Winchester (1805–73).

Society of Friends.

The proper designation of a Christian sect commonly called Quakers, which took its rise in England about the middle of the seventeenth century through the preaching of George Fox. They agree doctrinally with other Evangelical Christians, but lay greater stress on the doctrine of the personal presence and guidance of the Holy Spirit. They have no paid minister, and accept the ordinances of baptism and the Lord's Supper in a spiritual sense only, rejecting their outward observance as church rites. They condemn all oath-taking and all war. *v.* **Seekers.**

Society of the Cincinnati.

An association founded in 1783 by the regular officers of the Continental army at Baron Steuben's quarters on the Hudson River. The name was derived from that of the Roman dictator, L. Quinctius Cincinnatus, in allusion to the approaching change from military to civil pursuits. George Washington was its first president, and its chief immediate objects were to raise a fund for the relief of the widows and orphans of those who fell in the Revolutionary War, and to promote a closer political union between the States.

Socinians.

Those who hold the doctrines of the Italian theologians Lælius Socinus (1525–62) and Faustus Socinus (1539–1604) and their followers. The Socinians occupy theologically a middle position between the Arians, who maintain the divinity of Jesus Christ, but deny that He is coequal with the Father, and the Humanitarians, who deny His supernatural character altogether.

Soft Money.

A colloquial United States name for paper-money or greenbacks (*v.* **Greenback Party**), as distinguished from hard money or cash (gold and silver).

Soft-Money Party.

A nickname of the Independent National Party (*v.* **National Party**), organized in 1876 in the United States (*v.* **Soft-Money**).

Softshell Baptists.

A nickname given in the southern United States to Baptists holding Liberal views, as distinguished from the rigid or Hardshell Baptists.

Softshell Democrats.

A nickname given to the anti-slavery faction of the Democratic Party in New York State (c. 1848–54), their opponents being called Hardshells.

Soldiers' Friend, The.

A popular surname for Frederick Augustus, Duke of York (1763–1827), second son of George III, and commander of the British troops in the Low Countries at the time of the French Revolution. Through his exertions the system of favouritism was abolished, and political opinions became no longer a ground for preferment.

Solemn Doctor, The, *v.* Doctor Solemnis.

Solemn League and Covenant.

A treaty between Scotland and England, with the object of securing civil and religious liberty for both kingdoms. A modification of the **National Covenant** (q.v.) solemnly adopted by Parliament in 1643. Charles II accepted it August 16, 1650, but on his restoration in 1660 repudiated it.

Solid Doctor, The, *v.* Profound Doctor, The.

Solomon of England, *v.* British Solomon.

Solomon of France, The.

A surname given to Louis IX, King of France (1215–70). He was canonized in 1297. *v.* Sage, Le.

Solon of French Prose, The.

A surname given to Jean Louis Guez de Balzac, a noted French writer (1594–1654). Also called le grand épistolier de France.

Solon of Parnassus, The, *v.* Lawgiver of Parnassus, The.

Sonderbund (German " Separate League ").

A league of most of the Roman Catholic cantons of Switzerland, formed in 1843, and including eventually Lucerne, Uri,

Unterwalden, Schwyz, Zug, Fribourg and Valais. It was reactionary in its aims, and in favour of the Jesuits. The Swiss Confederation resolved (July 20, 1847) upon its abolition. War was begun in November, 1847, and the result was the overthrow of the Sonderbund and the adoption of a new constitution in 1848.

Son of the Last Man, The.

A surname given to Charles II of England (1630–85), in an offer, issued by Parliament, of reward for his apprehension. Cf. Last Man, The.

Sot, Le, v. Simple, The.

Sot, The.

A surname of Selim II, Sultan of Turkey (d. 1574), son of Solyman, the Magnificent, whom he succeeded in 1566.

South American Revolution.

The political movement and war by which the Spanish South American colonies became independent.

Southcottians.

A religious body of the nineteenth century, founded by Joanna Southcott (1750–1814) in England. This body expected that its founder would give birth to another Messiah. Also called New Israelites and Sabbatarians.

Southern Cross.

The name of a Norwegian whaler (previously named the Pollux), carrying the Newnes expedition to the Antarctic regions 1898–1900. Mr. Borchgrevink reached 78° 50′ S. lat. by sledge.

Southern Scott, The.

A surname given (by Lord Byron) to Ludovico Ariosto, a celebrated Italian poet (1474–1533), author of "Orlando Furioso." Also called the Tuscan Poet and the Homer of Ferrara.

South Sea Bubble.

A financial scheme which originated in England c. 1711, and collapsed in 1720. It was proposed by the Earl of Oxford to fund a floating debt of £10,000,000, the purchasers of which could become stockholders in a corporation, the South Sea Company, which was to have a monopoly of the trade with Spanish South America, and a part of the capital stock of which was to constitute the fund. The refusal of Spain to enter into commercial relations with England made the privileges of the company worthless ; but by means of a series of speculative operations and the infatuation of the people, its shares were inflated from £100 to £1,050. Its failure caused great distress throughout England.

Sovereign of the Seas.

The largest of the early English war-ships (100 guns), launched at Woolwich in 1637 (Charles I's reign). Length over all 232 feet, length of keel 128 feet, beam 48 feet. She had flush decks, a forecastle, half-deck, quarter-deck, and roundhouse. Supposed to have been burned in 1696.

Spanish Addison, The.

A surname given to Frey Benito, Feyjoo y Montenegro, a noted Spanish critic and scholar, a Benedictine monk (1676–1764).

Spanish-American War.

A war between Spain and the United States in 1898, waged by the latter for the liberation of Cuba. Treaty of peace signed at Paris, December 10, 1898. By the treaty Spain relinquished her sovereignty over Cuba, and ceded Porto Rico, Guahan in the Ladrones, and the Philippines to the United States.

Spanish Armada, The, *v.* Armada, The Invincible.

Spanish Brutus, The.

A surname given to Alphonso Perez de Guzman, a noted Spanish general (1258–1320).

Spanish Ennius, The.

A surname given to Juan de Mena, a Spanish poet (1411–56).

Spanish Fury, The.

A name given to the sack of Antwerp by Spanish troops in 1576. Cf. Furia Francesa.

Spanish Horace, The.

A surname given to both Bartolomeo Leonardo de Argensola (1562–1631) and his brother Lupercio Leonardo de Argensola (1559–1613), Spanish poets.

Spanish Jack.

A nickname given to a notorious felon, named Bli Gonzales (executed at Maidstone April 18, 1756), born at Alicante, Spain. In England he changed his name to John Symmonds.

Spanish Main, The.

A name applied, somewhat vaguely, to the northern coast of South America, from the mouth of the Orinoco westward. Sometimes it included the Isthmus of Panama and Central America, or all the continental lands bordering on the Caribbean Sea, as distinguished from the islands. The term was probably derived from the Spanish **Tierra Firme** or **Costa Firmi**, used in the sixteenth century for the continental coast from Paria to Costa Rica, and in a more restricted sense for the Isthmus. Many modern writers appear to suppose that the Spanish Main was the Caribbean Sea.

Spanish Mark, The.

A Frankish possession, conquered by Charles the Great, situated in the north-eastern extremity of Spain. It was ruled by counts of Barcelona, and became merged in Catalonia, and finally in Aragon.

Spanish Molière, The.

A surname given to Leandro Fernandez de Moratin, a Spanish dramatist and poet (1760–1828).

Spanish Petrarch, The, *v.* Prince of Spanish Poetry, The.

Spanish Tennyson.

A surname given to Gaspar Nuñez de Arce, a noted Spanish poet (b. 1834).

Spasmodic School, The.

A name given collectively to various nineteenth century writers, on account of their alleged unnatural style. Among them were Gerald Massey, Sydney Dobell, Bailey, Gilfillan, Alexander Smith and others.

Specie Circular, The.

An order by the secretary of the Treasury (United States), July 11, 1836, which directed that payment for public lands should be made to government agents in gold and silver only, except in certain cases in Virginia. It was designed to check speculative purchases of government lands.

Spectator, The.

An English periodical, published daily from March 1, 1711, to December 6, 1712. It comprised 555 numbers, of which 274 were by Addison, 236 by Steele, 1 by Pope, and 19 by Hughes. Eustace Budgell also contributed to it. It was revived in 1714.

Spectre of the Brocken.

An optical phenomenon seen on the Brocken (or Blocksberg), the chief summit of the Hartz Mountains, and the highest mountain in northern Germany, situated in the province of Saxony, Prussia. It is the traditional meeting-place of the witches on Walpurgis Night (q.v.).

Speedwell.

A ship of about 60 tons burthen, bought and fitted out in Holland, which sailed from Southampton with the " Mayflower " (q.v.) in 1615 for New England. She was sent back from Plymouth, England, owing to a series of mishaps, and those of the " pilgrims " who were disheartened turned back with her.

Spellbinders.

A nickname jokingly applied to the Republican political orators during the presidential campaign of 1888, from the speakers being said to have held their audiences " spellbound."

Spenser of English Prose-Writers, The, v. Shakspere of Divines, The.

Spheres of Influence.

The name given to large areas of land in Africa recognized as under the control of European powers. The phrase came into use c. 1885, and designates the region which may be occupied and developed by the power for which it is named. The European spheres of influence in Africa comprise a large part of the continent.

Spindle City, The, v. Manchester of America, The.

Spithead Mutiny.

A mutiny of the British sailors in the ships stationed at Spithead in 1797. It was settled amicably, and the sailors' grievances were remedied by Parliament.

Sport of Kings, The.

Horse-racing is sometimes so called.

Sporus, v. Lord Fanny.

Sprat Day.

A nickname for November 9, the day when sprats are first allowed to be sold.

Springer, Ludwig der, v. Ludwig der Springer.

Spring Garden.

A place of refreshment in St. James's Park, London, much frequented in the seventeenth century by persons of quality.

Squab Poet, The.

A nickname given to John

Dryden (1631–1700) by his antagonist Rochester, and afterwards adopted by lampooners of every degree.

Squatter Sovereignty.

A nickname given in derision by John Caldwell Calhoun (1782–1850) to the doctrine of popular sovereignty in the United States.

Stagirite, The, v. Pope of Philosophy.

St. Agnes' Eve.

The night of January 20. Superstitious people believe that it is possible on that date for a girl to see the form of her future husband. The name of a poem by Tennyson. Keats has also written one, " The Eve of Saint Agnes."

Stalwarts.

A nickname given to those Republicans—led by Senators Conkling, Cameron and Logan—who opposed President Hayes's policy of conciliation towards the south; also (later) to the wing of the party favouring General Grant's nomination for a third term of the Presidency, v. Half-Breeds.

Stammerer, The, v. Bègue, Le.

Also a surname of Michael II (Balbus), Byzantine emperor from 820–9.

Stamp Act.

An Act imposing or regulating the imposition of stamp duties. In American colonial history, an Act, also known as Grenville's Stamp Act, providing for the raising of revenue in the American colonies by the sale of stamps and stamped paper for commercial transactions, real estate transfers, lawsuits, marriage licences, inheritances, etc. It also provided that the royal forces in America should be billeted on the people. The Act was to become effective on November 1, 1765, but it aroused intense opposition led by the assemblies of Virginia, Massachusetts, and other colonies. The Stamp Act was repealed in March, 1766, but the agitation was one of the leading causes of the Revolution in America.

Star and Garter.

A famous tavern, formerly standing in Pall Mall, London.

Star Chamber.

(So called, it is said, because the roof was originally ornamented with stars.) A court of civil and criminal jurisdiction at Westminster. In 1640 the court of Star Chamber was abolished by an Act of 16 Charles I, reciting that " the reasons and motives inducing the erection and continuance of that court [of Star Chamber] do now cease." Cf. W. H. Ainsworth's novel of that name.

Star of South Africa Diamond, The, v. Dudley Diamond, The.

Star of the North, The, v. Lion of the North, The.

Star of the South Diamond, The.

A famous diamond found by a poor negress in Brazil in 1853. Original weight, 254½ carats; reduced, on being cut, to 125 carats.

Star of the West, The.

A United States Government vessel fired upon (January 9,

1861) by the Confederates in Charleston Harbour while attempting to convey men and supplies to Fort Sumter. Being a merchant vessel and unable to return the fire, it was compelled to put to sea without effecting its object.

Stars and Bars.

A nickname given to the flag of the late Southern Confederacy. It consisted of a field of three bars (red, white and red), and a blue union with as many white stars as States. Cf. **Stars and Stripes.**

Stars and Stripes, The, v. Old Glory. Cf. Stars and Bars.

Star-Spangled Banner, The.

An American national song, composed by Francis Scott Key, September, 1814, at the time of the bombardment of Fort McHenry (near Baltimore) by the British. It was set to the music of " Anacreon in Heaven."

Starvation Dundas.

A nickname given to Lord Melville (Henry Dundas), because in 1775, in a speech on American affairs, he invented (or brought into notice) the word " starvation."

States, The.

The name by which the United States of America are familiarly known.

States-General, v. États-Généraux.

Statute of Drogheda.

A statute passed by the Parliament of Drogheda, September 13, 1494, commonly called Poynings's Act (or Law), from the name of its author, Sir Edward Poynings, Lord Deputy of Ireland. It enacted that no Irish Parliament should be held without the consent of the King of England, and that no Bill could be brought forward in an Irish Parliament without his approval. Repealed in 1782.

St. Bartholomew's Day, v. Massacre of St. Bartholomew.

St. Benedict of Aviz, v. Order of St. Benedict of Aviz.

St. Crispin (Latin, Crispinus, Crispianus, "having Curly Hair ").

The patron saint of shoemakers. An early Christian martyr who, with his brother Crispinianus, fled to Soissons, and took up the trade of a shoemaker. He was put to death c. 287 by being thrown into a cauldron of molten lead. His fête day is October 25.

St. Cyprian (Latin, " Cyprianus, of Cyprus, Thasius Cæcilius Cyprianus ").

An ecclesiastic and martyr of the African Church, elected bishop of Carthage in 248. His festival was originally kept on Holy Cross Day, and was transferred to September 16. The present English calendar assigns to him September 26, which was at one time also given to another St. Cyprian, of Antioch, the magician.

St. Denis (or Denys).

The patron saint of France and apostle to the Gauls, beheaded according to tradition at Paris, 272.

St. Distaff's Day.

The 7th January is so called, because on that day the women, who have kept the Christmas festival till Twelfth Day (q.v.), return to their distaffs, or ordinary work. Sometimes named Rock Day, a distaff being also called a rock.

Steenie.

A nickname given by James I, king of England, to George Villiers, Duke of Buckingham (1592–1628), on account of a fancied resemblance to St. Stephen.

Stella.

A steamship belonging to the L. & S. W. Railway Co., wrecked in a fog on the Casquet Rocks, near Alderney, with 200 passengers and crew, March 30, 1899. Seventy-five persons were drowned.

Stella Polare (Italian, " Polar Star ").

The name of a ship (previously called " Jason," q.v.) in which H.R.H. the Duke of Abruzzi made his expedition to the Arctic regions (1899–1900), and from which the lat. of 84° 33′ N. was reached by sledge. This is about twenty miles farther north than Nansen's farthest.

St. Elmo's Fire.

A popular name for a luminous appearance, sometimes seen at the masthead and yardarms of vessels on stormy nights, or on land at the tops of church-spires and trees, etc. The phenomenon is due to the presence of electricity, and is named after St. Elmo, the patron saint of sailors.

Stern, The (Norwegian, " Hardrada ").

Surname of Harold III, King of Norway from 1046–66.

Steward, The.

A surname given to Robert II, King of Scotland (c. 1316–90). He was regent under David II, his uncle, whom he succeeded in 1370 or 1371.

Stewart Diamond, The.

A large diamond, found in 1872, on the claim of a Mr. Spalding, in South Africa. It weighed 288⅜ carats in the rough, and is of a light yellow tinge.

St. Felicitas.

An African martyr, killed in 203. *Milman*, " Hist. of Christianity," ii, 168.

St. Florian.

A German martyr (c. 190–230), who became, c. 1183, the patron saint of Poland. His fête is celebrated August 4.

St. Frideswide, Fritheswith, or Fredeswitha.

An English saint, who died possibly in 735. According to the legend, she was a royal princess, and fled from the importunities of her lover to Oxford, where she founded the monastery of St. Frideswide. Her fête is celebrated on October 19.

St. George.

The patron saint of England. A Christian martyr, a native of Cappadocia and military tribune under Diocletian, put to death at Nicomedia in 303.

St. Gertrude.

An abbess of Nivelles, in Brabant, daughter of Pippin of Landen, major-domo to Clotaire II and Itta. On the death of Pippin, Itta built a cloister at Nivelles, which included both a monastery and a nunnery, and Gertrude became abbess of the latter. She is commemorated throughout Brabant on March 17.

St. Gothard Tunnel.

The tunnel through the St. Gothard group of mountains, in the St. Gothard railway from Lucerne to Milan. Commenced in 1872, and opened in 1882. The longest tunnel in the world, extending to 9¼ miles. Height of central point, 3,786 feet.

St. Grouse's Day.

August 12 is jocularly so called, it being the first day of the shooting season.

St. Hilary's Day.

A feast commemorated on January 13 by the Church of England, and on January 14 by the Church of Rome. The Hilary Term at Oxford begins on January 14, and ends on the Saturday next before Palm Sunday. In law, the Hilary Term is one of the four terms of the Courts of Law in England. It begins January 11, and ends January 31. The Hilary sittings now begin January 11, and end the Wednesday before Easter. Formerly the sittings of the Courts of Chancery and Common Law were regulated by the terms (*Rapalie and Lawrence*, "Law Dict.").

Stinkomalee.

A slang nickname (originated by Theodore Hook) for the London University, in allusion to some question about Trincomalee (Ceylon) at the time, and to the University being in bad odour with members of other universities, because it admitted students from all denominations.

St. James's Coffee-House, The.

A famous coffee-house in St. James's Street, London, frequented by members of the Whig party, from the reign of Queen Anne down to that of George III. Demolished in 1806. It was a favourite resort of Dr. Samuel Johnson, Edmund Burke, Oliver Goldsmith, Dean Swift, David Garrick, and others.

St. Leger.

An English horse-race, second in importance only to the Derby. Established in 1776, and named after Colonel Anthony St. Leger, in 1778. It is a race for three-year-olds, and is run at Doncaster about the second week of September.

St. Luke's Summer, *v.* St. Martin's Summer.

St. Martin's Summer.

A period of fine weather, occurring between October 18 (St. Luke's Day), and November 11 (St. Martin's Day). Also called **St. Luke's Summer**. A similar period of mild, balmy weather in November is called in North America **Indian Summer**.

Stonewall Jackson.

A nickname given to Thomas Jonathan Jackson, a noted Confederate general (1824-63)

In the American Civil War. In rallying his troops, General Bernard E. Bee cried, " See, there is Jackson standing like a stone wall ! Rally on the Virginians ! " (whence " Stonewall Jackson "). Also called **Old Jack.**

Stormy Cape, *v.* **Cape of Storms.**

Stout Harry, *v.* **Bluff King Hal.**

St. Partridge's Day.

September 1 is popularly so called, it beginning the partridge-shooting season.

St. Perpetua.

An African female martyr, killed at Carthage in 203 (*Milman,* " Hist. of Christianity," ii, 168).

Strabo of Germany, The.

A surname given to Sebastian Münster, a German geographer, orientalist and mathematician (1489–1552).

Straight-out Democrats.

A nickname given to the Democrats who disapproved of the nomination by their party, in 1872, of Horace Greeley for United States President, and chose for their candidate Charles O'Conor, an American lawyer.

Street, The.

A popular name for the part of New York in and near Wall Street, famous as a financial centre. The name by which the market often continued in the street after the Stock Exchange is closed is familiarly known.

Street Prices.

The quotations ruling in the Street (q.v.) market, as distinguished from those in the House (q.v.).

Strong, The.

A surname given to Augustus II, as Saxon Elector, Frederick Augustus I (1670–1733). Elected king of Poland 1697. Also to Sancho II, king of Castile from 1065–72.

Strongbow.

A nickname given to Richard de Clare, second Earl of Pembroke and Strigul (d. 1176), in allusion to his strength and skill with the bow.

St. Swithin's Day.

July 15. Tradition has it that if it rains on St. Swithin's (or Swithun's) Day it will rain for forty days thereafter.

Stuffed Prophet, The.

A nickname given to Grover Cleveland (b. 1837), President (1885–9 and 1893-7) of the United States, by the " New York Sun," during the presidential campaign of 1892.

Stundists.

A Russian sect originated c. 1860. Its tenets and practices are in the main Evangelical and Protestant in character. Since 1870 the Stundists have been objects of persecution by the government. The sect has rapidly increased in numbers. (The name is derived from the Greek " stunde," hour, lesson, from their meetings for Bible-reading.)

Sturm und Drang (German, " Storm and Stress ").

A period in German literature (c. 1770–80), noted for the impetuosity of thought and style of the younger writers. So named from Klinger's drama, "Sturm und Drang." Among the representatives of this movement were Herder, Goethe (in "Werther"), Basedow, Klinger Lenz, etc.

Sublime Porte.

The building in which are the offices of the grand vizier and other high functionaries of the Ottoman empire; hence, the Turkish government itself. Also called the **Porte**.

Submerged Tenth, The.

A name sometimes given to those in the lowest depths of poverty.

Subtle Doctor, The, v. Doctor Subtilis.

Suburban, The.

The principal American horse-race—a handicap sweepstakes run annually at the June meeting of the Coney Island Jockey Club, at Sheepshead Bay, Long Island. Distance, 1¼ miles.

Succession Act, v. Act of Settlement.

Sucker State.

A nickname sometimes applied to the State of Illinois, especially by inhabitants of the other Western States.

Suffrage Party, The, v. Dorr's Rebellion.

Sunbeam.

Yacht in which Lady Anne Brassey (d. 1887 at sea) accompanied her husband, Thomas (afterwards Lord) Brassey, in various tours. Cf. her book, "A Voyage in the Sunbeam" (1878).

Sunday Gentleman, The.

A nickname given to Daniel Defoe (1661–1731), at Bristol (c. 1692), where he was hiding from the bailiffs during the week, but emerged in gorgeous raiment on Sunday.

Sunnites.

A Mohammedan sect, comprising the greater part of the Moslem world, usually claiming to be the traditional or orthodox sect. They recognize the first three caliphs as legitimate successors of Mohammed, and accept six books of the "Sunna," or rule, which purport to contain the verbal utterances of Mohammed, in contradistinction to the Koran, the written revelation. The Mohammedans of Turkey, Arabia, North Africa and India are mostly Sunnites, those of Persia and many in India being Shiites (q.v.).

Sun of Austerlitz (or "Soleil d'Austerlitz").

The bright sunlight which dispersed the clouds and mist on the morning of the Battle of Austerlitz (December 2, 1805). Alluded to by Napoleon on arriving at the battlefield of Moscow, September 7, 1812.

Sunset Cox.

A nickname given to Samuel Sullivan Cox, an American politician and diplomatist (1824–89), so called from an extremely rhetorical description of a sunset which he printed (May 19, 1853) in the "Statesman" (Columbus, Ohio), of which he was editor.

Superb, The.

A surname given to General

Winfield Scott Hancock (1824–86), in allusion to his brilliant repulse of General James Longstreet's brigade at Gettysburg, July, 1863.

Superba, La (Italian, " The Superb ").

A name given to Genoa, on account of its situation.

Supra Grammaticam (Latin, " Above Grammar ").

A surname applied by Carlyle to Sigismund, Emperor of the Holy Roman Empire (1361–1437), in allusion to a remark of his at the Council of Constance (1414).

Supplicants, The.

In Scottish history, those persons who (c. 1637–8) protested against Laud's policy in Scotland. Known later as Covenanters.

Surprise Plot, *v.* **Bye,** or **Surprise, Plot.**

Surtees Society, The.

A society (named after Robert Surtees, an English historian b. 1779, d. 1834) founded in 1834 for the publication of MSS. relating to the history of the north of England.

Swabian Emperors.

The German-Roman emperors who reigned from 1138 to 1254 (the Hohenstaufen line). So called because the founder was Duke of Swabia.

Swamp, The.

A low-lying region in the lower part of New York city, east of the Post Office, known as a centre of the hide and leather trade.

Swamp Angel, The.

A name given by the Federal soldiers to an 8-inch Parrott gun, which was mounted on a battery built on piles driven into a swamp outside of Charleston, and used during the siege of that city. It burst August 22, 1863.

Swan, The.

A playhouse opened at Bankside, Southwark, London, c. 1581.

Swan of Avon, Sweet.

A surname given to William Shakspere, the greatest of dramatists (1564–1616), by Ben Jonson. Also called the **Bard of Avon,** the **Bard of all Time,** the **Horace of our Dramatic Poets.**

Swan of Cambrai.

A surname of François de Salignac de La Mothe-Fénelon, a celebrated French prelate, orator and author (1651–1715). He was appointed Archbishop of Cambrai in 1695.

Swan of Lichfield, The.

A surname given to Miss Anna Seward, an English poet (1747–1809), the friend of Dr. Johnson.

Swan of Mantua, The, *v.* **Mantuan Swan.**

Swan of Padua.

A surname given to Count Francesco Algarotti, a noted Italian *littérateur* and art connoisseur (1712–64).

Swan of Pesaro, The.

A surname given to Gioachino Antonio Rossini, a celebrated Italian operatic composer (1792–1868), born at Pesaro, Italy.

Swan of the Meander, The, v. Father of Epic Poetry, The.

Swan of the Thames, The.

A surname given to John Taylor, an English poet (1580–1654). Also called the Water-Poet.

Swedenborgians.

The believers in the theology and religious doctrines of Emanuel Swedenborg, a celebrated Swedish philosopher and theosophist, founder of the New Church (1688–1772), first organized in London in 1778 under the name of "the Society of the New Church signified by the New Jerusalem."

Swedish Maccabæus, The, v. Lion of the North, The.

Swedish Nightingale, The.

A surname given to Jenny Lind (Madame Goldschmidt), a famous Swedish singer (1820–87).

Sweet Singer of the Temple.

A surname given to George Herbert, an English poet (1593–1633). After his death his religious poems were published in a volume called "The Temple of Sacred Poems and Private Ejaculations" (1633).

Sweet Swan of Avon, v. Swan of Avon, Sweet.

Swiss Guards, The.

A corps of Swiss mercenary troops in the French service, formed in 1616 and finally disbanded in 1830. They are celebrated for their valour in

the defence of the Tuileries, August 10, 1792, commemorated in the "Lion of Lucerne" (q.v.), at Lucerne.

Sword of God, The.

A name given to Khalid (or Kaled), a Saracen general (d. 642).

Sword of Rome, The.

A name sometimes given to Marcellus (Marcus Claudius), a celebrated Roman general and statesman (before 268–208 B.C.). Cf. Shield of Rome, The.

Synod of Dort.

An assembly of the Reformed Church of the Netherlands, with delegates from England and other countries, convened by the States-General for the purpose of deciding the Arminian controversy, and held at Dort (Dordrecht) 1618–9. It condemned the doctrines of the Arminians (q.v.) or Remonstrants.

Tabard, The.

An ancient London hostelry, made famous by Chaucer as the house at which his pilgrims assembled before starting for Canterbury; situated in the High Street of Southwark, near London Bridge. Demolished in 1866.

Table Diamond, The Great, v. Great Table Diamond, The.

Tables, The.

In Scottish history, an organization, consisting of members of the privy council and others, which took the lead in opposition to the introduction of episcopacy into Scotland, c. 1638–9. So called from the members sitting separately or conjointly at the tables in the Parliament House.

Taborites.

The members of the more extreme party of the Hussites. They were fierce and successful warriors under their successive leaders, Ziska and Procopius, causing widespread devastation, until their final defeat in 1434. (From a hill in Bohemia, named by them Mount Tabor.)

Taciturn, The, v. Hellmuth the Taciturn.

Taffy.

A popular nickname for a Welshman. A corruption of **Davy**, which is a shortening of **David**, the patron-saint of Wales.

Tall, The.

A surname given to Albert, Duke of Brunswick Lüneburg (1236–79); to Philip V, King of France (1239 ?–1322).

Tammany Hall.

A New York political organization, having its headquarters in Tammany Hall, the property of the " Tammany Society or Columbian Order." The latter was founded in New York city on May 12, 1789, with benevolent and fraternal purposes. In 1893, Tammany Hall, controlled virtually by one man, was in possession of every important office and avenue of public employment pertaining to the municipal administration, but was overthrown in 1894.

Tapissier de Notre-Dame, Le.

A surname given by the Prince de Conti to Francois Henri de Montmorency-Boute-

ville, Duc de Luxembourg (1628-95), a French marshal, in allusion to the number of flags sent to Paris after his numerous victories. At that time the custom was to hang on the walls of the cathedral flags taken from the enemy.

Tarasque.

A legendary monster, that ravaged the neighbourhood of Tarascon, France. A figure of him is carried in procession at a festival held annually at Beaucaire and at Tarascon, to celebrate his destruction.

Tariff of Abominations.

In United States history, a name given by its opponents to the high Tariff Act of 1828.

Tartuffe of the Revolution, The.

A surname given (by Carlyle) to Jean Nicolas, a French politician (1740–1823).

Tatler, The.

A periodical founded by Steele in 1709, and discontinued in 1711. Addison wrote forty-one papers, Addison and Steele together thirty-four. Steele wrote a much larger number alone.

Tattenham Corner, v. Derby, The.

Tavern of Europe, The (French, " Le Cabaret de l'Europe").

Paris was so called by Prince Bismarck.

Teacher of Germany, The.

A surname given to Philipp Melanchthon (or Melanthon), a German reformer (1497–1560), and the collaborator of Luther.

Teague.

A nickname for an Irishman

(from the former prevalence of Teague as an Irish name). It appears in the famous ballad, "Lillibullero" (q.v.).

Tear 'em.

A nickname given in Parliament to John Arthur Roebuck (1801–79).

Tearless Battle (Victory), The.

The name given to an engagement between the Lacedæmonians and the Arcadians (367 B.C.), in which the latter were defeated with great slaughter while the former did not lose a man.

Tea Water Spring.

A famous spring in New York, which issued from the ground in a hollow near what is now the junction of Chatham and Roosevelt streets, then out of the town. The water was the best on the island of Manhattan about the beginning of the eighteenth century, and was highly prized by housewives for making tea. Before the Revolution the old spring was a popular resort, and the wealth and fashion of the city gathered there on summer evenings to sip the water, fortified by other beverages.

Tecumseh.

An iron-clad vessel, a single-turreted monitor, of the United States navy. It was one of Admiral Farragut's fleet in the attack on Mobile, Alabama, commanded by Captain Craven, and was sunk by a torpedo in Mobile Bay, August 5, 1864.

Tegethoff.

An Austrian ship, commanded by Julius von Payer (b. 1842), who discovered Franz Josef Land during an Arctic voyage of exploration, 1872–4.

Teian Muse, The.

A surname given (by Lord Byron) to Anacreon, a famous Greek lyric poet (c. 563–478 B.C.), born in Teos.

Téméraire.

A British armoured warship, launched in 1876. Length 285 feet, breadth 62 feet, draught 27 feet, displacement 8,540 tons. *v.* also **Fighting Téméraire, The.**

Téméraire, Le (French, "The Bold").

A surname given to Charles, Duke of Burgundy (1433–77).

Temperance Sunday.

A Sunday (generally the last in November) annually set aside by Nonconformist churches for sermons directed against the evils of excessive drinking.

Tempest, The, *v.* **Tempête, La.**

Tempête, La (French, "The Tempest").

A surname given to Andoche Junot, a French general under Napoleon (1771–1813), from his impetuosity and daring.

Templars.

Also called Knights Templars, or Knights of the Temple, from the early headquarters of the order in the Crusaders' palace at Jerusalem. The order was founded c. 1118 at Jerusalem, and confirmed by the Pope in 1128. Its special aim was to protect pilgrims on their way to the holy shrines, and the distinguishing garb of the knights was a white mantle with a red cross. The Templars were accused of heresy, immorality, and other offences by Philip IV of France in 1307, and the order was suppressed in 1312 by the Council of Vienna.

Temple, Le.

A fortified lodge of the Knights Templars, established in Paris by the Council of Troyes in 1128, standing where the Marché du Temple now stands. After the abolition of the order in 1312, the old building was used for various purposes. The chapel (similar in general plan to that in London) stood until 1650, and the great square tower, made memorable as the prison of Louis XVI in 1792–3, was destroyed in 1810.

Temple, The.

A lodge in London of the religious and military establishment of the Middle Ages, known as the Knights Templars (*v.* Templars). The Temple Church, London, is the only part of it now existing. The first settlement of the Knights Templars of the Holy Sepulchre in London was in Holborn, where in 1118 they built a house which must have stood near the north-east corner of Chancery Lane. They removed to the New Temple in the Strand in 1184. When the order was suppressed in the reign of Edward II, their house was given by the king to the Earl of Pembroke; it went next to the Earl of Lancaster, and at his death reverted to the Crown. In 1338 it went to the Knights Hospitallers of St. John of Jerusalem (*v.* Order of the Hospitallers, etc.), at Clerkenwell, who leased part of it in 1346 to students of the common law, and on the site of the London Temple the two Inns of Court, called the Middle Temple and Inner Temple, now stand. The Inner Temple is so called because it is within the precincts of the city, the Middle Temple because it was between the Inner and Outer Temple. The Outer Temple remained in the possession of the Bishop of Exeter, when the remainder was leased, and was afterwards converted into the Exeter Buildings.

Temple Bar.

A famous gateway before the Temple in London, which formerly divided Fleet Street from the Strand. According to ancient custom, when the sovereign visited the city he asked permission of the Lord Mayor to pass it. In its last form it was a rather ugly archway, built by Wren in 1670. In 1878 it was removed and re-erected at Waltham Cross, Herts. The spot is now marked by a monument called the Temple Bar Memorial, a tall pedestal surmounted by a griffin (sometimes called "The Griffin" in consequence).

Teniers of Comedy, The.

A surname given to Florent Carton Dancourt, a French playwright and comedian (1661–1725). He excelled in putting village scenes on the stage.

Tenth Muse, The.

A surname given to Mme. Antoinette du Ligier de la Garde Deshoulières, a celebrated French poet (c. 1635–94). Also called the **French Calliope** and **Amaryllis**. *v.* French Sappho, The.

Terence of England, The, *v.* Man without a Skin, The.

Terreur Blanche, La.

A name given to the bloody royalist reaction of 1815. A-mong the victims were Brune at Avignon, Ramel at Toulouse, Protestants at Nîmes, Mamelukes at Marseilles, etc. Cf. Ernest Daudet," La Terreur Blanche," 1878.

Terrible, The.

A surname of Ivan IV, Czar of Russia (1530–84). Assumed the title of Czar of Russia in 1547.

Terror.

An arctic exploring vessel which sailed from England with the " Erebus," under Sir John Franklin, in 1845. A document was discovered on the shore of King William's Land by Captain McClintock, stating that both ships were abandoned about a year after the death of Sir John Franklin in 1847, and that the survivors had started for the Great Fish River. They all perished on their journey southward, and no traces of the vessels appear to have been found. The " Erebus " and " Terror " had previously been the vessels of the Antarctic expedition, under command of Sir James Clark Ross.

Terror, The, *v.* **Reign of Terror, The.**

Terror of France, The, *v.* **Achilles of England, The.**

Terror of the World, The.

A surname given to Attila. *v.* **Scourge of God, The.**

Terry Alts.

The name given to a lawless body in Clare, Ireland, which sprang up after the Union, and committed various outrages. Similar societies were " The Thrashers," in Connaught, and " The Carders " (so called from their method of flaying their victims with a wool-card).

Tertullianists.

A branch of the African Montanists of the third and fourth centuries, who held the doctrines of Montanism as modified by Tertullian.

Test Acts, The.

The name given to several Acts of Parliament, but more especially to that of 1672, enforcing upon all persons filling any office, civil or military, the obligation of taking the oaths of supremacy and allegiance, etc. Repealed in 1829 (10 Geo. IV, c. 7).

Teutonic Order.

A military order founded at Acre, in Palestine, in 1190, and confirmed by the emperor and the Pope. Its chief objects were at first the care of the sick and wounded pilgrims and the defence of the Holy Land. The ancient inhabitants of the duchy of Prussia were conquered by the Teutonic Knights in the thirteenth century.

Thanksgiving Day.

The last Thursday in November, a day of national rejoicing in the United States. First observed as a harvest festival by the Pilgrim Fathers (q.v.) at Plymouth, Massachusetts, in September 1621. The festival has been observed annually in New York since 1817.

Thaumaturgus of the West, The.

A name given to St. Bernard (1091–1153).

Theatins, or Theatines.

A monastic order of regular clerks, founded at Rome in 1524, principally by the Archbishop of Chieti, with the object of combating the Reformation. There were also Theatin nuns. The order flourished to some extent in Spain, Bavaria and Poland, but its influence is now confined chiefly to Italy.

Théâtre de Monsieur.

A theatre existing in the Foire St.-Germain, Paris, in the latter part of the eighteenth century. It was founded by a coiffeur of Marie Antoinette, named Léonard Autre, and was named after " Monsieur," the king's brother, who gave it his support. Italian opera and French comedy were played there, and it had a brilliant existence from 1789–91, when a new house was built for it in the Rue Feydeau, named the Théâtre Feydeau.

Théâtre Italien.

The name given to the old Italian opera house, in the Rue Le Peletier, Paris. The new opera house was opened in 1875.

Theban Eagle (Bard or Lyre).

A surname given to Pindar, the greatest of the Greek lyric poets (c. 522–443 B.C.).

Thelusson's Act.

The name given to an Act of Parliament, passed in 1800 (39 & 40 Geo. III, c. 98), rendering it illegal to bequeath property to accumulate for more than twenty-one years. So-called from Peter Thelusson, a London merchant (d. 1798), who by his will left £800,000 to accumulate until his grandson's grandson reached the age of twenty-one.

Theologian, The (Latin, " Theologus ").

A surname of St. Gregory of Nazianzus (or St. Gregory Nazianzen), one of the fathers of the Eastern Church (c. 325–90). Made bishop of Constantinople in 380.

Theophrastus of France, The.

A surname given to Jean de La Bruyère, a celebrated French moralist (1645–96).

Thespian Maids, The.

The Muses.

Third Founder of Rome, The.

A surname given to Caius Marius, a celebrated Roman general (c. 155–86 B.C.). He was driven from Rome (88 B.C.), but returned, and with Cinna captured Rome in 87 B.C.

Thirteen Communes (Italian, " Tredici Comuni ").

A locality in the province of Verona, Italy, near Badia. It has long been noted for the preservation of a Germanic dialect (Cimbro), now nearly supplanted by Italian. Chief town, Giazza. Cf. **Seven Communes.**

Thirteenth Apostle, The.

A surname given to St. John Chrysostom, a celebrated father of the Greek Church and patriarch of Constantinople (c. 347–407).

Thirty-nine Articles, The.

The name by which the **Articles of the Church of England** (see the Book of Common Prayer) are usually known. Originally, in 1553, the number was forty-two: seven were omitted in 1562, and four (V, XII, XXIX and XXX) were added.

Thirty Tyrants, The.

An aristocratic body which usurped the government of Athens, 404–403 B.C. The most notable was Critias. They were expelled by the democratic party, under the lead of Thrasybulus. Also a popular name given collectively to the body of pretenders to the Roman Empire, under the reigns of Valerian, Gallienus, etc. Among them were Tetricus and Odenathus. *v.* also the **Mother of the Camps.**

Thirty Years' War, The.

A religious and political war in Central Europe, which involved Germany and various countries. It was caused by the friction between the Protestants and Catholics in the Empire; and the immediate occasion was the infringement by the Court of Austria of the rights of the Bohemian Protestants, who in May, 1618, rose in revolt under the leadership of Count Thurn. In 1648 the war was terminated by the peace of Westphalia (q.v.). In general the Protestants were strong in northern Germany, and the Catholics in southern Germany.

Thistle.

A steel yacht (cutter), designed by George L. Watson, and launched at Glasgow April 21, 1887. Length over all, 108·05 feet; beam, 20·03 feet; displacement, about 138 tons. Designed expressly to contest the America Cup, but lost the cup races to Volunteer (q.v.). She was afterwards sold to the Emperor of Germany, and rechristened "Meteor."

Thistlewood Conspiracy, *v.* Cato Street Conspiracy.

Thomas the Rhymer.

A surname given to Thomas Learmont of Ercildoune, a Scottish poet (fl. c. 1225–1300).

Thomists.

The followers of St. Thomas Aquinas (or Thomas of Aquino), a famous Italian theologian and scholastic philosopher (c. 1225 or 7–1274).

Thorough Doctor, The, *v.* Doctor Fundatus.

Thousand Islands, The.

A collection of islands in the expansion of the St. Lawrence from the north-eastern end of Lake Ontario for about forty miles. Their number is estimated at from 1,500 to 1,800.

Thracian, The, *v.* Great, The (Leo I).

Thrashers, The, *v.* Terry Alts.

Three Bishoprics, The.

In French and German history, the three bishoprics of Metz, Toul and Verdun. They were taken by France in 1552.

Three Chapters, The.

An edict issued by Justinian, c. 545, condemning the writings of Theodore of Mopsuestia, those of Theodoret in defence of Nestorius and against Cyril, and the letter of Ibas to Maris. Also applied to the writings so condemned. The edict was intended to reconcile the Monophysites to the Church by seeming to imply a partial disapproval of the Council of Chalcedon, which had admitted Theodoret and Ibas, after giving explanations, to communion.

Three Estates of the Realm, The.

A name generally applied to King, Lords and Commons, but more properly meaning the Lords, the Clergy and the Commons, these three orders—with the King or Queen—constituting the Parliament of the United Kingdom. Cf. Tiers-État.

Three-fingered Jack.

A popular nickname for a notorious negro robber, the terror of Jamaica in 1780. He was hunted down and killed in 1781.

Three Kings of Cologne, The.

Name applied in medieval legend to the three magi who followed the Star of Bethlehem from the East, to lay their gifts before the Infant Jesus. Their names were Gaspar, Melchior and Balthazar. It is claimed that their bones are deposited in Cologne Cathedral. " The three days after New Year's Day bear their names in the calendar, and their memory is preserved in the feast of the three Holy Kings—the Epiphany." *Chambers*.

Three R's, The.

A familiar way of referring to reading, (w)riting and (a)rithmetic.

D.N.

Three Sisters, The.

The Fates or Parcæ.

Three Wise Men, *v.* Three Kings of Cologne, The.

Thule, *v.* Ultima Thule.

Thunderbolt, The.

A surname (Ilderim) given to Bajazet I (Bayazid or Bajasid), Sultan of the Turks (1347–1403), on account of his rapid movements. Defeated by Timur, 1402.

Thunderbolt, The.

A surname given (by Mozart) to Georg Friedrich Händel, a celebrated German composer (1685–1759).

Thunderbolt of Italy, The.

A surname given to Gaston de Foix, Duc de Nemours, a celebrated French general (1489-1512). In 1512 he conducted a brilliant campaign against the Spaniards in Italy, and was killed in the pursuit after a great victory won by him at Ravenna, April 11, 1512.

Thunderbolt of Painting, The, *v.* Furioso, Il.

Thunderer, The.

A surname given to Stephen II, King of Hungary (c. 1114–31).

Thunderer, The.

A nickname given to " The Times " newspaper, founded in 1785, under the title of " The London Daily Universal Register." The present name was adopted in 1788. According to Carlyle's "Life of Sterling," the name was originally given to Captain Edward Sterling, who

X

was called the **Thunderer** of the " Times " newspaper.

Thundering Legion, The.

In Christian tradition, a legion of Christians in the army of Marcus Aurelius, in battle with the Quadi, whose prayers for rain were answered by a thunder shower, which refreshed the thirsty Romans, while it destroyed numbers of the enemy by lightning.

Tichborne Claimant, The, v. Tichborne Trial.

Tichborne Trial, The.

A famous trial—the longest known in England, lasting from June 1871 till February 28, 1874—in which Arthur Orton (alias Thomas Castro), who called himself Sir Roger Charles Tichborne, claimed the baronetcy and large estates in Hampshire. The trial resulted in the claimant being non-suited (March 6, 1872), but he was soon afterwards committed for perjury, the second trial lasting 188 days. He was found guilty, and sentenced to fourteen years' imprisonment with hard labour, but released on a ticket-of-leave in 1884, confessed his imposture in 1895, and died April 1, 1898. The real heir was born January 5, 1829, and died at sea 1854, being on board the " Bella," which sailed from Rio de Janeiro for New York, April 20, 1854, and was lost. There have been other famous claimants, notably General William Knollys, who in 1806 claimed the earldom in the Great Banbury Case, but was non-suited. The suit lasted from 1660-1811, and the question was

whether William Knollys, treasurer of Queen Elizabeth's household, who died in 1632, aged 88, left any issue. His widow, after his death, announced that there were two children of the marriage—Edward and Nicholas—born in 1628 and 1630 respectively. Edward died, and Nicholas in due time took his seat and voted in the Parliament of 1660. In 1661 a Bill was read a first time, declaring Nicholas illegitimate. He died in 1673, and his son Charles continued the suit in the reigns of James II, William III, Anne and George II. The question, after Charles's death, remained in abeyance until General Knollys petitioned George III, and on June 18, 1813, the House resolved that he was not entitled to the earldom. The present Lord Knollys is the grandson of the William Knollys who made the eighth and last attempt to secure the Banbury peerage.

Tiddy-doll.

A nickname given to Richard Temple Grenville, Earl Temple (1711-79), an English politician. Also called **Lord Gawkey.**

Tiers État (French, " Third Estate ").

In France, that portion of the nation which belonged neither to the nobility, nor the clergy (the two privileged classes), nor the peasantry. It consisted chiefly of the burghers who sent representatives to the States-General. The name became famous, owing to the struggles of the representatives of this order in the last French States-General for power equal to that of both the other orders, and their final assumption of supreme authority, consummating the French Revolution.

Tiger of Central America, The.

A surname given to General Santos Guardiola, a rough and cruel soldier (1810–62), President of Honduras from February 17, 1856.

Tiger of Tacubaya, The.

A surname given to the Mexican general Leonardo Marquez (b. c. 1820), in allusion to his massacre of prisoners at Tacubaya (April, 1859).

Tintoretto of England, The, *v.* English Tintoretto, The.

Tintoretto of Switzerland, The.

A surname given to Johann Rudolphe Huber, a Swiss painter (1658–1748).

Tin Wedding, *v.* Wedding Anniversaries.

Tippecanoe, *v.* Old Tip.

Tirynthian Swain, The.

A surname given to Hercules, a mighty hero in Greek and Roman mythology, famous for his Twelve Labours.

Tityre Tus.

Under this name and those of Muns, Hectors, Scourers and afterwards Nickers, Hawkabites (q.v.) and Mohawks (or Mohocks, q.v.), dissolute young men, often of the better class, perambulated the streets of London by night towards the end of the seventeenth and beginning of the eighteenth century, breaking windows, upsetting sedan-chairs, insulting women and citizens. The **Tityre Tus**

took their name from the first line of the first Eclogue of Virgil :—

" Tityre tu patulæ recubans sub tegmine fagi."

Tityrus, *v.* Father of English Poetry, The.

Tombs, The.

A former prison in New York city, built in 1838 and demolished in 1897. Its front was in Centre Street, in the block bounded by Leonord, Elm and Franklin Streets. The new criminal law courts, on the opposite side of Franklin Street, were connected with the Tombs by a bridge from the second story, known as the " Bridge of Sighs."

Tom Folio.

A nickname given to Thomas Rawlinson, a noted book and MS. collector (1681–1725).

Tommy Atkins.

A generic name for a private in the British army; also, the rank and file collectively (cf. the French " Dumanet "). The name is said to be derived from the usage of making out blanks for military accounts, etc., with the name, " I, Tommy Atkins," etc.

Tom o' Bedlam.

An incurable male lunatic. A female lunatic was called **Bess o' Bedlam.** *v.* Bedlam.

Tom Pepper.

An imaginary character in sailors' legends, said to have been kicked out of heaven for lying.

Tom Piper.

A character in the English morris-dance.

Tom Quad.

The great quadrangle of Christ Church College, Oxford.

Tom's.

A famous coffee-house, named from its proprietor, Thomas West, formerly situated in Russell Street, London. Removed in 1865. In 1764 a club of nearly 700 members was formed here, consisting of the most noted men of the age, and called Tom's Club.

Tom's Club, v. Tom's.

Tom (or John) Styles (or Stiles).

A fictitious name formerly used by lawyers in actions of ejectment. v. John Noakes.

Tom Thumb.

The sobriquet of Charles Sherwood Stratton, an American dwarf (1838–83), exhibited by P. T. Barnum in various parts of the world. He married in 1863 Mercy Lavinia Bump, (Lavina Warren), also a dwarf. When first exhibited he was about 2 feet high, but grew to a height of 40 inches.

Tonnante.

The first ironclad, one of five floating batteries, built by Napoleon III during the Crimean War. Launched at Brest March, 1855. Length, 172 feet; breadth, 44 feet; draught, 9 feet. The armoured casemate carried 4½-inch armour and 17-inch wooden backing, and mounted 16 guns.

Tontine System.

The name given to a system of life-insurance or annuities, invented by Lorenzo Tonti, an Italian banker (fl. c. 1650), by which when one annuitant dies his share goes to benefit the survivors.

Torgau Articles.

A document, drawn up at Torgau in 1530, which formed the basis of the Augsburg Confession (q.v.).

Tories.

One of the two great political parties which arose at the end of the seventeenth century. It may be regarded as the successor of the Cavaliers, Court Party, and Abhorrers. It favoured Conservative principles in Church and State. One branch after the revolution of 1688 became known as Jacobins; it was the peace party in the reign of Queen Anne; and from the Hanoverian succession (1714) it was in opposition for about half a century. It took stronger ground than the Whig party against the American colonies and against the French Revolution. Pitt, Canning and Wellington were among its leaders. From about the time of the Reform Bill of 1832, which the Tories opposed, the name began to be replaced by Conservatives (v. Conservative Party). The word Tory, however, is still in common use. Also the loyalist or British party during the American Revolutionary period.

Tower of the Winds, The.

The water-clock (or horologium) erected at Athens (first century, B.C.), by the Syrian Andronicus Cyrrhestes, a Greek astronomer. Towards the top of each face is sculptured the figure of a Wind, with appropriate attributes. The structure is octagonal in plan, 26 feet in diameter and 42 feet high, and was surmounted by a bronze Triton, which served as a weather-vane.

Towers of Silence.

The name given to the structures used by the Parsees for the disposal of their dead. The most notable of these dakhmas are in the neighbourhood of Bombay. These dakhmas or towers are open at the top, and the bodies are placed upon iron gratings at the top, where they remain exposed to the elements and birds of prey until the flesh has disappeared and the bones have fallen into a pit beneath. They are afterwards removed to a neighbouring cavern.

Town and Gown Riots.

The name given to disturbances between the students (or gownsmen) of Oxford University and the townspeople of Oxford.

Tractarians.

The followers of a movement, the basis of which is to be found in Tracts for the Times, or Oxford Tracts, a series of 90 pamphlets, published at Oxford (*v*. **Oxford School**), 1833–41. The fundamental principles of the movement were that the Christian religion involves certain well-defined theological dogmas, and a visible Church with sacraments and rites and definite religious teaching on the foundation of dogma, and that this visible church is based upon and involves an unbroken line of episcopal succession from the apostles, and includes the Anglican Church. Also called **Puseyites** (q.v.).

Traitors' Gate.

The Southwark end of London Bridge, where, after 1577, the heads of persons executed for treason were exhibited.

Translator General.

A surname given to Philemon Holland, a noted English translator (1552–1637).

Trappists.

A monastic body, a branch of the Cistercian Order. It is named from the village of Soligny - la - Trappe (Orne), France, where the abbey of La Trappe was founded in 1140 by Rotrou, Count of Perche. The rules of the order are noted for their extreme austerity, and inculcate extended fasts, severe manual labour, almost perpetual silence, abstinence from flesh, fish, etc., and rigorous asceticism in general.

Travellers' Club.

A London club, originated shortly after the peace of 1814, by the Marquis of Londonderry (then Lord Castlereagh). The present house in Pall Mall was built in 1832.

Treasury of Peru, The.

A surname given to the Andes, the principal mountain-system of South America, rich in gold, silver and other metals.

Treaties.

In addition to the following, *v*. also **Peace of, etc.**

Treaty Elm, The.

A tree, formerly standing near Philadelphia, beneath which Penn negotiated a treaty with the Indians in 1682.

Treaty of Baden.

A treaty between the German Empire and France, concluded at Baden, Switzerland, September 7, 1714, which, with the treaties of Utrecht (*v.* **Peace of Utrecht**) and Rastatt (q.v.), ended the War of the Spanish Succession (q.v.). The Peace of Ryswick was ratified, the elector of Bavaria and Cologne were re-instated in their lands and dignities, and Landau was left in the possession of France.

Treaty of Falczi, *v.* Peace of the Pruth.

Treaty of Ghent.

A treaty between the United States and Great Britain, concluded at Ghent, December 24, 1814, terminating the war of 1812.

Treaty of Hanover.

An alliance for mutual aid, concluded between England, France and Prussia, September, 1725. It was directed against the union between Austria and Spain.

Treaty of Madrid.

A treaty between the Emperor Charles V and Francis I of France, signed January 14, 1526. Francis was released from captivity in return for the cession of Burgundy and other concessions.

Treaty of Mangalore.

A peace concluded 1784 between the British and Tippoo Saib, on the basis of a mutual restitution of conquests.

Treaty of Nanking.

A treaty between Great Britain and China, concluded at Nanking in 1842. By it Hong Kong was ceded to Great Britain; Canton, Amoy, Shanghai, Fuhchow and Ningpo were opened to British commerce, and China paid an indemnity.

Treaty of Newport.

The name given to negotiations at Newport, Monmouthshire, between Charles I and the English Parliament, September to November, 1648. The king made great concessions, but apparently only to gain time.

Treaty of Péronne.

A conference in 1468 between Charles the Bold, Duke of Burgundy, and Louis XI of France (who had gone to Péronne with a small escort, and was imprisoned by the duke). Louis made important concessions.

Treaty of Ripon.

A truce concluded at Ripon by Charles I with the Scots in October 1640.

Treaty of San Stefano.

A treaty concluded between Russia and Turkey, March 3, 1878, at San Stefano (a small port on the Sea of Marmora), which put an end to the Russo-Turkish war. The provisions of this treaty were, however, greatly altered by the Congress of Berlin, June—July, 1878 (*v.* **Berlin Congress**).

Treaty of Schönbrunn.

A treaty concluded at Schönbrunn, December 15, 1805, between Napoleon I and Haugwitz (acting for Prussia). Prussia ceded Cleves, Anspach and Neuchâtel to France, and received Hanover. A treaty (called also the Treaty of Vienna), concluded October 14, 1809, at Schönbrunn between Napoleon I and Francis I of Austria.

Treaty of Seville.

A treaty between Great Britain, Spain and France, concluded at Seville in 1729. It put an end to the war between England and Spain, left England in possession of Gibraltar, and established a close alliance between the three powers.

Treaty of Shimonoseki.

A treaty of peace concluded between China and Japan at Shimonoseki, April 17, 1895. China recognized the independence of Korea; ceded to Japan the southern portion of the province of Shing-king (Liautung peninsula), the island of Formosa and the Pescadores Islands; agreed to pay a war indemnity of 200 million Kuping taels (about £35,000,000); and made other important concessions. Japan later agreed, in deference to Russia's objections, to give up the Liautung peninsula.

Treaty of Tafna.

A treaty concluded between the French general Bugeaud and Abd-el-Kader, May 30, 1837.

Treaty of Troyes.

A treaty between Henry V of England and France, 1420, by which Henry V was to marry Catharine, daughter of Charles VI, to become regent of France, and to succeed to the throne on the death of Charles.

Treaty of Verdun.

A treaty made at Verdun in 843 by the sons of Louis le Débonnaire. Lothaire was confirmed as emperor, and received Italy and the region lying in general west of the Rhine and Alps, and east of the Rhone, Saône, Meuse and Schelde. Ludwig the German received the region between the Rhine and the Elbe (the nucleus of Germany), and Charles the Bald obtained the region west of Lothaire's dominions (the nucleus of France).

Treaty of Washington.

A treaty between Great Britain and the United States, signed May 8, 1871, which provided for the settlement of the Alabama claims (q.v.) by the Geneva tribunal, and for the settlement of the San Juan boundary and fisheries disputes.

Tredici Comuni, *v.* Thirteen Communes.

Tremont.

The original name of Boston, Massachusetts, given to it in allusion to the three hills on which it was built. Also Trimount or Trimountain.

Trent, The.

A British steamer, on which were seized, in the Bahama Channel, November 8, 1861, the Confederate Commissioners to Europe, Mason and Slidell, by the American captain Wilkes. The disavowal of Wilkes's act by the United States government prevented serious complications arising between the United States and Great Britain.

Trent Affair, The, *v.* Trent, The.

Trial of the Pyx.

A term used to express the annual official inquiry to determine the weight and fineness of the standard coins issued from the Mint during the preceding year. So called from the pyx, the box or chest in which the specimen gold and silver coins of the realm are kept. The trial now takes place at Goldsmiths' Hall, a jury of goldsmiths being presided over by the King's or Queen's Remembrancer.

Trianon, Decree of the, *v.* Decree of the Trianon.

Tribune of the People, The, *v.* Apostle of Free Trade, The.

Tricoteuses, Les (French, " The Knitters ").

A class of women who frequented the tribunals and places of execution during the French Revolution, and sat knitting while they expressed their approval or disapproval of the turn of events. From their violence they have received the name of " Furies of the Guillotine." They were not seen after 1794.

Tridentine Council, *v.* Council of Trent.

Triennial Act.

An Act of Parliament, passed in 1694, which limited the duration of Parliaments to three years, and forbade a period of three years to pass without a Parliament being summoned.

Superseded by the Septennial Act (q.v.) of 1716.

Trimmers.

An English political party which followed the Marquis of Halifax, c. 1680–90, in trimming between the Whigs and the Tories.

Trimount (or Trimountain), *v.* Tremont.

Trinity House, Corporation of, *v.* Corporation of Trinity House.

Trinity Jones.

A surname given to William Jones, of Nayland, an English clergyman and theological writer (1726–1800).

Trinovant (or Trinovantum).

An old name for London, corrupted from Troja Nova (New Troy). Also written Trinobant and Troynovant. Called Augusta by the Romans. Michael Drayton, in his " Polyolbion " (viii), calls it **Brute's City.**

Triple Alliance.

A league between England, Sweden, and the Netherlands, formed in 1668, and designed to check the French aggression. A league between France, Great Britain and the Netherlands, formed in 1717, and directed chiefly against Spain. After the accession to it of Austria in 1718, it was known as the **Quadruple Alliance.** An alliance between Germany, Austro-Hungary and Italy, formed c. 1883, and designed to check Russia and also France. Chiefly the creation of Prince Bismarck. By its provisions the three powers are bound to support one another in certain contingencies. Its influence has succeeded to that of the League of the Three Emperors (German, Austrian and Russian).

Tripolitan War.

A war between the United States and Tripoli, 1801–5. Declared by Tripoli June 10, 1801, because the United States refused to increase its payment for immunity from the depredations of the Tripolitan corsairs. Peace concluded June 4, 1805.

Truce of God.

A suspension of private feuds, which was observed, chiefly in the eleventh and twelfth centuries, in France, Italy, England and elsewhere. The terms of such a truce usually provided that such feuds should cease on all the more important church festivals and fasts, or from Thursday evening to Monday morning, or during the period of Lent or the like.

Truce of Nice.

A truce concluded at Nice, in 1538, between Francis I of France and the emperor Charles V.

Truce of Ulm.

A truce concluded in 1647 between the Franco-Swedish forces and the Bavarians.

Tugendbund.

A German association formed at Königsberg, 1808, with the acknowledged purpose of cultivating patriotism, reorganizing the army, and encouraging education, and with the secret aim of aiding in throwing off the French yoke. Frederick

William III was forced to dissolve it in 1809, but it continued in secret for several years, and exerted a very considerable influence, especially in 1812. It was vehemently attacked in 1816 by reactionary politicians.

Turnip-hoer, The.

A nickname given to George I of England (1660–1727), in allusion to his having, it is said, talked of turning St. James's Park into a turnip ground.

Turpentine State, The.

A popular surname for the State of North Carolina, which produces annually great quantities of turpentine.

Tuscan Poet, The, *v.* Southern Scott, The.

Twelve Knights of the Round Table.

The name given to twelve famous knights of King Arthur's Court. The most famous among them were Launcelot, Tristram, Lamoracke, Tor, Galahad, Gawain, Gareth, Palomides, Kay, Mark, Mordred. Various names, not so well known, supply the twelfth. Cf. Sir Thomas Malory's "Morte d'Arthur," Tennyson's "Idylls of the King," and Sir Walter Scott's "Bridal of Triermain."

Twelve Peers (or Paladins) of Charlemagne, The.

The name given to twelve famous peers (so called on account of the equality between them) of Charlemagne's court. The most famous among them were Orlando, Rinaldo, Astolfo, Oliver, Ogier le Danois, Ganelon, Florismart, Namo, Otuel,

Ferumbras, Malaggi. Various names, not so well known, supply the twelfth.

Twelve Peers of France.

A collective name for the peers of France, fixed at twelve (viz., six lay and six ecclesiastic) under Philip Augustus in the twelfth century. The six lay peers were the Dukes of Burgundy, Aquitane and Normandy, and the Counts of Flanders, Toulouse and Champagne ; and the six ecclesiastic peers the Archbishop of Rheims, and the Bishops of Laon, Langres, Beauvais, Châlons and Noyon. By the date of the French Revolution the number had been increased to thirty-eight peers of the realm.

Twopenny Tube.

A popular name for the underground electric railway, from the City to Shepherd's Bush. The fare is 2d. any distance.

Two Thousand Guineas.

An annual horse-race, run in the spring, at Newmarket, Cambridgeshire. Distance, 1 mile 11 yards.

Tyburn.

A tributary of the Thames, which rose in the clay-beds at the foot of the Hampstead Hills. It went through Regent's Park, crossing Oxford Street at Sussex Court, then to Green Park, through Buckingham Palace Gardens, and through St. James's Park to Thorney, Westminster. The manor at Tybourne, which took its name from this, adjoined that of Marylebone. There was a place

of execution on the Tyburn, near what is now the Marble Arch, Hyde Park. " Tyburn Tree " was the public gallows till the executions were transferred to Newgate in 1783.

Tyburnia.

A fashionable quarter of London, north of Hyde Park, named from the former Tyburn (q.v.).

Ultima Thule.

The furthest of the " Britannic Isles." " It has been identified with all sorts of localities since the time when Pytheas sailed with his Cimbric guides to the country of the midnight sun. The controversy is boundless, and its details are too tedious to be examined at length. But we may select sufficient evidence to show why the story of the journey should be believed, and to justify the selection of Lapland as the northern limit of the expedition." *Elton*, " Origins of Eng. Hist." p. 64. Thule was the name given by Pytheas of Marseilles to a region or island north of Great Britain, the position of which has been for more than two thousand years a matter of controversy. Some say Pytheas embraced the Orkney and Shetland Islands under the general name of Thule. Poetically, the word Thule (or Ultima Thule) may be considered as applying to some unknown, far-distant, indefinite, northern or mythical region, or even goal.

Ultramontane Party.

In German politics, the centre party, which opposes legislation supposed to be inimical to the Church of Rome.

Ulysses, v. Achilles of Germany, The.

Ulysses of the Highlands, The.

A surname given to Sir Evan Cameron, Lord of Lochiel (d. 1719).

Uncle Sam.

The government of the people of the United States; a jocular extension of the initials U.S.

Unconditional Surrender Grant.

A nickname given to General Ulysses Simpson Grant, eighteenth President of the United States (1822–85).

Uncrowned King of Ireland, The.

A surname given to Charles Stewart Parnell, an Irish statesman (1846–91).

Underground Railroad, The.

A popular term used in the United States to indicate the numerous ways in which fugitive slaves from the southern states were assisted to gain a place of safety in Canada or the North. The movement began with the Pennsylvania Quakers, became organized in 1838, and continued till the Civil War. Often jokingly contracted to U.G.R.R.

Unfair Preacher, The.

A surname given (by Charles II) to Isaac Barrow, a noted English theologian, classical scholar and mathematician (1630–77). He was chaplain to Charles II, and his sermons were so exhaustive that it was " unfair " to those who followed him.

Unfortunate Peace, The.

The name sometimes given to the Treaty of Cateau-Cambrésis, between France, England and Spain, April 2–3, 1559, under which France retained Calais, and France and Spain restored most of their conquests.

Uniformity Act.

An Act of Parliament, passed in 1549, which provided for uniformity of religious service. Also an Act passed May 19, 1662. It obliged holders of church livings to be ordained by a bishop; to assent to the Prayer-Book; to renounce the Covenant; to declare the unlawfulness of bearing arms against the sovereign; and to make oath of canonical obedience. Many clergymen resigned their benefices.

Union, The.

The United States of America. Also a statute of 1800, which united the kingdoms of Great Britain and Ireland on and after January 1, 1801.

Unionists.

Those politicians who are opposed to the dissolution or rupture of the legislative union existing between Great Britain and Ireland, and especially to the separatist principles and tendencies of those who desire to establish home rule in Ireland (v. Home Rule Bills). The name is applied to the Conservatives and Liberal-Unionists.

Union Jack.

The national ensign of the United Kingdom and Ireland, used in a small form as a jack—

that is, displayed at the end of the bowsprit. The name " union jack " has come wrongly to be applied to the larger union flag itself. It is formed by the union of the Cross of St. George (red on a white field), the diagonal cross or saltier of St. Andrew (white on a blue field), and the diagonal cross or saltier of St. Patrick (red on a white field).

Union League Club.

A social and political (Republican) club, organized in New York city in 1863, and incorporated in 1865. Its stated objects at the time of its organization during the War of the Rebellion were " to promote, encourage and sustain, by all proper means, absolute and unqualified loyalty to the government of the United States ; to discountenance and rebuke, by moral and social influences, all disloyalty to said government, and every attempt against the integrity of the Nation "; and also to establish a library and art gallery for the collection of literature, works of art and military trophies, relating to the war. Similar clubs were formed in other cities.

Union of Heilbronn.

An alliance between the Swedes and the German Protestants, for the prosecution of the war against the Imperialists, concluded at Heilbronn in 1633.

Union of Utrecht.

The union, concluded in 1579, of the seven united provinces, Holland, Zealand, Utrecht, Gelderland, Overyssel, Groningen and Friesland, which be- came the Dutch republic. *v.* United Provinces, The.

Unitarians.

A name generally applied to those Christians who do not accept the doctrine of the Trinity. The title dates from the sixteenth century.

United Brethren, *v.* Moravians.

United Irishmen.

An Irish society, formed in 1791 by Wolfe Tone, for the purpose of procuring parliamentary reform and the repeal of the penal laws. It afterwards became a secret society with revolutionary aims, and was influential in causing the Irish rebellion of 1798.

United Kingdom.

A common abbreviation for the official name of the British kingdom since January 1, 1801, viz. the United Kingdom of Great Britain and Ireland (including England, Wales, Scotland, Ireland and the neighbouring smaller islands). *v.* Union, The.

United Provinces, The.

The seven provinces of the Low Countries—Holland, Zealand, Utrecht, Friesland, Gelderland, Groningen and Overyssel—which in 1579 formed the Union of Utrecht, and laid the foundation of the republic of the Netherlands.

United States.

An American frigate, launched at Philadelphia in 1797, which, under command of Decatur, captured the British frigate " Macedonian," October 25, 1812. The " United States " before the war was nicknamed " Old Waggon," from her indifferent sailing qualities, but these were subsequently much improved.

Universal Doctor, *v.* **Doctor Universalis.**

Universal Genius, The.

A surname given to Sir William Petty, an English statistician and political economist (1623–87). He was in 1651 professor of anatomy at Oxford and professor of music at Gresham College. In 1652 he was appointed physician to the army in Ireland, and in 1663 he invented a double-bottomed ship.

Universalists.

A denomination of Christians founded in England in 1750 by James Reilly, and in America twenty years later by John Murray. They believe in the ultimate salvation of all rational creatures.

Universal Spider, The.

A surname given to Louis XI, King of France (1423–83), in allusion to his craftiness and unscrupulousness.

Unlearned Parliament, *v.* **Parliament of Dunces.**

Unready, The.

A surname given to Ethelred II, King of England (968–1016).

Unser Fritz, *v.* **Our Fritz.**

Untamed Heifer, The.

A surname given to Elizabeth, Queen of England (1533–1603) in the Martin Mar-Prelate Tracts. These are attributed to John Penry (or Ap Henry), who was executed May 29, 1593, for uttering seditious words against the queen.

Unter den Linden (German, " Under the Lindens ").

A famous street in Berlin, extending from the Brandenburger Thor eastward about three-fifths of a mile. Width, 160 feet. In it are the imperial and princely palaces, the university, the academy, the statue of Frederick the Great, etc.

Upholsterer of Notre-Dame, *v.* **Tapissier de Notre-Dame.**

Upper Crust, The, *v.* **Upper Ten Thousand, The.**

Upper Ten, The, *v.* **Upper Ten Thousand, The.**

Upper Ten Thousand, The.

A collective name given to the aristocratic or higher circles of society. Said to have been invented by Nathaniel Parker Willis, an American author (1806–67), and originally applied by him to the fashionable society of New York, numbering, he considered, about ten thousand. Often shortened to the **Upper Ten,** and sometimes the **Upper Crust** is used with the same meaning. The phrases **Upper Ten** and **Lower Five** (meaning the lower classes), are often repeated in a song (duet) called " St. Giles's and St. James's," which was at one time very popular.

Upright, The.

A surname of Frederick IV, Elector Palatine (1574–1610).

Ursa Major, *v.* **Great Moralist, The.**

Useless Parliament, *v.* **Parliamentum Vanum.**

Utraquists, *v.* **Calixtines.**

Vaishnavas, *v.* **Smartas.**

Valiant, The.

A surname given to Alfonso VI (or Alphonso), King of Leon, as Alfonso I of Castile (1030–1109). Also to John V, duke of Brittany (d. 1399).

Valkyrie II.

A keel cutter built at Glasgow in 1893 for Lord Dunraven. She went to America in October, 1893, to race for the America Cup, and was defeated in three races by the " Vigilant " (q.v.). Sunk in a collision with the " Satanita," July 5, 1894, at the Mud Hook Regatta, on the Firth of Clyde. Length over all, 126 feet; draught, 16·6; beam, 20·06; load water-line, 85·50.

Valkyrie III.

A cutter built in 1895 for Lord Dunraven to compete for the America Cup. The cup was defended by the " Defender " (q.v.). In the first race, September 7, the " Defender " won; in the second, September 10, the yachts fouled, and the race was awarded to the " Defender," which was injured, though the " Valkyrie's " time was 47 seconds less; in the third race the " Valkyrie " withdrew immediately after crossing the line, while the " Defender " sailed over the course. The cup was awarded to the latter.

Valley of Humiliation.

The scene of the contest between Christian and Apollyon, in Bunyan's " Pilgrim's Progress."

Valley of the Shadow of Death.

A valley traversed by Christian, in Bunyan's " Pilgrim's Progress."

Van Dyck in Little, *v.* **Apelles of His Age, The.**

Vandyke (or Van Dyck) of Sculpture, The.

A surname given to Antoine Coysevox, a French sculptor of Spanish origin (1640–1720).

Vanguard.

A British line-of-battle ship of 74 guns and 1,603 tons. She served in the Channel squadron of Lord Howe in 1793, and was flag-ship of Vice-Admiral Sir Horatio Nelson in the battle of the Nile, August 1–2, 1798. Also an armoured battleship, of the " Iron Duke " (q.v.) class. She came into collision with the " Iron Duke " off the Irish coast in 1875, and was sunk.

Vanity Fair.

A fair described in Bunyan's " Pilgrim's Progress." It was held in the town of Vanity, and the phrase is often used as a synonym for the present world and its worldliness. Also the title of a novel by Thackeray.

Vatican Council.

The twentieth Ecumenical Council, according to the reckoning of the Church of Rome, which met in the Vatican, December 8, 1869, and declared belief in the infallibility of the Pope, when speaking *ex cathedrâ*, to be a dogma of the Church. It was closed October 20, 1870, owing to the occupation of Rome by Victor Emmanuel.

Vauxhall Gardens.

A popular and fashionable London resort, formerly situated on the Thames above Lambeth. Vauxhall Gardens were laid out in 1661, and were at first known as the New Spring Gardens at Fox Hall, to distinguish them from the Old Spring Gardens at Whitehall. They were finally closed in 1859, and the site is now built over. *Hare,* " London," ii, 422. Cf. also Smollett's " Humphrey Clinker " and Thackeray's " Vanity Fair."

Vega.

The vessel in which Baron Nils Adolf Erik Nordenskjöld made his expedition of 1878–9 to the Arctic regions, accomplishing the North-East Passage.

Vehmgerichte (German, from " Fehm," a criminal tribunal so named, and " Gericht," judgment).

Medieval tribunals which flourished in Germany, chiefly in Westphalia, in the fourteenth and fifteenth centuries. The sessions were open for the adjudication of civil matters, but secret when persons accused of murder, robbery, heresy, witchcraft, etc., were summoned. Those convicted of serious crimes, or those who refused to appear before the tribunal, were put to death. Cf. Sir Walter Scott's " Anne of Geierstein."

Vendeans, *v.* War of La Vendée.

Vendôme Column, *v.* Colonne Vendôme.

Venerable Bede (or Bæda), The.

A celebrated English monk and ecclesiastical writer (c. 673–735). Sometimes called the Father of Ecclesiastical History.

Venerable Doctor, *v.* Doctor Venerabilis.

Venerable Initiator, The, *v.* Invincible Doctor, The.

Vengeur, Le.

A French vessel of 74 guns, which sank off Ushant, June 1, 1794, with all on board, after Lord Howe's victory on that date. The captain and his son (127 of the crew in all) were prisoners on board the " Culloden " at the time. (For details, cf. Carlyle's essay, " On the sinking of the ' Vengeur.' ")

Venice of the East.

A name occasionally given to Bangkok, Siam, its houses being built largely in the river.

Venice of the North.

A name sometimes given to Stockholm and to Amsterdam.

Venice of the West.

A name occasionally given to Glasgow.

Venus of Arles.

A Greek statue found at Arles in 1651, now in the Louvre, Paris. The goddess is represented standing, undraped to the hips, with the head slightly inclined towards the left.

Venus of Medici.

An antique Greek original statue of marble, probably of the time of Augustus, in the

Tribuna of the Uffizi, Florence. A very graceful, highly-finished figure of the goddess, undraped, as Anadyomene, with her arms held before her body, and a dolphin to her left. While without the dignity of earlier Greek work, it has long ranked as a canon of female beauty.

Venus of Melos.

A famous Greek statue in the Louvre, Paris, perhaps the most admired single existing work of antiquity. Found in 1820 in the island of Melos, and in date appears to fall between the time of Phidias and that of Praxiteles, or c. 400 B.C. The statue represents a majestic woman, undraped to the hips, standing with the weight on the right foot, and with the head turned slightly towards the left. The arms are broken off, and there is a dispute as to their original position. Also called the **Venus of Milo.**

Venus of Milo, *v.* Venus of Melos.

Venus of the Forest, The.

A surname given to the ash-tree.

Vêpres Siciliennes (French, " Sicilian Vespers ").

A name given to the massacre of the French in Sicily by the Sicilians, 1282. So called from its commencement at vespers on Easter Monday. Cf. Verdi's opera of the name, produced in Paris 1855; also a play by Casimir Delavigne.

Vermilion Sea, The.

A name formerly given to the Gulf of California, on account of the red-coloured infusoria it contains.

Vesta, *v.* Arctic.

Vicar of Bray, The.

A well-known song, written by an officer in the British army, in the reign of George I. Bray is a parish in Berkshire, England, 26 miles west of London, and a " Vicar of Bray," Simon Alleyn, was twice a Papist and twice a Protestant in the reigns of Henry VIII, Edward VI, Mary and Elizabeth (according to Fuller), but always Vicar of Bray.

Vicar of Christ, The.

A title assumed by the Pope of Rome.

Victoria.

A British armoured battle-ship (tonnage, 10,400; indicated horse-power, 12,000) sunk in a collision off Tripoli, Syria, June 22, 1893. It was the flag-ship of Vice-Admiral Sir George Tryon, and was lost in manœuvring through orders issued by him, which led to its being rammed by a companion vessel, the Camperdown. The admiral and 338 officers and men were drowned.

Victoria, La.

One of the vessels composing the squadron of Magalhães, 1519–21. She was the only one to return to Europe around the Cape of Good Hope, and was thus the first vessel to circumnavigate the globe. " La Victoria " was of about 90 tons burthen, and carried 45 men. The official seal of the Hakluyt Society (q.v.) bears a representation of this ship.

Victorieux, Le (French, " The Victorious ").

A surname given to Charles VII, king of France (1403–61). Joan of Arc delivered Orleans (1429) in his reign.

Victorious, The, *v.* **Victorieux, Le.**

Victorious, The.

A surname of Frederick I, Elector Palatine (1425–76); of Osman (or Othman) I, founder of the Ottoman empire (1259–1326); of Waldemar II, king of Denmark, from 1202–41.

Victory.

A British line-of-battleship of 100 guns. She was the flag-ship of Vice-Admiral Lord Howe before Toulon and Corsica, 1793–4; the flag-ship of Sir John Jervis in action with the Spanish fleet off Cape St. Vincent, February 14, 1797; and the flag-ship of Vice-Admiral Lord Nelson at Trafalgar, October 21, 1805.

Victory's Darling Child, *v.* **Enfant chéri de la victoire, L'.**

Vigilant.

A centre-board sloop, selected to defend the America Cup against the Valkyrie. She won three races October 5, 9 and 13, 1893. In July, 1894, she went to Great Britain for the racing season, in which she was unsuccessful. Her racing length for the America Cup was 93·31 feet; height of topmast, 56·88 feet; load water-line, 86·34 feet; boom, 74·62 feet. She has been somewhat altered, and is owned by George J. Gould.

Villa Medici.

A Roman villa built in 1540,

south of the Pincio, for Cardinal Ricci da Montepulciano. About 1600 it came into possession of the Medici family, and afterwards into that of the grand dukes of Tuscany. Galileo was confined there 1630–3. The French Academy of Art, founded by Louis XIV, was transferred to it in 1801, and it has a fine collection of casts.

Violet-Crowned City.

A name sometimes given to Athens.

Virgil of the French Drama, The.

A surname given to Jean Racine, a French tragic poet (1639–99). So called by Sir Walter Scott. Cf. **Homer of the French Drama, The.**

Virginian Plan, The.

An outline plan of a constitution for the United States, presented to the Constitutional Convention of 1787 by Edmund Randolph, of Virginia. It projected a national union, differing radically from the old confederacy.

Virgin Modesty.

A surname given by Charles II to John Wilmot, Earl of Rochester (1647–80), because he blushed so easily.

Virgin Queen, The, *v.* **Maiden Queen, The.**

Voltaire of Germany, The.

A surname given to Christopher Martin Wieland, a German poet and author (1733–1813). *v.* also **Meister, Der.**

Volunteer.

A steel centre-board sloop, built to defend the America Cup,

D.N.   Y

challenged by the "Thistle" (q.v.), a Scotch cutter. She won the trial race with the "Mayflower" (September 17, 1887), and both the cup races against the "Thistle" (September 27 and 30). She was afterwards re-modelled into a schooner, and called the "Phœnix." Originally designed by Edward Burgess for General J. C. Paine, of Boston, and launched June 30, 1887. Length over all, 106·23 feet; beam, 23·2 feet; draught, 10 feet; displacement, 130 tons.

Vorhees Bill, v. **Sherman Bill.**

Vorwärts, v. **Marshal Forward.**

Votre Solidité (French, "Your Solidity").

Name given by Louis XIV to Madame de Maintenon (1635–1719), in allusion to her solid virtues.

Wacht am Rheim, Die (German, "The Watch on the Rhine").

A German popular song, words by Schneckenburger (1840), music by Karl Wilhelm (1854). It enjoyed great vogue in the war of 1870–1, becoming a national song.

Waggon Boy, The.

A surname given to Thomas Corwin, an American statesman and orator (1794–1865), he having, when a lad, conveyed a waggon-load of provisions to General William Henry Harrison, who was then at war with the Indians on the northern frontier. Or **Waggoner Boy.**

Wake, The.

A surname (according to John of Peterborough) given to Hereward, a noted English outlaw and patriot, who defended Ely against the Normans (fl. c. 1070). Cf. "Hereward the Wake," a novel by Charles Kingsley, published in 1866.

Walcheren Expedition.

An unsuccessful British expedition against the French. The troops landed on Walcheren in July, 1809, the land force (40,000) under Lord Chatham, and the naval force under Strachan. They bombarded and took Flushing in August; failed to take Antwerp; and retired from Walcheren, after sustaining great losses, in December.

Waldensians.

(From the founder Waldo or Valdo.) The members of a reforming body of Christians, followers of Peter Waldo (Valdo), of Lyons, formed c. 1170. Their chief seats were in the Alpine valleys of Piedmont, Dauphiné and Provence. The Waldensians joined the Reformation movement, and were often severely persecuted, especially in the sixteenth and seventeenth centuries.

Walhalla, or Temple of Fame.

A building founded by Ludwig I, 1830, at Ratisbon, Bavaria. The interior forms a hall 50 feet by 180 feet, and 56 feet high, and is surrounded by a frieze representing the early history of the Teutonic race. The hall contains 101 busts of celebrated Germans, and six Victories by Rauch.

Walking Library, v. **Ever Memorable, The.**

Walking Stewart.

A surname given to John Stewart, a famous English traveller (d. 1822). He traversed India, Persia, Arabia, Abyssinia, Nubia, the United States and parts of Europe on foot. Cf. Charles Lamb's " Pindaric Ode to the Tread-Mill," last line (" A ' Walking Stewart! ' ").

Wallace of Switzerland, The.

A surname given to Andreas Hofer, a Tyrolese patriot (1767–1810), head of the Tyrolese insurrection in 1809.

Wallace's Larder.

A name given to the dungeon of Ardrossan, Ayrshire, into which Sir William Wallace (c. 1274–1305) caused the dead bodies of the garrison to be thrown in Edward I's reign. *v.* also **Douglas Larder, The.**

Wall of Antoninus.

A rampart erected in the first part of the reign of Antoninus Pius, to check the northern barbarians of Britain. It extended from the Firth of Forth to the Firth of Clyde.

Wall of China, Great, *v.* Great Wall of China.

Wall of Hadrian, *v.* Picts' Wall.

Wall of Severus.

A wall built c. 208 A.D. by the emperor Septimius Severus, between the Tyne and the Solway in Britain, as a defence against northern inroads. It followed the lines of the fortifications of Hadrian.

Walloon Guard, The.

A Spanish body-guard of Walloon troops, formed in 1703 and disbanded in 1822.

Wall Street.

A street in the lower part of New York city, extending from Broadway, opposite Trinity Church, to the East River, famous as a financial and speculative centre, and often used figuratively in this sense. Cf. **Capel Court.**

Walpurgis Nacht (German, " Walpurgis Night ").

So called from the day of St. Walpurgis, Walburgis, or Walpurga, the name of an abbess, who emigrated from England to Germany in the eighth century. The night before the first of May. According to German popular superstition, on this night witches are said to ride on broomsticks, he-goats, etc., to some appointed rendez-vous, especially the Brocken in the Harz Mountains, where they hold high festival with their master, the devil.

Walpurgis Night, *v.* Walpurgis Nacht.

Walter Scott of Belgium, The.

A surname given to Hendrick Conscience, a Flemish novelist (1812–83).

Walter Scott of the Middle Ages, The.

A surname given to Jean Froissart, a celebrated French chronicler (1337–c. 1410).

Wandering Jew.

A legendary character who, according to one version, was a servant of Pilate, by name Cartaphilus (afterwards baptized Joseph), and gave Christ a blow when he was led out of the palace to execution. According to a later version, he was a cobbler, named Ahasuerus, who refused Christ permission to sit down and rest when He passed his house on the way to Golgotha. Both legends agree in the sentence pronounced by Christ on the offender, " Thou shalt wander on the earth till I return." A prey to remorse, he has since wandered from land to land, without being able to find a grave. The story has been turned to account by numerous painters and novelists. Cf. Edgar Quinet's " Ahasuerus," and Eugène Sue's " Le Juif Errant."

Wapping of Denmark, The.

A surname given to Elsinore (Helsingor), a seaport in Zealand. Associated with the story of " Hamlet, Prince of Denmark."

Warlike, The.

A surname of Frederick I, margrave of Meissen (Elector and Duke of Saxony (1369–1428). Founded the University of Leipsig in 1409.

Warming-pan Hero, The, v. Chevalier de St. George.

War of Jenkins's Ear.

The name popularly given to the war between Great Britain and Spain, which broke out in 1739, and became merged in the War of the Austrian Succession. Its immediate cause was the grievance of an English mariner, Robert Jenkins, who alleged that he had been tortured by the Spaniards, who cut off his ear.

War of La Vendée.

The royalist war against the French republic, which was carried on chiefly in La Vendée and in Brittany. It broke out in La Vendée in March, 1793, and reached its height in the Vendean victory at Saumur in June, 1793. The Vendeans, under La Rochejacquelin, suffered a decisive defeat at the hands of the republicans under Westermann and Marceau at Le Mans, December 12, 1793. The war was continued in Brittany (v. Chouans),and was suppressed in La Vendée by Hoche in 1796. The complete submission of the Chouans was effected by Napoleon Bonaparte in 1800.

War of Liberation, v. Befreiungskrieg.

War of Secession.

The American Civil War, 1861–5, is sometimes so called. Its chief causes were the anti-slavery agitation and the development of the doctrine of State sovereignty.

War of the American Revolution, v. American Revolution.

War of the Barons.

An insurrection of English barons (1263–5), under Simon de Montfort, against the arbitrary government of Henry III.

War of the Pacific (Spanish, " Guerra del Pacifico ").

The name commonly given to the war waged by Chile against Bolivia and Peru, 1879–83.

War of the Polish Succession.

A war which broke out in 1733, owing to a disputed election to the throne of Poland. Stanislaus Leszczynski was supported by France, Spain and Sardinia, and Augustus III (elector of Saxony) by Austria and Russia. The war was ended by the Peace of Vienna (1738), by which Augustus III was acknowledged.

War of the Spanish Succession.

A war arising out of disputes about the succession in Spain on the death of Charles II, fought from 1701–14 between the emperor and the naval powers on the one hand, and France and its allies on the other. The war was ended by the peace of Utrecht (q.v.) in 1713, and that of Rastatt (q.v.) 714. v. also **Treaty of Baden.**

War of the Succession, v. War of the Spanish Succession.

War of Toulouse.

A war in 1159, caused by the claim of Henry II of England to the countship of Toulouse. He reduced a large part of the territory.

War of William and Mary, v King William's War.

War of 1812.

The war between Great Britain and the United States, 1812–5. Declared June 18, 1812; peace signed at Ghent, December 24, 1814, and ratified at Washington, February 18, 1815, but the news did not reach the ocean cruisers till later, 1815.

Warrior.

The first English ironclad ship constructed entirely of iron, launched in 1860. Length, 380 feet; breadth, 58·4 feet; displacement, 9,210 tons. The central part was protected for 218 feet by 4½-inch armour on 18-inch wooden backing. Her sides could not be penetrated by any guns then afloat.

Warrior, The.

A surname of Michael VI, Byzantine emperor from 1056–7.

Wars of Reunion.

A name sometimes given to the wars between France and the allied powers, waged in consequence of the annexation of territory determined by the Chambers of Reunion (q.v.) in 1680.

Wars of the Roses.

The prolonged armed struggle between the rival houses of Lancaster and York, so called from the red rose and white rose badges respectively of the adherents of the two families. The wars began in the reign of Henry VI (third of the Lancaster line), and ended with the defeat and death of Richard III at Bosworth (August 22, 1485), and the succession of Henry VII, representative of a Lancaster offshoot, who, by his marriage with a Yorkist princess, united the conflicting interests.

Warwick Vase.

A celebrated antique marble vase, discovered in Hadrian's Villa, Tivoli, Italy, and purchased from its finder by Sir Wm. Hamilton. Its capacity is 168 gallons, and it is now at Warwick Castle, England.

Washington Elm.

An elm in Cambridge, Massachusetts, under which Washington took command of the American army in 1775.

Washington of Colombia, The, *v.* **Libertador, El.**

Washington of South America, The, *v.* **Libertador, El.**

Washington of the West, The, *v.* **Old Tip.**

Wasp.

An American ship of war of 18 guns, built at Washington in 1806. On October 18, 1812, she fell in with six merchantmen, under convoy of the British brig "Frolic" (q.v.). The action began at 11.32 a.m., and the "Frolic" struck at 12.15 p.m. It was fought in a very heavy sea. Both ships were captured the same day by the "Poictiers." Also an American ship-rigged sloop of war (22 guns and 160 men), built at Newburyport in 1814. On June 28, 1814, she fell in with the British sloop "Reindeer" (18 guns and 118 men). The battle began at 3.17 p.m., and the "Reindeer" struck at 3.44. On September 1 she met the British brig "Avon" (18 guns). The battle began at 8.38 p.m., and the "Avon" struck at 10.12. On October 9 she spoke and boarded the Swedish brig "Adams," and took out of her Lieutenant McKnight and a master's mate, late of the United States ship "Essex," on their way from Brazil to England. The "Wasp" was never heard from again.

Watch on the Rhine, The, *v.* **Wacht am Rhein, Die.**

Waterloo Hero, The.

A surname given to Viscount Rowland Hill, an English general (1772–1842), who distinguished himself in the Battle of Waterloo.

Water-Poet, The, *v.* **Swan of the Thames, The.**

Watling Street.

One of the principal Roman roads in Britain. It commenced at Dover, passed through Canterbury to London, and thence went by St. Albans, Dunstable, Stony Stratford, etc., passing along the boundary line of the present counties of Leicester and Warwick to Wroxeter on the Severn, and then north to Chester. It had a number of branch roads diverging from it.

Weathercock, The.

A nickname given to Charles Townshend, an English politician (1725–67), from the instability of his political opinions.

Weaver-Poet of Inverurie, The.

A surname given to William Thom, a Scottish poet (1799–1850). Wrote "Rhymes and Recollections of a Handloom Weaver."

Wedding Anniversaries.

The following is a list of the names given to the various anniversaries:—

    1st, Cotton Wedding.
    2nd, Paper Wedding.
    3rd, Leather Wedding.
    5th, Wooden Wedding.
    7th, Woollen Wedding.
    10th, Tin Wedding.
    12th, Silk Wedding.
    15th, Crystal Wedding.
    20th, China Wedding.
    25th, Silver Wedding.
    30th, Pearl Wedding.
    40th, Ruby Wedding.
    50th, Golden Wedding.
    75th, Diamond Wedding.

Wedding the Adriatic, *v.*
Bride of the Sea.

Weeping Philosopher.

A surname given to Heraclitus, a celebrated Greek philosopher (b. probably c. 535; d. probably c. 475 B.C.). Cf. **Laughing Philosopher, The.**

Welcome Nugget, The.

The largest gold nugget ever found, weighing 184 lb., and sold for £10,000. Found at Ballarat, Victoria, Australia.

Well-beloved, The, *v.* **Bien-aimé, Le.**

Well-Founded Doctor, The, *v.* **Doctor Fundatissimus.**

Well-Languaged Daniel, The.

A surname give by William Browne (in his " Britannia's Pastorals ") to Samuel Daniel, an English poet (1562–1619), whose writings are remarkable for purity and grace of language.

Welsh Shakspere.

A surname given to Edward Williams, a Welsh poet (1745–1826).

Wesleyan Methodists, *v.* **Methodists.**

West End.

A name by which the aristocratic western part of London is familiarly known. *v.* **East End.**

Western Empire.

The distinctive designation of the western portion of the Roman world after its division into two independent empires in 325 (*v* **Eastern Empire**). Its power very rapidly declined under the inroads of barbarians and other adverse influences, and it was finally extinguished in 476. *v.* **Holy Roman Empire.**

Westminster Assembly.

A convocation summoned by the Long Parliament, to advise " for the settling of the Liturgy and the government of the Church of England." Most of its members were Presbyterians, and nearly all were Calvinists. It met July 1, 1643, and continued its sessions until February 22, 1649. The chief fruits of its labours were the Directory of Public Worship, the Confession of Faith, and the Larger and Shorter Catechisms, which were rejected in England, but established in Scotland.

Whigs.

(Originally a contemptuous epithet in Scotland, the primary application of which is not known) One of the two great political parties arising in England at the end of the seventeenth century. It may be regarded as succeeding the Roundheads, Country Party, and Exclusionists (Petitioners). It professed more liberal principles than the Tory Party (*v.* **Tories**), and favoured and defended the revolution of 1688, Parliamentary control and the Hanoverian succession. The great Whig families controlled the government for many years from the beginning of the reign of George I. About the time of the Reform Bill of 1832 (which the Whigs favoured), the name began to be replaced by Liberal (*v.* **Liberal Party**). Also the patriotic or American party during the Revolutionary period. Also an American political party, formed under the leadership of Henry Clay, and known until c. 1834 as the National Republican. It became divided on the slavery question, lost the election of 1852, and soon after disappeared.

Whisky Insurrection or Rebellion.

An outbreak in the four western counties of Pennsylvania, in 1794, against the enforcement of an Act of Congress of 1791, imposing an excise duty on all spirits distilled within the United States, and on stills. A large body of militia, under Governor Lee, of Virginia, was sent to the disturbed district, but the insurrection was suppressed without bloodshed.

Whisky Ring.

A conspiracy of distillers and United States government officials, formed to defraud the government of the excise taxes. It existed c. 1872-5.

Whisky Van.

A nickname given to Martin Van Buren, eighth President of the United States (1782–1862), by his political opponents.

White, The.

A surname of Hugues (or Hugh), Count of Paris and Duke of France (d. 956). Also called " The Great."

Whiteboys.

The members of an illegal agrarian association, formed in Ireland c. 1761, whose object was " to do justice to the poor by restoring the ancient commons, and redressing other grievances " (Lecky). The members of the association assembled at night with white frocks over their other clothes (whence the name), threw down fences and levelled enclosures (being hence also called Levellers), and destroyed the property of harsh landlords or their agents, the Protestant clergy, the tithe-collectors, and any others who had made themselves obnoxious to the association. Cf. John Banim's novel, " The Peep o' Day."

Whitecaps.

In the United States a self-constituted body or committee of persons who, in Indiana and other States, generally under the guise of rendering service or protection to the community in which they dwell, commit various outrages and lawless acts.

Whitechapel Murders.

A series of extraordinary and atrocious murders committed in London, especially in Whitechapel, by an unknown person, popularly called " Jack the Ripper," c. 1888-9. The victims were in all cases fallen women.

White Company, The.

The name given to a band of adventurers, led by Sir John Hawkwood, who ravaged the northern part of Italy with them in the fourteenth century. *v.* also **Compagnie Blanche, La.**

White Cross Knights.

A surname given to the Knights of Malta. *v.* **Order of the Hospitalers of St. John of Jerusalem.**

White Cross Society, The.

A society organized in England in 1883 by Miss Ellice Hopkins, for the encouragement of personal purity among men. Its further objects are: " to raise the tone of public opinion upon the subject of morality," and " to secure proper legislation in connection with morality—one law only for men and women."

White Czar (or King), The.

A name sometimes given to the Czar of Russia.

White Devil of Wallachia, The.

A surname given by the Turks to Scanderbeg (or Skanderbeg), originally George Castriota, an Albanian commander (1403–68).

Whitefriars' Theatre.

In 1580 the Whitefriars' Monastery was given up to a company of players, and known as Whitefriars' Theatre. It was not used after 1616.

Whitehall Palace.

A palace in London, originally built by Hubert de Burgh, in the reign of Henry III. It became the residence of the Archbishops of York in 1248, and was called York Place for three centuries. (It should not be confounded with York House) In 1615 it was nearly destroyed by fire, and James I undertook to rebuild the palace, but only the banqueting hall, designed by Inigo Jones, was finished at the opening of the Civil War. Through an opening broken in the wall, between the upper and the lower central windows, Charles I walked to the scaffold. The banqueting hall was turned into a chapel by George I, but has never been consecrated. It is called " The Chapel Royal of Whitehall," and was dismantled in 1890.

White Hart, The.

A noted tavern in Southwark, London.

White Horse, The.

A nickname given to the 3rd Dragoon Guards. Also called " The Prince of Wales's."

White House, The.

The official residence of the President of the United States of America, at Washington, the capital.

White King, The, *v.* Royal Martyr, The.

White League, The.

A military organization in Louisiana, in the period succeeding the Civil War, formed for the purpose of securing white supremacy. *v.* also Ku-Klux Klan.

White Man's Grave, The.

Sierra Leone, on the west coast of Africa, has been so named from the unhealthiness of the climate to Europeans.

White Quakers.

A name given to those Quakers who seceded from the main body c. 1840. So called from their white garments.

White Queen, The.

A surname given, by the French, to Mary Queen of Scots (1542–87), alluding to the white mourning which she wore for her husband, Lord Darnley.

White Rose of Raby.

A surname given to Cecily Nevill, daughter of the Earl of Westmorland, and mother of Edward IV of England. A novel with this title was published in 1794.

White's.

A noted club in St. James's Street, London, established in 1698 as a chocolate-house, and called after the name of its keeper. It was from the beginning principally a gambling club.

White Sheep, The.

The Turcoman conquerors of Persia, c. 1468.

White Ship, *v.* Blanche Nef.

White Surrey.

The favourite horse of Richard III (cf. Richard III, Act 5, sc. 3).

White Terror, The, *v.* Terreur Blanche, La.

Whitfield of the Stage, The.

A surname given to James Quin, an English actor (1693–1766). So called by David Garrick (1716–79), to whom the name is sometimes also applied.

Wickliffites, *v.* Lollards.

Wide-Awakes.

A name given to certain electoral campaign clubs, organized by the Republican party during the 1860 presidential election. The members paraded at night, wearing black oilskin hats and capes, and carrying torches.

Wild Boar of Ardennes.

Nickname of William de la Marck (d. 1485), on account of his resemblance to the animal, both in looks and disposition. Cf. Sir Walter Scott's novel, "Quentin Durward."

Wilde Jager, Der (German, "The Wild Huntsman").

A spectral hunter in German folk-lore, the subject of a ballad by Bürger.

Wild Huntsman, The, *v.* Wilde Jager, Der.

Wild West, *v.* Buffalo Bill.

Willis's Rooms.

A later name of Almack's (q.v.) assembly-rooms in London.

Will's Coffee-House.

A famous coffee-house in Russell Street, London, named from its proprietor, whose first name was William. It was the resort of gamblers, and of poets and wits, in the time of Dryden, when it was also known as "The Wits' Coffee-House." It was at the corner of Bow Street.

Wily, The, *v.* Catholic, The. (Ferdinand V).

Windsor Knights, *v.* Military Knights of Windsor.

Windsor of Denmark, The.

A surname given to the castle of Kronborg, Elsinore.

Windward.

The vessel in which the Jackson-Harmsworth expedition made its voyage to the Arctic regions, 1894–6, and in which Nansen and Johansen returned to Norway. The expedition returned to England in the autumn of 1897.

Winged Lion, The, *v.* **Lion of St. Mark.**

Winter King, The.

A name given to Frederick V, Elector of the Palatinate (1596–1632), and King of Bohemia through the winter of 1619–20. Also called **Goodman Palsgrave.** *v.* also **Winter Queen, The.**

Winter Queen, The.

A surname given to Elizabeth Stuart (1596–1632), wife of Frederick V, Elector Palatine, daughter of James I of England. Also called **Goody Palsgrave.** *v.* **Winter King, The.**

Wise, The.

A surname given to Albert IV, Duke of Bavaria (1447–1508), third son of Albert III; Albert II, Duke of Austria (1298–1358] Alfonso X (or Alphonso), King of Leon and Castile (1221–84), also called the **Astronomer;** *v.* **Sage, Le;** Frederick II, Elector Palatine (1482–1556); Frederick III, Elector of Saxony (1463–1525); *v.* **British Jeremiah, The ;** Leo VI, Byzantine emperor. (d. 911), also surnamed " The Philosopher"; Robert of Anjou, King of Naples (c. 1275–1343).

Wise Doctor, The.

A surname given to Johann Wessel, a Dutch divine and philosopher (1419–89).

Wise Men of the East, *v.* **Three Kings of Cologne, The.**

Wisest Fool in Christendom, The, *v.* **British Solomon, The.**

Wisest Man of Greece, The.

A surname given to Socrates, a famous Greek philosopher (c. 470–399 B.C.).

Witches' Sabbath.

A midnight meeting supposed, in the Middle Ages, to be held annually by demons, sorcerers and witches, under the leadership of Satan, for the purpose of celebrating their orgies.

Witchfinder, The (or Witch-finder-General).

A name given to the Englishman Matthew Hopkins, a pretended discoverer of witches, c. 1645.

Without Fear and without Reproach, *v.* **Chevalier sans peur, etc.**

Witling of Terror, The, *v.* **Anacreon of the Guillotine, The.**

Wizard of the North, The.

One of the surnames given to Sir Walter Scott (1771–1832). *v.* **Ariosto of the North, Great Unknown, The, Minstrel of the Border, The, Border Minstrel, The.**

Wolfland.

A surname sometimes given to Ireland in the time of William III, owing to a belief then prevalent that wolves abounded there.

Wolverine State, The.

A popular surname for the State of Michigan, from the number of wolverines it contained.

Wonderful Doctor, The, *v.* **Admirable Doctor, The.**

Wonderful (or Wonder-making) Parliament, *v.* **Merciless Parliament, The.**

Wonder of the World, The.

A name given, on account of his intellectual endowments, to Otto III, Emperor of the Holy Roman Empire (980–1002); also given to Frederick II of Germany (1194–1250).

Wondrous Maid, The, *v.* Maid of Orleans, The.

Wondrous Three, The.

A collective name for Charles James Fox (1749–1806), William Pitt (1759–1806) and Edmund Burke (1729–97) applied to them by Lord Byron in his " Monody on the Death of Sheridan."

Wooden Wedding, *v.* Wedding Anniversaries.

Woollen Wedding, *v.* Wedding Anniversaries.

Worldly Wiseman, Mr.

A character in Bunyan's " Pilgrim's Progress."

World's Fairs.

A series of international exhibitions, the most important of which were those held in London (1851 and 1862), Paris (1855, 1867, 1878, 1889 and 1900), Vienna (1873), Philadelphia (1876), and Chicago (1893). The first universal exhibition was held in the Crystal Palace, Hyde Park, London, at the instigation of the Prince Consort (May 1 to October 11, 1851). Total number of visitors, 6,039,195. The total attendance at the World's Columbian Exposition at Chicago (May 1 to October 30, 1893) was 27,529,400.

World's Wonder, The, *v.* Maiden Queen, The.

Wyandotte Constitution.

The constitution under which Kansas was admitted to the Union, adopted at Wyandotte (now a part of Kansas City, Kan.) in 1859.

Wyclifites (or Wyckliffites), *v.* Lollards.

X.Y.Z. Mission.

An American embassy to France in 1797, consisting of C. C. Pinckney, Marshall and Gerry. An attempt was made by three French agents (disguised as X, Y and Z) to bribe them. The correspondence was disclosed in 1798.

Yankee Doodle.

An American national air, probably of English origin in the middle of the eighteenth century. Its traditional author is Dr. Schuckburgh, a surgeon in the French and Indian war, c. 1755. The original name of the song (not the air) was " The Yankee's Return from Camp."

Yellow Jack.

A popular name among sailors for the yellow fever. Probably from the yellow flag (or jack) customarily displayed from lazarettos and vessels in quarantine.

York House.

A former palace in London, situated in the Strand, west of Salisbury House and the Savoy: a town residence of the Archbishops of York after Wolsey. (It should not be confounded with York Place.) The only archbishop who actually resided here was Heath, Queen Mary's Chancellor. It became the official residence of chancellors and keepers of the great seal; hence Sir Nicholas Bacon went to reside there. Francis Bacon was born there.

York Place, *v.* **Whitehall Palace.**

Young Adventurer, The.

A title given to Prince Charles Edward Stuart, on account of his leading the desperate insurrection of 1745. *v.* **Young Pretender, The.**

Young Chevalier, The.

Charles Edward Stuart, son of the Pretender. *v.* **Young Pretender, The.**

Young Cub, The.

A nickname given to Charles James Fox, a celebrated English statesman and orator (1749–1806). Also called **Carlo Khan,** from the supposition that, from the Bill he introduced into Parliament (1783) respecting the East Indies, he intended to establish a dictatorship in his own person. *v.* **Man of the People, The.**

Young Democracy, *v.* **Barnburners.**

Young Europe, *v.* **Young Italy.**

Young Germany.

A literary and political school in Germany, of innovating tendencies. Its chief representative was Heine.

Young Ireland Party (or Young Ireland).

A group of Irish politicians and agitators, active c. 1840–50, who were at first adherents of O'Connell, but were separated from him by their advocacy of physical force, and took part in the rising of 1848.

Young Italy.

An association of Italian republican agitators, active c. 1834, under the lead of Mazzini. Analogous republican groups in other countries were called **Young Germany, Young Poland, Young France,** etc., and these republican associations collectively were known as **Young Europe.**

Young Juvenal, The.

A surname given (by Robert Greene) to Thomas Lodge, an English novelist, dramatist, lyric poet and miscellaneous writer (c. 1556–1625).

Young Pretender, The.

Surname of Charles Edward Louis Philip Casimir (1720–88), eldest son of the Chevalier de St. George (called James III by the Jacobites), and Princess Clementine, daughter of Prince James Sobieski. Also called the **Young Adventurer,** the **Young Chevalier** and the **Highland Laddie.**

Young Roscius.

Surname given to William Henry West Betty, an English actor, especially famous for his precocity (1791–1874). He made his first appearance August 19, 1803, as Oswyn, in " Zara "; left the stage in 1806; returned to it in 1812, and finally abandoned it in 1824. Also known as **Master Betty** and the **Infant Roscius.**

Youth, The.

A surname given to Diego de

Almagro (born at Panama 1520, and executed at Cuzco 1542). The conspirators who killed Pizarro (1541) had met at his house. He was proclaimed Governor of Peru, but defeated September 16, 1542, by the royalists, and soon after beheaded. Also called the **Lad.**

Zany of Debate, The, *v.* **Cicero of the (British) Senate, The.**

Zanzalians.

The Jacobites of the East; so called occasionally from Zanzalus, a surname of Jacobus Baradæus. *v.* **Jacobites.**

Butler & Tanner, The Selwood Printing Works, Frome, and London.